I0210158

Self-Supply

Praise for this book

'Self-supply has long been overlooked because it is largely unmapped, unmonitored and unregulated, and therefore invisible to policy-makers and decision-takers. This wonderful new book shows what they are missing by providing an accessible but comprehensive overview of self-supply in its many forms and contexts, from the lowest income countries to the highest. It puts people at the centre of the challenge to achieve universal water access and is a celebration of ingenuity and resilience – and highlights that household investment and remittances can play a vital role in plugging the investment gap in rural water infrastructure. This book is destined to become a classic reference that all rural water supply professionals should become familiar with.'

Sean Furey, Director, Rural Water Supply Network (RWSN)

'In Ethiopia, self-supply is a simple investment against poverty, and millions of people depend on it in rural areas. This is the first book that discusses how to support and improve their efforts.'

Tamene Hailu (PhD), Director General of Ethiopian Water Technology Institute

'It is a pleasure to endorse this skilfully written and well researched book on self-supply for our most precious of resources – water. The authors provide evidence, from several parts of the world, where self-supply of water has proven to be totally invaluable and often vital for people's survival.'

Peter Morgan, researcher and consultant; Stockholm Water Prize winner

'Self-supply is a critical, and under-examined component of access to basic water services globally. If we are to achieve the Sustainable Development Goals for universal access to safe drinking water, strengthening best practices and support for self-supply is imperative. These expert authors have produced a well-researched and thoughtful guide to help communities, practitioners, service providers, researchers, governments and donors learn about, and contribute to, community capacity for drinking water self-supply.'

Evan Thomas, University of Colorado, Boulder

'Self-supply – when households and communities take their own initiatives to gain access to water – is an important component of both rural and urban water services, and this book is the resource for understanding its place. The authors demonstrate the potential to incorporate self-supply into national strategies which recognize the need for multiple solutions to the challenges of water supply and its financing and management. I strongly commend the book to all who are working in or interested in the water sectors of nations.'

Professor Richard Carter, WASH specialist

'Whether as temporary stop-gap or long-term 'service model', self-supply has the potential to reach those people and places that public utilities cannot. This timely and useful book, at once rallying cry, history and how-to manual, provides a wealth of useful detail for anyone interested in promoting self-supply as part of delivering safe water for all, forever.'

Dr Patrick Moriarty, IRC Chief Executive Officer

Self-Supply

Filling the gaps in public water supply provision

Sally Sutton with John Butterworth

Practical
ACTION
PUBLISHING

Practical Action Publishing Ltd
27a, Albert Street, Rugby,
Warwickshire, CV21 2SG, UK
www.practicalactionpublishing.com

© IRC, Sally Sutton and the contributors, 2021
The moral right of the author to be identified as author of the
work has been asserted under sections 77 and 78 of the
Copyright Design and Patents Act 1988.

The PDF version of this book is distributed under a Creative Commons Attribution
Non-commercial No-derivatives CC BY-NC-ND licence. This allows the reader to
copy and redistribute the material; but appropriate credit must be given, the material
must not be used for commercial purposes, and if the material is transformed or
built upon the modified material may not be distributed. For further information see
https://creativecommons.org/licenses/by-nc-nd/4.0/legalcode

Product or corporate names may be trademarks or registered trademarks, and are used
only for identification and explanation without intent to infringe.

A catalogue record for this book is available from the British Library.
A catalogue record for this book has been requested from the Library of Congress.

ISBN 9781-7-8853-0-439 Paperback
ISBN 9781-7-8853-0-422 Hardback
ISBN 9781-7-8044-8-275 Epub
ISBN 9781-7-8044-8-190 PDF

Citation: Sutton, S. with J. Butterworth (2021) *Self-Supply:
Filling the gaps in public water supply provision,* Practical Action Publishing, Rugby
<http://dx.doi.org/10.3362/ 9781780448190>.

Since 1974, Practical Action Publishing has published and disseminated books and
information in support of international development work throughout the world.
Practical Action Publishing is a trading name of Practical Action Publishing Ltd
(Company Reg. No. 1159018), the wholly owned publishing company of Practical
Action. Practical Action Publishing trades only in support of its parent charity
objectives and any profits are covenanted back to Practical Action
(Charity Reg. No. 247257, Group VAT Registration No. 880 9924 76).

The views and opinions in this publication are those of the author
and do not represent those of Practical Action Publishing Ltd
or its parent charity Practical Action.

Reasonable efforts have been made to publish reliable data and information, but the
author and publisher cannot assume responsibility for the validity of all materials or
for the consequences of their use.

Cover photo shows a self-financed household
water supply in Zambia. Photo R. Haanen, Jacana, Zambia.
Cover design by RCO.design
Typeset by vPrompt eServices, India

Contents

Figures, photos, tables, and boxes	vi
Acknowledgements	xvi
Preface	xvii
Foreword	xix
Abbreviations	xxii
Glossary	xxiv
1. Why public water supply can't fill all the gaps	1
2. Introducing self-supply	27
3. The scale of rural self-supply	47
4. The scale of urban and peri-urban self-supply	83
5. Ownership and investment in self-supply in sub-Saharan Africa	103
6. Early stage self-supply technologies	131
7. Self-supply and well water quality	165
8. Community and self-financed supplies: complementary services in sustainability	185
9. Supporting self-supply acceleration	215
10. Conclusions and recommendations	249
Part 2: Self-supply case studies	267
1. The role of self-supply in Scotland	271
2. Self-supply in the Danube region	281
3. The shining example of domestic rainwater harvesting in Thailand	289
4. The National Upgraded Well Programme, Zimbabwe	297
5. Introducing alternative and affordable technologies for rural water supply in Tanzania	305
6. The pitfalls and positives of introducing support to self-supply in Zambia	313
Index	323

http://dx.doi.org/10.3362/9781780448190.000

Figures, photos, tables, and boxes

Figures

1.1 Percentage of population using at least basic drinking water services, 2017   5

1.2 Regional changes in rural coverage with improved and unimproved supplies from 2000 to 2017 in selected regions   6

1.3 Trends in rural and urban 'at least basic' and 'less than basic' water supplies in sub-Saharan Africa   11

1.4 Population densities in Africa   15

1.5 Examples of distribution of community size   16

1.6 Liberia – community size and coverage   17

1.7 Projected trends in sub-Saharan rural water supply coverage to 2030   19

1.8 ODA disbursements to the WASH sector at global and sub-Saharan Africa regional levels, 2002–2017   20

1.9 Summary of main trends which may affect future progress towards universal coverage in sub-Saharan Africa   21

2.1 An example of affordable steps towards a basic or safely managed household supply   29

2.2 Dutch Woman and her Maid in a Courtyard, by Pieter de Hooch (1660). Note the household hand pump, guttering, and downpipe to tank or well   36

2.3 Core support service elements needed to facilitate self-supply   41

2.4 Service delivery models and framework for assessing rural water supply sustainability   43

3.1 Proportion of rural households with own non-piped improved and unimproved on-premises water supplies in selected sub-Saharan countries/regions   50

3.2 Privately owned well-construction in Sierra Leone   53

3.3 Thailand changing from point improved sources to piped water supply – a typical middle-income economy trend   56

3.4 Proportion of total population depending on private supplies (individual plus group), relative to HDI in the WHO European region   63

3.5 Generalized evolution of rural water service delivery with growing rural economy   74

3.6 Stages in the evolution of water supply management structures: the persistence of self-supply   75

4.1 Proportion of urban households with own non-piped improved and unimproved water supply on premises   86

5.1 Water supply ownership responsibilities   105

5.2 Examples of ownership patterns of traditional water supplies   106

5.3 Numbers of households sharing traditional supply   108

5.4 Level of education and well-ownership and sharing in SNNP region of Ethiopia   110

5.5 Wealth characteristics of well-owners and sharers   111

5.6 Top 12 perceived benefits of water supply close to the house   113

5.7 Annual official development assistance and official remittances to sub-Saharan Africa, 2012–2018   120

5.8 Sources of funds for self-supply well-construction in Zambia and Malawi   126

6.1 Growth in well-construction rates in parts of three sub-Saharan countries   135

6.2 Schematic diagram of a rope pump   147

6.3 EMAS promotional material showing basic household water and sanitation technologies   150

6.4 Trends in uptake, costs, and impact relating to technology introduction   158

7.1 (a) Low and (b) high levels of contamination in different source types in four sub-Saharan countries   167

7.2 Water quality with Afridev pumps on three different source types   168

7.3 Progressive improvement in quality with higher technology in Ethiopia from RADWQ 2010 and RiPPLE results   169

7.4 Water quality in traditional wells before and after improvement, compared with fully protected wells   174

7.5   Proportion of water samples without detectable faecal coliform
      at source and at point of consumption in Sierra Leone   175

7.6   Point of consumption water quality relative to source water in
      four countries   176

7.7   Estimated use of household water treatment   178

8.1   Numbers of wells per region   189

8.2   Motivating factors for changing household primary water
      source, Milenge District, Zambia   192

8.3   Factors affecting user satisfaction   193

8.4   Reliability of different supply technologies in Ethiopia   196

8.5   Examples of distribution of community water supply and
      self-supply water point user numbers   198

8.6   Committee management responsibilities in community
      water supply   205

9.1   Roles and responsibilities developed by Ministry of Water
      and Energy Uganda for self-supply support in 2015   218

9.2   Local service providers and range of products required to
      support basic household supply investment   219

9.3   Funding types and purpose   222

9.4   Stages in the process of establishing a self-supply service
      delivery model   225

9.5   Progress in scaling-up supported self-supply in selected countries   228

9.6   Complementary public and private sector roles in self-supply
      support   233

9.7   Variations in unit/uptake costs (including software costs)
      during piloting and scaling up. An example in Cambodia   241

9.8   The example of Zambia. Cost savings to government of including
      self-supply support as an option to reach the last 20 per cent 243

10.1 A generalization of the difference between the professional
      and household perspectives   251

10.2 Illustration of the scale of self-supply in rural sub-Saharan
      Africa (owners and sharers of self-supply sources) shown in
      comparison with levels on the JMP water supply ladder   254

10.3 The mix and fluidity of public, private, and commercial
      service delivery   256

10.4 Multi-sectoral potential in supporting self-supply   261

CS.1.1   Overall compliance for samples taken from larger (regulated)
         private water supplies in Scotland, year on year, with
         comparison against public water supply   275

CS.2.1   Countries included in the review of rural water and sanitation
         services in the Danube region   282

CS.2.2   Rural sector structure and indicative estimates of provision
         of piped rural services   283

CS.2.3   Share of self-supply households and their service level
         characteristics by management model and by country   285

CS.6.1   Stakeholders' roles in Zambian self-supply activities   314

Photos

2.1   Early steps in rainwater harvesting Mozambique (lowest cost)   31

2.2   Early steps in rainwater harvesting Mozambique (mid cost)   32

2.3   An Ethiopian self-supplied household well, protected and
      convenient for domestic purposes'   33

3.1   Upgraded Zimbabwean family with cistern for small-scale irrigation   52

3.2   A typical house in rural Thailand with several Thai jars   61

3.3   Late 19th century American homestead domestic and farm water
      supply, Oklahoma   66

4.1   Typical peri-urban household supply, Lagos State, Nigeria   88

4.2   Typical peri-urban development with its own water supply, Lafia,
      Nassawara State, Nigeria   90

4.3   Household (improved?/unimproved?) self-supply well used for
      washing and family laundry business in Freetown, Sierra Leone   93

5.1   Household well in Bo, Sierra Leone, sited for use by neighbouring
      houses and passers-by   107

5.2   Household well with cattle trough and cow-shed; domestic and
      productive uses from on-premises self-supply well, Mali   116

5.3   Women's cooperative in South Africa, watering vegetables from
      their own well   116

5.4   Brick-making in Zambia   117

5.5   Ethiopian family well with investment in wellhead protection   125

6.1   Small diameter well-digging and underlining for additional
      shaft support   135

6.2   Unprotected well, Meskan woreda, Ethiopia   136

6.3   Protected? A household well in Luapula Province, Zambia   136

6.4   Protected self-supplied well in Ziguinchor, Senegal   137

6.5   Brick lining for well and drainage channel (part completed)
       with foundation for top slab, Northern Province, Zambia   138

6.6   Concrete well rings for traditional family well improvement
       (well in background) Luapula Province, Zambia   139

6.7   Hand-augering in Senegal   141

6.8   SHIPO drilling in Tanzania   141

6.9   Laban Kaduma demonstrating the principles of the rope pump
       to trainees in Tanzania   143

6.10   Community self-supply spring protection, Northern Province,
       Zambia   144

6.11   Drawing water by pulley, Senegal   145

6.12   Locally made handpump on a household well in Niger   146

6.13   EMAS pumps for demonstration in Sierra Leone   149

6.14   Kickstart treadle pump   151

6.15   Household Afridev with animal watering tank, Ethiopia   152

6.16   Homemade shower using storage pot and watering can
       rose, Ethiopia   152

6.17   Basic roof water collection jars, Ghana   155

6.18   High cost expansion of rainwater in-series storage, Ghana   155

6.19   Constructing domestic wired-brick rainwater storage with
       cement lining, Malawi   156

6.20   Low-cost trickle irrigation, Ethiopia   157

6.21   SMART Centre in Mzuzu, Malawi   159

7.1   Unimproved household well in Mbala district, Zambia   170

7.2   Unimproved wellhead, Luapula province, Zambia   171

7.3   Household well covered but with no other protection, Luapula
       Province, Zambia   171

7.4   The well in photo 7.1 improved by the household, but still
       lacking a cover or drainage   172

7.5   The well in Photo 7.2 with basic improvements including a
       pole for hanging up the rope and bucket   172

7.6   The well in Photo 7.3 with basic improvements including
       lockable cover   173

8.1   A traditional Malian family well   190

8.2   Drawing water by hand from 80 metres down, Maradi, Niger   194

8.3   Household well upgrading financed by an NGO in Niono, Mali   206

9.1   Well-lining rings made by local artisans at Sila Mumba's house   221

9.2   Artisans trained by WaterAid in techniques for self-supply water
       and sanitation, Luapula province, Zambia   232

CS.1.1   A reasonably well-designed and maintained private surface
         water abstraction in rural Scotland, with a 'stilling pool'
         upstream and a screen to remove coarse debris   272

CS.1.2   Two private water supply treatment systems: (a) supplying
         a large estate and (b) a simple 'point of use' ultraviolet
         disinfection unit in a kitchen cupboard   276

CS.1.3   A leaflet that has been sent to users of domestic private water
         supplies to raise awareness of risks   278

CS.3.1   Dragon jars at a pottery in Ratchaburi   290

CS.3.2   (a) Thai Jar factory; (b) Thai Jars being delivered to customers 293

CS.4.1   Well built during Zimbabwe's National Upgraded Well
         Programme   298

CS.4.2   Family well showing a lack of attention and maintenance   301

CS.5.1   SHIPO hand-drilling   307

CS.5.2   Contractors sell low cost options for community projects as
         well as self-supply. This school supply was installed 15 years ago 308

CS.6.1   Family well upgraded in Northern Province Zambia using
         the training from Mvuramanzi Trust, Zimbabwe   315

CS.6.2   Family borehole and rope pump installed by Jacana,
         in Eastern Province, Zambia   319

Tables

1.1   The SDG ladder for household drinking water services   7

1.2   MDG and SDG classifications of supply   8

1.3   Summary of sub-Saharan urban water supply trends towards
       SDG 6.1 from 2000   12

1.4   Summary of sub-Saharan rural water trends towards SDG 6.1   12

2.1   Forms of self-financed water supply   30

2.2   The relationship between self-supply and MUS water use   33

3.1   Population estimated from MICS data, using own
       on-premises supply   49

3.2   Top 20 sub-Saharan countries for use of unprotected groundwater 51

3.3   Self-supply provision in Danube Basin middle-income countries 56

3.4   Examples of individual rural self-supply (up to 50 people) in high-
       income countries   65

3.5   Examples of European group/cooperative supply coverage   67

3.6   Phases in the evolution of Finnish cooperatives   68

3.7   Meeting *E. coli* standards – example from Ireland, compliance
       per private water supply type   70

3.8   SWOT analysis of group/cooperative water schemes versus
       public supply   71

3.9   SWOT analysis of individual self-supply in high-income countries 73

4.1   Urban population using own on-premises supply estimated
       from MICS data   87

4.2   Examples of large urban area self-supply in sub-Saharan Africa 89

5.1   Well-ownership and national education level, population
       percentages with secondary or higher education   110

5.2   Proportion of households using water from self-financed wells
       for domestic and productive use in three countries   115

5.3   Changing food security in 420 well-owning households   118

5.4   Examples of the widespread tradition of savings schemes
       in sub-Saharan Africa   121

5.5   Progression (bottom to top) in financing mechanisms
       for savings and loans   123

6.1   Progressive steps towards a self-financed, safely managed
       groundwater supply   133

6.2   Main advantages and disadvantages of hand-dug wells   139

6.3   Comparative features of low-cost drilling and well-digging   140

6.4   Drilling methods and their basic characteristics   142

6.5   Summary of starter level handpump design characteristics
      affecting customer choice   152

6.6   Summary of higher level pump types for household
      and group supply   153

7.1   Selected HWTS technologies and products   179

8.1   Some differences in communal and individual thinking relevant
      to WASH sustainability   187

8.2   The influence of type of supply ownership on functionality   195

8.3   User satisfaction and supply performance, an example
      from Ethiopia   199

8.4   Stakeholder contribution to life-cycle costs   201

8.5   Proportion of users paying for rural supply regularly or
      on breakdown   202

9.1   Core indicators for sustainable self-supply support   220

9.2   Situation summary for countries in Figure 9.5   228

9.3   Summary of merits and drawbacks of introducing a new concept
      through commercial, government, and NGO channels   238

9.4   Per capita costs of facilitating sanitation and water self-supply   240

CS.1.1   Private water supply source types in Scotland   273

CS.1.2   Compliance for most commonly failing parameters in larger
         (regulated) private water supplies and comparison with public
         water supplies in Scotland, 2017   274

CS.2.1   Rural sector structure and indicative estimates of provision
         of piped rural services   283

CS.4.1   Levels of contamination (E. coli) for unimproved and improved
         family wells   299

CS.4.2   Levels of contamination (E. coli and faecal streptococci) for
         unimproved and improved family wells, January to March 1988   299

CS.6.1   Strengths and weaknesses of different stakeholder-led self-supply
         acceleration initiatives in Zambia   320

Boxes

1.1	Parallels with self-supply in the energy sector	3
1.2	Community size and user numbers in Liberia	16
3.1	Self-supply in Sierra Leone	53
3.2	Honduras report proposing strategies for dispersed populations	59
3.3	Thai rainwater harvesting	61
3.4	Collective action for water supply in Ireland	67
3.5	The paradox of Ireland	72
4.1	Typical tales of urban supply	85
4.2	Indian government support to self-supply	95
4.3	Triggers to self-supply, examples in high-income urban environments	96
5.1	Cultural aspects of traditional water supply	107
5.2	The experience of Zambian research into improving traditional sources	109
5.3	Changes in food security with investment in a well or a pump	118
5.4	Savings circles and self-supply	122
5.5	How households paid for their well or its upgrading in SNNP Region, Ethiopia	125
6.1	Making drilling into a business – a Tanzanian success story	143
6.2	Economic impact of the rope pump in Nicaragua and beyond	148
6.3	EMAS technologies and self-supply in Sierra Leone	150
6.4	Moving up the ladder	152
6.5	SMART and EMAS centres	159
8.1	Binta Koli in Ziguinchor Senegal: individual or communal responsibility?	188
8.2	Mali: a typical tale of public and private supplies	189
8.3	Household decisions on water source	191
8.4	Convenience in water lifting in Niger	194
8.5	CMP approach in Ethiopia	201

8.6   Integrating a perspective on gender and vulnerability in WASH
      in Uganda   209

9.1   Introducing new products   221

9.2   Background to the human rights fulfilment for water and sanitation   230

9.3   Combined water and sanitation programmes   231

9.4   Self-supply policy, targets and gaps in Ethiopia   234

9.5   Government role in group water supply in Meru County, Kenya   235

9.6   The Tanzanian experience (see also Part 2, Case Study 5)   236

9.7   Self-supply progress in Nicaragua   237

10.1 Recommended high-level actions for donors and international
      aid agencies   263

10.2 Recommended actions for governments   263

10.3 Recommended actions for NGOs   264

10.4 Areas of missing research on self-supply   264

CS.4.1 Construction quality and maintenance   301

CS.4.2 Costs and financing of family wells   303

CS.5.1 Alternative and affordable technologies introduced by SHIPO
        in Njombe Region   306

Acknowledgements

The following are gratefully acknowledged for their contributions to this book:

Sandy Cairncross (London School of Hygiene & Tropical Medicine) for his contribution to the first chapter;
Richard Carter for peer review;
Peter McIntyre for editing;
Patrick Moriarty (IRC) for review of the first chapter;
Tom Slaymaker (WHO/UNICEF Joint Monitoring Programme) for vetting the method used for estimating self-supply scale from MICS surveys;
Rik Haanen (Jacana Zambia) and Henk Holtslag (SMART centre group, The Netherlands) for inputs on technology;
Matt Bower (Scottish Water), Susanna Smets (World Bank consultant), Matthias Saladin (SKAT Foundation Switzerland), Peter Morgan (Aquamor, Zimbabwe) and Walter Mgina (Tanzania and the Netherlands) for their case studies.
Lars Osterwalder (IRC) – water quality and HWTS;

Inputs were also provided by:

Brian MacDonald (Irish Federation of Group Water Schemes) – Irish private water sector;
Stef Smit, IRC – Latin America;
Lemessa Mekonta – Ethiopia;
Marieke Adank (IRC) – reference acquisitions;
Jenny Gronwall – human rights;
Yahya Kargbo (Welthungerhilfe) – Self-supply Sierra Leone;
Bret McSpadden (IRC) and Stuart Sutton – reference checking;
Dechan Dalrymple (IRC) – graphics.

Finally thanks to my husband Stuart for endless (almost) patience and support over two years of being sorely tested when this book has taken precedence.

Preface

I have been motivated in writing this book partly by my amazement on discovering the scale, ingenuity, and universal spread of self-financed water supply while working and travelling in various parts of the world. The second stimulus can be summed up by two incidents picked from recent years working on rural water supply in sub-Saharan Africa. They are snapshots of situations which are occurring all over the region every day, as people strive to create a better life for themselves and their families.

In the late 1980s I was working for the Department of Water Affairs in Zambia. The Department was building up capacity to provide sustainable community water supply for over half a million people in the Western Province – an area bisected by the Zambezi on its way through to Kariba and the Victoria Falls. A village headman came to apply for a borehole and handpump for his village as they were several kilometres from the valley and easy access to water. I explained the procedure for application via councillors and local government and eventually we were all called to the village, only to find it consisted of just eight widely scattered houses – too small to be prioritized while so many larger ones remained unserved. We explained the problem to the headman and he asked that the authorities should visit again later in the month. Returning as requested, the village had grown to 40 or more households and a beaming headman asked for a recount. His tenacity and the spirit in which so many had uprooted and moved house to support his request won the day. Once their job was done, a few moved permanently to enjoy the convenience of passing trade on the road and a new water supply, but most returned to their more remote houses and the lands which provided them with subsistence. Their struggle drove home the problem of the large number in smaller scattered communities whose needs as individuals are equal to those of bigger groups but who seldom have a voice to call for change. For them most governments offer no solution because of the enormously increased per capita costs where pumps would provide for so few.

Twenty years later wandering around the outskirts of Kofridua in Ghana, I came across Abdul Rahman. His house had been large enough for him to let a room to guests and he had then expanded into making a separate guesthouse next door. He found someone to dig him a well and furnished it with a rope and bucket. The easy availability of water meant he could charge his guests more per night, and he began also to sell water to his neighbours. One of the guests who was a mechanic informed him about different pump types and costs. He then ploughed back the money from the guesthouse and water sales into protecting the well and pumping the water up into a small storage tank. Sales rose as his water didn't need to be lifted out by hand and was regarded as safer than other wells nearby. He bought a bigger pump and forwarded water to a larger elevated tank, employed a caretaker to collect payments and began to dream of selling house connections. A friend who was in government service explained he would need to guarantee the water quality when selling on that scale, and that he should contact the district water office and get his water tested. This he did and added in-line chlorination. So Abdul Rahman developed his own supply, helped up the technology ladder by those he knew around him, both in the public and private sectors.

Abdul Rahman's story illustrates the ingenuity and drive that exist to improve quality of life among many motivated people. In his case he had useful connections who gave him good advice and had social connections to traders in the town who stocked pumps. But for millions who long for change those supporting elements are lacking. Their efforts to improve access to water hit a brick wall, leaving them dependent on poor quality traditional sources or the vagaries of passing NGOs and local governments whose ability to respond is severely limited by the resources available to them.

Everywhere I have worked across Africa I have found households taking the first steps, investing their own cash and efforts in affordable, but therefore mainly very low, levels of supply technology in their battle to achieve a better quality of life. I have also found their investment is being almost totally ignored by the sector despite the millions of dollars they have spent and the millions of water collecting hours and calories this has saved them. I began to explore how this picture fits with the evolution of water supplies and the scale of such developments in higher income countries. It has led to piloting ways in which the public and private sector and consumers can combine forces to solve their problems where government alone is unable to provide an adequate supply. This book reflects some of the findings, assisted by others (led by John Butterworth) with an interest in making more options available to those who have seen no improvement in their water supply during their lifetime and little prospect of change during their children's lifetime: unless they do it themselves. May the contents stimulate curiosity and a desire to listen to what people are doing to solve their own problems, and raise donor and government interest in supporting self-supply to become one of several accepted options to reach universal access and maximize user satisfaction. That way lies true sustainability.

Foreword

Although some progress has been achieved in the last several decades, hundreds of millions of people still lack access to safe water services and billions lack access to even basic sanitation. In rural areas, the level of access is inferior to that in urban areas in practically all countries around the world and progress seems slower than it ought to be. Ensuring access to safe drinking water and sanitation for all will require much greater effort and engagement from states, international organizations, service providers, and civil society. Nevertheless, one might ask, will it really be possible to 'leave no one behind' by 2030? The authors of this book invite us to confront the idea that our Sustainable Development Goal targets might not be reached – at least in rural sub-Saharan Africa – within the confines of the dominant approach that has driven the water sector.

In the last years during which I undertook several country visits as the Special Rapporteur on the human rights to safe drinking water and sanitation, I have had the opportunity to witness the frequent omissions of governments in ensuring an adequate rural water supply for all, sometimes justified by the challenges of dealing with a diversity of complex situations, including indigenous peoples, nomadic populations, and populations living in hard to reach, remote areas. In fact, from Botswana to Lesotho, from India to Mongolia, from Malaysia to Tajikistan, from Mexico to El Salvador and Portugal, what I generally have found is little attention being paid to rural populations, non-existent or weakly targeted policies and programmes, and lack of budgets and of participatory mechanisms.

This book, instead of merely lamenting or simply ignoring the challenges of water supply in rural areas, highlights an approach to address them: self-supply. Self-supply may be roughly defined as the construction of infra-structure by households themselves or by a small group of households utilizing primarily their own means. It basically means people using their own skills and resources in order to improve their lives, rather than complaining, demanding, and waiting for external assistance which may not appear anyway. It means neighbours backing each other up and enhancing bonds of solidarity. Building on direct experience and numerous examples, mainly in sub-Saharan Africa where a significant portion of the world's population with no access to improved water, sanitation, and hygiene services live, the book makes a fair point: practitioners, academics, and even activists are not paying attention to self-supply. As a result it is a rather unknown phenomenon while being a very common one, with millions of households addressing challenges and filling the gap where government attention is so far lacking.

The human rights framework provides compelling views on the self-supply of water. After all, ensuring access to a minimum essential amount of water to all for personal and domestic uses, commensurate with the prevention of disease, is the minimum core state obligation under international law. The human rights to safe drinking water and sanitation must be progressively realized and duty bearers must use their maximum available resources, taking deliberate, concrete and targeted measures towards the fulfilment of their human rights obligations. The right to water requires that services are available, accessible, safe, acceptable, and affordable for all without discrimination. Thus, it requires an explicit focus on the most disadvantaged and marginalized groups and on those that are unserved or underserved.

The principle of equality and non-discrimination and the state's obligation to progressively realize the human rights to water and sanitation frame the normative context in which self-supply may be considered and best assessed. Self-supply of water raises concerns of availability, accessibility, quality, and affordability. Since rural dwellers are rights holders in the same manner as urban dwellers, acknowledging self-supply as a definitive solution for water supply might appear to be legitimizing a discriminatory practice or endorsing state failure to comply with its immediate obligations. Because rural dwellers are among those that are the most deprived of services, a policy oriented by the human rights framework ought to put those populations at the forefront of its priorities. Under international human rights law, states should thus take deliberate action to prioritize the access to services for those that rely on unacceptable levels of access.

However, as the book argues, people will not wait for state action, sometimes because they cannot even be sure that any public authority will come and help. These cases, where people take matters into their own hands and do things by and for themselves, empowering communities and improving their life conditions, can be seen as a first step in the process of progressive realization of human rights. But as a first step only. Thus, it is important to focus one eye on supporting community initiatives for self-supply and the other eye on state obligations. States need to be compelled – and must be granted the capacities – to meet their human rights obligations, ensuring that adequate support systems are in place for the upgrading of self-made solutions to a level of services compliant with the normative content of the right to water. Seen in these terms, self-supply of water might be understood as a seed that was planted by the rights holders. In order for it to blossom, it relies on public authorities to water it and to ensure it can grow healthily. In this sense, acknowledging self-supply has less to do with bowing down and accepting the inevitable and more to do with urging stakeholders to take a stand.

The human rights framework further emphasizes the principles of participation, accountability, and transparency. The application of these principles together with the obligation of progressively realizing the rights to water and sanitation provides guidance for states. Empowering the most disadvantaged in rural areas may be the key to taking self-supply more seriously and to including it in the realm of human rights. By promoting involvement of rights holders in decision-making, public authorities trigger change more rapidly and are held accountable for their efforts to reduce inequalities. Raising this relevant debate through a very realistic and concrete approach is one of several contributions of this book. But it does even more. While shining light on this unacknowledged phenomenon the authors remind us that granting access to water and sanitation is urgent and that 2030 is knocking at the door. And for this endeavour to succeed, everyone's help – including those innovative households already taking action – is earnestly needed.

Léo Heller
Former UN Special Rapporteur on the human rights to
safe drinking water and sanitation

Abbreviations

ADB   Asian Development Bank
AMCOW   African Ministers' Council on Water
CBO   Community-based organization
CDF   Community development fund
CLTS   Community-led total sanitation
CWS   Community water supply
DFID   Department for International Development (UK)
DHS   Demographic health survey
DRC   Democratic Republic of the Congo
DWI   Drinking Water Inspectorate (UK)
EMAS   Mobile water & sanitation school (Spanish acronym, Escuela móvil de agua y saneamiento)
FAO   Food and Agriculture Organization of the United Nations
GIS   Geographic information system
GLAAS   UN-Water Global Analysis and Assessment of Sanitation and Drinking-Water
HDI   Human Development Index
HWTS   Household water treatment and storage
IDE   International Development Enterprises
IWRM   Integrated water resources management
JICA   Japanese International Cooperation Agency
JMP   Joint Monitoring Programme (UNICEF/WHO)
KAP   Knowledge, attitude and practice
MDG   Millennium Development Goal
MFI   Microfinance institution
MICS   Multiple index cluster survey (UNICEF)
MUS   Multiple use water services
NGO   Non-governmental organization
ODA   Official development assistance
ODF   Open defecation free
ROSCA   Rotating credit and savings association
RWH   Rainwater harvesting
RWSN   Rural water supply network
SDG   Sustainable Development Goal
SHIPO   Southern Highlands Participatory Organisation (Tanzania)
SKAT   Swiss Resource Centre and Consultancies for Development
SMART   Simple, market-based, affordable, repairable technologies
SME   Small and medium-sized enterprise
SNNPR   Southern Nations, Nationalities People's Region (Ethiopia)
TAF   Technology Assessment Framework

TIP	Technology Introduction Process
UNICEF	United Nations Children's Fund
VSLA	Village savings and loans scheme
WASH	Water, sanitation, and hygiene
WHO	World Health Organization
WSP	Water and Sanitation Program, World Bank

Glossary

Community water supply. Point water supplies, commonly a borehole or lined hand-dug well with a handpump, managed by the community but provided almost completely by government/donor funding. Some may have a bucket and windlass or pulley for lifting water.

Coverage. The proportion of the population who are served by an improved supply.

Drinking water. Water for domestic purposes of drinking, cooking, and personal hygiene (bathing and clothes washing).

Family/traditional well. A hand-dug well, usually unlined except near the surface. May be protected from inflowing water and wind-blown debris, and with a cover or may be unprotected.

Hardware. Physical water supply components, tools, machinery, equipment.

Improved/protected well. Protected from runoff water by a (partial) or full) well lining, headwall and an apron that diverts spilled water away from the well. It is also covered so that contaminated materials (including bird droppings and small animals) cannot enter the well. Water is delivered through a pump or manual lifting device.

Improved supply. SDG definition – as above plus bottled, sachet or tankered water if from an improved supply.

Millennium Development Goals (MDGs). UN Goals set in 2000 to halve world poverty by 2015.
  Target 7C. Halve, by 2015, the proportion of people without sustainable access to safe drinking water and basic sanitation.

Private sector. Mostly artisans providing products and services in support of private water supply or sanitation. May include formal SMEs but in sub-Saharan Africa this is often informal. This does not therefore refer to a sector beholden to shareholders as with big water companies (unless specifically mentioned as companies), and also contrasts with public sector services provided by government, municipalities or as sizeable public–private partnerships.

Private supply. Belonging to an individual family or group, usually self-funded and not for profit.

Productive use. Water used for income-generating activities.

Safe water. Water with no detectable faecal coliform/100 ml.

Served. Those using an improved supply.

Shallow well. A large diameter hand-dug well.

Software. Non-material components of infrastructure development such as institutional support to training, marketing, advisory services, policy, and guideline development.

Sustainable Development Goals (SDGs). Goal 6. Ensure access to water and sanitation for all

6.1 By 2030 achieve universal and equitable access to safe and affordable drinking water for all.
6.2 By 2030, achieve access to adequate and equitable sanitation and hygiene for all and end open defecation, paying special attention to the needs of women and girls and those in vulnerable situations.

Unimproved supply. Surface water, unprotected well or spring which allows windblown debris or surface water seepage/inflow into the source through lack of cover, parapet or apron.

Unserved. Those using an unimproved supply.

CHAPTER 1

Why public water supply can't fill all the gaps

The gap between those served with improved WASH services and the global population has narrowed dramatically over the last decade, but a significant number of households are still partly or wholly dependent on their own solutions (self-supply). This chapter examines the global challenge in closing the gap to achieve universal WASH access, particularly to safe and reliable water supply in sub-Saharan Africa which presently has the largest deficit. Relevant factors include past trends in coverage (reflecting construction capacity and financing), the characteristics of remaining unserved communities, and the challenges of keeping existing services functioning. They are examined in the context of changes arising from the progression from the Millennium Development Goals (MDGs) to the Sustainable Development Goals (SDGs), and a range of increasing calls upon sector funding. New thinking is needed to accelerate progress, especially among small, remote, and marginalized communities, and greater inclusion of users in decision-making, funding, and imple-mentation if universal access is to be achieved among the most difficult to reach.

Keywords: MDG, SDG, global, water, sanitation, sub-Saharan Africa, self-supply

Key messages

1. Self-supply is one of a range of service delivery options. As economies improve, more and more households take the initiative to provide their own on-premises supply or augment less than basic supplies provided by public or commercial services.
2. Sub-Saharan Africa is the main focus of this book because it has a sixth of the world population but more than half of all those still without adequate water supply or sanitation.
3. The gap in provision is much greater in rural areas of sub-Saharan Africa, but numbers of urban people using a less than basic supply are gradually growing as peri-urban and slum areas expand.
4. There are over 330 million rural people currently unserved by 'at least basic' supplies in the region. Trends to date indicate that, being largely in dispersed or remote communities, this number will probably slightly increase by 2030 as those with a limited supply are the fastest growing group.
5. Indications are that among those remaining unserved, user numbers for each new water supply will decrease significantly, increasing per capita costs and slowing progress.

http://dx.doi.org/10.3362/9781780448190.001

6. The total costs of operation and maintenance will grow as supply numbers and the age of infrastructure increase. The ability to cover these and long-term capital maintenance costs (replacement) will require greater public financial support, which may reduce funding available for new works.
7. Available official development assistance (ODA) and public (government) funding are not increasing fast enough. Each year's deficit in progress means that even greater funds are needed in subsequent years if SDG targets are to be reached.
8. Household initiative has become the basis for new approaches in sanitation but no similar fresh thinking has been adopted widely in the water sector.
9. New sources of funding (e.g. household savings and remittances) and a reassessment of strategies are necessary if supplies are to be sustainable and universal access is to be achieved. Continuing to replicate only the solutions developed to date will not lead to improvement in water supply and sanitation for all.
10. This book focuses on self-supply, particularly for rural water in sub-Saharan Africa but referring also to lessons learned from other countries and from sanitation. It argues that providing support services to improve the performance of widespread self-supply (self-supply acceleration) would leverage new funds and provide practical alternatives for those unserved or with inadequate facilities.

Introduction

Where there are gaps in supply that public provision does not reach, or not adequately, households the world over may invest in their own facilities (**self-supply**). Originally all water supply was from surface water or self-supplied groundwater or rainwater harvesting, which has been developed, augmented, or replaced to varying degrees over time. Even in the highest income countries, some households (particularly those more isolated or hard to reach) invest to improve access to water, and globally self-supply forms a permanent or transitory phenomenon at a surprisingly large scale in both urban and rural environments.

Moves to improve water services in developing countries have focused on public provision and to some extent on the role of the private sector and community management in rural areas. Analysis of progress in service provision and sector strategies assume all is government or donor provided with little or no reference to the significant contribution from, and potential in, self-financed water provision.

This book is the first to examine the prevalence of self-supply, its role in water supply evolution, the potential it offers, and ways in which supporting self-supply can help to bridge the gap in, and improve the quality of, water provision. It sets out evidence and research findings for policy makers,

---

Box 1.1 Parallels with self-supply in the energy sector

In the energy sector self-supply is already well-recognized in providing off-grid power through household or group initiatives in diesel, solar, or hydro-generation. Resulting systems can be expanded or their capacity increased in affordable steps among the global 1.4 billion still not connected to a grid. Sub-Saharan Africa has 17% of the global population but 60% of households without electricity (see 'Electrifying Africa', Oxford Institute for Energy Studies, 2018), indicating a need to prioritize the region.

As with water, self-supply in the energy sector does not only provide for those without access to centralized supplies. It also supplements erratic public supplies especially in urban areas and those marginal to grids and can be superseded or augmented if or when grid extent and capacity allow. Private off-grid supplies in lower income countries are often shared (e.g. phone charging, television watching) especially in remote villages. Larger group supplies can feed into the grid or act autonomously.

Self-supplied energy can also be controversial where it rivals mainstream commercial production and raises costs for consumers connected to centralized networks. The justification for subsidies at group and household level is also an issue for debate.

The water sector raises similar issues and offers a comparable mosaic of public and private options, requiring enabling policies for each to function effectively, and to enable off-grid households to develop their own solutions.

---

practitioners, and researchers to assess the relevance of self-supply to the sector, to consider its role, and how to harness its potential. It argues that self-supply will always form an important part of the service mix for households in sparsely populated regions and an interim supply for many others. It is divided into two parts: the first part is an analysis of existing self-supply and potential for its support; and the second part is a set of country case studies which are referred to in the main text.

Personal investment in water results from a combination of household aspirations surpassing government capacities to deliver an acceptable service, and family prosperity rising sufficiently to support their chosen improvements to quality of life. Families are increasingly investing in water supply primarily as an option for domestic use but also sometimes conjunctively for productive use. Such investment offers a complementary path to fill some of the significant gaps left in public service delivery, in much the same way as in the energy sector (see Box 1.1) with which it forms a nexus.

A powerful driving force for private investment is that drinking/domestic water must be available every day and accessing this can consume considerable time and effort. If this effort can be reduced within the means of the family, it brings relief, especially to the female members of the household, and benefits to the quality of life of the whole household which they can easily identify. Alongside the growth in public supplies, it has led to the development of large numbers of self-financed supplies on which families place great value. This value is increasingly being recognized by the sector in higher income countries, but elsewhere is still largely ignored.

Because self-financed progress occurs only in small steps (especially in lower income economies), many have not gone beyond the lowest steps of a rope and bucket or a basin collecting rainwater. In most countries, rural economies have developed hand in hand with water supply, but the process can be speeded up in weaker economies by improving the availability of affordable technologies, advisory services, microfinance, a skilled private sector, and sometimes by incentives or subsidies. In this way the efforts already made can be built upon and new ones stimulated, to upgrade self-provision where public supplies are inadequate. Delivery of these support services which help families to get onto, or to accelerate up, the ladder to safely managed supply largely through their own initiative is called **supported self-supply**. The first part of this book explores existing self-supply and how it can be accelerated to provide service delivery alongside conventional community supply. The second part presents six case studies in high, middle, and low income settings.

Analysis of present-day gaps in supply and factors limiting progress in closing them, form the major part of this first chapter, justifying the call for greater attention to what people are already doing for themselves. Self-supply in sanitation and the processes to encourage it, are generally only touched upon where it has lessons for the water sector, since this element of water, sanitation, and hygiene (WASH) is widely covered by others.

Chapters 2 to 4 look first at the characteristics of self-supply and the scale of it in both rural and urban contexts in countries at different stages of development, and historically in that the coexistence of state and private provision is nothing new. In rural water supply it is shown to be an integral part of the evolution of universal coverage.

Chapters 5 onwards look principally within the sub-Saharan context, at what sort of people invest in household-level water provision and why. Chapter 6 discusses a range of affordable starter technology options suitable for household investment. These options create a progression in improved access and water quality linked to increasing costs. Water quality issues of different technologies and importance of investing in household water treatment are explored in Chapter 7.

With community water supply (boreholes/wells and handpumps) still by far the most widely adopted state-supported option in sub-Saharan Africa, the performance of and relationship between self-supply and community water supply (CWS) are examined in Chapter 8 to see how they compare and how they fit together. Models for, and experience of, supporting self-supply acceleration and the ascent of households to higher levels of technology are examined in Chapter 9 in the light of going to scale through government or private sector support. Chapter 10 looks at the lessons from existing self-supply and the potential and challenges faced in supporting it, and recommends the way forward for different stakeholders – strategy-makers, donors, practitioners, and researchers. In Part 2 six country case studies give more detailed examples of self-supply and support for it in higher and lower income countries.

Overall the book demonstrates that as part of a mosaic of options, community water supply and self-supply can cover a wider range of situations than either can achieve on its own, alongside the growth of small piped supplies and multi-village schemes for more densely populated rural areas and the fringes of urban utilities.

The basic challenge

The global growth in population in this millennium has been largely in urban areas rather than rural ones. Part of the reason for the drift away from rural areas is that levels of investment in essential services (roads, power, water supply, sanitation, and work opportunities) have been far greater in concentrated urban areas that are easier to serve. Although the rise of urban populations has been seen as a major challenge, it is rural households who have largely been left behind. Many young rural people feel they are less privileged and look longingly at the bright lights of the cities.

The overall global challenge comes not only from the high rate of population growth but also from the large extent to which this growth takes place in countries which already have the biggest deficit in services. This includes the degree to which the gap in safe water services (and sanitation) has remained stubbornly high in specific parts of the world, and especially in rural areas. The Millennium Development Goals (MDGs) set a target to halve the number of people without access to safe water by 2015. Globally, the target was reached in 2010, but two regions (sub-Saharan Africa and Oceania) did not achieve it (World Bank, 2017). Sub-Saharan Africa was by far the most populous with the highest population growth rate and the largest number of people without access to safe water (see Figure 1.1) globally (WHO/UNICEF, JMP, 2017; WHO/UNICEF JMP, 2019).

This region accounted for less than 10 per cent of the world's urban population in 2015 but contained more than 25 per cent of global urban dwellers who were without access to an improved water source (for definitions see Glossary). In rural populations the disparity is even greater: only a sixth of the world's rural population live in sub-Saharan Africa, but the region contains more than half

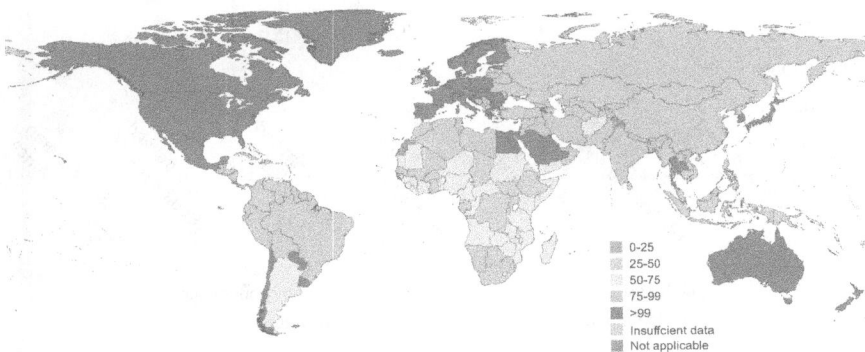

Figure 1.1 Percentage of population using at least basic drinking water services, 2017
Source: WHO/UNICEF, 2017

(52 per cent) of the global total of rural people who remain unserved. The region is predicted to account for half of the global population growth in the period to 2050 (UNDESA, 2017). For these reasons, sub-Saharan Africa forms the focus of this book and especially the rural potential, but it also explores the scale and lessons to be learned from self-supply in other regions and economies.

Global statistics show the worldwide rural progression from unimproved groundwater (self-supply) and surface water to improved non-piped water points (community water supply plus self-supply) and on to piped supplies (see Figure 1.2). They also show the falling rural population (-260 million) in Eastern and South-eastern Asia and its significant growth in Central and Southern Asia and sub-Saharan Africa. In richer economies such as North America and Europe, Australia and New Zealand, and to a lesser extent Latin America, the situation has stabilized as piped supplies (from utilities, companies, and self-supply) have almost reached their maximum extent. In Northern Africa and Western Asia piped provision continues to grow, and in East and South-east Asia development is moving away from non-piped (community water points and widespread self-supply) to piped supplies mainly on premises, with a big reduction in those using unprotected groundwater and surface water. In Central/Southern Asia and sub-Saharan Africa the emphasis is still on gains in non-piped supplies and to a lesser degree in piped supplies, greatly reducing the numbers using unimproved groundwater in the former but having yet to make in-roads in the

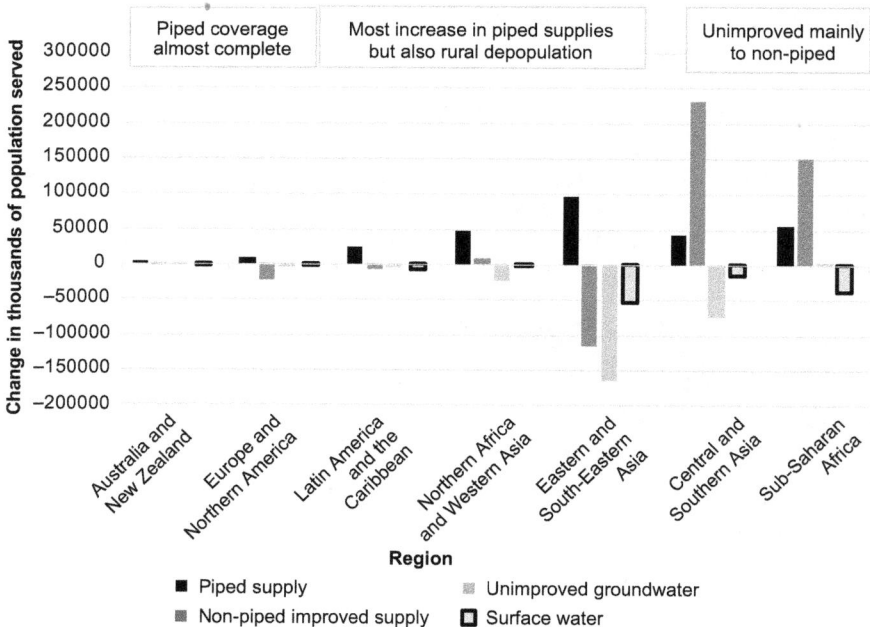

Figure 1.2 Regional changes in rural coverage with improved and unimproved supplies from 2000 to 2017 in selected regions
Source: WHO/UNICEF JMP, 2019

latter. Surface water users are consistently decreasing with both small public supplies and self-supply largely depending on groundwater.

In sub-Saharan Africa over 200 million more people gained access to improved supply in the 17 years since 2000. As the region with the fastest rural population growth in the world, over 230 million in 2017 remained without access to an improved supply, increasingly made up of those using unimproved groundwater. Understanding the reasons for continued dependence on unimproved groundwater and the adoption of new strategies to speed up progress are pre-requisites to reducing their number by 2030. For many millions, nothing has changed in the past 30 years or is predicted to change in 15 or 20 years' time, unless a wider spectrum of solutions can be developed. Those being left behind need to be listened to and become more involved, especially in remote areas where public services seldom operate effectively. The priority must be as Carter (2019) says 'to deliver at least basic services for everyone, rather than an ideal service for a few' in line with the SDG 1.4.1 on equality for the poor and vulnerable. This book explores the situation for those being left behind and aims to introduce new thinking about additional ways to develop basic water services for them.

The changing context with SDGs

Moving from the MDGs to SDGs involves a shift in emphasis from the absolutes of being 'served' or 'not being served' by specific technology types, to step-wise progression in service delivery (see Table 1.1) towards the goal of universal coverage with 'safely managed' supplies. At the bottom end of the ladder, unimproved supplies remain essentially the same as before, consisting of unprotected groundwater or surface water. Improved sources constitute piped supplies, boreholes, protected wells and springs, with rainwater, bottled, or tankered water derived from such sources added in, at a safely managed, basic, or limited service level. The different categories are summarized in Table 1.2.

Table 1.1 The SDG ladder for household drinking water services

Service level	Definition
Safely managed	Drinking water from an improved water source which is located on premises, available when needed and free of faecal and priority chemical contamination
Basic	Drinking water from an improved source provided collection time is not more than 30 minutes for a roundtrip including queuing
Limited	Drinking water from an improved source where collection time exceeds 30 minutes for a roundtrip to collect water including queuing
Unimproved	Drinking water from an unprotected dug well or unprotected spring
No Service	Drinking water collected directly from a river, dam, lake, pond, stream, canal or irrigation channel

Source: UNICEF/WHO JMP, 2017

Table 1.2 MDG and SDG classifications of supply

Level of service	MDG classification	SDG classification
Safely managed	Improved	At least basic
Basic		
Limited		Less than basic
Unimproved	Unimproved	
No service		

The new SDG monitoring process (UNICEF/WHO JMP, 2017) takes a ladder approach, not by technology but by using three conditions linked to improved sources which contribute to a safely managed service. A major change is that proximity to the source and availability/reliability become more strongly represented.

To reach the top of the ladder and be 'safely managed' an improved source must meet three conditions:

- source should be located on premises (within dwelling, yard or plot);
- water should be available when needed; and
- water supplied should be free from fecal and priority chemical contamination.

If any one of the three conditions is not met but the round trip for collecting water takes less than 30 minutes, it will be categorized as a basic service. If water is more than 30 minutes' return trip from the house, it is regarded as only being a 'limited' service, giving a substandard level of access to an improved supply. The aim is to bring improved water supply successively closer until it is on premises, to increase its reliability so it is always available, and to achieve undetectable levels of fecal coliform. The ladder therefore assists in setting targets and benchmarking progress towards SDG Goal 6.1 which is 'By 2030, achieve universal and equitable access to safe and affordable drinking water for all'. The indicator for this objective is the 'Proportion of population using safely managed drinking water services'.

For sanitation a similar ladder indicates progression from open defecation through to safely managed facilities which are not shared, with excreta safely disposed in situ or transported and treated off-site.

Hygiene indicators culminate in hand-washing facilities with soap and water in the house. Indicators for WASH all aim for water in the house for maximum benefit. This is a marked difference from the MDG which implied different goalposts for sanitation (household facility) and water (community facility). As Cumming et al. (2014) pointed out,

> When equivalent benchmarks are used for water and sanitation, the global deficit is as great for water as it is for sanitation, and sanitation progress in the MDG-period (1990–2015) outstrips that in water. As both drinking water and sanitation access yield greater benefits at the household-level than at the community-level, we conclude that any post–2015 goals should consider a household-level benchmark for both.

The significance of 'on-premises' supply

Sandy Cairncross of the London School of Hygiene and Tropical Medicine writes:

> The WHO/UNICEF Joint Monitoring Programme, which compiles the global figures of coverage by country, and year by year, has evolved historically from surveys which mainly reflected concerns about drinking water quality, rather than the increased convenience and savings in time spent carrying water which are associated with water supply improvements. As a result, the figures (WHO/UNICEF JMP, 2019) for rural sub-Saharan Africa alone show that roughly 382 million people officially have access to an improved water supply, but to collect the water and bring it home would require, for 103 million (27%) of those people, a round trip journey of more than 30 minutes.
>
> It is hard to argue that those 103 million people have any access to water which is worthy of the name. Such a gross misclassification would never be admissible in a setting where self-supply was an option. If consumers are to be convinced to help finance their own water supplies, as they do in self-supply, they first need to see that their money will buy them a saving in time and drudgery spent carrying water. In most self-supply schemes, the level of access to which most consumers aspire is on-site, the level at which time-saving is greatest.
>
> When water is made available on the consumer's plot, it stimulates a substantial increase in per capita water usage by each household. This is usually accompanied by considerable reductions (24–80 per cent) in the incidence of diarrhoeal disease (Esrey et al., 1990), noticeably greater than the reductions of 15–30 per cent normally associated with the public tap level of water service. Esrey's review is old, but similar patterns can be seen in more modern and more rigorous studies (Brown et al., 2013) and systematic reviews (Overbo et al., 2016; Wolf et al., 2018). It appears that provision of a public water point has limited impact on health, even where the water provided is of good quality and it replaces a traditional source which was heavily contaminated with faecal material. By contrast, moving the same tap from the street corner to the yard produces a substantial reduction in diarrhoeal morbidity. How is this recurring pattern to be understood?
>
> The first step to an explanation is an understanding that most endemic diarrhoeal disease is transmitted by water-washed routes and is not water-borne. This means that the germs which cause it are transported to the next victim's mouth on food, hands, and other surfaces which are not kept clean enough because of a shortage of water. While water-borne *epidemics* of diarrhoeal diseases such as cholera and typhoid (in which many people caught the disease in a short space of time by drinking contaminated water) have been notorious in the history of public health, the *endemic* pattern of transmission

(causing continuous but sporadic cases) seems to be different, particularly in poor communities.

1. *Negative health impact studies.* As mentioned above, Esrey et al. (1985, 1990) cite a number of studies of the health impact of water supplies, where water quality improvements have failed to produce a significant impact on diarrhoeal disease incidence.
2. *Food microbiology.* Studies of the microbiology of foods in low income countries, particularly the weaning foods fed to children in the age group most susceptible to diarrhoeal disease, have shown them to be far more heavily contaminated with faecal bacteria than their drinking water (Lanata, 2003; Touré et al., 2011), even when the water has been stored in open pots.
3. *Seasonality of diarrhoea.* In countries with a seasonal variation in temperature, bacterial diarrhoeas peak in the warmer season, whereas viral diarrhoeas peak in the winter (Rowland, 1986). This suggests that the bacterial pathogens show environmental re-growth at some stage in their transmission route, which means that they must have a nutritional substrate. Water is thus a less likely vehicle than food.
4. *Fly control studies.* Trials in rural Asia and Africa have shown that fly control can reduce diarrhoeal disease incidence by 23 per cent (Chavasse et al., 1999; Emerson et al., 1999).
5. *Hand washing studies.* A systematic review of the impact of hand washing with soap has shown that this simple measure is associated with a reduction of 43 per cent in diarrhoeal disease, and 48 per cent in diarrhoeas with the more life-threatening etiologies (Curtis and Cairncross, 2003).
6. *Intervention studies of weaning food hygiene.* Two recent randomized trials of weaning food hygiene promotion in Nepal (Gautam et al., 2017) and in the Gambia (Manjang et al., 2018) added secondary outcomes to their protocol, and so detected significant reductions in diarrhoea prevalence, by 75 per cent and 61 per cent, respectively. These outcomes have not yet been subject to peer review, but the reductions are large enough to suggest that they are robust.

The second step is to understand how the level of service and convenience of a water supply influences such hygiene practices in the home. Taking the amount of water used per capita as an indicator of hygiene changes, other things being equal, one finds that providing a public source of water closer to the home, and therefore more convenient to use, has very little impact on water consumption unless the old source was substantially more than 1 kilometre (30 minutes' round trip journey) away from the user's dwelling.

Water consumption doubles or trebles when water is provided on the plot (White et al., 1972), and there is reason to believe that much of the additional consumption is used for hygiene purposes. For example,

Curtis et al. (1995) found that provision of a yard tap nearly doubled the odds of a mother washing her hands after cleaning her child's anus, and more than doubled the odds that she would wash any faecally soiled linen immediately.

To conclude, self-supply of water is likely to involve provision of an on-plot level of service, and this offers the greatest time-saving benefits and the best hope of health improvements, particularly when the old source of water was more than 30 minutes' round trip away.

Sandy Cairncross

Trends in the progress of water supply in sub-Saharan Africa

In the period 2000–2017 urban coverage (see Figure 1.3) increased by significantly more than rural (185 million and 109 million, respectively). Inequalities between the two environments have therefore been perpetuated with 84 per cent of those with a less than basic supply being rural dwellers.

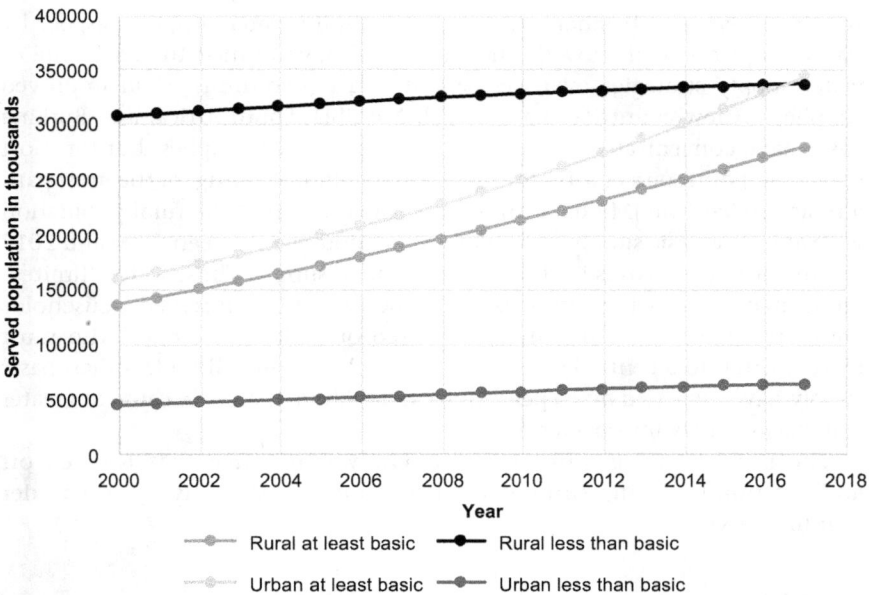

Figure 1.3 Trends in rural and urban 'at least basic' and 'less than basic' water supplies in sub-Saharan Africa
Source: WHO/UNICEF JMP, 2019

Recent progress in sub-Saharan urban water supply

The proportion of the urban population with an 'at least basic' supply has doubled in the past 17 years and those with a 'less than basic' supply have

Table 1.3 Summary of sub-Saharan urban water supply trends towards SDG 6.1 from 2000

Level of service	2000	2017	Growth to 2017 (%)
Safely managed	85,697,505	203,876,368	138
Basic	73,220,571	140,339,379	92
Limited	18,707,516	32,267,727	72
Unimproved groundwater	17,502,871	24,880,504	42
Surface water	7,512,480	6,036,985	−20

increased by over 50 per cent. Surface water users have decreased, but users of unimproved groundwater are very gradually increasing (see Table 1.3). They in part augment public supplies with rural types of point water supply (unimproved wells, springs). The number of urban dwellers who have a limited service because water collection time is greater than 30 minutes has almost doubled, reflecting the growth of peri-urban and slum populations (see Chapter 4).

Rural water supply trends in sub-Saharan Africa

In rural areas of sub-Saharan Africa, community water supplies, especially handpumps on shallow wells and boreholes, have formed the backbone of water supply strategies over the past 40 years (two-thirds of all improved supplies). A few countries (e.g. Senegal, Namibia, South Africa, and Burkina Faso) have concentrated more on multi-village piped supplies, but for most countries, point sources form the major rural option, offering for the most part, a basic service. The JMP data[1] shows (see Table 1.4) that the rural population with at least a basic supply of drinking water doubled between 2000 and 2017 but the fastest growth is in those with a limited supply. Those in the 'limited' group may be growing fastest because the remaining unserved households are increasingly in smaller, more dispersed or peripheral groups who must travel further to a centralized supply. As a result, those with a less than basic supply have increased by 10 per cent to 336 million, mainly because of greater distance to a new improved source.

The number using unimproved groundwater sources has levelled off and the number using surface water is falling consistently by just under 4 million a year.

Table 1.4 Summary of sub-Saharan rural water trends towards SDG 6.1

Level of service	2000	2017	Growth to 2017 (%)
Safely managed	28,730,821	71,475,234	149
Basic	107,241,669	207,285,268	93
Limited	38,783,287	103,163,015	166
Unimproved groundwater	152,000,404	154,632,317	2
Surface water	115,610,009	78,725,660	−32

By 2017 11.6 per cent of rural sub-Saharan Africa had achieved 'safely managed' status (WHO/UNICEF JMP, 2019), and 45 per cent 'at least basic'. The definitive publication by WHO/UNICEF JMP (2017) advises that 'individual countries will therefore need to establish customized national targets focused on increasing coverage of basic and safely managed services in line with national strategies for sustainable development'. At the same time, they must reduce inequalities of service and aim to leave no one behind. While many country targets are for safely managed supply for all (WHO, 2019), SDG Indicator 1.4.1 on equality looks for the 'proportion of population living in households with access to basic services (including access to basic drinking water, basic sanitation and basic handwashing facilities)'. To achieve the goal of universal access, few sub-Saharan countries can realistically look at doing so for everyone beyond the 'basic' level by 2030. Even that is a distant dream for many of the harder to reach. The ultimate aim must be for the highest level of service for all, but interim targets may need to be set for progress to be seen as successful rather than designed to fall short.

Combining the elements of WASH

The transfer of new approaches developed in Asia to other parts of the developing world has accelerated progress in sanitation especially in the last decade, and also shows the care necessary in transferring between different cultures and between high- and low-density populations. Over a hundred million sub-Saharan urban dwellers and almost 60 million rural ones have gained an 'at least basic' sanitation facility since 2000. Largely as a result of population growth, the number of rural people in the region practising open defecation has remained essentially the same (190 million in 2000, 181 million in 2017). With projected rural population growth of a further 140 million by 2030 (World Bank, 2017), the trends of the past 17 years imply open defecation-free numbers in rural areas will fall short of the targets of 2030. Roche et al. (2017) found that only 15.4 per cent of sub-Saharan African households have both improved water supply and sanitation. The common challenges that water and sanitation face especially for low-density rural populations and relevant sanitation approaches (community-led total sanitation and sanitation marketing) suggest a great potential to tackle the challenges of both together and/or to use shared resources when looking for household level response.

New approaches are needed to get households to analyse their priorities and how to achieve them for long-term sustainability. Perhaps it is, as Anderson et al. (2012) exhort us, 'time to listen' and give more attention to household priorities and aspirations and pay more heed to their solutions and decisions. Some fundamental changes are needed in strategies, not least because of the changing context facing those looking to provide a range of WASH services to the last 10 or 20 per cent.

The changing context in sub-Saharan rural water supply

The environment within which the first 50 per cent of coverage was achieved varies considerably from that which now pertains. Changing circumstances in terms of:

- sources of water and climate change;
- size of communities;
- projections from trends in progress to date;
- trends in per capita costs and official development assistance (ODA).

all point to an urgent need for new thinking.

Sources of water

The number of people depending on surface water has fallen by 32 per cent since 2000 (WHO/UNICEF JMP, 2019). Those who mostly use unprotected groundwater have roughly stabilized in number (2 per cent increase over the same period). The numerical persistence of unprotected groundwater users suggests a greater reluctance (and/or a lesser opportunity) to change. This may in part link to the small size of communities or preference for the familiar, but also to the degree to which people are investing in their own wells for greater convenience and flexibility of use and are reluctant to abandon their investment.

Reduced dependence on surface water is also linked to climate change as closer sources begin to dry up, and groundwater is better buffered for increasingly frequent droughts. Shallow wells and springs or lakes and streams may all equally be affected by changing patterns of rainfall, stimulating action by communities to seek more reliable supplies and some of those already covered seeking replacement of wells which have dried up. Pressure on construction capacity and budgets can only grow.

The size of unserved communities

The growth in numbers of those with a 'limited' water supply reflects the higher proportion of newly served communities where a centralized point can only conveniently supply relatively few people. This hypothesis is supported by figures on population density and user numbers.

During the earlier years of community water supply construction, much effort was put into identifying larger communities for cost-effective results. Planning of water point coverage largely depended on defining groups of 250–300 people, regarded as the optimum number to be served by one handpump. To achieve this within a radial distance of 500 metres is equivalent to a density of 318 people/km². Low densities (see Figure 1.4) do not have to mean scattered households but with a regional average of 23 people/km² (Wikipedia, 2018), equivalent to about four households

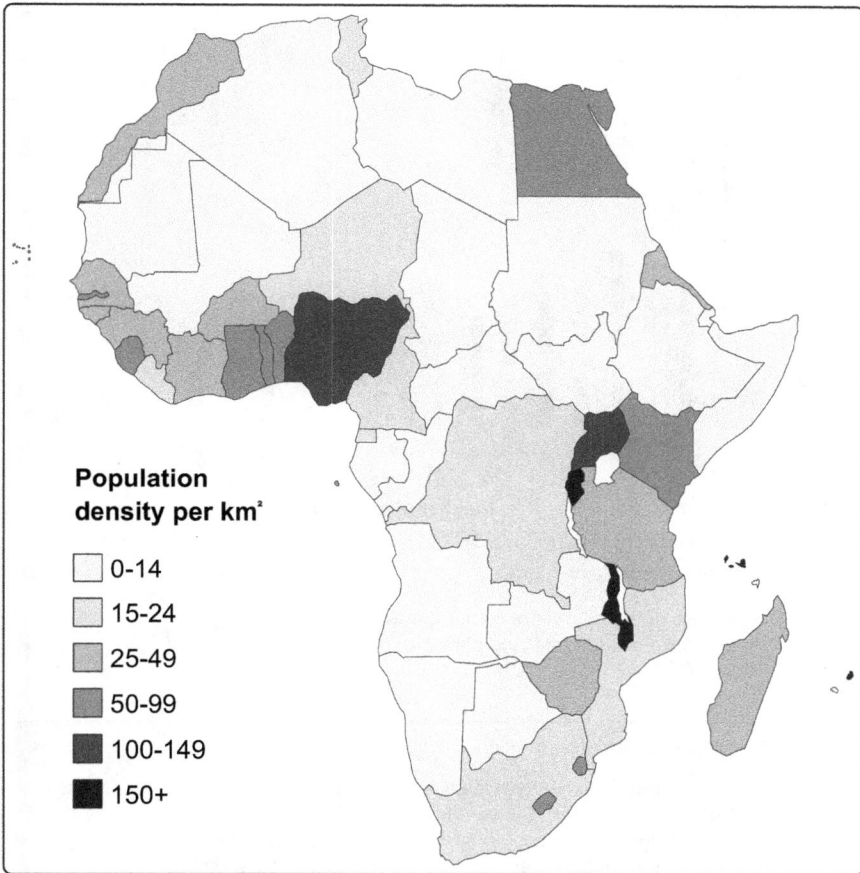

Figure 1.4 Population densities in Africa

per km², districts with lower densities and smaller communities are not rare especially in resettlement areas, or among those depending on rain-fed crops or livestock farming. Figure 1.5 gives some examples from four countries with 20–54 per cent of communities smaller than 100 inhabitants. In Ethiopia, combining GIS and census data (A. Smith, personal communication on research being carried out using GIS and Python software to identify population densities from census data, 2019), 7–24 per cent of the rural population in two randomly chosen *kebeles* live in areas with a density which would only result in 125 or fewer users per handpump within 500 m. Surveyed districts in Sierra Leone and Malawi (GOAL and PumpAid field data) show a similar pattern. Regionally, indications are that some 15–20 per cent of rural people live in communities of less than 15 households (or approximately 100 people) and that these form more of the target communities as coverage increases (see Box 1.2).

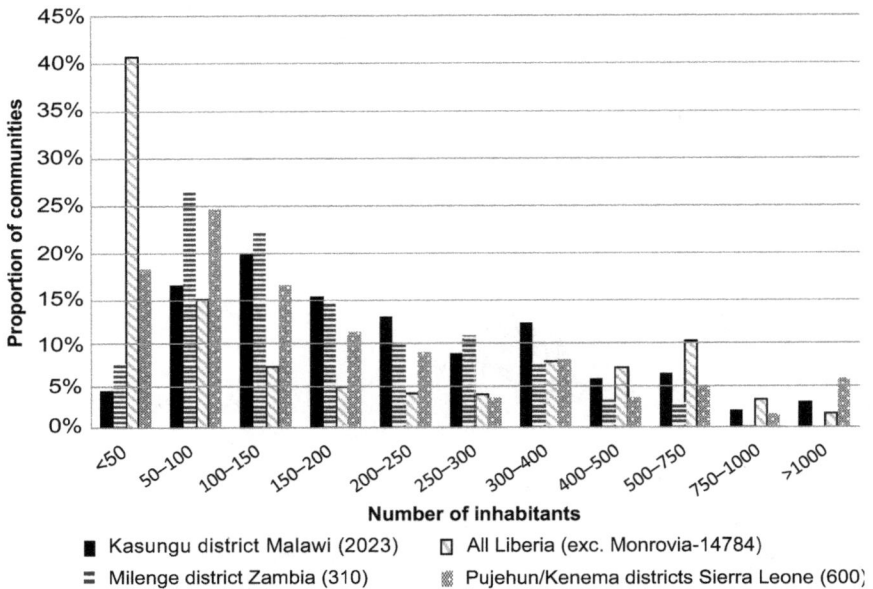

Figure 1.5 Examples of distribution of community size
Note: Figure in brackets is the total sample size.
Source: Sutton, 2017

Box 1.2 Community size and user numbers in Liberia

Liberia is unusual for having countrywide information on community sizes and on those that have an operating water supply. It is possible to examine the size of communities that in 2011 had not been served. In a country with many small groups of rural households, more than 4,000 communities have fewer than 50 inhabitants and are without functioning water supplies (see Figure 1.6). As coverage increases, the number of people served by each new water point is likely to be smaller compared with those constructed some time ago.

For example, in 2011 when coverage was 60 per cent the average user number per water point was 280 and the average number of inhabitants of unserved communities was 114. When coverage reaches 80 per cent, if the focus has continued to be on larger unserved communities, the average size of remaining unserved communities will be 60. The decrease in numbers served per unit will lead not only to a slowing in progress unless borehole construction rates increase, but also to a significant increase in per capita costs. The capital costs of a borehole and handpump are effectively the same, regardless of how many people are served. In the Liberian case this would lead to a per capita increase in costs by at least a factor of four for the last 20 per cent of communities.

The potential future reduction in numbers per water point is likely to have a significant effect on rates of progress in coverage and on per capita costs, since capital costs remain the same (or even higher mobilizing to remote areas) divided by a smaller number of consumers. Lower cost options are needed for affordable capital costs (to the state) and simpler maintenance requirements in remote areas.

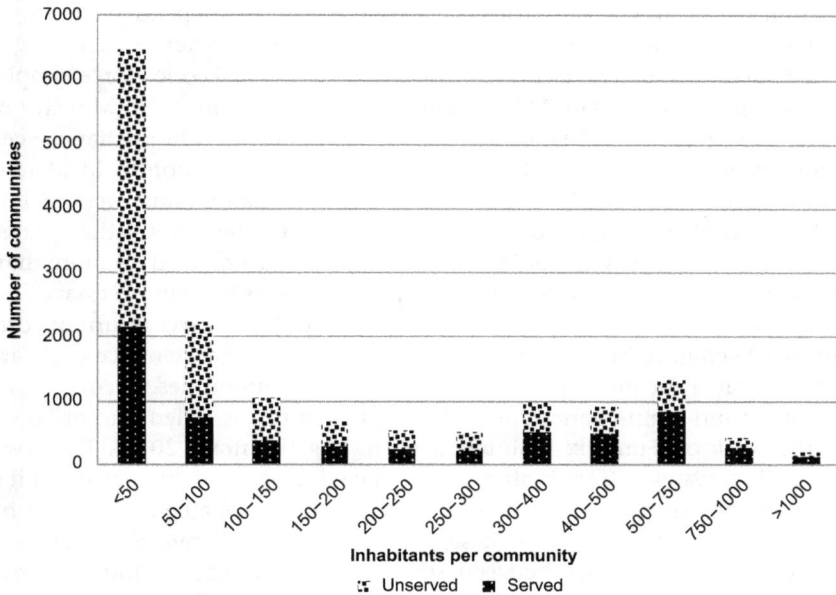

Figure 1.6 Liberia – community size and coverage
Source: Personal communication, Abdul Koroma, Ministry of Public Works Monrovia, 2014, and waterpoint inventory raw data held by Ministry of Public Works

The challenge of keeping existing supplies functioning

Providing new supplies is popular with politicians and contractors, while the 'low hanging fruit' of refurbishing or replacing handpumps which have been out of action for prolonged periods tends to be popular as a cost-effective intervention with local government and NGOs. This equates to deferred maintenance and underlines the degree to which funding of repairs has tended to be a low priority with national governments and often unaffordable or not a priority for communities. The result has been continuous slippage where initial capital investment is slowly lost where communities are unwilling or unable to provide all the necessary resources to keep their supply operating in the long term, without continued inputs from government or donors (Foster, 2013). Foster found that the degree of water point failure was linked most to the age of the pump and strength of management.

In 2009 an assessment (RWSN, 2009) put the proportion of non-functioning supplies in sub-Saharan Africa at around 35 per cent. Later estimates range from 22 per cent (Banks and Furey, 2016) to 26 per cent (Foster et al., 2019), the latter being equivalent to some 175,000 water points. This represents a fall in the proportion of non–functioning water points, suggesting improved maintenance systems and/or an increasing rate of rehabilitation or replacement; still one in four supplies is out of action and long-term maintenance is generally not included in government budgets.

Pump downtime greatly affects whether users can depend on a single source. Most households collect water every day or every other day. The length of a breakdown period is therefore critical. In Sierra Leone, for example, 56 per cent of more than 23,000 handpumps surveyed in 2016 (Ministry of Water Resources (Sierra Leone), 2016) had broken down for more than a week before their last repair and 46 per cent for more than a month. In Malawi (Mwathunga et al., 2017) 45 per cent of surveyed handpumps were of low yield or out of action for more than a month a year. The result is that a large proportion of people with 'at least basic' supplies must depend on more than one source during the year and use of multiple sources is often necessary.

Sector strategies have put the onus on communities to cover recurrent costs but it is becoming increasingly apparent that capital maintenance costs are not affordable for most. It may be possible for communities to cover basic operation and maintenance costs, although even this is called into question by the work on Fundifix maintenance funding (Dahmm, 2018). The costs of keeping systems functioning are predicted to exceed projected capital requirements for basic supplies by 2029 and will not be able to be borne by users alone (Hutton and Varughese, 2016). Studies in Kenya note that it is difficult to get a balance between sustainable fee structures and universal access without additional support (Foster and Hope, 2017). Pay-as-you-fetch generates higher income and better operational performance than a flat rate tariff per household, but also increases the probability that households will revert to free, less protected supplies (self-supply sources). Because their income is seasonal, many rural families find difficulty in maintaining cash payments through all seasons and may opt for cheaper sources of water at least for high volume uses such as washing or bathing.

Failure rates tend to be highest in communities which are far from district or county capitals (Foster, 2013) highlighting the special problems faced by more remote communities. Greater financial support and/or different technologies need to be considered for remote areas if supply systems are to be sustainable in the long term. There is real concern that poorer countries and poorer households will not be able to cover such costs, and a growing acknowledgement that sustainability cannot be achieved without better targeting of public funds and a greater choice in technology options.

If a far greater part of public funding has to be diverted to maintenance issues, the result is that either budgets for new construction will reduce or more water points will go out of action. Either way, the rate of coverage increase will slow down, and those now being left behind will have an even longer wait for change.

Projection from trends in service levels to date

Figure 1.7 shows the projected best-case scenario for 2030. It assumes that there is a constant acceleration in rates of progress as in the past five years. The prediction on this basis is that in 2030 some 53 per cent of rural people (just over 400 million) will use an 'at least basic' supply, and a further 22 per cent a limited supply.

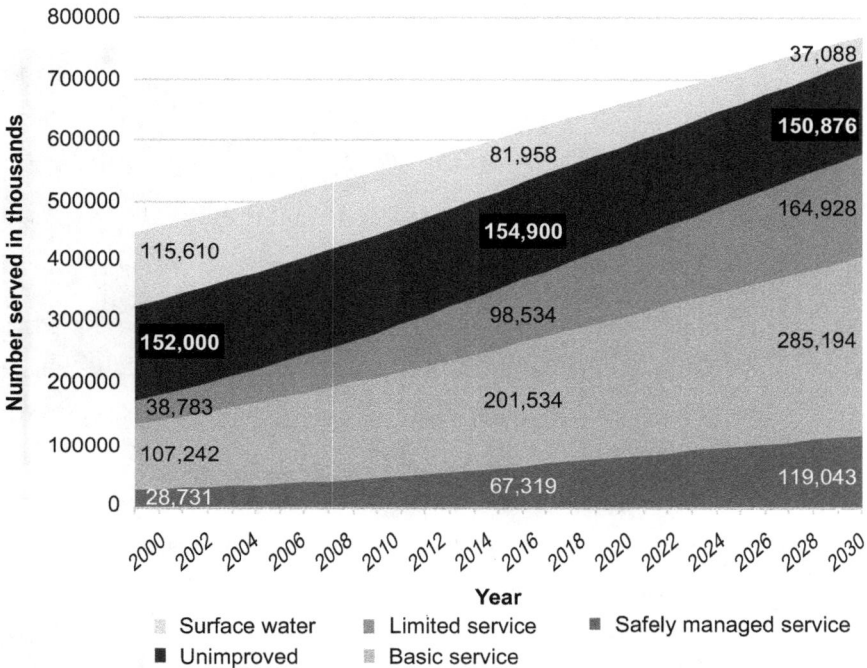

Figure 1.7 Projected trends in sub-Saharan rural water supply coverage to 2030
Source: Based on WHO/UNICEF JMP, 2019 data and World Bank, 2017 population projections

People have been abandoning surface water sources at an accelerating rate since 2000. If that rate continues to grow, surface water users would decrease to around 37 million (5 per cent) by 2030 as a result of distance to the source, climatic variability, and their growing understanding that groundwater is safer and usually more convenient. Projections using the latest trends from JMP data would see groundwater user numbers in 2030 reduce marginally to some 150 million. The growth in coverage with improved supplies assumes that existing rates of functioning can be maintained and combined with an increase in supply construction in line with trends to date.

Funding trends and requirements

Adjusting for the smaller size of communities still to be covered, more than a six-fold increase in investment and construction capacity was required in 2016 to ensure universal access to an improved supply ('limited' plus 'at least basic') by 2030. A multiplier is needed for each year coverage rates are not escalated, so by 2018 it had already risen to more than seven times the previous investment rates and will increase every year that coverage rates are not escalated. In addition, there is the cost of keeping all existing water points in operation through maintenance and rehabilitation or replacement. This cost

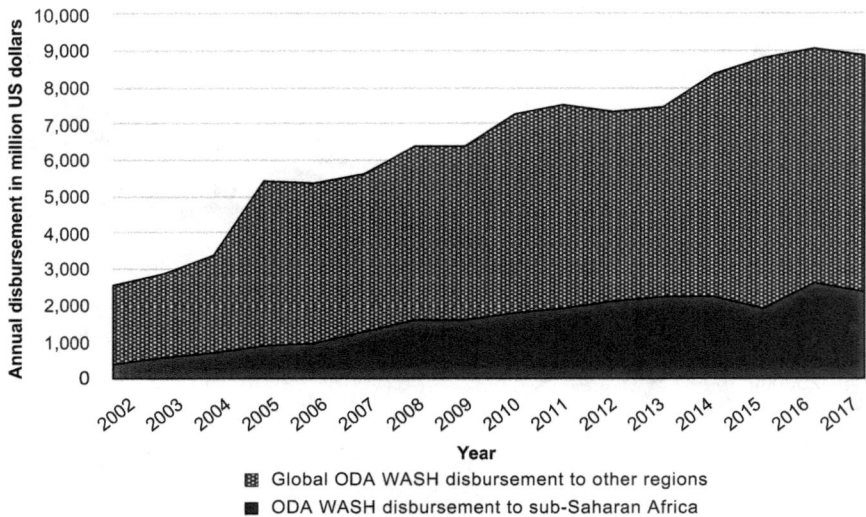

Figure 1.8 ODA disbursements to the WASH sector at global and sub-Saharan Africa regional levels, 2002–2017
Source: African Development Bank, 2019, UN Stats, 2019

is put at US$3–6 per head per year by the WASHCost team (2012) and at around $10 per head by OECD (2005) for a borehole and handpump, with a suggestion by Foster (2013) and others that the major part of rehabilitation or replacement will need to be borne by government.

The largest part of water supply investment in sub-Saharan Africa comes from ODA, with inputs also by local governments and NGOs. WaterAid (2015) identifies 45 countries still largely dependent on ODA for investment in the sector, and 36 of these are in sub-Saharan Africa. ODA for WASH has risen gradually from 2005 (UnStats 2019), peaking in 2016. From 2008 sub-Saharan Africa has received 25–30 per cent of disbursements (see Figure 1.8) reflecting its high population growth rate and continued deficit in coverage. Meanwhile government contributions to date have increased by an average of 4.5 per cent per annum (Fonseca and Pores, 2017).

In summary, capacity to achieve target levels of coverage may be strongly affected by pressure from additional calls upon public funding (left side of Figure 1.9) and from factors affecting the per capita cost of new supplies and maintenance of existing ones (right side of Figure 1.9).

The calls to give sanitation higher priority than in the past combined with a growing awareness of the need for public funds for maintenance means that money allocated for WASH has to go further. In addition, several countries in the region including Tanzania, Uganda, and Ethiopia and Malawi are looking to introduce or increase multi-village water supplies. The experiences of Ghana are that these have capital costs which are twice as high as for a handpump supply and that such schemes are

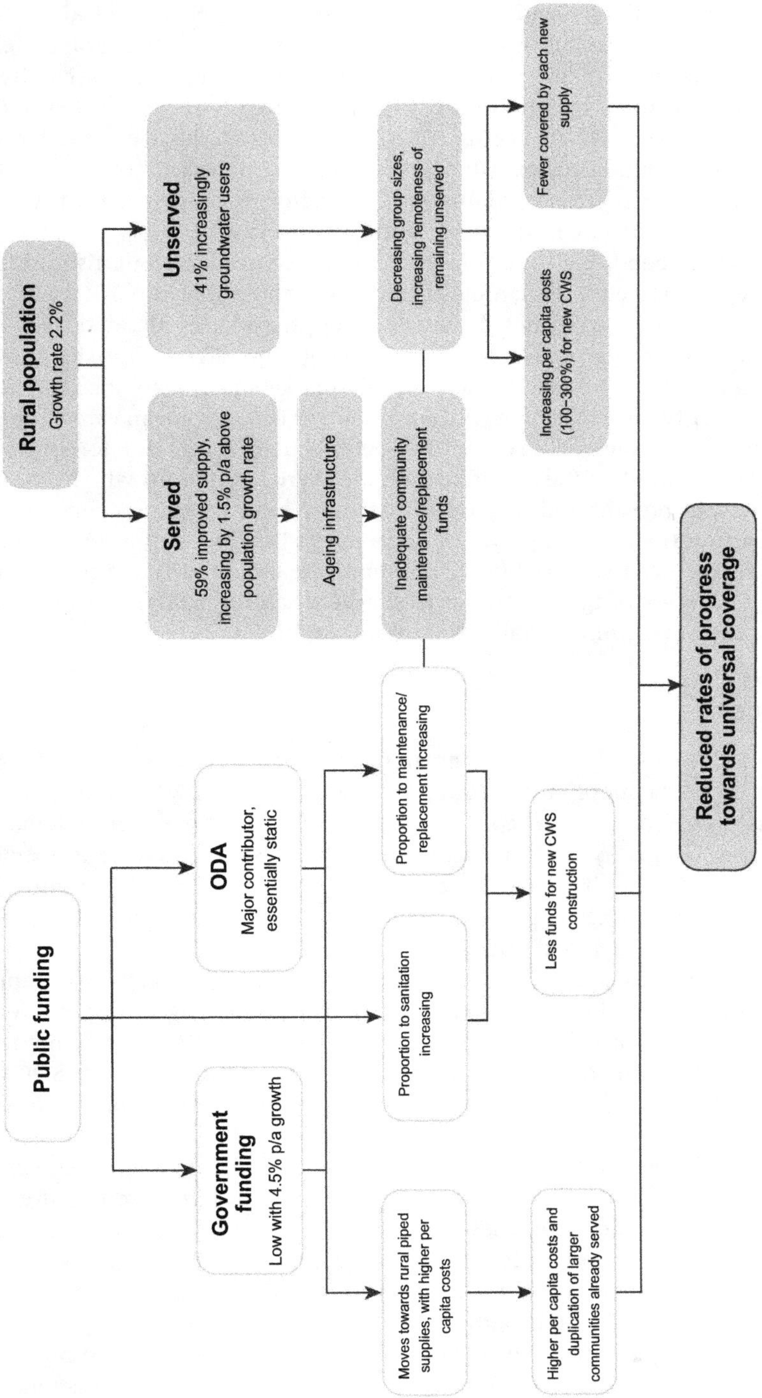

Figure 1.9 Summary of main trends which may affect future progress towards universal coverage in sub-Saharan Africa

best suited to villages with more than 300 people (Nyarko et al., 2010). Any move towards small piped supplies is therefore likely to involve higher per capita costs than for point supplies and to be applied principally to larger communities which are most likely to already have point supplies. As coverage nears 80 per cent it is to be expected that the smaller size of remaining communities will slow the rate of increased coverage unless WASH funding increases dramatically, and/or strategies adjust to the specific needs of smaller and more remote communities.

Progress depends not only on what funds are available but also on how well they are targeted. Pullan et al. (2014) conclude that the SDGs will not be achieved unless countries deliberately adopt strategies aimed at reaching the lowest coverage areas and population groups. These are often areas which are poorest and with few available markets and materials; this does not necessarily mean they are without resources but may mean careful design of targeted subsidies to leave no one behind. It is important for strategies to be well-tailored to the specific needs and varied scenarios which 'the last to be served' present and to ensure that those who have to depend wholly or in part on their own supply, can do so safely. Dealing with water supply as a personal rather than a public asset requires new ways of thinking, and new ways of using existing support services rather than regarding the situation as being simply a technical challenge of water supply.

Conclusion

Sub-Saharan Africa remains the greatest challenge in achieving WASH SDG targets. In water supply terms it appears obvious that in 2030 there will still be major gaps not just in coverage, but also in the time that systems are functional in quality and quantity terms. Sector strategies already in place need to be added to if large numbers of rural people, and smaller numbers of urban dwellers, largely depending on unimproved groundwater, are not still to lack access to improved water supply in 2030.

Sanitation has seen an enormous shift towards household-financed sanitation approaches (CLTS and sanitation marketing) since universal coverage with subsidized sanitation services was seen to be unachievable. A similar shortfall in human and financial resources to achieve SDG 6.1 (WHO, 2019) through public water supply alone requires similar innovative thinking.

This book therefore looks at the existing roles and potential of self-supply to speed up progress, to access additional (household) funds, and ensure that all families can achieve some level of improved access to and quality of water supply. It is an option which enables households themselves, wherever it is technically feasible, to take positive steps to ensure that they are not left behind. It builds on what many families already do in providing a (usually low) level of supply themselves. This can be strengthened through provision of support services accelerating progress and increased personal investment.

Note

1. JMP figures are being continuously refined. Figures and trends (including those from 2000–2010) have significantly changed from those apparent at the time of the review of MDGs (WHO/UNICEF, 2017). Particularly where values are interpolated from very few surveys, they have changed again with new data for 2017, made available in July 2019. Figures given in publications from different dates may therefore not be the same, and the figures given here may again change in the future even for data from more than a decade ago.

References

African Development Bank (2019) African Information Highway [online], AFDB Socio Economic Database, 1960–2020 <https://dataportal.open dataforafrica.org/nbyenxf/afdb-socio-economic-database-1960-2020> [accessed June 2020].

Anderson, M., Brown, D. and Jean, I. (2012) *Time to Listen: Hearing People on the Receiving End of International Aid*, CDA Collaborative Learning Projects, Cambridge, MA.

Banks, B. and Furey, S. (2016) *What's Working, Where, and for How Long: A 2016 Water Point Update to the RWSN (2009) statistics* [online], GWC/Skat, RWSN, St Gallen, Switzerland <http://www.rural-water-supply.net/en/resources/details/787> [accessed 13 June 2018].

Brown, J., Vo Thi Hien, McMahan, L., Jenkins, M., Thie, L., Liang, K., Printy, E. and Sobsey, M. (2013) 'Relative benefits of on-plot water supply over other "improved" sources in rural Vietnam', *Tropical Medicine & International Health* 18(1): 65–74 <http://dx.doi.org/10.1111/tmi.12010>.

Carter, R. (2019) 'Editorial: Leave no one behind in rural services', *Waterlines* 38(2): 69–70 <http://dx.doi.org/10.3362/1756-3488.18-00028>.

Chavasse, D.C., Shier, R.P., Murphy, O.A., Huttly, S.R.A, Cousens, S.N. and Akhtar, T. (1999) 'Impact of fly control on childhood diarrhea in Pakistan: community-randomised trial', *Lancet* 353(9146): 22–5 <https://doi.org/10.1016/s0140-6736(98)03366-2>.

Cumming, O., Elliott, M., Overbo, A. and Bartram, J. (2014) 'Does global progress on sanitation really lag behind water? An analysis of global progress on community- and household-level access to safe water and sanitation', *PloS One* 9(12): e114699 <https://doi.org/10.1371/journal.pone.0114699>.

Curtis, V. and Cairncross, S. (2003) 'Effect of washing hands with soap on diarrhea risk in the community: a systematic review', *Lancet Infectious Diseases* 3(5): 275–81 <https://doi.org/10.1016/s1473-3099(03)00606-6>.

Curtis, V., Kanki, B., Mertens, T., Traore, E., Diallo, I., Tall, F. and Cousens, S. (1995) 'Potties, pits and pipes: explaining hygiene behaviour in Burkina Faso', *Social Science & Medicine* 41(3): 383–93.

Dahmm, H. (2018) *Handpump Data Improves Water Access* [online], SDSN TReNDS, UN Sustainable Developments Solutions Network, Paris <https://www.sdsntrends.org/research/2018/11/27/case-study-smart-handpump-project> [accessed 17 January 2019].

Emerson, P.M., Lindsay, S.W., Walraven, G.E., Faal, H., Bøgh, C., Lowe, K. and Bailey, R.L. (1999) 'Effect of fly control on trachoma and diarrhea', *Lancet* 353(9162): 1401–3.

Esrey, S.A. and Habicht, J.P. (1985) *The Impact of Improved Water Supplies and Excreta Disposal Facilities on Diarrheal Morbidity, Growth, and Mortality among Children*, Cornell International Nutrition Monograph Series no. 15, Division of Nutritional Sciences, Cornell University, Ithaca, NY.

Esrey, S., Potash, J., Roberts, L. and Shiff, C. (1990) *Health Benefits from Improvements in Water Supply and Sanitation: Survey and Analysis of the Literature on Selected Diseases*, WASH Technical Report no. 66, Environmental Health Project for USAID, Rosslyn, VA.

Fonseca, C. and Pores, L. (2017) *Financing WASH: How to Increase Funds for the Sector while Reducing Inequities: Position Paper for the Sanitation and Water for All Finance Ministers Meeting, April 19, 2017* [pdf], Water.org and IRC <https://water.org/documents/48/Water.org_Financing_SDG_Position_Paper_April_2017.pdf> [accessed 18 May 2020].

Foster, T. (2013) 'Predictors of sustainability for community-managed handpumps in sub-Saharan Africa: evidence from Liberia, Sierra Leone, and Uganda', *Environmental Science and Technology* 47: 12037–46 <http://dx.doi.org/10.1021/es402086n>.

Foster, T. and Hope, R. (2017) 'Evaluating waterpoint sustainability and access implications of revenue collection approaches in rural Kenya', *Water Resources Research* 53(2): 1473–90 <https://doi.org/10.1002/2016WR019634>.

Foster, T., Furey, S., Banks, B. and Willetts, J. (2019) 'Functionality of handpump water supplies: a review of data from sub-Saharan Africa and the Asia-Pacific region', *International Journal of Water Resources Development* <https://doi.org/10.1080/07900627.2018.1543117>.

Gautam, O.P., Schmidt, W.P., Cairncross, S., Cavill, S. and Curtis V. (2017) 'Trial of a novel intervention to improve multiple food hygiene behaviors in Nepal', *The American Journal of Tropical Medicine and Hygiene* 96(6): 1415–26 <http://dx.doi.org/10.4269/ajtmh.16-0526>.

Hutton, G. and Varughese, M. (2016) *The Costs of Meeting the 2030 Sustainable Development Goal Targets on Drinking Water, Sanitation, and Hygiene* [pdf], Technical paper 103171, WSP, World Bank <http://documents.worldbank.org/curated/en/415441467988938343/pdf/103171-PUB-Box394556B-PUBLIC-EPI-K8543-ADD-SERIES.pdf> [accessed June 2018].

Lanata, C.F. (2003) 'Studies of food hygiene and diarrheal disease', *International Journal of Environmental Health Research* 13(suppl 1): S175–S183 <https://doi.org/10.1080/0960312031000102921>.

Manjang, B., Hemming, K., Bradley, C., Ensink, J., Martin, J.T., Sowe, J., Jarju, A., Cairncross, S. and Manaseki-Holland, S. (2018) 'Promoting hygienic weaning food handling practices through a community-based programme: intervention implementation and baseline characteristics for a cluster randomised controlled trial in rural Gambia', *BMJ Open* 8(8): e017573 <http://dx.doi.org/10.1136/bmjopen-2017-017573>.

Ministry of Public Works and Liberian Institute of Statistics (2011) *Liberia Waterpoint Atlas* [pdf], Final review version <https://www.acaps.org/sites/acaps/files/key-documents/files/waterpoint_atlas_-_wsp.pdf> [accessed 10th December 2019].

Ministry of Water Resources (MWR) Sierra Leone (2016) 'Sierra Leone WASH data portal: Water point functionality' [website] <https://washdata-sl. org/water-point-data/water-point-functionality/2016/> [accessed 18 May 2020].

Mwathunga, E., MacDonald, A.M., Bonsor, H.C., Chavula, G., Banda, S., Mleta, P., Jumbo, S., Gwengweya, G., Ward, J., Lapworth, D., Whaley, L. and Lark, R.M. (2017) *UPGro Hidden Crisis Research Consortium: Survey 1 Country Report, Malawi* [online] (OR/17/046), British Geological Survey, Nottingham <http://nora.nerc.ac.uk/id/eprint/518402/> [accessed June 2018].

Nyarko, K., Dwumfour-Asare, B., Appiah-Effah, E. and Moriarty, P. (2010) 'Cost of delivering water services in rural areas and small towns in Ghana', in *IRC Symposium 2010 Pumps, Pipes and Promises* [pdf] <https://www. safewaternetwork.org/file/774/download?token=kR6ygpUP> [accessed 15 January 2019].

OECD (2005) *Rural Cost Functions for Water Supply and Sanitation* [pdf], OECD EAP Task Force Secretariat (EXD/PCM/EN/NMC/04/125) <https://www. oecd.org/env/outreach/36228167.pdf> [accessed June 2020].

Overbo, A., Williams, A.R., Evans, B., Hunter, P.R. and Bartram, J. (2016) 'On-plot drinking water supplies and health: a systematic review', *International Journal of Hygiene and Environmental Health* 219(4–5): 317–30 <http://dx.doi.org/10.1016/j.ijheh.2016.04.008>.

Oxford Institute for Energy Studies (2018) 'Electrifying Africa', *Forum* 115 [online] <https://www.oxfordenergy.org/wpcms/wp-content/uploads/2018/ 09/OEF-115.pdf> [accessed 7th February 2020].

Pullan, R.L., Freeman, M.C., Gething, P.W. and Brooker, S.J. (2014) 'Geographical inequalities in use of improved drinking water supply and sanitation across sub-Saharan Africa: mapping and spatial analysis of cross-sectional survey data', *PLoS Medicine* 11(4): e1001626 <https://doi. org/10.1371/journal.pmed.1001626>.

Roche, R., Bain, R. and Cumming, O. (2017) 'A long way to go: estimates of combined water, sanitation and hygiene coverage for 25 sub-Saharan African countries', *PLoS One* 12(3): e0173702 <https://doi.org/10.1371/ journal.pone.0173702>.

Rowland, M.G. (1986) 'The Gambia and Bangladesh: the seasons and diarrhea', *Dialogue on Diarrhea* (26): 3.

Rural Water Supply Network (RWSN) (2009) 'Handpump data 2009: selected countries in Sub-Saharan Africa' [website] <http://www.rural-water-supply. net/en/resources/details/203> [accessed 29 August 2015].

Sutton, S. (2017) 'Trends in sub-Saharan rural water supply and the essential inclusion of self-supply to achieve universal access', *Waterlines* 36(4) <https:doi.org/10.3362/1756-3488.2017.36>.

Touré, O., Coulibaly, S., Arby, A., Maiga, F. and Cairncross, S. (2011) 'Improving microbiological food safety in peri-urban Mali; an experimental study', *Food Control* 22(10): 1565–72 <https://doi.org/10.1016/j.foodcont.2011.03.012>.

United Nations, Department of Economic and Social Affairs, Population Division (UNDESA) (2017) *World Population Prospects: The 2017 Revision. Key Findings and Advance Tables* [pdf], Working Paper no. ESA/P/WP/248 <https:// population.un.org/wpp/Publications/Files/WPP2017_KeyFindings.pdf> [accessed 7th February 2020].

UN Stats (2019) 'Goal 6: Ensure availability and sustainable management of water and sanitation for all' [website], United Nations Statistics Division, New York <https://unstats.un.org/sdgs/report/2019/The-Sustainable-Development-Goals-Report-2019.pdf> [accessed 19 May 2020].

WASHCost (2012) 'Providing a basic level of water and sanitation services that last: cost benchmarks', Info sheet 1 October 2012 [website], IRC, The Hague, Netherlands <https://www.ircwash.org/resources/providing-basic-level-water-and-sanitation-services-last-cost-benchmarks> [accessed 19 May 2020].

WaterAid (2015) *Essential element: why international aid for water, sanitation and hygiene is still a critical source of finance for many countries: A WaterAid report with analysis provided by Development Initiatives* [pdf], July 2015, London <https://washmatters.wateraid.org/sites/g/files/jkxoof256/files/Essential_element.pdf> [accessed 19 May 2020].

White, G.F., Bradley, D.J. and White, A.U. (1972) *Drawers of Water: Domestic Water Use in East Africa*, Chicago University Press, Chicago.

WHO (2019) *National Systems to Support Drinking-Water, Sanitation and Hygiene: Global Status Report*, UN-Water Global Analysis and Assessment of Sanitation and Drinking Water (GLAAS) 2019 report, WHO, Geneva.

WHO/UNICEF (2016) *Safely Managed Drinking Water Services: Thematic Report on Drinking Water* [pdf], WHO, Geneva, Switzerland <https://data.unicef.org/wp-content/uploads/2017/03/safely-managed-drinking-water-JMP-2017-1.pdf> [accessed 19 May 2020].

WHO/UNICEF JMP (2017*) Progress on Drinking Water, Sanitation and Hygiene: 2017 Update and SDG Baseline* [pdf] <http://www.who.int/mediacentre/news/releases/2017/launch-version-report-jmp-water-sanitation-hygiene.pdf> [accessed June 2018].

WHO/UNICEF JMP (2019) 'Global household database 2017 update' [online] <washdata.org/data/household> [accessed 20 July 2020].

Wikipedia (2018) File:Africa densidade pop.svg [website] <https://commons.wikimedia.org/w/index.php?curid=7465928> [accessed March 2018].

Wolf, J., Hunter, P.R., Freeman, M.C., Cumming, O., Clasen, T., Bartram, J., Higgins, J.P.T., Johnston, R., Medlicott, K., Boisson, S. and Prüss-Ustün, A. (2018) 'Impact of drinking water, sanitation and handwashing with soap on childhood diarrheal disease: updated meta-analysis and meta-regression', *Tropical Medicine & International Health* 23(5): 508–25 <http://dx.doi.org/10.1111/tmi.13051>.

World Bank (2017) Population data [website] <https://data.worldbank.org/indicator/SP.POP.TOTL> [accessed June 2018].

CHAPTER 2
Introducing self-supply

Self-supply, to which this chapter provides an introduction, is relatively new as a term in water supply. Definitions of unsupported self-supply are followed in this chapter by an outline of its common characteristics and how progress can be accelerated by the support of an enabling environment. The principle is of a ladder of small, affordable steps which allow achievement of basic and safely managed supply largely through self-financing. This financing is by individuals or groups and may evolve into higher level piped supplies for households or whole communities. Providing one's own supply is nothing new and has been part of the evolution of supply provision throughout history. Historically, progress in acceleration up the technology ladder shows just how slowly ideas are transmitted between different societies and regions. Self-supply principles are much better developed and documented in sanitation, but there has been growing awareness in the last 15 years of their wider potential in WASH and the need to provide similar support services for a very large number of people for whom any other form of service delivery may still be a distant dream.

Keywords: self-supply, sanitation, supply history, support services, acceleration

Key messages

1. WASH self-supply is the provision of services through the initiative of householders (and usually at their cost), complementing publicly or commercially funded provision.
2. Limitations in affordability mean it often takes time to reach at least basic levels of service, and progress tends to proceed incrementally in small steps.
3. The scale and potential of self-supply is largely hidden by lack of information fuelling lack of strategic interest. Examination of disparate evidence is presented in Chapters 3 and 4 with the aim of triggering greater curiosity and interest to bring self-supply into sector thinking, budgeting, and planning.
4. The scale of private initiative in water is only just beginning to become apparent in numerical terms as national surveys are geared mainly to conventional public supplies. Sector financial analyses, however, suggest the scale globally is enormous.
5. The natural process of improving such supplies can be accelerated to reduce risks and increase convenience especially where gaps in adequate public supply drive people to look for their own, often sub-standard, solutions.
6. Support for the acceleration process has much in common with sanitation marketing and to a lesser degree with community-led

http://dx.doi.org/10.3362/9781780448190.002

total sanitation (CLTS) (see also Chapter 6) in which business development, and government support through indirect subsidy, play important parts.

7. Public water supplies are a feature of civilization, allowing the growth of cities. However even in the best organized societies self-supply has tended to form a necessary stage in development for those being left behind or wanting a better service than the state can provide.

8. Despite the long-known links to health and well-being, the slow rates of progress in adoption of good practices for improved supply suggest many social and psychological aspects are yet to be understood. Unrealistic time frames may therefore be being set for sustainable achievements of targets.

9. The water sector can learn lessons from sanitation in being more open to adopting new ways of thinking and starting from the household perspective.

10. As with sanitation, focusing on the household level requires significant changes in ways of thinking, skills, and greater dependence on market dynamics. All of these cannot happen overnight, but require long-term support, knitted into the fabric of service provision.

Definitions

The natural occurrence of **self-supply** in WASH is defined as the construction of, or incremental improvement to water supplies and sanitation by households and small groups, largely using their own means. Improvements to supply may be in bringing the supply closer to home and improving its quality, reliability, or adequacy. Self-supply is a common phenomenon in all economies, but is particularly relevant in supply evolution for rural and urban areas in low and lower-middle income countries. It may also be called private individual (drinking) water supply where it reaches a safely managed level of service.

Self-supply initiatives reflect the gaps in public supply delivery. In **unsupported self-supply** all resources are provided by consumers, and consequently progress can only be made in steps that are affordable to the family or families concerned and, being market-driven, depend on the skills and technologies which are available to them. Incremental progress towards a safely managed supply or sanitation takes time, the start and speed of achievement varying with the economic situation of the household, and the hydro(geo)logical, political, social, and economic (and thus technological) context of the country around them.

Ladders of progress in improvement are locally specific and can be derived in part from the range of existing supplies found and added to with other affordable technologies. A composite example is given in Figure 2.1, moving from no source protection to maximum security of supply. Those who use surface water directly, just scooping water from a stream or pond, are at the bottom rung of the ladder, having made no investment, and have no improvement to supply unless they treat the water.

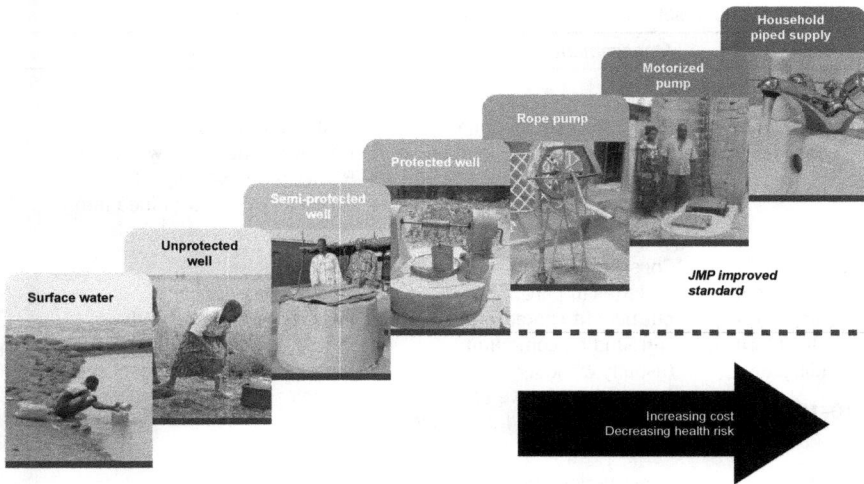

Figure 2.1 An example of affordable steps towards a basic or safely managed household supply

Conducive self-supply refers to the add-ons to supply a household may invest in to achieve their aspirations for water quality, quantity, or cost. Add-ons include water storage to increase reliability or reduce cost and household water treatment to improve quality.

Supported self-supply is the process by which households or groups are enabled to move incrementally up the ladder, still largely by their own means, but supported by government, NGOs, and the private sector, to improve the level of service they can provide for themselves. It is particularly relevant in sub-Saharan Africa and other rural areas with poor economies, where there are millions of traditional wells with potential for upgrading by their owners (see Chapter 3), but, as yet, rural economies are not strong enough for relevant markets and skilled businesses to have developed spontaneously. Similar affordable steps allow achievement of safely managed rainwater harvesting, sanitation, and hygiene and can be locally derived as part of the process of support to accelerated progress.

In higher income countries government financial support to communities and households for hardware is limited but has helped some to higher levels of service, while others have had the means to do it themselves often using government and commercial advisory services.

Common characteristics of self-supply provision

Key features of self-supply systems

Private investment in water supply can take many forms and be given many different names in different countries. Table 2.1 summarizes the commonest forms.

Table 2.1 Forms of self-financed water supply (* denotes improved level of service)

Level	Management	Source technologies
Individual investment		
1. Individual – one family **1–10 users**	Paid for/constructed/managed personally, high willingness to invest and may include income generation. Single household use	• Traditional well/spring • Improved traditional well/spring* • Rainwater harvesting (RWH)* • Borehole/well water piped into house*
2. One household/ individual/ shared without obligation **10–100 users**	Construction paid for or undertaken personally, but benefit shared with surrounding community (usually without charge). Invest and improve at owners' cost. Productive use limited to owner.	• Traditional well • Unprotected spring • Improved traditional well* • Protected spring* • Borehole/well water piped into houses or standpipes*
3. One household/ shared with joint obligation **50–200 users**	Construction and/or improvements/maintenance undertaken by lead family/ headman with assistance of neighbours and benefit shared with them and others. Productive use usually still for owner only unless with communal gardening.	
Group investment		
4. Communal/ small cooperative **50–5,000 users**	Constructed as communal effort at communal cost. Traditional community management structure/ committee/(legally constituted board or contracted management in small piped supplies). Productive use may be as household multiple use services (MUS), or communal gardens.	• Traditional well • Improved traditional well* • Borehole* • Spring • Improved spring* • Surface water intakes (*if treated) • Piped supply with house connections/standpipes*

Self-supply is not necessarily the domain of individuals, but, depending on population distribution and community cohesion, may be provided by a community group either managing on its own behalf or contracting the private sector to do so for them (group/cooperative water schemes). One essential element is that the water provision is from the potential users themselves, at least initially and that they own the supply and form their own system of management. A second element is that this is investment rather than purchase. The payments made establish a service and continue to yield a benefit (water), rather than just buying a bottle of water or a cubic metre from a utility, which is a simple commercial transaction. In rare cases the users buy water in bulk from a utility or water company but invest cooperatively in and manage their own reticulation system, forming a hybrid of public and self-supply provision.

Self-financed rural water supply is commonest where public supplies are not available, especially where households are widely dispersed (such as in prairie farmlands), but also on the periphery of small rural towns with piped supply systems of limited capacity in terms of volume or extent, and in more remote villages. Much depends on the degree to which the resident population can be served by piped supplies or by point sources such as boreholes, or improved wells or springs. Those for whom a public supply is most costly to establish and run are those most likely to need to provide their own supply, if water resource conditions allow.

Rainwater harvesting (RWH) constitutes self-supply in its simplest ownership and management form, easily upgraded with investment from, and benefit to an individual household (see Photos 2.1 and 2.2).

Most self-suppliers in developing economies base their supply on groundwater and share their water supply with their neighbours. Water in this instance is regarded as a social rather than an economic good, and there are widely held and strong cultural views that water is not a commodity but something of common benefit which fellow beings should not be denied. An owner of a well will therefore generally share its use

Photo 2.1 Early steps in rainwater harvesting Mozambique (lowest cost)

Photo 2.2 Early steps in rainwater harvesting Mozambique (mid cost)

with neighbours, and in rural areas particularly, or systems using human-powered lifting devices, do so without charge. It then forms a privately managed mini-community supply, benefitting more than just the family which owns it.

For those who have no other options, their own investment (cash/energy) provides all their water (single-supply). Many others, especially in urban areas, find their public supply unreliable, inconvenient, and/or expensive and so augment it (conjunctive use) by rainwater storage or their own wells. Public funding may help legally constituted groups to construct or expand piped supplies as public-private partnerships, but the latter retain control of the system. Far more rarely and mostly in higher income countries, public funding helps individuals with the cost of upgrading their supply to national standards without changing ownership or management.

Domestic and multiple uses

The chief value of self-supply is that it is 'on premises'. Bringing water closer to or into the house (see Photo 2.3) favours its expanded use for domestic purposes such as bathing and washing as well as drinking and cooking, and at higher income levels also to flush toilets and supply hot showers and other modern day uses. It also allows for water-related productive use where self-supply includes adequate water for basic domestic uses and multiple

Photo 2.3 An Ethiopian self-supplied household well, protected and convenient for domestic purposes'
Source: Photo Tsegaw Hailu

Table 2.2 The relationship between self-supply and MUS water use

Domestic	Multiple use water services	Irrigation plus
	Public/community supplies, designed also for productive use	
	Domestic plus	
Drinking	Domestic needs plus small scale:	Satisfy all domestic uses
Cooking	Livestock (including poultry) watering	Main use for irrigation of cash crops (beyond watering-can)
Washing		
Bathing	Vegetable garden watering (watering-can level)	Fish ponds
Fire fighting	Brick making	
Household hygiene	Beer making	
Dust settling	Food processing	
Domestic supply to neighbours	Craft needs	
Car washing		

use services (MUS) (see Van Koppen et al., 2009). The supply use extends beyond purely basic domestic purposes into domestic plus, where it includes small-scale economic use (Moriarty et al., 2004), or where irrigation supplies are also used for household purposes (See Table 2.2).

While domestic plus and MUS have much in common, the main criterion for self-supply remains that of the supply being funded principally by the users themselves and used for domestic purposes, while MUS looks more at the productive use at household level of publicly funded supplies (primarily piped or canalized systems), with livelihoods as the starting point. The core of self-supply stems from the demand to fill the gap that public supply for domestic purposes does not reach, and acknowledges that for many, domestic water is all they are looking for, and even those looking for productive water use will ensure their own domestic supply first.

Self-supply for water: a historic feature of society

Self-supply has been a part of the evolution of water supply and sanitation throughout history. Civilizations have generally depended to a great degree on the ability of the state to provide water as a public service, so that cities and towns can flourish. As Juuti et al. (2008) put it: 'one could say that our whole civilization is built on the use of water'. Mass provision of water supply is an early indicator of civilization and a prerequisite to urbanization, reducing the time and energy burden of finding and collecting water, and liberating the individual to develop new ideas and be more productive. However well-organized it may have been, state provision could not always satisfy the individual. Self-supply is not a new phenomenon but demonstrates the fundamental need, not just for humans to have water somewhere, but the specific desire to have it as near as possible to the home and to have control over it. This, in public supply terms, ultimately leads to piped water into the house, but any lesser level of provision generally leaves the householder yearning for something more, and seeking ways to bring a reliable supply into, or as near as possible to the house.

Civilizations such as the Chinese, Aztec, Inca, Nabatean, Roman, Persian (Achaemenid and Sassanid empires), and Arab societies have demonstrated great ingenuity in providing water to the masses, on a communal scale, but this did not necessarily remove the desire of individuals to improve upon it for their own use. For example, the Roman Empire developed very sophisticated large-scale water distribution systems with aqueducts, canals, piping, and public drinking fountains, and included supplies to individual households as well as standpipes and public bathhouses for the less well-off. This did much to enable the development of large urban areas and to minimize the health risks of living in them. But householders also improved their own supplies, for instance by bribing officials to connect their houses illegally to aqueduct water giving them priority of access (Vitruvius, 50 BC). Less influential families dug wells (Lorenz and Wolfram, 2014) to provide a reliable supply when their piped supply was too far away or unreliable. Rainwater harvesting was also a common feature of housing, with the water diverted in gutters to a central cistern within the house (*impluvium*). Thus, despite a well-developed communal system, many invested in alternatives to provide them with closer, safer, or more reliable water over which they had some control.

The Roman state also provided communal latrines connected to sewers (e.g. the Cloaca Maxima). However, many houses preferred their own pit latrines since water seals had not been invented (Koloski-Ostro, 2015) and the resulting smell from the sewers meant that the communal systems were not for the faint-hearted. So early on it became established that when even the most organized state cannot supply services adequately in the eyes of the householder, those with resources will develop solutions they perceive as suiting them better.

The link between health and water was not to be universally acknowledged for many centuries but Andrew Boorde, an early 16th-century English doctor, contributed greatly to the growth in the understanding of the health implications (Boorde, 1547) of water supply in his *Dyetary of helth*. He urged that water supply should be annexed to the house to cater for all water demands of drinking, washing, baking, brewing, and also for fire-fighting. A latrine should, however, be positioned far from the house.

His works illustrate the fact that water quality was an integral part of domestic self-supply hundreds of years ago and explain that treatment should vary according to the use of the water. The treatment he suggested (Boorde, 1547: Chapter 10) for water used in cooking and brewing is that having collected running water, it should be left to stand for 2–3 hours before use, and then the top part filtered through a thick linen cloth and the lower part discarded. He disapproved of drinking neat water, preferring it mixed with wine or made into ale, and prescribed filtering and then boiling and cooling it before adding it to the wine. He also recommended handwashing before eating, stating that before 'the Lorde' eats he should be brought a bowl of water to wash his hands, and then all others who will sit at the table must follow suit. Thus even 500 years ago, Boorde was establishing the basic principles of self-supply for water, where individuals bring water supply near to the house, ensure its safety within the household for consumption and its use for hygienic purposes. These remain the fundamental objectives of self-supply in water, five centuries on.

A century later, a picture by Pieter de Hooch in 1660 (National Gallery London) shows a typical house courtyard with its own hand pump and rainwater harvesting system providing an on-site supply with hygienic surroundings (Figure 2.2) and a drain from an indoor sink. De Hooch's painting represents typical features of Dutch life at that time (National Gallery, 2019) as the Rhine became more and more polluted and households resorted to their own wells or storing rainwater (Boom and de Vrede, 2002). A similar handpump appears in the painting of 'the Cobbler' by van Ostade a few years later. The widespread abstraction of easily accessible groundwater or stored rainwater allowed privacy, control of the system, and 24-hour availability. Both Boorde and de Hooch show the historical value given to good water supply at household level and highlight the very slow progress in spreading what has been well-known for centuries, but which is not universally applied today. Barriers to uptake are complex and challenging to the time scales needed to bring about sustainable change and the targets of development goals.

While water has remained well-linked to health over the centuries, the link to fire-fighting that Boorde raised is largely being forgotten and yet is most critical.

Figure 2.2 Dutch Woman and her Maid in a Courtyard, by Pieter de Hooch (1660). Note the household hand pump, guttering, and downpipe to tank or well
Source: ©National Gallery, London, UK

A hand-pump a kilometre away is a poor weapon for fighting a blaze in any house let alone one made of grass or wood. This fact was well understood with respect to the wooden houses of Finland in the mid-19th century. Here the General Fire Assurance Company of the Grand Duchy of Finland financed the city water works of Helsinki in 1832 and a few years later the Finnish Rural Fire Assurance Company offered loans at advantageous interest rates for rural water supplies to individual farms. Both aimed to reduce the fire-damage claims that could be made against the company. In Switzerland loans or grants from fire insurance companies for water supply projects continue to this day (Saladin, 2002). While health remains the main sector interest for water supply, and increasingly its economic benefits, its role in fire-fighting should not be forgotten.

Growing awareness of the potential of household investment in water supply and sanitation

Emergence of self-supply as a concept

Before the turn of the Millennium the term self-supply was not mentioned in relation to water supply in developing countries. There was almost no international focus on what people do for themselves, since water supply is usually regarded as requiring very expensive investment and as the domain of large public utilities and the state, or equity funding and powerful banks, or more indirectly through NGOs channelling donor funding particularly into rural areas. The idea that there is any capacity among households to provide for themselves was hardly mentioned and certainly not that they could have significant effect on water provision at scale. This seems paradoxical when the sustainability of community water supplies is so dependent on the capacity of households in the community to operate and maintain supply systems built on technologies, finance, and management models which are foreign to them. Meanwhile rural private drinking water supplies are well-recognized in developed countries and the long-term need for them to fill the gaps in public supplies (see Chapter 3) is readily acknowledged particularly where there are sparse rural populations and connection to mains is not affordable either to households or water utilities.

The introduction of the term 'self-supply' began when the Rural Water Supply Network (RWSN) introduced the self-supply theme in 2004. At that time there was little wider recognition of what people are doing for themselves without support and of the hidden resources this can bring to the sector. The lack of awareness was linked closely to the widespread lack of definitive data on household level supplies in all countries (developed and developing) in urban and rural contexts.

The recognition of the contribution of household investment in WASH only really became apparent through economic/financial analyses rather than inventory/census information. In 2014 Global Analysis and Assessment of Sanitation and Drinking-Water (GLAAS) reports (WHO, 2014) on sector financing began to include mention of household contribution to the sector as a whole. By 2017 the reports began to split household contributions into tariff payments and self-supply, and to emphasize the growing role of household finance. According to the latest GLAAS report (WHO, 2019) 66 per cent of WASH funding is estimated to come from household contribution in the 35 countries with relevant data, but with self-supply undifferentiated. In 2017 self-supply exceeded tariff payments in Bangladesh, Ghana, and Peru of the seven countries for which differentiated information was available. 'The majority of countries could only provide tariff data, which may be a small percentage of household contributions in less developed areas without formal service providers, where households may make significant investments' (WHO, 2017: 18). The report writers felt throughout that self-supply data, if available at all, was under-reported. This illustrates the frustrating degree to which self-supply appears to be a topic of global significance but also one for which so little is known, a bit like the abysses of the deep oceans – one of the 'known un-knowns'.

Measuring the 'known un-known'

Privately owned supplies contribute to coverage figures for improved supplies throughout the world. Many others, especially in lower income countries, are unimproved, and offer a reservoir of sources which have potential, but also present greater risks. Knowing how many people depend on them and where they are is a first step, to be followed by monitoring progress in improvements. At various points in this book the lack of numerical and spatial data is bemoaned as being the largest constraint to getting policy makers and sector professionals to recognize the potential that is largely being overlooked.

Available information gets scarcer as one progresses from high- to low-income countries, and institutional capacity and resources for monitoring reduce. Only high-income countries which require registration of private household supplies and a very few others which try to include them in water point inventories can identify the actual number and location of self-supply water points. Most countries exempt small private supplies from registration unless there is a commercial use for the water. National water point inventories are almost all confined to those sources regarded as 'improved', and mostly only to public supplies. Present household surveys are also not generally well-designed to reflect the roles that private supplies play.

Considerable efforts have been made therefore to piece together as much evidence as possible, but the variety of ownership models, regular sharing of private supply, the provision of sometimes indistinguishable individual, group, or public piped water supply into the home, conjunctive and multiple uses, and variable degrees of protection all provide a range of situations which do not yet fit most survey categories. Multiple indicator cluster survey (MICS) data summaries and some Living Conditions surveys do provide relevant data by including the proportion of houses with:

A. On premises improved supplies.
B. Piped supply into the home or yard plus any improved tanker/vendor or sachet/bottled water. (A) minus (B) can be assumed to be almost completely attributable to own on-premises improved water points, which are mainly groundwater but include rainwater harvesting, and a small amount of surface water or springs.
C. The proportion of unimproved supplies on premises gives a measure of unimproved self-supply.

The contribution of total self-supply will however be an underestimate from these summaries especially in urban areas where bottled/sachet water are popular primary drinking water sources and if the secondary source of domestic water is not given. Country data cannot give a measure of the (usually larger) number of people sharing the owner's supply. Group self-financed supplies are also not often differentiated from public piped supplies.

Rather than being exact figures, most derived statistics should be taken as indicative not definitive, with margins of error continually reducing as more survey data become available. Chapters 3 and 4 analyse as far as possible the available evidence of the scale of household level self-supply in rural and urban environments.

Supporting self-supply: accelerating progress in sanitation and water

Supporting self-supply in sanitation

The sanitation sub-sector of WASH has led the way in promoting self-supply and provides parallels and experiences to learn from. In the late 1990s the very slow increases in sanitation coverage, linked to small public budgets and a high dependence on subsidizing facilities at household level, led to rethinking in sanitation and new strategies to reduce the enormous numbers still resorting to open defecation. Motivating people to take action and invest in latrines for themselves is at the heart of Community-Led Total Sanitation (CLTS). The social pressure of shame has been used to motivate households to dig latrines in sub-Saharan Africa, as well as in South Asia where the CLTS approach was initially developed and in Latin America where it has also spread widely. Through government or NGO services, communities are 'triggered' to become open-defecation-free (ODF) (Chambers, 2009) using the power of peer pressure and community level planning. Triggering household level action and use of resources encourages not only latrine construction but also their continued use (a common failing in total subsidy approaches). CLTS is an effective example of social marketing at work, and is often combined with government or NGO support in building private sector capacity to provide relevant services.

While an effective way to get people onto the first step of the sanitation ladder, CLTS has been less successful in ensuring latrines are of good quality and in moving families up the ladder. Widespread slippage has been observed with significant numbers going back to open defecation (Jerneck et al., 2016). To encourage sustainability of impacts and movement up the technology ladder, public investment in more continuous follow-up support to communities and market development through sanitation marketing prove necessary. This requires continued public funding and combined public and private sector inputs (Munkhondia et al., 2016). Countries which have set out to support self-supply in both water and sanitation are finding that the approach is not an instant fix but one which requires a different way of thinking at all levels and incorporation into long-term plans.

Supported self-supply in water also has households as the main target, and similarly mixes public sector promotion and social marketing with local private sector entrepreneurship (Harvey, 2011). There is a concept in common of households moving up a technology ladder over time. The social dynamics built up for sanitation promotion, and the technical skills and advisory and training services developed for latrine construction can also be employed for water supply. However it is not necessary that one precedes the other, and services should if possible be built up to cater for both, depending on the priorities of communities/individual households and the structure of responsibilities in local government and line ministries.

Introducing support services to self-supply for water

Self-supply can and does spread without support from governments or development partners. Relying largely on locally available technologies and their own financial resources, households do invest in improving their access to water, but are limited in what they can achieve on their own, especially in lower income countries with poorly equipped rural businesses. This raises the question of whether government has a role in stimulating self-supply and good quality support services. The response of governments, with existing information and their responsibilities to provide access to water arising from constitutional obligations, human rights legislation, international agreements, and other laws and policies, is varied. Typical positions are:

- To reject self-supply as a form of provision and take measures to restrict its development. This is most common in urban areas where utilities offer an alternative whose economic viability may be threatened by competition or there are concerns about the levels of pollution of groundwater (see Chapter 4). Or
- To largely ignore and not get involved in self-supply, while leaving households to do whatever they can to help themselves. Others – including NGOs – may step in to support small-scale self-supply in generally unharmonized projects. Or
- To accept self-supply as a form of provision and to develop official policies and strategies to scale up support enabling owners/users to improve their own supplies and manage their risks. Or
- To take over responsibility for the supply and provide individual household level options.

Stances taken by government depend on context and the different water supply options that are available, the stage of economic development and availability of resources, and capacities to provide alternatives. However, most professional staff engaged in advising policy makers on these decisions will be unlikely to have had training related to self-supply and may be ill-equipped with information on its scale or their role in supporting it. These limitations contribute to inertia in government policy with respect to self-supply, including a lack of any strategies geared to smaller communities and dispersed households.

Strategies to provide an enabling environment (Olschewski, 2016) centre on self-supply investors so they can drive progress, make informed choices, and implement them (see Figure 2.3). They revolve around four supporting elements (see Chapter 9 for more details) common to both water and sanitation which can be created through indirect subsidy by government or NGOs:

- technical advice and guidelines on, introduction of, and demand creation for affordable technologies (see Chapter 6) and of water resource management issues;
- strengthened supply chains and markets for products and services typically through the local private sector (market and business development);
- improved access to microfinance (savings and loans are discussed further in Chapters 5 and 6);
- supportive policies and an appropriate regulatory framework.

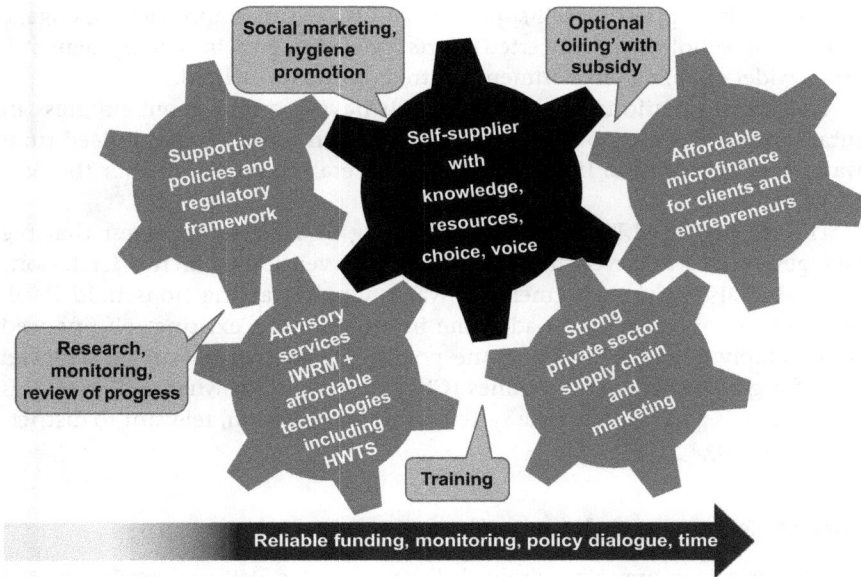

Figure 2.3 Core support service elements needed to facilitate self-supply
Source: Modified from Olschewski, 2016

With the self-supplier as the main driving force, the four supporting cogs can work more effectively if lubricated by:

- improved access to information (similar to the provision of primary healthcare and agricultural extension services) with awareness raising, social marketing, and campaigns (in Chapter 5 access to information is identified as a critical need);
- monitoring of progress to identify problems and bring self-financed water supplies into planning;
- direct subsidies in cash or materials for households or groups;
- training of public and private sector personnel in technical, financial, and business and resource management issues which may affect quality service provision;
- and in some cases regulation.

The support services which create this enabling environment are available to all who invest in their own supply, to encourage supplies which at least meet minimum standards. The additional factor of direct subsidy to capital costs and targeted promotion provides the oil which helps the four revolving elements to work together more efficiently by strengthening demand where it is most needed. It is usually geared to remote and dispersed groups and households being left behind, to ensure they can achieve at least a basic level of service.

Essentially, supporting self-supply demands a systems approach, to engage multiple stakeholders in concerted efforts focused on growing supply, demand, and a wider enabling environment centred on the household.

The transformations in strategy which have brought about progress in rural sanitation have not so far been reflected in water supply, indeed rural water supply provision has changed little overall in approach over the past 30 years.

The impact of CLTS and social marketing in sanitation suggest that big changes can be achieved from low level interventions which offer lessons applicable also to improvement of water supplies at the household level. For that to happen requires adequate information on existing self-financed water supply (Chapter 3–8) and the potential gains which can be achieved both for governments and families (Chapters 9 and 10) where self-supply is considered as part of the whole system of water provision, relevant to district-wide planning.

Service delivery models and self-supply

The water sector organizes around distinct service delivery models which are defined principally by institutional structure. They are built around the roles of the public and private sectors and critically in the case of rural water supply, the community. They define who builds new infrastructure and who operates and manages it, and how it is financed and regulated. In a review of the sustainability of service delivery models for rural water supply, the International Bank for Reconstruction and Development (World Bank, 2017) identify five main models: community-based management, direct local government provision, public utility provision, private sector provision, and supported self-supply (see Figure 2.4).

Community management with all its strengths and weaknesses remains the most widespread service delivery model in sub-Saharan Africa and many lower income countries. Mainly employed for the most numerous rural point water supplies such as springs, wells or boreholes with a handpump, its key feature is volunteerism, which requires sustained institutional support to provide effective long-term management (Schouten and Moriarty, 2003). Water supply committees are often not legal entities. Public utilities are, by contrast, legal and accountable entities run by professional salaried and trained staff. They have better access to funds and are subject to more monitoring and regulation. Utilities are most widely associated with towns but there is interest currently in extending professionalization and utility-like models to rural areas with high population density, as stand-alone or multi-village schemes.

Private sector water providers come in a variety of sizes and degrees of formal management structure, from large private water companies such as Suez or Thames Water, to small piped supplies serving small peri-urban areas. Most, especially the larger, are profit making and all are subject to government regulation.

Country context: economic development, population growth and urbanization, decentralization, geography and hydrology, aid dependency

Sector governance: political prioritization, aid-effectiveness, private sector participation, human rights and inclusion, institutional arrangements and service delivery models, service levels

National sector level

Service authority level

Service provider level

Community-based management
Direct local government
Public utility provision
Private sector
Supported self-supply

Institutional capacity

Financing

Asset management

Water resource management

Monitoring and regulation

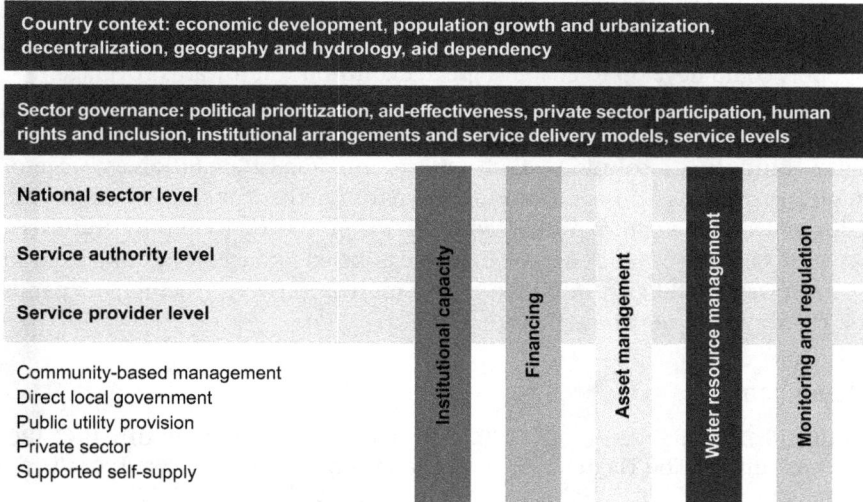

Figure 2.4 Service delivery models and framework for assessing rural water supply sustainability
Source: World Bank, 2017

The World Bank sustainability review includes consideration of self-supply only in Ethiopia, where it exists in embryonic form as a government-supported service delivery model. This does not reflect the true potential or present contribution of self-supply to the sector. The contribution and influence of self-supply in its unsupported (and commonest) form was not considered despite the review including many countries where it provides for a significant proportion of the rural population (see Chapter 3). For example in Bangladesh, India, Indonesia, Vietnam, and Nicaragua it interacts with and may affect the sustainability of the other service delivery models considered. Where analysis of the sector is based on institutional frameworks and conventional public systems, a substantial gap is being left in a systems approach to water provision, overlooking elements which widely interact with formal delivery models, replace them, or are replaced by them but do not fit the institutional frameworks of conventional water supply.

Conclusions

Self-supply is a natural development from which many have benefitted over the centuries. It is an inherent response where inequalities in supply exist and where people feel they have resources which can improve their situation. As it is regarded as a privilege to have easy access to water, supplies are generally shared with others and so form an informal community service.

Sanitation is perhaps not lagging behind in progress towards universal coverage if household-level facilities are considered the norm for both sanitation and water, and in terms of supporting or accelerating self-supply it is certainly leading the way. Since it is already well-documented it is less explored in this book and more used to provide pointers in the way self-supply support could develop to enable a greater contribution towards coverage.

The situation is not one of 'have's' and 'have nots' but of a dynamic where self-supply may be temporarily or permanently a solution for those being left behind. It is a solution which reflects the present evolutionary stage of supply provision in different economic environments, but also to a degree the gaps between the values prioritized by sector professionals and by end-users. As with sanitation, household initiative can be encouraged and supported in various ways to fill gaps in public supply more effectively. Chapter 9 expands on the ways this may be achieved.

References

Boom, S. and de Vrede, E. (2002) *Drinking Dutch Water* [pdf], IRC JPO Programme, The Hague, The Netherlands <https://www.ircwash.org/sites/default/files/Boom-2002-Drinking.pdf> [accessed 19 May 2020].

Boorde, A. (1547) *The fyrst boke of the introduction of knowledge made by Andrew Borde, of physycke doctor. A compendyous regyment; or, A dyetary of helth made in Mountpyllier* [online], edited by F.J. Furnivall for the Early English Text Society 1870, Keegan Paul, Trench, Trübner & Co, London, UK <https://archive.org/details/fyrstbokeofintro00boorrich> [accessed 6 November 2018].

Chambers, R. (2009) *Going to Scale with Community-Led Total Sanitation: Reflections on Experience, Issues and Ways Forward*, IDS, Brighton, UK <http://www.communityledtotalsanitation.org/sites/communityledtotalsanitation.org/files/media/Chambers_Going%20to%20Scale%20with%20CLTS.pdf> [accessed 19 May 2020].

Harvey, P. (2011) 'Zero subsidy strategies for accelerating access to rural water and sanitation services', *Water Science and Technology* 63(5): 1037–43 <http://dx.doi.org/10.2166/wst.2011.287>.

Jerneck, M., van der Voorden, C. and Rudholm, C. (2016) *Sanitation and Hygiene Behaviour Change at Scale: Understanding Slippage* [pdf], Global Sanitation Fund <https://www.ircwash.org/sites/default/files/sanitation-and-hygiene-behaviour-change-at-scale-understanding-slippage-reflections-paper-gsf.pdf> [accessed 19 May 2020].

Juuti, P., Katko, T. and Vuorinen, H. (2008) *Environmental History of Water: Global Views on Community Water Supply and Sanitation*, IWA Publications, London <http://www.iwapublishing.com/books/9781843391104/environmental-history-water> [accessed 19 May 2020].

Koloski-Ostrow, A.O. (2015) *The Archaeology of Sanitation in Roman Italy: Toilets, Sewers, and Water Systems*, University of North Carolina Press, Chapel Hill, NC.

Lorenz, W.F. and Wolfram, E.J. (2014) 'The wells of Pompeii', *Groundwater* 52(5): 808–11 <http://dx.doi.org/10.1111/gwat.12221>.

Moriarty, P., Butterworth, J. and Van Koppen, B. (2004) *Beyond Domestic Case Studies on Poverty and Productive Uses of Water at the Household Level*, Technical paper no. 41, IRC International Water and Sanitation Centre, Delft, The Netherlands.

Munkhondia, T., Simangolwa, W.M. and Maceda, A.Z. (2016) 'CLTS and sanitation marketing: aspects to consider for a better integrated approach', in P. Bongartz, N. Vernon, and J. Fox (eds), *Sustainable Sanitation for All: Experiences, Challenges and Innovations*, pp. 99–120, Practical Action Publishing, Rugby.

National Gallery (2019) 'Pieter de Hooch: A Woman and her Maid in a Courtyard' [website], <https://www.nationalgallery.org.uk/paintings/pieter-de-hooch-a-woman-and-her-maid-in-a-courtyard> [accessed 19 May 2020].

Olschewski, A. (2016) 'A business case for supported self-supply as service delivery approach to achieve SDGs', *Proceedings of the 7th RWSN Forum, Abidjan, Côte d'Ivoire* [pdf], pp. 514–9 <https://rwsnforum7.files.wordpress.com/2018/03/proceedings-of-the-7th-rwsn-forum-2016-28feb.pdf> [accessed June 2020].

Saladin, M. (2002) *Community Water Supply in Switzerland: What can we learn from a century of successful operation?* [pdf], SKAT Foundation, St Gallen, Switzerland <https://www.ircwash.org/sites/default/files/community_water_supply_in_switzerland_0.pdf> [accessed 19 May 2020].

Schouten, T. and Moriarty, P. (2003) *Community Water, Community Management: From Service to System in Rural Areas*, Practical Action Publishing, Rugby, UK.

Van Koppen, B., Smits, S., Moriarty, P., Penning de Vries, F., Mikhail, M. and Boelee, E. (2009) *Climbing the Water Ladder: Multiple Use Services for Poverty Reduction*, IRC International Water and Sanitation Centre and International Water Management Institute TP Series no 52, The Hague, The Netherlands.

Vitruvius (50 BC) *On Architecture*, VIII.6.1ff, Rome, Italy.

WHO (2014) *Investing in Water and Sanitation: Increasing Access, Reducing Inequalities,* GLAAS 2014 Findings, Special report for Africa WHO Document Production Services, Geneva, Switzerland.

WHO (2017) *Financing Universal Water, Sanitation and Hygiene under the Sustainable Development Goals,* GLAAS 2017 Report, UN-Water Global Analysis and Assessment of Sanitation and Drinking-Water, World Health Organization, Geneva, Switzerland.

WHO (2019) *National Systems to Support Drinking-Water, Sanitation and Hygiene*, GLAAS 2019 Report, UN-Water Global Analysis and Assessment of Sanitation and Drinking-Water, World Health Organization, Geneva, Switzerland.

World Bank (2017) *Sustainability Assessment of Rural Water Service Delivery Models: Findings of a Multi-Country Review*, World Bank, Washington, DC.

CHAPTER 3
The scale of rural self-supply

This chapter looks at the scale of self-supply in different rural economies (progressing from low to high income countries), and the part that governments are playing. The more developed the economy the more information is available and there is a greater likelihood of government intervention. The scale of existing self-supply in lower income economies indicates potential for supported or accelerated improvement. The experience of higher income countries is that high levels of service can be achieved and that self-supply is important as a temporary or permanent step in water supply evolution. Information on the scale of self-supply is rare, dispersed, and difficult to compare between countries. This chapter compiles, for the first time, information from a wide range of sources to indicate the scale and forms it takes.

Keywords: self-supply, community, cooperative, rural, public supply

Key messages

1. Self-supply is an almost universal phenomenon but also widely ignored. The highest personal investment appears to be in middle-income countries, but few countries have reached universal coverage without some interim or permanent household investment in their own supply.
2. In sub-Saharan Africa, approximately 7.4 per cent of rural households have a non-piped (mainly self-financed), on-premises improved supply. One in six households of the 45 per cent with an at least basic supply provided it for themselves in the 15 countries for which data is available. A further 5 per cent of the population have an on-premises unimproved supply. Some supplies may potentially be upgraded to a 'safely managed' level.
3. Self-supplied water sources are normally shared with neighbours, markedly increasing the number of people for whom it forms a basic supply, or an alternative supply if the community water supply fails. National survey data does not allow quantification of numbers sharing, but spot surveys suggest at least a third of rural sub-Saharan people may depend fully on self-financed, privately owned improved wells (see Chapter 5) and many others partially.
4. Sub-Saharan Africa rural economies, especially in remoter areas, are still mostly only developing slowly, and private sector capacity is weak. If Sustainable Development Goal (SDG) 6.1 and 6.2 are to be reached by 2030, then in this region public and private sector capacity building to support greater self-supply investment is essential for water and sanitation and as part of the building blocks for rural economic transformation.

http://dx.doi.org/10.3362/9781780448190.003

5. The main need is for government recognition (as in high income countries) of the specific needs of dispersed rural households, provision of adequate advice or support to umbrella organizations, and monitoring of supply performance. The private sector needs to have sufficient capacity to provide sustainable technical support services including marketing and advice.

6. Official recognition and inclusion of rural self-supply in planning for dispersed households is difficult to achieve without more comprehensive data than is available at present.

7. Regulation and monitoring are expensive and mainly a very recent development in higher income countries and the onus is generally on the individual supply owner to inspect (or pay for the inspection of) the supply. For lower income countries recovery of the full cost of regulation may deter personal investment in supply or lead to reluctance to register but is also a stimulus to continued improvement in performance.

8. Globally, even where regulation of rural water supply is well developed, supplies for less than 10 m³/day or 50 people are almost always exempt from such regulation and are seldom recorded or provided with support, yet are most likely to be sub-standard.

9. In high-income countries regulation for smaller supplies is recent and linked to funding for a 'carrot and stick' approach to raise standards, driven by a growing understanding of the higher risk they present. Similar systems are needed for middle- and lower-income countries and are starting to be developed especially in Latin America.

10. Individual self-supply is an almost universal phenomenon, but group supplies are most common (and serve more people) in higher-income countries. Group schemes can be very effective initially, and an important stepping-stone, but supplies which depend long term on voluntary management will require growth of private sector management capacity to replace or strengthen it in the long term.

Self-supply in lower income countries: sub-Saharan Africa

Scale of individual self-supply

Sub-Saharan Africa has made great strides in rural public water provision, but still has by far the largest unserved population in the world. By 2017 almost 280 million people in the region had access to an 'at least basic' supply (WHO/UNICEF, 2019), but 233 million remained without access to an improved supply, two-thirds of these (155 million) using unimproved groundwater sources. These 155 million have remained remarkably constant over the past 20 years and are generally assumed to be the majority of those providing their own supply (springs and hand-dug wells) as communities or individuals. Analysis of recent MICS survey summary data (UNICEF 2019), although limited in the countries covered, allows a better understanding of those households with their own non-piped supply (see Chapter 2, 'Measuring the known un-known').

Table 3.1 Population estimated from MICS data, using own on-premises supply (– signifies no data recorded)

Country	People using rainwater harvesting	People with on-premises improved groundwater supply	People with on-premises unimproved groundwater supply	Proportion of improved on-premises groundwater supplies (%)
Nigeria 2017	2,156,000	10,094,000	11,368,000	47
Ethiopia 2017*	1,086,800	2,508,000	2,006,400	56
Guinea 2016	16,330	1,739,145	408,250	81
Côte d'Ivoire 2016	48,273	1,568,862	832,704	65
Zimbabwe 2014	11,201	1,209,725	470,449	72
Mali 2015	97,506	975,060	1,213,408	45
Malawi 2014	–	884,047	201,625	81
Benin 2014	124,930	392,637	368,841	52
Cameroon 2014	31,911	372,295	202,103	65
Kenya Nyanza 2013/14	258,617	371,468	141,064	72
DRC 2010	–	365,184	228,240	62
Ghana 2011	12,858	205,724	141,436	59
Madagascar South 2012	275,942	194,783	113,623	63
Sierra Leone 2017	57,343	180,851	57,343	76
Congo 2014–15	68,835	169,440	33,535	83
Kenya Bungoma County 2013/14	–	144,000	56,400	72
Kenya Kakamega County 2013/14	17,662	125,238	48,169	72

Note: * Data source Central Statistical Agency of Ethiopia 2017

The countries and counties listed in Table 3.1 represent over half the population of sub-Saharan Africa. For these countries more than half (56 per cent) of on-premises (mostly self-financed) supplies are improved (boreholes, protected dug wells or springs). Those with their own improved groundwater supply (6.2 per cent) provide an at least basic supply often with potential for further improvements. To these should be added those harvesting rainfall as their main drinking water supply (1.2 per cent). If these countries are representative of the whole region, then some 78 million rural people in sub-Saharan Africa are drinking on-premises water they provided themselves. Of these, around 46 million use improved groundwater and rainwater supplies. They account for some 16 per cent of 'at least basic' coverage, and so contribute significantly to official coverage rates.

Table 3.1 illustrates the numerical dominance of Nigeria in the numbers adopting self-supply among the countries for which information is available, both as improved and unimproved sources, totalling over 21 million people. In regional terms, looking at the largest country populations, the exceptional

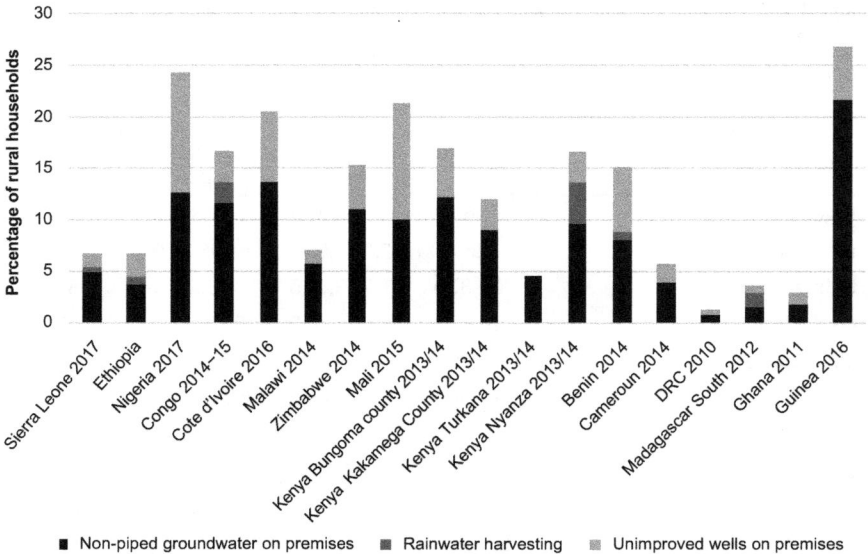

Figure 3.1 Proportion of rural households with own non-piped improved and unimproved on-premises water supplies in selected sub-Saharan countries/regions
Source: Data from most recent multiple indicator cluster surveys (MICS) and Central Statistical Agency of Ethiopia 2017. (not including households using bottled/sachet water as primary drinking water source)

development of household self-supply in Nigeria is balanced by its rarity in Ethiopia and DRC. Projections from this group of 15 countries may therefore reasonably provide a first estimate of the regional scale of self-provision of supply. User numbers indicate that Nigeria has by far the most, but as a percentage of population served (see Figure 3.1), self-supply is relatively important in many other countries. Mali, Guinea, and Côte d'Ivoire all have a fifth or more of their rural population with their own supply. Nigeria is the country with the greatest potential for upgrading on-premises self-financed supplies but there are others, as Figure 3.1 shows, where, within smaller rural populations, there is a significant proportion for whom self-supply is an important option. To some degree this reflects conventional supply coverage, socio-economic differences, and density of population.

The total impact of household investment on coverage is considerably greater than the numbers given in Table 3.1 which only refer to the families owning the supply.

While rainwater harvesting may be household specific, groundwater supplies are mostly privately owned but shared with neighbours (see Chapter 5, 'Supply ownership and sharing'), unless almost all have their own well. The number using a neighbour's self-financed improved supply cannot be identified from surveys but would further contribute to 'at least basic' coverage. Only 6.2 per cent of households may have their own improved (non-piped) groundwater supply but sharing with an average of four neighbours can provide a basic supply for over 30 per cent of the population (some 190 million) and for many more as an alternative source. The ratio of sharing households to those owning a supply can be estimated approximately from the totals using unimproved wells (JMP figures) and those with their own on-premises unimproved supply (MICS figures). The average ranges from less than three households per well in Mali, Guinea, and Nigeria, to 11.5 in Ethiopia, similar to the RiPPLE findings of 11.7 from seven *woredas* (Sutton et al., 2012). In the Democratic Republic of the Congo (DRC) only 1 per cent of households have their own supply, but 24 million depend on unimproved groundwater with an average of over 100 houses per source. Different technologies and marketing strategies may be needed to maximize the impact of upgrading for supplies owned by individuals or by larger groups. Water quality and the effects of upgrading are discussed in Chapter 7.

JMP figures (WHO/UNICEF JMP, 2019) can give a more regional view for unimproved supplies. If it is assumed that most wells and springs which are counted as unprotected are not publicly funded, then JMP figures indicate the potential impact of upgrading unimproved self-supply sources (see Table 3.2) and the levels of support needed through policy, advisory, and private sector services, which are at present lacking.

The absence of traditional unprotected systems in most national level water point inventories means that spatial distribution is unknown and so 1) those areas where people have greatest difficulty in providing their own water may not be prioritized and 2) more cost-effective and sustainable solutions may not be developed for communities with plentiful, reliable, on-premises supplies.

Table 3.2 Top 20 sub-Saharan countries for use of unprotected groundwater

Rank	Country	Unimproved groundwater users	Rank	Country	Unimproved groundwater users
1	DR Congo	24,088,038	11	Burkina Faso	4,177,242
2	Ethiopia	23,205,481	12	Zambia	3,393,080
3	Nigeria	22,558,281	13	Cameroon	3,251,715
4	Tanzania	9,226,396	14	Côte d'Ivoire	2,779,139
5	Madagascar	7,058,079	15	Mali	2,629,284
6	Niger	6,592,811	16	Zimbabwe	2,478,899
7	Chad	5,354,062	17	Angola	2,359,493
8	Kenya	5,309,240	18	Senegal	2,110,982
9	Uganda	4,764,283	19	Somalia	1,866,665
10	Mozambique	4,318,337	20	South Sudan	1,803,712

Source: WHO/UNICEF JMP, 2019

Well-owning families tend to be larger than the norm, the larger amounts of domestic water needed stimulate action for a more convenient water source. At 8–10 people per well-owning household, unimproved groundwater sources at household level in sub-Saharan Africa would then number 3–4 million and improved ones a further 4–5 million. Estimates are still rough, but the apparent high numbers of self-supply water points indicate the potential of a presently ignored service delivery model.

The few national level water point inventories which include private and unprotected sources suggest that such very large numbers of self-financed mainly traditional wells are indeed credible. In 2004 a water point inventory of Mali (DNH, 2004) found over 170,000 household wells serving a rural population which comprises less than 2 per cent of the sub-Saharan total. At an average of 10 people per household this tallies well with the proportions in Figure 3.1, using 2004 populations. Such large households signify either that 'on premises' may include extended family compounds sharing a yard but not kitchens (common in Mali), or an underestimate of supply numbers, noted as likely in the survey. Despite these high numbers, national rural water strategy makes no reference to them but includes support to group-financed piped water supplies, as in Kayes region (Maizama, 2015).

In the same year, a UNICEF/NAC inventory in Zimbabwe identified over 129,000 upgraded family wells (see Photo 3.1). According to the MICS 2014 survey approximately another 37,000 unprotected wells were found at

Photo 3.1 Upgraded Zimbabwean family well with cistern for small-scale irrigation

household level in addition to any communal wells (see also Part 2, Case study 4). Comparison between the 2004 supply survey and 2014 MICS data suggests that some 10–15 per cent more improved private wells may have been constructed or upgraded in the intervening 10 years. Mali and Zimbabwe constitute just over 3 per cent of the sub-Saharan rural population. The implication, based on these examples, is that sub-Saharan self-supply sources could, pro rata, number around 10 million. Since Mali and Zimbabwe appear to have above average self-supply provision, the MICS surveys suggest a lower range of 7–9 million sources.

Sierra Leone's more recent national water point survey (Ministry of Water Resources, Sierra Leone, 2019) and the 2017 MICS survey indicate lower levels of self-supply, but its continued growth (see Box 3.1).

Box 3.1 Self-supply in Sierra Leone

The national water point inventory in Sierra Leone (Ministry of Water Resources, Sierra Leone, 2019) is exceptional in its recent inclusion of unprotected as well as protected sources, and also in recording the type of supply management/ownership. It shows that although public rural water coverage has increased rapidly in the years since the war, the rate of private well construction is also speeding up, partly fuelled by problems of access to community supplies during the Ebola epidemic of 2014–15. More private wells are now being properly protected as they are constructed, and so contributing to coverage figures (see Figure 3.2), while those previously dug can also be upgraded. Approximately a third of all Sierra Leone water points are privately funded and managed.

Comparison between Sierra Leone WASH Portal water point inventory and JMP data suggests an average of 32 people (5–6 households) per private well.

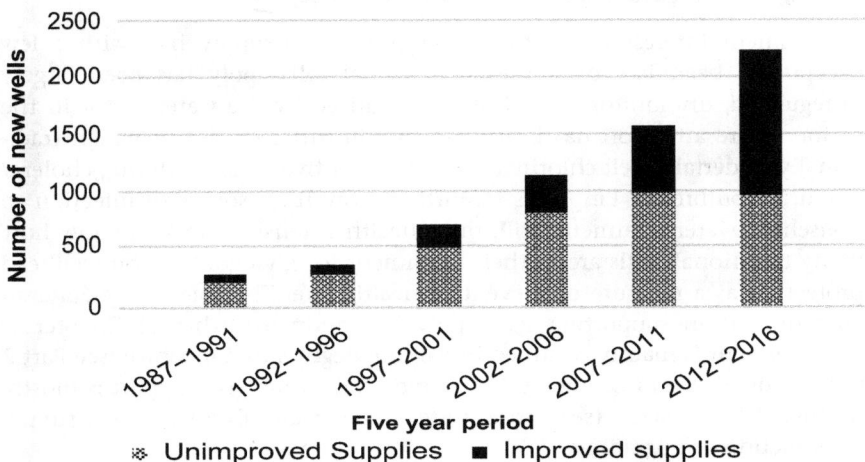

Figure 3.2 Privately owned well-construction in Sierra Leone
Source: Data from the Ministry of Water Resources, Sierra Leone, 2019

Improved group supplies

While the majority of self-financed supplies provide a basic or less than basic level of service, and most communally constructed supplies are unimproved, there are certain areas where self-financed improved group supplies have been developed. An example is the group self-help schemes in central and western Kenya (Arvonen et al., 2017). These are mainly gravity-fed systems serving rural towns and peri-urban areas which are small enough and cohesive enough for communities to organize cooperative systems. In Kenya, there are over 1,200 such schemes serving over 3.6 million people (Advani, 2010), an average of 3,000 per system. Most have been running for more than 20 years and are based on the Kenyan principle of *'harambee'* (a tradition of self-help). Examples are also to be found in Cameroon (Njoh, 2009) and Ghana (Nyarko et al., 2008) employing motorized pumps on wells or boreholes and in Mali (Maizama 2015) especially in the Kayes region river intakes and boreholes which have been constructed using remittances and some funding from government. The common features are strong community leadership, formation of legal entities, and cash raised from remittances and savings, but also a tradition of communal work and ability to raise funds from government and from outside.

Conditions for encouraging group supply development have generally been little explored but may offer an additional way to increase coverage in rural towns. It does, however require a tradition of self-help and strong community leadership. The former may have been somewhat undermined over the past half century by increased donor dependency and the latter by a move away from traditional social structures towards emphasis on the democracy of committees.

Existing roles of government in sub-Saharan self-supply

Government interest in existing unsupported self-supply has, with a few exceptions, been low or non-existent. Rural self-supply has been largely unregulated, unmonitored, and little recognized by the water sector in the region. More attention has been paid by Ministries of Health which traditionally undertake well chlorination as a preventive measure during cholera/dysentery outbreaks. Emphasis is shifting away from source disinfection to household water treatment; still, most health extension workers know how many traditional wells are in their catchment for giving advice on wellhead protection as a measure of preventive health care. The role of sub-Saharan governments in supporting self-supply is examined further in Chapter 9, but at present is mainly confined in varying degrees to Zimbabwe (see Part 2 Case study 4), Sierra Leone, Ethiopia, and Mali. Otherwise support is mostly through NGO projects (see Part 2, Case studies 5 and 6) for low cost supply construction or upgrading.

Sierra Leone, with the best information on private supplies (improved and unimproved), has recognized self-supply as a service delivery model. This is, so far, more a recognition of the acceptability of low-cost technologies than support through inclusion in rural water budgets. The Ethiopian government has included self-supply as a service delivery option in the ONE WASH (National rural WASH strategy 2016–2021) but has yet to formalize and take implementation to scale. Zimbabwe has for years supported the upgrading of family wells, especially through the Ministry of Health, but this level of service does not now appear in WASH policy (MWRDM, 2012), which refers only to community water supply (see also Chapter 9 and Part 2, Case study 4).

A few countries are now seeking to learn more about private supply development and to make it mandatory that even low-cost drillers and well-diggers must register and provide information on wells they construct and that well-owners must make themselves known to water or health departments and are responsible for the quality of water in their supply. Malawi is at present undertaking a full inventory of water points while Zambia is imposing regulation on drillers which requires them to register and record the boreholes they complete. Tanzania is introducing a tax on any well more than 15 m deep and requiring all drilling enterprises, however small, to be registered.

Government intervention in low-income country household water supply seems to be mainly regulatory in a context where resources are already mostly insufficient to monitor community supplies adequately. In addition, there are few, if any, elements of professional development for the private sector or grants or loans for end-users to compensate for the burden being put on a still embryonic private sector.

A stronger case for regulation could be made for the development of self-financed small piped water supplies. Chapter 9 explores the roles of government in supporting self-supply.

The scale of rural self-supply in middle-income economies

Middle-income countries provide a view of an intermediate step between low- and high-income self-supply and offer a rich (but as yet largely unexplored) experience of ways to enable the move from traditional supplies into those piped into the house (World Bank, 2018) or of amalgamation into group or municipal water supplies. While governments are focussing on expansion of piped supplies as economies improve, the rate of higher service provision has yet to catch up with the aspirations that rural people have for a better quality of life. Markets have therefore built up to satisfy the demand for private investment in improved access and service levels in water supply and sanitation.

Experiences in central and eastern Europe, Latin America, and South Asia indicate some elements of the future for lower income countries, but also the degree to which the enormous number of private supplies are mostly still ignored. Their recognition is perhaps greatest in Latin America.

While low-income countries are still mainly moving towards community water supply (see Figure 1.2), in middle-income countries community handpumps and self-supply for drinking water are most actively being replaced

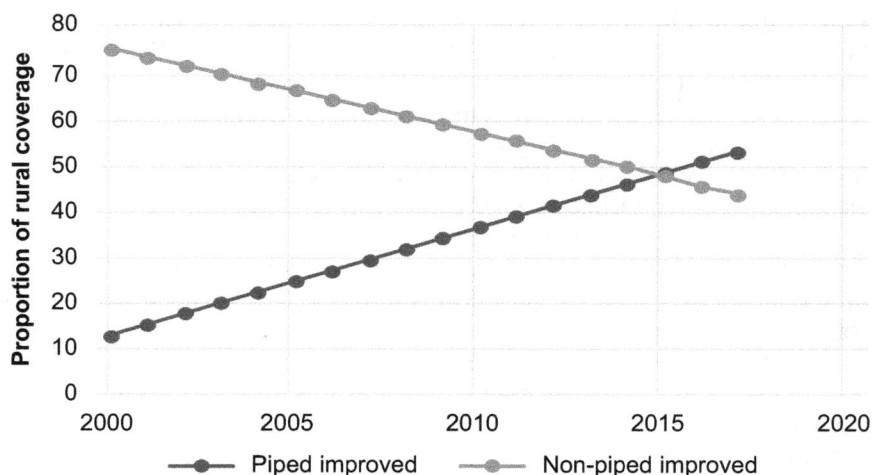

Figure 3.3 Thailand changing from point improved sources to piped water supply – a typical middle-income economy trend
Source: WHO/UNICEF JMP 2019

by public piped supplies often through expansion of utilities as trends in Thailand show (see Figure 3.3). There is little stimulus for governments to support self-supply while the focus is on making public utilities viable and centralizing supply operation and management for economies of scale, but household investment still plays an enormous part in domestic water provision for hundreds of millions of people.

Examples in Central and Eastern Europe

Middle-income Danube basin countries (see Table 3.3 and Part 2, Case study 2) provide a range of dependence on self-supply and of technology levels.

Table 3.3 Self-supply provision in Danube Basin middle-income countries

Country	HDI	Total privately supplied	Number served (non-piped)	Number served (piped)	Total self-supply to rural population (%)
Ukraine	88	n/a	8,910,000	n/a	66[1]
Romania	52	5,340,000	3,560,000	1,780,000	60
B/Herzegovina	77	1,344,000	252,000	1,092,000	64
Moldova	112	1,311,000	1,026,000	285,000	69
Albania	68	n/a	228,000	n/a	19[1]
Kosovo	140	330,000	220,000	110,000	30

Note: [1] Non-piped access only. Self-supply and local operator piped access not differentiated; HDI: Human Development Index
Source: Data from World Bank, 2018

Almost half (49 per cent) of rural households (14.2 million people) depend on non-piped access by self-supply, and of these over a third in Ukraine and Romania collect water by hand. Ukraine and Albania do not differentiate between local operator and self-supplied piped water but for the other four countries almost a quarter (23 per cent) of households provide their own piped supply into the house.

The region presents a microcosm ranging from situations found over much of Africa to those found in the United States or Australia. The policy environments and socio-economic conditions which have helped propel some countries into the latter group and retained some in the former are being studied by the World Bank and will have valuable lessons for sub-Saharan Africa (see Part 2 Case study 2).

Examples in Latin America

Size and scope of self-supply in Latin America. Latin America has relatively high rural water supply coverage, with about 88 per cent having at least basic services (WHO/UNICEF JMP, 2019). Most of that is through connections to piped supplies (75 per cent of the rural population), some largely communally self-financed, others through municipal or state provision. Most water is supplied on premises (80 per cent). These statistics indicate that there is a small, but important, part of the population who are currently served through non-piped improved supplies on premises. It is not possible to ascertain what percentage of piped and non-piped supply have been self-supplied; that is, where the households have made all or most of the investments, either individually or as a community, since governments have intervened to some degree to upgrade or provide individual household supplies.

Another 6 per cent are currently accessing unimproved supplies. These tend to be unprotected wells or spring captures, often for single households or groups of households. They are likely to be self-supplied; that is, the (groups) of households have developed these wells or spring captures, though not up to an improved standard. Finally, some 5 per cent of the rural population still takes water from surface water sources.

Self-supply and supported individual supplies. Though comprehensive statistics are lacking, it is likely that most of those not on public reticulation systems live in the most remote and dispersed rural areas, where piped communal supplies are often financially or technically not feasible. The provision or upgrading of improved individual supplies is an important alternative for serving those populations. Such improved supplies may be a product of household investment and publicly funded programmes to upgrade them, or publicly funded investment to provide an individual supply to those who cannot afford their own solution, especially with rainwater harvesting.

Policies and programmes for support to individual supplies. Relevance of individual supplies is officially recognized, and to varying degrees supported, in countries such as Brazil, Colombia (Domínguez et al., 2016), Nicaragua (Lockwood and Smits, 2011), and, in the past, Honduras (Smits, 2017).

Some examples:

- The One Million Rainwater Harvesting Programme in Brazil (Noguiera, 2008). In some of the dry north-eastern states, rainwater harvesting tanks are provided to vulnerable households (female-headed households or those with small children, people with disabilities, or elderly people). This builds up rural businesses and enables others to buy for themselves from local contractors.
- In Nicaragua, there has been a combination of NGO-supported programmes to provide wells with rope pumps and households investing in such technologies. Estimates of rope pump sales and unimproved household wells amounted to over 320,000 in 2015. No MICS surveys are available, but the 2017 JMP database records over a quarter of the rural population depending on unprotected groundwater sources and 30 per cent using non-piped improved supplies, which suggests a large self-financed element and potential for improvement or upgrading. Developments in Nicaragua in the 1980s led to an estimated 25 per cent increase in rural coverage (Alberts, 2004), increased productive water use, and transfer of affordable technologies (a range of rope pump models and hand-drilling technology) to El Salvador, Guatemala, and, to a small extent, Honduras (Brand, 2004). The rope pump is an officially recognized technology option in Nicaragua and Colombia (Lockwood and Smits, 2011) and Bolivia (Maccarthy, 2014).
- Technologies originating from the EMAS centre in Bolivia for low cost drilling, well protection, hand pumps, rainwater harvesting (RWH), household piped supply and plumbing, latrines, showers, and irrigation systems have also spread to the private sector in this region (see also Chapter 6). All these products have been specifically designed to be affordable to families in the self-supply market, with hundreds of artisan entrepreneurs trained in production and installation. They are established in Bolivia and active in at least eight other Latin American countries.
- In Honduras, there are numerous spring captures, whereby households convey water from those springs with hosepipes to individual houses, or groups of houses. These offer the greatest opportunity for self-supply upgrading (see Box 3.2) among highly scattered rural households, but with requirements for new strategies to accommodate them.

Examples in South Asia

Scale of development. In numerical terms, the highest incidence of self-supply is in Southern Asia. Figure 1.2 shows the big increase in non-piped improved supplies in Central and Southern Asia, and the move in Eastern and

---

Box 3.2 Honduras report proposing strategies for dispersed populations

Fifteen per cent of the rural Honduran population of 1.3 million live in dispersed communities of less than 200 inhabitants. In this group, access to water is still largely from informal sources (see Table 3.2). The widespread use of water from unprotected springs, either directly or brought by hosepipe to the house, provides ample opportunity for upgrading to achieve improved supplies at home. Since 2003 the Ministry of Health has had a specific policy for rural water and sanitation, including dispersed populations. However, the responsible municipalities receive many demands from larger communities and have limited capacity and even more limited knowledge of the situation in small dispersed communities, so little has changed.

Self-supply among dispersed population in Honduras

Supply type	Proportion of dispersed population using supply (%)
Piped supply	46
Improved self-supply	3
Other improved supply	1
Unimproved self-supply	
Hosepipe from spring	29
Well with windlass/rope	1
Open source	21

Report recommendations:

The need is for a different strategy from that for high-density populations to address needs in technology, unit costs, and marketing methods among populations with aspirations for piped water but not the means to achieve them. The strategy, to be cost effective, also needs to combine water and sanitation and look at incremental change. The first step would be to define the status quo so that there is increased awareness of the problems scattered households face. Earmarking a budget for WASH and part of it for dispersed groups can be tied to performance-related fiscal incentives, and compliance in planning and monitoring as conditions for budget release. Strengthening capacity at all levels from national to district and community will also be needed if the situation is to improve.

Source: Smits, 2017

South-eastern Asia away from non-piped (largely self-supply handpumps) to water piped into the home. Both changes have led to significant reduction in unimproved groundwater use, due to a combination of expanded piped supplies and households upgrading wells and investing in hand- or motorized pumps.

Foster et al. (2019) note that there are 29 million households with their own handpump in India and at least 10 million in Bangladesh. Dave (2014) estimates that over 340 million people in India depend on self-supply, with over 1 million new tubewells (mainly private) being drilled annually. Household investment appears not to be diminishing, and the same is true in rural Pakistan. Here piped systems are struggling to provide a reliable supply and piped coverage fell 10 per cent between 2000 and 2017, the resultant gap increasingly being filled by non-piped supply, especially self-supply. In the Punjab region, while there is theoretically 98 per cent coverage with improved water supply into the home (Cooper, 2018), the World Bank (Sami, 2018) attributed 84.9 per cent of coverage to household investment in electric and hand pumps on their own wells, rather than provision by utility piped supplies. The Asian Development Bank (ADB, 2009) earlier remarked that 'Highly convenient access through hand and/or motor pumps represents a very high investment that communities have made in the self-provision of water, and it is hard to envisage this supply being replaced in the short- to medium-term by government-led interventions'. Increasing emphasis is being put on women's participation (e.g. women as ambassadors for change in the World Bank sanitation and nutrition project, 2017) and on civil society involvement (e.g. teacher student WASH clubs) to improve their own WASH facilities. The combination of community and household private investment appears to provide the greater part of basic or safely managed water supply to reach near universal coverage.

High levels of rural self-supply are remarked on in Viet Nam (Wegener, 2015) (RWH and groundwater), Lao (mainly groundwater) (SNV, n.d.), and Bangladesh (Fisher, 2017) among others. Strong private sector development of local support services (mechanics, masons, drillers) encourages households to upgrade their own supplies. In Viet Nam with 92 per cent coverage, 80 per cent have a non-piped improved water supply on their premises mainly provided by households themselves (UNICEF Viet Nam, 2014). In 2014 the Water and Sanitation Program predicted households to be the major source of capital funding for water supply but did not include their existing contri- bution in the sector assessment. Community mobilization for finance and construction of group supplies by women's groups and provision of unsub- sidized loans by the Vietnam Bank for Social Policies both contribute to the enabling environment.

Household investment in rainwater harvesting is traditionally common in Thailand (see Box 3.3 and Part 2, Case study 3). Here government promotion of roof water harvesting has led to convenient provision of water for large numbers of households, either as sole supply or, more often, as a dual supply to reduce costs of piped water or the inconvenience of off-site water collection. An enormous campaign from the 1980s built on a strong tradition for rain- water harvesting to promote upgrading to larger, safer storage (Thai rain jars). As key factors in this successful campaign, Saladin (2016) cites:

- strong government commitment;
- building on existing tradition of rainwater as a highly valued commodity;
- options at affordable cost;
- well-developed supply chains and skills;
- absence of alternatives.

Despite the apparent high levels of self-supply in South and South-east Asia, there appears to be little documentation of government recognition or inputs to support improvements except in Thailand.

Box 3.3 Thai rainwater harvesting

Photo 3.2 A typical house in rural Thailand with several Thai jars
Source: EnterpriseWorks/Vita

Rainwater harvesting is a tradition in Thailand, with almost every house having some level of storage (Saladin, 2016). By 2013 rural coverage with improved supplies had reached 95%. Over 40% of households named RWH as their primary drinking water source (see Photo 3.2), with people adopting modern options beyond the traditional jars. Piped supplies have however increased by over 30% since 2000.

Shifting service delivery models in middle-income countries

The move away from basic self-supply into higher technology levels has partly been stimulated by the spread of rural electrification and solar power. This is often a key factor in the dynamics of rural water supply, opening up more private and public options. The wider availability of low-cost motorized pumps (largely Chinese) is also changing the face of self-supply and is cited as a major reason for the fall in demand for rope pumps in Cambodia (Smit, personal communication, 2018). Electric power, like water, is being developed as an expanding network in these rural economies, and both will continue with elements of 'off-grid' self-financing for many years to come. The public sector emphasis will, however, continue to be mainly on the development of larger public networks for both.

For many middle-income countries self-supply has formed an intermediate step, enabling rural development and better quality of rural life many years in advance of the arrival of public supplies. When reliable household connections are available they will become the preferred option. The challenge is to make them reliable enough from the start for people not to continue also to use their own supply, which may undermine the necessary demand base for network supplies to be sustainable. In most middle-income countries dependence on self-supply is falling as governments become more able to afford to support construction and expansion of piped supplies. Additional strategies may need to be considered as self-supply still plays a major role, especially among highly dispersed rural communities, where small urban supplies are not yet able to extend into more rural areas and among those reluctant to lose their autonomy. A two-pronged approach to development is therefore needed to facilitate household improvements to their own supplies as well as connections for those best situated to become part of municipal or commercial networks.

Studies in Central Europe (e.g. World Bank, 2018) and in Latin America (e.g. Smits, 2017) offer recommendations that are relevant to many middle- and lower-income countries. They include:

- A better balance between urban and rural investments and policies, with earmarked rural WASH funding.
- Essential inclusion of the health sector in rural water and sanitation (already has full responsibility in Honduras).
- Improved understanding of the status quo (inventories, establishing the relationship between public and self-supply and needs assessments for future support).
- Incentives, conditionality of funding, and accountability to encourage urban utility expansion into rural areas.
- Incremental improvements for self-supply which include:
  - specific planning, technologies, and marketing methods for scattered households;
  - subsidy schemes for piping water into the house;
  - awareness campaigns for water quality and monitoring;
  - inventories with risk assessments;
  - campaigns and incentives to connect to public supply where feasible, including micro-loans to the poorest;
  - combined water and sanitation interventions for economies of scale;
  - targeted capacity building at different levels, for the relevant provision of technical advice, practical assistance, micro-finance, and regulation/monitoring;
  - identification of priority areas and fiscal incentives for tackling them.

These aspects are discussed more fully in Chapter 9.

The scale of rural self-supply in higher-income countries

Despite well-developed economies investing in public infrastructure over much of the urban and rural environment, high-income countries still often depend to a significant degree on consumer investment in their own water supply. Government roles in support are evolving and there is also more information available from which lessons can be learned.

In Europe as a whole, there is a significant relationship between coverage with private supplies and Human Development Index (HDI) ranking (see Figure 3.4). The main exceptions are Moldova, Armenia, and Serbia, which have a lower coverage with private supply than the norm for their relative HDI. Ireland, Denmark, Sweden, and Germany have a higher dependence on private supply coverage than their HDI ranking would indicate, linked to the evolution of group (cooperative) as well as household investment, more widely scattered populations and supportive government policies.

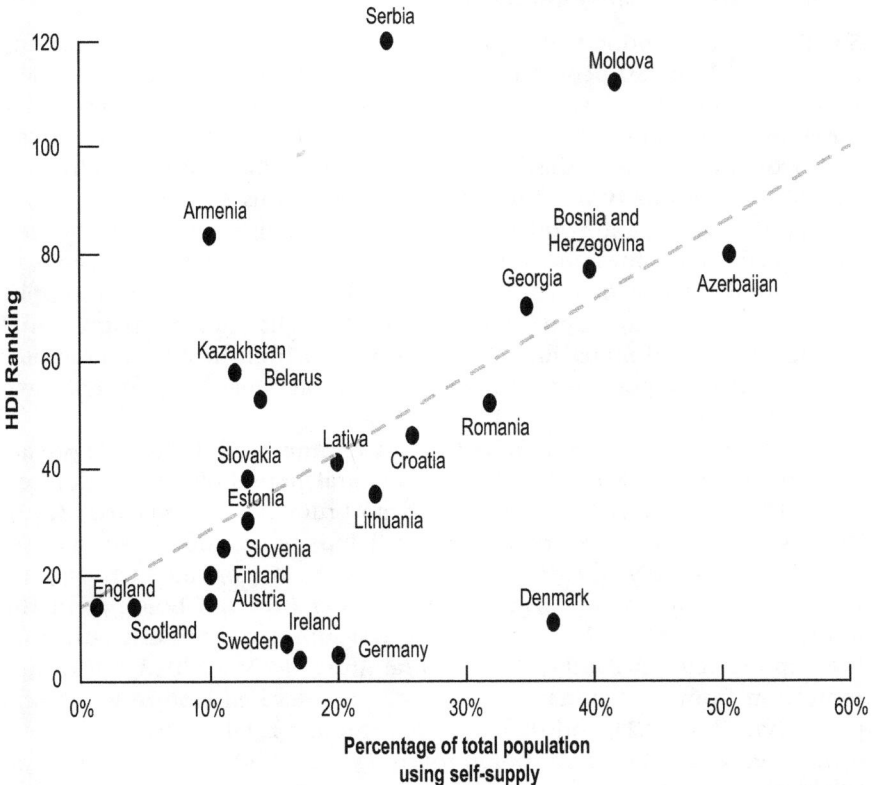

Figure 3.4 Proportion of total population depending on private supplies (individual plus group), relative to HDI in the WHO European region
Source: Data from Rickert et al., 2016; UNDP, 2018

Although there is often a move to consolidate private supplies into small groups, or to get small groups to amalgamate, in most high-income countries there is a growing acceptance that self-supply provision is a cost-effective solution for highly dispersed households if they are to have a reliable and affordable supply (for example Scotland; Part 2, Case study 1). The main need is to provide them with adequate advice and monitoring of performance and for the private sector to have the necessary capacity (monitored with certification) to provide technical support services.

Total provision by public supply tends to occur where there is a dense rural population or around rural towns whose density leaves little truly rural land in between, as with the Netherlands and Belgium which provide public supply to all properties. The Netherlands banned private water supplies in 2004. In contrast, Denmark relies heavily on small user-owned cooperatives supported by an Association of Waterworks which serve 35 per cent of the total population.

Scale of individual supply ownership

Small private or individual supply typically means rural systems serving fewer than 25 or 50 people (see Table 3.4) or with consumption of less than 10 m³ per day. These are more usually groundwater sources (wells, boreholes, and springs) but may also include surface/gravity water sources, as in Scotland (see Part 2, Case study 1). In high-income countries individual supplies can normally be shared by only a few houses before regulations are applied. In England two-thirds of all self-supply is to individual houses. In Sweden they appear to serve almost the total population because of the high incidence of second homes, 'cabins' with their own supply, and in parts of Central Europe household dug wells remain a part of rural life. In the United States and Canada scattered high income households lead to a high proportion of the rural population depending on their own supplies.

The United States seems to have the greatest number of individual private wells or boreholes, with over 10 million rural households depending on them. This constitutes 45 per cent of the most rural population (AHS, 2017). These very small supplies are not regulated and are regarded by most states as the responsibility of their owners/consumers. Almost all such supplies in North America now consist of piped water into the house from the home well or borehole but most started as a supply not too different from the unprotected wells and springs in rural Africa (Pa Mac, 2012). Over time protection from contamination increased and elevated storage with wind power (see Photo 3.3), and then powered through rural electrification, was introduced as rural economies improved. Water could then be piped into the home.

The WHO survey (Rickert et al., 2016) of the European region found some 20 million people (7 per cent of the total population of the 27 responding

Table 3.4 Examples of individual rural self-supply (up to 50 people) in high-income countries

High income countries	HDI	Number served by individual rural self-supply	Percentage rural population served	Percentage total population served	Information source
United States	13	25,726,950	45	8	AHS, 2017
Canada	12	2,197,800	33	10	Hardie and Alaysia, 2009
Sweden	7	1,200,000	87	12	Hendry and Akoumianaki, 2016
Lithuania	35	861,872	91	30	Orru and Rothstein, 2015
Austria	20	701,840	24	8	Hendry and Akoumianaki, 2016
Germany	5	700,000	4	1	Hendry and Akoumianaki, 2016
Slovakia*	38	700,000	28	13	Rickert et al., 2016
England	14	567,261	6	1	DWI, 2015
Ireland	4	480,000	27	10	Cooney, 2016
Croatia	46	423,280	25	10	World Bank, 2018
Latvia*	41	420,000	66	22	Rickert et al., 2016
Finland	15	250,000	16	5	Hendry and Akoumianaki, 2016
Estonia*	30	250,000	60	19	Rickert et al., 2016
Slovenia*	25	200,000	19	10	Rickert et al., 2016
Scotland	14	195,961	21	4	DWQR, 2017
Denmark	11	105,000	15	1	Hendry and Akoumianaki, 2016

Note: * Denotes supplies categorized as 'individual de-centralized and local supplies and supplies serving up to 50 people'. Country definition of 'rural' varies.

countries) to be served by individual self-supply (a similar proportion to sub-Saharan Africa). In terms of rural population, individual self-supply still seems to provide an essential service to some of the 'developed' world. The form it takes may however be indistinguishable from public piped supply, with water being piped into the house from their own source.

Small group schemes

Small group schemes typically cover communities of up to 5,000 people, which may be regarded as rural towns and villages. Overall in the WHO European region (Rickert et al., 2016) 16 per cent (144 million) of the

Photo 3.3 Late 19th century American homestead domestic and farm water supply, Oklahoma

population is served by small-scale water supplies. Community-run schemes arise from the amalgamation of individual supplies or when community members decide that they want to solve their problems of access by creating a new shared supply. This requires a level of community cohesion but is a common form of supply for villages and small towns, filling in between municipal/utility and individual supplies. Countries listed in Table 3.5 have a significant number of group supplies in the form of cooperatives which have largely provided their own funding and offer a second way of harnessing private finance to reach higher levels of service, also providing for some larger urban areas.

The United States also has over 3,300 water cooperatives for rural towns and new peri-urban developments (Deller et al., 2009).

Overall self-supply can still be seen to play an important part in rural water supply in a range of high- income countries. In most it is the more isolated individual households or very small groups for which self-supply is a permanent solution. Cooperatives systems are fewer but since they cover larger groups, their members in Europe constitute about half of those outside of public systems in total.

Table 3.5 Examples of European group/cooperative supply coverage

Country	HDI	Number served by group supplies	Proportion of total population served (%)	Information source
Germany	5	16,000,000	20	Hendry and Akoumianaki, 2016
Austria	20	2,700,000	31	Rickert et al., 2016
Denmark	11	1,995,000	35	Pietilä et al., 2016
Finland	15	715,000	13	Pietilä et al., 2016
Ireland	4	336,000	7	Cooney (IEPA) 2016)
WHO European region		43,826,087	16	Rickert et al., 2016

Note: Total population used as many group supplies are for small urban areas

Government roles in high-income self-supply

Evolving roles. Government involvement is generally engaged to speed up the process of amalgamating suppliers into larger groups to provide economies of scale, and/or to accelerate the move to safer supply for small groups or individuals. The trigger for the formation of group water schemes may be from government, but at least in the case of Ireland, the first move came from women who began to campaign for a better and more convenient water supply than the village pumps which were still the main source of water for many well into the second half of the 20th century (see Box 3.4). Government finance was limited so communities largely had to solve the problem for themselves (National Federation of Group Water Schemes (NGWS), 2012).

Box 3.4 Collective action for water supply in Ireland

In the early 1960s only 12% of rural houses had a piped water supply, compared with 97% of urban households. The village pump or local well/ spring were the only options.

The 'Turn on the Tap' campaign was a combined effort of the Irish Countrywomen's Association and the Department of Local Government. It was essentially a grass-roots initiative which galvanized community members to volunteer both their time and their cash to work together to form a group water supply. Small grants were available towards the cost of the supply (made more cost effective by one well serving many houses), but the major investment was from the contribution of households themselves, and their digging of trenches and laying of pipes.

Within 10 years more than five times as many properties had piped supply, largely through their own investment. The final push came with joining the EEC whose requirement for higher supply standards (starting with the Directive 98/83/EC) fortunately coincided with higher prices for farm produce enabling households to finance or borrow funds for upgrading.

Source: NFGWS, 2012: 64

Irish local authorities facilitated the process by:

- providing water for groups from their own sources where possible;
- taking potential group development into consideration when developing public schemes;
- encouraging the infill of regional schemes by private groups.

Ireland in the 1960s and Finland in the 1940s faced many of the water problems rural Africa faces today and provide many useful and documented lessons on how consumers can help solve them (Katku, 1992). The evolution of Finnish cooperatives has followed a similar path (see Table 3.6) to that in Ireland (and reflecting those in Kenya and Mali), linked to pressure exerted by women, especially in sparsely populated areas and the need for water for productive use. Some 15 per cent of Finland's population is served by individual wells and cooperatives and rural water supply has always been based on consumer initiative. Katku acknowledges that this is a slower path than the externally funded route but has left no inequity between rural and urban coverage. The growth of cooperatives has occurred in several phases (Pietilä et al., 2016) which reflect changes in government policies. Government support, however small (less than 10 per cent of total costs), appeared to provide a strong incentive, alongside municipal funding to reduce urban drift.

More recent moves are to amalgamate cooperatives. This may, however, be weakening management structures which remain essentially voluntary as more villages are incorporated, leading to bigger financial risks. As in

Table 3.6 Phases in the evolution of Finnish cooperatives

	Type/ funding sources	Role of state	Comment
1. Before 1950	Funded and constructed by user(s)	Little or no state input	Stimulated by needs of dairy farmers and women's pressure groups
2. 1950s to 1970s	Small loans/subsidy, most of cost borne by users	State supervision improved quality of works	Loans/subsidies only available to rural groups
3. 1980s and 1990s	Extension of municipal supplies to rural areas at cost to group	Municipalities provided advice, and subsidy or loan guarantees	Managed by users, EU grants since 1995
4. Since 2000	Increased incorporation of individual supplies into groups	Mostly as connections to larger municipal supplies, co-financed and with wastewater	User management, bulk buying water
5. All rural towns	Small town linkages of large numbers of households with own wells	As the management and income strengthened these expanded to rural areas	Most included sewerage from the start as housing density is higher

Source: Derived from Pietilä et al., 2016

Ireland, management strength is also being threatened by the ageing of the original founders and the lack of training of the younger generation and their reluctance to get involved. This is a problem shared with community supplies in many lower income countries. Commercial management services need to grow to fill the widening gap in both. Larger urban cooperatives are better placed in that they have a higher financial turnover and generally employ outside management capacity from the start.

Initially it is common to try to enforce house connections to maximize the enormous investments in providing piped water supply, which may conflict with the strong desire of those with their own supply to cling onto it and not lose their autonomy. In the United States this was particularly so in the 1990s (Stone, 1998), when those who would not connect to public supply were jailed (New Jersey) or fined as much as $500 a day (Wisconsin). That pressure is no longer so strong, but increasingly it has become mandatory to register private wells (e.g. Oklahoma State). Despite the legislation to register them, supplies are not monitored or regulated by the Safe Drinking Water Act (1974) and are regarded as being the responsibility of the owner who bears all risks.

Strong pressure is still put on European households in several countries to join group schemes or public ones, especially if a supply is found to be non-compliant with quality standards (e.g. Denmark); while in Austria connection is mandatory if piped supply is available. Despite this rule in Austria, 8 per cent of rural households still provide their own supply, since connection is too expensive for those users and for the cooperatives or municipalities providing the nearest supply. Elsewhere local authorities accelerate the improvement of existing supplies and development of new ones through support to advisory groups and services, provision of grants (e.g. Scotland, Wales), and low interest loans (United States).

Growing awareness of the higher risks of self-supply. Quality of supply is a major concern for governments where there are group and individual self-supply systems. In all countries private provision seems to perform less well than public systems and smaller systems worse than larger ones. Taking Ireland as an example, with the highest incidence of VTEC (a strain of more harmful *E. coli* bacteria (O157), which causes serious infection) in Europe, patients with VTEC were found to be four times more likely to have consumed untreated water from a private household supply than any other, despite them only serving 10 per cent of the population. The pattern for *E. coli* counts (Table 3.7) illustrates a similar pattern, with public supplies performing consistently better than private ones – a pattern repeated across most of Europe according to WHO/UNECE (Rickert et al., 2016).

Poorer performance of smaller supplies is partly because they are less likely than larger systems to have staff trained for and dedicated to supply management (Brady and Gray, 2010), and also lesser frequency of water sampling. The WHO study (Rickert et al., 2016) found that among small supplies half had only low qualification staff and half had staff without any qualification.

Table 3.7 Meeting *E. coli* standards – example from Ireland, compliance per private water supply type (to zero faecal coliform)

All private supplies	1. Public group water	2. Private group water	3. Small private (<50)	3. Household individual supply
96.2%	99.8%	96.1%	94.8%	68%
All non-public, average of 1–3	Group water schemes, community managed using public water supply	Group water schemes with community management + own source	Small commercial or public entity e.g. school, pub	Mostly wells and boreholes to one property

Source: Data for 1, 2, 3 from Cooney, 2016; column 4 from Hynds et al., 2013

For individual systems there are also constraints to improvement noted in Ireland and Scotland and echoed in many lower income countries. The reluctance to shift to public supplies has its origins in consumers feeling they:

- are responsible for their own health;
- perceive that they have drunk the water without ill-effects for considerable periods of time;
- are nervous of the unknown cost implications of improvement or enforced connection to public supply;
- are often happy with the status quo; and
- may not be the owners of the supply.

These factors can lead to supply owners preferring to forgo grants or loans (Box 3.4) to avoid getting drawn into regular testing regimes with the possibility of enforced improvements at their own cost. Targeted awareness raising campaigns and greater consultation with owners are gradually changing views (see Part 2, Case study 1)

Growing realization that small private supplies are generally a greater risk is leading to increased efforts to provide advice and monitor water quality in most high-income countries. It is the main driver for introduction of regulation where none previously existed. This is a relatively recently established role in the sector requiring adequate funding to cover both effective regulation and the means to support supply owners unable to cover the costs of required improvements.

Regulation of group/cooperative supplies. There is generally a differentiation between the regulatory obligations for group schemes, small supplies covering a few households and single house self-supply. Group schemes, while owned by the users, are regarded as being in effect a supply to the public and so are regulated to much the same degree as a public utility. Their numbers and status are better known; they operate as legal entities and tend to have greater access to grants to accelerate improvements. They can often more easily refer to umbrella organizations (e.g. American National Groundwater Association, Irish National Federation of Group Water Schemes) for advice alongside the support of Environmental Protection Agencies and health authorities.

The EU Framework for Action guidance for the management of small supplies (European Commission, 2014) and the EU Drinking Water Directive (Council Directive 98/83/EC) have had much influence in the region for the introduction of a light regulatory framework for supplies to more than 50 people. The threat of national fines for non-compliance is driving new efforts to improve water quality in all small supplies, with each country setting its own regulatory framework, or in the case of the UK, each water company region, overseen by the Drinking Water Inspectorate. The Irish government (DHPLG, 2016) under the same threat, has introduced local authority grants (of up to €7,650 per household) to encourage consolidation of small group schemes, improved water treatment and amalgamation into public supplies for the advantages brought by economies of scale and improved management (See Table 3.8).

Regulation of individual private supply. Individual private supply in EU terms covers all supplies of <10 m³/day or for less than 50 people and with no commercial use, but confusingly there is a further sub-division for single dwellings. Both tend to be regarded differently from small group supplies, in much the same way that if a household kitchen only provides food for itself or a neighbour/family member, governments do not regulate activities but offer advice. Only when food is sold do rules and inspection come in, and for domestic scale production the role of authorities is simply

Table 3.8 SWOT analysis of group/cooperative water schemes versus public supply

Strengths	Opportunities
– Largely independent of public funding – High sense of ownership/solidarity – Local knowledge of systems – Low political influence on decision-making – Non-profit making – Clear charging framework to cover costs – Not bound by local administrative boundaries – Usually with a central umbrella organization/cooperative of cooperatives – Not for profit organization	– Supply maintenance burden can be shared among many households – Merging to create larger, more cost-effective unit – Large enough to employ professional rather than volunteer management – Sometimes large enough to purchase water from utility – A legal entity which can access public funding
Weaknesses	**Threats**
– Reliance on volunteers – Dependence on community cohesion – After construction members lose interest – Individual interests may cause conflict – Lack of necessary business or technical skills – Not all countries provide easy access to public funding if needed	– Members tire of voluntary work – Members age and retire but no new volunteers – Amalgamation with other cooperatives may lead to loss of commitment – Inter-personal relationships – Regulations become too onerous for management

---

Box 3.5 The paradox of Ireland

Since 1972 Ireland is the only OECD country not to charge for public water supply. Those on group water schemes, however, constructed and ran their supply at their own cost. To remove this inequity the Irish government now pays them a subsidy to cover most running costs so their members are not disadvantaged. The same does not apply to the greater number of households which have their own supply, but which tend to be more remote and difficult to serve in any other way, and more likely to be non-compliant with EU regulations. The exclusion of individual supplies from regulation is widespread but needs to be linked to access to funds for upgrading if those most at risk are not to be permanently disadvantaged.

---

to provide information on risks and good practice and to investigate any outbreak of food-related diseases. Much the same is true for domestic level water supplies. Individual supplies are exempt from regulations in over half the 45 respondent countries in the European region (Rickert et al., 2016) and only regulated if commercial in a further third. The role of government has been chiefly one of supporting these two groups with advice, information, and guidelines, creating awareness of health risks and measures to reduce them. Investment in supply construction or improvement has been regarded largely as the responsibility of individual well owners (e.g. Ireland; see Box 3.5).

With growing awareness that the smaller the water supply the greater the risk to consumers, and that the light touch of 'guidelines and advice' has not led to sufficiently rapid improvement to water quality, regulations are increasingly being extended to individual supplies. UK Regulation 10 (DWI, 2018) requires registration with the local authority and a risk assessment of each private supply serving more than one household, every five years, undertaken at cost to the well owner (£500 each time). Only single households remain exempt.

In the United Kingdom and Ireland, loans specific to water supply are quite widely available, but in Scotland and Ireland grants (as opposed to loans) tend to be linked to non-compliant supplies where the owner is unable to pay for improvements. Wales is something of an exception with grants towards new supplies to farms for drilling boreholes, and new rainwater harvesting systems rather than improvements to existing supplies.

Other governments have encouraged greater attention to household supply water standards by linking it to necessary disclosure when selling or renting a property. For example, in New Zealand no house can be sold without certification that its supply is wholesome and reliable, and compliant with local authority standards.

Acceleration in high-income countries now increasingly seems to employ a 'carrot and stick' approach, requiring a good knowledge of the status quo by regulating authorities. Monitoring remains largely the responsibility of the individual owner. Again, it is the responsibility of the supply owner to report any health issues and to undertake remedial actions largely at their own cost.

Table 3.9 SWOT analysis of individual self-supply in high-income countries

Strengths	Opportunities
– Strong sense of ownership – Lowest level decision-making structure – Instant response to problems possible – Control of users and uses – User oversight of site hygiene – Serves households other systems cannot reach – Lowest cost option for state and consumers	– Loans or grants for improvements – Possible centralizing of supply with other small units to form group – Relatively low public investment can leverage user funds to bring significant improvements

Weaknesses	Threats
– No professional expertise in management/technology – Likely user under-estimation of risks – Usually not officially recognized unless problems occur – Lack of monitoring	– Higher health risks – Not enough users to finance professional management – Regulations may force closure

Monitoring is usually the responsibility of the health sector within local government but water supply or the environmental sector may provide the regulatory framework and enforcement. Regulation tends to be closely tied to funding, since the provision of grants or loans can accelerate improvement in performance and compliance where it is most needed. Low interest loans or loan guarantees may be available, especially where there is concern over rural depopulation. Essentially the official attitude to self-supply at household level lays responsibility at the home-owner's door but recognizes that it is the only affordable alternative both for state and individual and so may provide advisory and, to a limited extent, financial assistance where needed. Despite being high-income countries, many acknowledge the cost- effectiveness of self-supply in specific circumstances (see Table 3.9) and support its long-term role in gap-filling between more centralized supplies through efforts to improve supply performance.

Findings on the evolution of supplies relating to country economy

The experience across the range of countries and economies shows different service delivery models are operating depending largely on the income level of the country (see Figure 3.5). In the low-income countries of sub-Saharan Africa (Type 1), piped supply in rural areas is generally negligible, exceeded by both publicly provided community water points and almost equally by self-supplied groundwater or rainwater harvesting. Exceptions within the region include South Africa, Burkina Faso, and Senegal where rural piped supplies are well-established. The wide public provision of non-piped improved supplies (community boreholes and wells with handpumps) stimulates self-supply where households or communities are a step ahead of

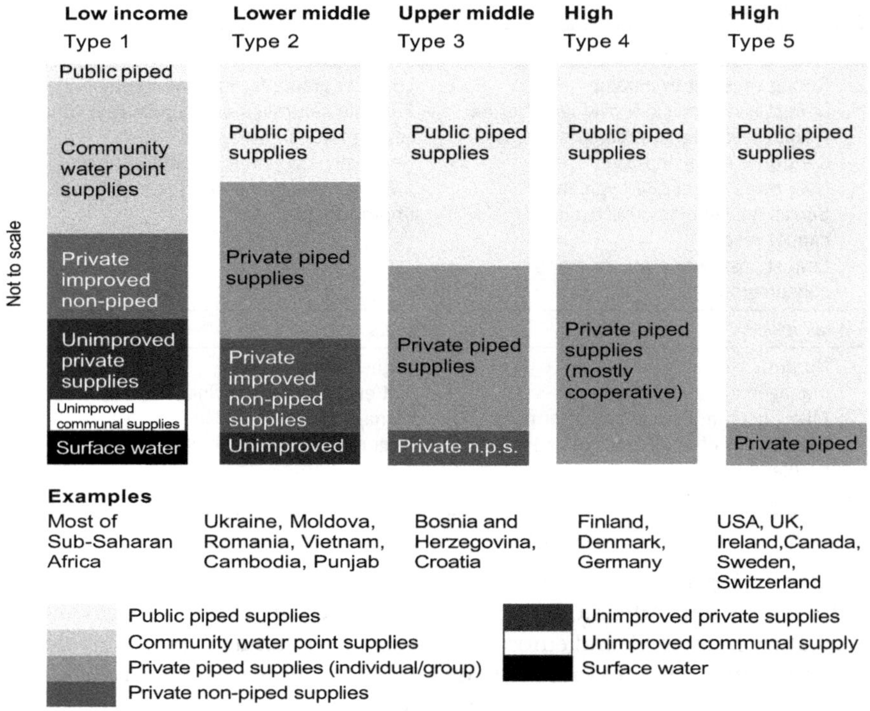

| Low income | Lower middle | Upper middle | High | High |
| Type 1 | Type 2 | Type 3 | Type 4 | Type 5 |

Public piped

Community water point supplies | Public piped supplies | Public piped supplies | Public piped supplies | Public piped supplies

Not to scale

Private improved non-piped | Private piped supplies | | |

Unimproved private supplies | Private improved non-piped supplies | Private piped supplies | Private piped supplies (mostly cooperative) |

Unimproved communal supplies | | | |

Surface water | Unimproved | Private n.p.s. | | Private piped

Examples

| Most of Sub-Saharan Africa | Ukraine, Moldova, Romania, Vietnam, Cambodia, Punjab | Bosnia and Herzegovina, Croatia | Finland, Denmark, Germany | USA, UK, Ireland,Canada, Sweden, Switzerland |

Public piped supplies
Community water point supplies
Private piped supplies (individual/group)
Private non-piped supplies

Unimproved private supplies
Unimproved communal supply
Surface water

Figure 3.5 Generalized evolution of rural water service delivery with growing rural economy

governments in feeling they can afford a more convenient supply. Surface water use is diminishing (see Figure 1.2) but improved and unimproved private groundwater supplies and rainwater harvesting continue to grow.

Among lower middle-income countries, rural or particularly small rural town populations are increasingly depending on their own investment to create improved, mainly non-piped supplies. Public piped supplies are extending but not necessarily with high reliability, so private non-piped supplies still play a major part (Type 2).

In Type 3 public piped supply is still expanding and private provision increasingly replaces basic rope and bucket wells with piped water to the yard or into the house where public piped supply is still not available.

Cooperative initiatives increase with higher income and in Type 4, households have amalgamated into groups for economies of scale and cooperatives developed among communities where public supply has not reached. Where cooperatives are strongly developed (e.g. Finland, Germany, and Denmark), these tend to provide for smaller towns and rural areas, amalgamating into bigger groups or merging with municipal supplies when expedient.

An alternative among higher income countries (Type 5) is that most are served by public piped supply except a relatively small proportion of the most rural. These provide their own piped supply into the house, either as a group or individually. There is larger inherent capacity for self-supply investment in higher income countries, because there tend to be:

- umbrella organizations and advisory services;
- access to cash and government safety nets for those unable to pay;
- a skilled private sector;
- stability because there is less expectation or desire for expansion of piped supply;
- a preference for autonomy and security of legislation for those forming group supplies.

Settlement patterns already have much influence the type of management structure adopted for water supply (see Figure 3.6), and this in turn affects

Evolutionary supply options

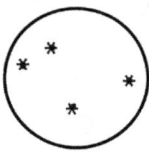

Individual self-supply
Single unconnected source, family owned, all levels from unprotected well up to piped into house.

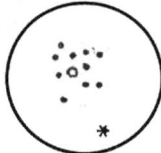

Community water supply
Shared communally owned source. Protected supply usually donor/ government funded.

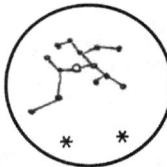

Group water supply
Small group interconnected source. houses, piped supply, common in higher rural economies.

Cooperative water supply
Larger groups, privately owned but management may be contracted out for sustainability.

Small municipal supply
Publicly owned, generally only urban area, insufficient revenue to cross subsidize connection to small isolated villages/ households.

Small utility supply
Publicly owned, founded in urban area but extending into rural villages Connection to isolated households limited by cost to householder or utility.

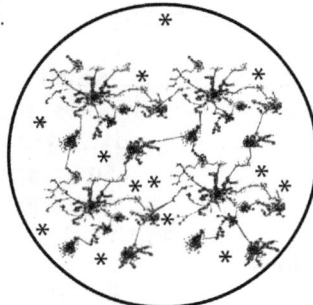

Major utility supply
Commercially or publicly owned, amalgamating many municipal, small utility supplies, and accessible small rural supplies. Outliers still use own supplies unless connection cross-subsidized.

Figure 3.6 Stages in the evolution of water supply management structures: the persistence of self-supply
Note: Some communities may remain at any one stage; others may omit some transition stages

the level of government involvement. Where several households are close enough together, in high-income countries they may combine resources and develop the most reliable/best quality supply. These supplies may amalgamate over time to form a cooperative and in time the cooperative may link to a larger municipal supply to avoid the costs of maintaining the source and treatment of supply. Community water supplies mostly take a different development path in sub-Saharan Africa, which is shaped by donor dependency rather than the type of progression which many other equally rural and poor communities have followed, using water in part as a self-financed route out of poverty. Learning from the experience of high-income countries, a range of interim and permanent service delivery models is needed.

Conclusion

Self-supply seems almost universally prevalent, providing both improved and unimproved supplies. It appears to peak in middle-income countries where rural economies are growing stronger and the desire for on-premises supplies is growing faster than piped networks are growing. Low-income countries are only in the early stages of this type of rural development and it is one which can have a big effect on rural economies but is as yet officially largely unacknowledged. It is in these conditions that group water supplies have grown up in higher income countries, but are still rare in lower income ones. However, there are enough examples to show they may be a possible solution for rural towns and villages, which tend to be on community water points.

Self-supply appears to be an agent stimulating rural development but one which should be prepared to be superseded or augmented where higher level on-premises technologies can reliably take over. This is especially so in middle-income economies, which tend to exhibit a dynamism in infrastructure development which is less obvious in higher income countries (infrastructure well-established) and in lower income countries (rural infrastructure generally resource-constrained and not reliable or convenient). Middle-income countries are finding out the degree to which governments can afford to fill the gaps and where self-supply will continue to provide long-term services – in electrification as well as water. Links with the growth in home level off-grid power generation and the spread of mains electricity are as yet mostly unexplored but offer combined potential for the future.

The lessons learned so far from other regions are:

- enable small initiatives where the state cannot provide, offering advice, performance monitoring, and strengthened private sector capacity for technical services;
- build up umbrella organizations;
- encourage piped connections but have an alternative strategy where this is not cost effective;

- be aware and spread awareness of the risks of private supplies but don't dismiss their value;
- make cost-effective subsidies where this can accelerate positive changes;
- support alternative management structures and capacity building to augment or replace community volunteer management systems over time;
- allow time for new systems to develop and embed themselves in government, private sector, and communities. Successful sustainable systems are seldom rapidly established.

These and other factors of acceleration are explored more fully in Chapter 9.

References

ADB (2009) *Impact of Rural Water Supply and Sanitation in Punjab, Pakistan* [pdf], IES: PAK 2009-26 Impact Evaluation Study, August 2009 <https://www.adb.org/sites/default/files/evaluation-document/35047/files/ies-pak-2009-26.pdf> [accessed May 2020].

Advani, R. (2010) *Using Market Finance to Extend Water Supply Services in Peri-Urban and Rural Kenya (English)* [online], IFC smart lessons brief, Washington, DC: World Bank <http://documents.worldbank.org/curated/en/340501468047725311/Using-market-finance-to-extend-water-supply-services-in-peri-urban-and-rural-Kenya> [accessed March 2019].

AHS (American Housing Surveys) (2017) Data 2013-2017 [online], US Census Bureau <https://www.census.gov/programs-surveys/ahs.html> [accessed June 2020].

Alberts, J.H. (2004) 'The rope pump: an example of technology transfer', *Waterlines* 22(3) <http://dx.doi.org/10.3362/0262-8104.2004.010>.

Arvonen, V., Kibocha, S., Katko, T. and Pietilä, P. (2017) 'Features of water cooperatives: a comparative study of Finland and Kenya', *Public Works Management and Policy* 22(4): 356–77 <https://doi.org/10.1177/1087724X17715267>.

Brady, J. and Gray, N. (2010) 'Group water schemes in Ireland: their role within the Irish water sector', *European Water* 29: 39–58.

Brand, A. (2004) *Low Cost Pump Alternatives for Rural Communities in Honduras* [online], WSP Field note <https://www.rural-water-supply.net/en/resources/details/289> [accessed March 2020].

Central Statistical Office of Ethiopia (2017) *Drinking Water Quality in Ethiopia* [website} <https://washdata.org/report/who-unicef-radwq-ethiopia-report> [accessed June 2020]

Cooney, E. (2016) *Focus on Private Water Supplies 2016* [online], Environmental Protection Agency, Co. Wexford, Ireland <https://www.epa.ie/pubs/reports/water/drinking/focusonprivatewatersupplies2016report.html> [accessed May 2020]

Cooper, R. (2018) *Water, Sanitation and Hygiene Services in Pakistan*, K4D Helpdesk Report, Institute of Development Studies, Brighton, UK.

DAVE, S. (2014) 'Manual drilling in India', webinar 2.1, in K. Danert, *2nd UNICEF–RWSN Webinar on Manual Drilling, 18 February 2014* <http://www.rural-water-supply.net/en/resources/details/565> [accessed 20 May 2020].

Deller, S., Hoyt, A. and Sundaram Stukel, B. (2009) *Research on the Economic Impacts of Cooperatives* [online], University of Wisconsin Report <http://reic.uwcc.wisc.edu/water/> [accessed March 2020].

Department for Housing, Planning and Local Government (Ireland) (DHPLG) (2016) 'Group water schemes and rural water issues' [website] <https://www.housing.gov.ie/water/water-services/rural-water-programme/group-water-schemes-and-rural-water-issues> [accessed 16 January 2020].

Direction Nationale d'Hydraulique (DNH) (2004) *Situation des points d'eau modern au Mali*, DNH Bamako, Mali.

Domínguez, I., Torres-López, W., Restrepo-Tarquino, I., Paterson, C. and Gowing, J. (2016) 'Self-supply as an alternative approach to water access in rural scattered regions: evidence from a rural microcatchment in Colombia', *Ingeniería y Universidad* 20(1): 175–95 <https://dx.doi.org/10.11144/Javeriana.iyu20-1.ssaa>.

Drinking Water Inspectorate (DWI) (2015) *Drinking Water 2014: Private Water Supplies in England* [pdf], Drinking Water Inspectorate <http://dwi.defra.gov.uk/about/annual-report/2014/pws-eng.pdf> [accessed June 2020].

Drinking Water Inspectorate (DWI) (2018) *Information Note on Regulation 10* [pdf], Private Water Supply (England) Regulations <http://www.dwi.gov.uk/private-water-supply/regs-guidance/Guidance/info-notes/england/reg-10.pdf> [accessed 20 May 2020].

DWQR (Drinking Water Quality Regulator, Scotland) (2017) Drinking Water Quality in Scotland, 2017, Private Water Supplies <https://www.gov.scot/news/drinking-water-quality-in-scotland-2017-private-water-supplies/> [accessed June 2020].

European Commission (2014) *Framework for Action for the Management of Small Drinking Water Supplies* [pdf] <https://ec.europa.eu/environment/water/water-drink/pdf/Small%20drinking%20water%20supplies.pdf> [accessed June 2020].

Fisher, A. (2017) 'Reconciling polycentric administrative data to improve drinking water security in rural Bangladesh', *2017 International Conference on Sustainable Development, Trends Thematic Research Network on Data and Statistics* [pdf], Pretoria, South Africa <https://resources.unsdsn.org/reconciling-polycentric-administrative-data-improve-drinking-water-security-in-rural-bangladesh> [accessed June 2020].

Foster, T., Furey, S., Banks, B. and Willetts, J. (2019) 'Functionality of handpump water supplies: a review of data from sub-Saharan Africa and the Asia-Pacific region', *International Journal of Water Resources Development* <https://doi.org/10.1080/07900627.2018.1543117>.

GWA/DOW (Government of Western Australia Department of Water) (2015) *Private Drinking Water Supplies* [pdf], Water Quality Protection Note 41 <https://www.water.wa.gov.au/__data/assets/pdf_file/0006/5955/82330.pdf> [accessed June 2020].

Hardie, D. and Alasia, A. (2009) 'Domestic water use: the relevance of rurality in quantity used and perceived quality', *Rural and Small Town Canada Analysis Bulletin* 7(5) [online] <https://www150.statcan.gc.ca/n1/en/pub/21-006-x/21-006-x2007005-eng.pdf?st=DseNkiF3> [accessed June 2020].

Hendry, S. and Akoumianaki, I. (2016) *Governance and Management of Small Rural Water Supplies: A Comparative Study*, CRW2015/05 [pdf], Centre of Expertise for Waters (CREW) Facilitation Team, James Hutton Institute<https://discovery.dundee.ac.uk/ws/portalfiles/portal/11591546/CRW2015_05_Final_report.pdf> [accessed June 2020].

Hynds, P., Misstear, B. and Gill, L. (2013) 'Unregulated private wells in the Republic of Ireland: consumer awareness, source susceptibility and protective actions', *Journal of Environmental Management* 127: 278–88 <https://doi.org/10.1016/j.jenvman.2013.05.025>.

Katku, T. (1992) *The Development of Water Supply Associations in Finland and Its Significance for Developing Countries* [pdf], Water and Sanitation Discussion Paper Series DPS 8 Feb 1992 <https://www.ircwash.org/sites/default/files/202.2-92DE-9439.pdf> [accessed 20 May 2020].

Lockwood, H. and Smits, S. (2011) *Supporting Rural Water Supply: Moving Towards a Service Delivery Approach*, Practical Action Publishing, Rugby, UK.

Maccarthy, M. (2014) *Low-Cost Household Groundwater Supply Systems for Developing Communities* [online], PhD dissertation <http://scholarcommons.usf.edu/etd/5261> [accessed July 2019].

Maizama, D. (2015) 'Self water supply in Sahelian context', presentation in *Does the Government Have a Role in Self-supply?* [webinar], RWSN Secretariat, Switzerland <https://vimeo.com/121332803> [accessed March 2020].

Ministry of Water Resources Sierra Leone (2019) 'Water point management' [website] <https://washdata-sl.org/water-point-data/water-point-management/> [accessed November 2019].

Ministry of Water Resources Development and Management (MWRDM) (2012) *Zimbabwe National Water Policy* [pdf] <http://ncuwash.org/newfour/wp-content/uploads/2017/08/National-Water-Policy.pdf> [accessed 20 May 2020].

National Bureau of Statistics (NBS, Nigeria) and UNICEF (2017) *Multiple Indicator Cluster Survey 2016–17, Survey Findings Report*, National Bureau of Statistics, Abuja, Nigeria and United Nations Children's Fund <https://www.unicef.org/nigeria/reports/multiple-indicator-cluster-survey-2016-17-mics> [accessed June 2020].

National Federation of Group Water Schemes (NFGWS) (2012) *Submission on the establishment of Irish Water and the future delivery of rural water services as part of the DECLG public consultation process*, 24 February 2012, NFGWS, Monaghan, Ireland.

Njoh, A. (2009) *Self-Help, a Viable Non-Conventional Urban Public Service Delivery Strategy: Lessons from Cameroon* [pdf], Case study prepared for Revisiting Urban Planning: Global Report on Human Settlements, UN Habitat <https://staging.unhabitat.org/downloads/docs/GRHS2009CaseStudyChapter03Cameroon.pdf> [accessed June 2020].

Noguiera, D. (2008) 'Brazil: Rainwater harvesting in semi-arid region helps women' [online], Department of Sociology, University of Brasilia (SOL/UNB), Source Bulletin September 2008 <http://genderandwater.org/en/gwa-products/knowledge-on-gender-and-water/articles-in-source-bulletin/brazil-rainwater-harvesting-in-semi-arid-region-helps-women-1> [accessed 20 May 2020].

Nyarko, K., Awuah, E. and Ofori, D. (2008) 'Self supply schemes for community water supply in Ghana', in H. Jones (ed.), *Access to Sanitation and Safe Water – Global Partnerships and Local Actions: Proceedings of the 33rd WEDC International Conference, Accra, Ghana, 2008*, pp. 421–5.

Orru, K. and Rothstein H. (2015) 'Not "dead letters", just "blind eyes": the Europeanisation of drinking water risk regulation in Estonia and Lithuania', *Environment and Planning A: Economy and Space* 47: 356–72 <http://dx.doi.org/10.1068/a130295p>.

Pa Mac (2012) 'How'd they used to get water?' [website] <http://www.farmhandscompanion.com/how_did_they_used_to_do_that_files/0df278b1eba607f271aed8a585fbd6c2-5.html> [accessed 20 January 2019].

Pietilä, P., Arvonen, V. and Katku, T. (2016) 'Role of water cooperatives in water service production: lessons from Finland and Denmark', in N. Achour (ed.), *Proceedings of the 20th CIB World Building Congress 2016: May 30 – June 3, 2016 Tampere Finland*, vol. V, pp. 1152–61, Tampere University of Technology, CIB World Building Congress, 1/01/00.

Rickert, B., Samwel, M., Shinee, E., Kožíšek, F. and Schmoll, O. (2016) *Status of Small-Scale Water Supplies in the WHO European Region: Results of a survey conducted under the Protocol on Water and Health* [pdf], WHO, Geneva, Switzerland <http://www.euro.who.int/__data/assets/pdf_file/0012/320511/Status-SSW-supplies-results-survey-en.pdf?ua=1> [accessed 20 May 2020].

Saladin, M. (2016) *Rainwater Harvesting in Thailand: Learning from the World Champions*, RWSN Field Note 2016-1, RWSN, St Gallen, Switzerland.

Sami, M. (2018) *Concept Project Information Document-Integrated Safeguards Data Sheet - Punjab Rural Sustainable Water Supply and Sanitation Project - P169071* [online], World Bank Group <http://documents.worldbank.org/curated/en/377341538557978297/Concept-Project-Information-Document-Integrated-Safeguards-Data-Sheet-Punjab-Rural-Sustainable-Water-Supply-and-Sanitation-Project-P169071> [accessed May 2020].

Smits, S. (2017) 'Propuesta para modelos de intervención en agua y saneamiento el área rural dispersa de Honduras', IRC, The Hague.

SNV (no date) *Functionality of Rural Water Supply Services: Water Supplies in Savannakhet and their Role in Development* [pdf] <http://www.snv.org/public/cms/sites/default/files/explore/download/promo_papers_watersupply-types_final_small.pdf> [accessed 20 May 2020].

Stone, A. (1998) 'Groundwater for household water supply in rural America: private wells or public systems?', *Proceedings of the Joint Conference of the International Association of Hydrogeologists and the American Institute of Hydrology*, Las Vegas, September 1998.

Sutton, S., Butterworth, J. and Mekonta, L. (2012) *A Hidden Resource: Household-Led Rural Water Supply in Ethiopia* [online], IRC International Water and Sanitation Centre, The Netherlands <https://www.ircwash.org/resources/hidden-resource-household-led-rural-water-supply-ethiopia> [accessed July 2019].

UNDP (2018) *2018 Statistical Update: Human Development Indices and Indicators* [website], Human Development Report, HDRO/UNDP <http://www.hdr.undp.org/en/2018-update> [accessed 10 March 2019].

UNICEF (2019) *Multiple Index Cluster Surveys: Country surveys for selected countries* [online] <https://mics.unicef.org/surveys> [accessed June 2020].

UNICEF Viet Nam (2014) *Viet Nam Multiple Indicator Cluster Survey 2014, Final Report*, Ha Noi, Viet Nam.

Wegener, A. (2015) *Domestic Water Supply in Rural Viet Nam – Between Self-supply and Piped Schemes*, Doctoral thesis (Natural Sciences), Karlsruhe Institute of Technology, Germany.

WHO/UNICEF JMP (2019) *Global household database 2017 update* [online] <washdata.org/data/household> [accessed June 2020].

World Bank (2018) *Beyond Utility Reach: How to Achieve Sustainable Service for All?' A Review of Rural Water Supply and Sanitation Services in Seven Countries of the Danube Region*, World Bank, Washington, DC.

CHAPTER 4

The scale of urban
and peri-urban self-supply

This chapter looks at the roles that urban self-supply plays in different economic contexts. In sub-Saharan Africa those living at the economic or geographical margins of urban networks are particularly driven to look for their own solutions. They fall into two main categories – poorer households depending on hand-dug wells, and richer households and community-based organizations constructing boreholes with submersible pumps to bring water onto the premises as an individual or shared piped supply. The future challenges of urban growth in sub-Saharan Africa are exemplified by experiences in India which show how self-supply can contribute positively as well as negatively. Investment in self-supply does not necessarily cease when piped supply into the house or yard is achieved in high-income countries and households may continue to invest in supply improvements. Perhaps surprisingly in lower income economies self-supply plays a significant part in bringing improved water on to premises. The question is whether the efforts of those augmenting or providing their own supply threaten the sustainability of utilities and water companies or help to fulfil consumer expectations where utilities cannot provide acceptable supply or are unable to extend the piped network. The answer is always very context specific.

Keywords: urban, peri-urban, informal water supplies, vendors, self-supply

Key messages

1. Self-supply is looked on as a rural phenomenon, but many urban people still depend at least in part on similar approaches (technologies, organization, finance) which should not be overlooked.
2. For the poorest, water from self-financed shallow wells (owned or shared at low or no cost) is a practical necessity. For the richest, especially in peri-urban areas, self-supply investment at higher levels (boreholes and submersible pumps) offers greater autonomy and assurance of a reliable supply. For both self-supply is an integral part of access to water, but requiring different policies.
3. Those using self-financed improved water points for urban drinking water are a significant proportion (some 12 per cent) of the total in sub-Saharan Africa. They have the potential to contribute to basic, and some to safely managed, supply coverage.
4. In lower income countries households tend to use a variety of water sources conjunctively, but despite evidence of large numbers of

http://dx.doi.org/10.3362/9781780448190.004

household wells, low use of unimproved supplies for drinking water suggests some selectivity on the basis of perceived water quality.

5. Urban self-supply is well-developed in South Asia but is now increasing in sub-Saharan Africa because of rapid urban population growth and poorly operating utilities with limited capacity to expand. The latter region should prepare to face similar challenges to those already confronting Indian cities in how to cope with self-supply.

6. Urban self-supply needs better quantification and official recognition so that cohesive planning can compensate for utilities' limitations but not check their effectiveness and expansion. Context-specific regulation is necessary to accommodate different source types, uses, and water quality, in various urban, peri-urban, and rural environments.

7. Lack of information about who is providing their own improved supplies leads to the danger that at higher technology levels they are ignored in planning and at lower levels they are equated with unimproved supply and therefore condemned without sufficient attention as to why they exist, and options for improvement or conjunctive use.

8. The growth of large urban areas leads to increased pressure on water resources. Rainwater harvesting is under-developed but can provide water for aquifer recharge as well as household consumption.

9. With the increasing pressure that most urban supplies now face throughout the world, a move towards greater understanding of informal supplies, and their greater inclusion in planning and regulation in the urban environment seems essential.

10. Water supply is a fundamental service. Even when all households have a good piped supply in their house there is still motivation to invest in alternative supplies or better quality. Self-supply in terms of private wells or boreholes may be superseded, but the desire to improve the service as a householder never completely goes away.

The global picture

With global urban water supply coverage put at 97 per cent (UNICEF/WHO JMP, 2019), there would seem to be little role for self-supply initiatives. However, towns grow into cities, people live in closer and closer proximity and in greater numbers, lifestyle changes engender ever expanding per capita water demand, power supply fluctuations interrupt pumping into storage, and deteriorating pipe networks and water losses increase. As a result, piped water supplies struggle more and more to provide a 24/7 supply, or in some cases to reach the peri-urban areas at all. Consequently, households are also using both improved and, to a lesser degree, unimproved self-financed supplies in cities and towns throughout the developing world. This high level (97 per cent) of urban coverage hides an important feature. Previously unimproved supplies have been regarded as the indicator of urban self-supply, but it would seem that awareness of health risks is high, and the major proportion of urban self-supply used for drinking water comprises improved supplies which contribute to 'basic coverage' especially in lower economy countries. But it is also here that inequities between rich and poor are greatest.

Self-supply activities are related to the strength of the local economy and the cost and performance of local public supplies. At the higher levels they range from the luxury of water filters to remove water hardness, or the cost saving of water butts to provide rainwater for garden watering. At the lower end they embrace more fundamental provision for basic domestic needs in rapidly growing cities particularly in South Asia and sub-Saharan Africa. The drivers of change are similar but the solutions differ. In all a feeling of ownership and a desire to improve what is provided lead to investment and improvement of water reliability, adequacy, and/or quality.

Self-supply in urban sub-Saharan Africa

Self-supply in large urban areas

The sub-Saharan urban population of just over 400 million formed 10 per cent of the global total in 2017 but 44 per cent of the world's urban population with a less than basic supply. This reflects the growing urbanization of the region but also the greater inability of supply services to cope (see Box 4.1). The two main challenges for sub-Saharan cities are:

- 55 per cent of the urban population live in squatter settlements (World Bank, 2018) often renting rather than owning their house in areas with limited service provision; and
- much urban growth for the better-off is in new peri-urban housing estates, beyond the reliable reach of utility networks.

Since 2000 those using a limited supply more than 30 minutes from home (see Table 1.3) have almost doubled, reflecting the growth in less dense peri-urban housing and more peripheral, unserved squatter settlements.

Box 4.1 Typical tales of urban supply

1. Mulenga in Groenwall et al. (2010) on George Compound, Lusaka, Zambia:

    'Water supply was only once or twice a fortnight and then the pressure so low the water only came out as a trickle.'

2. Household head interviews (Neville, 2017), Akaki Kality, peri-urban Addis Ababa, Ethiopia:

    'We knew about the [citywide system of] rationing [to balance the supply-demand deficit] and accepted there would be some days our tap would not work. But it has been over two months since a drop of water came out, and we have to pay for this "luxury"'.

    And perhaps justifiably if not seriously 'the water quality is absolutely terrible, zero. There is never any water in the taps for us to use so the quality must be zero'.

    It is frustrations like these which lead people to water vendors or to develop their own supplies, or if well-placed for piped supply to take out loans to get connected, or make illegal connections.

Cities and large towns in the region have grown up mainly where surface freshwater was accessible. The associated accessibility of groundwater in alluvial aquifers often gives the opportunity for those without a piped supply to provide for themselves and their neighbours. Regionally 25 million urban dwellers use unprotected groundwater as their main supply. This is higher than any other region in the world and is still increasing. Just over 6 million (1.5 per cent) use surface water (JMP, 2019 update) but their number is slowly falling.

While the number of unprotected groundwater supply users is growing gradually (increasing by 7 million since 2000), improved private supplies provide a significant proportion of water consumed in many cities and may be growing much faster (Foster et al., 2018). Rainwater harvesting, other than casual roof and bucket capture, appears to be rare in most countries, adding only 1 per cent to improved on-premises supplies.

Multiple indicator cluster survey (MICS) data for 15 countries representing over half of the regional total shows that most urban private (on-premises, non-piped) groundwater supplies used for drinking are improved (average 86 per cent), and some 12 per cent of households have their own on-premises (non-piped) improved supply. The picture is dominated by the situation in Nigeria (see Figure 4.1 and Table 4.1), which has almost a quarter of the regional

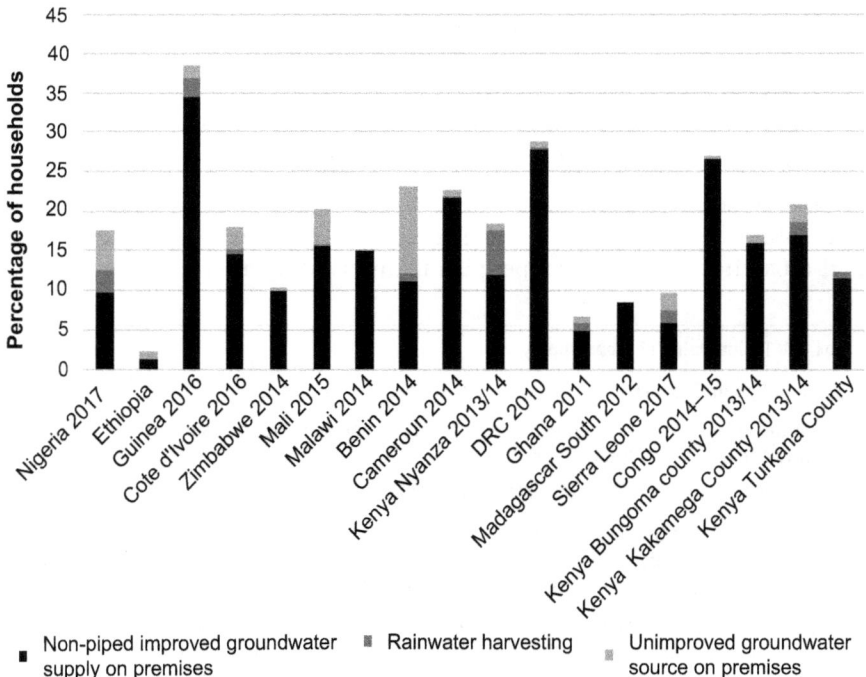

Figure 4.1 Proportion of urban households with own non-piped improved and unimproved water supply on premises
Source: Data from most recent MICS surveys

urban population and of on-premises wells and boreholes. The small percentage of the regional population using unimproved on-premises (less than 2 per cent) or off-premises unimproved (0.2 per cent) supplies indicate that generally there are few unimproved private or shared supplies used for drinking water. Nigeria and Benin appear to be the only countries with significant potential for upgrading unimproved urban supplies (Oluwasanya, 2009) if protection proves effective for water from urban aquifers.

This low incidence does not, however, mean there are not many more shallow wells used principally for other domestic purposes (higher volume uses such as washing or bathing). Nor may 'improved' have any real meaning, in the shallow groundwater of an urban environment, where contamination of the aquifer may be a much greater risk than anything caused locally by use of the well.

The service delivery figures for domestic water do not include the secondary sources of those households using bottled or sachet water as a primary drinking water source (see Table 4.1). This means there may be an underestimate in Nigeria, Ghana, and Sierra Leone in particular, of those with their own supplies. Nor is there any indication of how many households share their improved supplies with their neighbours to provide them with an at least basic supply.

While the scale of growth in urban coverage has been enormous it perhaps masks: 1) the degree to which alternative or additional sources are used especially where piped supplies are unreliable or too expensive for bulk water uses such as bathing and laundry; and 2) the significant investment by

Table 4.1 Urban population using own on-premises supply estimated from MICS data

Urban	Numbers using rainwater harvesting	Numbers with on-premises non-piped improved supplies	Numbers with on-premises non-piped unimproved supplies	Numbers using bottled water and undefined other supplies
Nigeria 2017	2,660,000	9,310,000	4,845,000	15,200,000
DRC 2010	25,818	7,177,319	206,542	154,906
Cameroon 2014	12,004	2,604,868	96,032	216,072
Côte d'Ivoire 2016	60,000	1,752,000	348,000	192,000
Guinea 2016	113,796	1,565,839	72,830	–
Ghana 2011	159,758	766,841	127,807	4,569,093
Zimbabwe 2014	–	524,700	26,500	5,300
Benin 2014	46,460	520,352	506,414	–
Mali 2015	2,754	432,378	121,176	2,754
Malawi 2014	–	410,346	8,262	5,508
Congo 2014-15	–	278,290	–	189,892
Ethiopia 2017	–	277,121	213,170	63,951
Sierra Leone 2017	53,499	185,673	69,234	327,288

Note: – Signifies no data recorded

entrepreneurs and wealthier peri-urban residents in boreholes and wells with pumps and elevated storage which may be counted as safely managed supplies but are not funded by the public sector. Some of the latter self-supply systems may be individually owned and act as improved supplies for neighbours, who may buy the water or be given it for free. Others are run by community-based organizations (CBOs) or as small businesses, selling piped connections or water to households or to vendors to distribute more widely, and are not included in the implied self-supply figures (Table 4.1). Groenwall et al. (2010) found that informal (improved and unimproved) groundwater supplies provided for 59 per cent of urban Nigerians, 70 per cent of Liberians, and 69 per cent of Bangladeshis in 2008/2009.

The figures for urban areas in Table 4.1 are based mainly on cluster surveys of households and supplies and only cover wells used for drinking and main domestic use, and those which are household level, not community/group investments. In 2017 one in eight urban Nigerian households provided their own on-premises supply (see Photo 4.1); but this is counterbalanced by less than 2 per cent of urban Ethiopian households doing the same. The latter is atypical of the region and arises in part from policies and in part from groundwater conditions. In Addis Ababa, with the largest urban population, the state water company provides all household water (even to vendors) since alternative supplies are prohibited.

Photo 4.1 Typical peri-urban household supply, Lagos State, Nigeria
Source: Photo A. Healy

An approximate estimate of the number of urban sharers of unimproved private supplies can be made from JMP figures. The JMP (2019) estimates that 25 million people are using unimproved groundwater sources. The MICS indicate some 13 million with on-premises unimproved supplies, and so only an average of two sharing households, implying that improved sources are available to and used by most people. The MICS survey indicates four times as many improved self-financed supplies used for drinking, and if shared even with equally few neighbours, these would then serve some 100 million people of the urban total. The preference of people for water from improved supplies suggests the number may be even higher. In total, urban self-supply may provide water to a minimum of 125 million urban dwellers (over 30 per cent) in the region. This is far higher than indicated by unprotected sources alone, and does not allow for conjunctive use or group-financed piped supplies.

Figures from well inventories in several cities (see Table 4.2) suggest even higher figures of self-supply reflecting local conditions or widespread conjunctive use. It is apparent that informal gap filling is very common across the region, where groundwater conditions allow, supplementing other sources, especially unreliable piped supplies, with self-financed but usually improved water supplies.

The poor condition of some urban shallow wells may in part reflect owners and users regarding them only as sources for bulk domestic purposes. Their condition to a casual observer would suggest neglect and high risk. The consequence may be a negative view of all self-financing and the danger that good and bad, rural and urban all get covered by a single policy decision when source types, uses, and alternatives vary widely in different contexts.

Groenwall et al. (2010) looked at trends in unimproved groundwater use in 13 sub-Saharan countries from 1990 onwards and found particularly steep increases in Nigeria and Ghana, countries with major city expansions. In Nigeria that trend has continued up to the present, as it also has in

Table 4.2 Examples of large urban area self-supply in sub-Saharan Africa

Town/city	Population	Scale of self-supply	Source of information
Tamatave, Madagascar	250,000	60% with own well and pump	Maccarthy, 2014
Awka, Nigeria	500,000+	73% with own well	Ezenwaji, 2018
Abeokuta, Nigeria	250,000	45% with own well	Oluwasanya et al., 2011
Peri-urban Lagos, Nigeria	n/a	51% owned a borehole	Capstick et al., 2017 Sample survey
Kisumu, Kenya	900,000	68% with own well	Ayelew et al., 2014
Ndola, Zambia	450,000	79% get at least some water from private wells	Liddle et al., 2014
Dodowa, peri-urban Accra, Ghana	12,000	38% depend on private boreholes and dug-wells for main supply	Groenwall and Oduro-Kwarteng, 2017

Source: From source surveys

Angola and the Democratic Republic of the Congo. In contrast in Ghana and Mozambique unimproved groundwater use has decreased by two-thirds. In Mozambique this results from a large increase in reliable piped supplies, but in Ghana household connections have actually decreased. In 2013 the Ghana Water Company only met some 60 per cent of residents' needs in Accra (metropolitan population *c.* 4 million) (Peloso and Morinville, 2014). The gap is filled partly by the growth in bottled/packaged water but also as Mosello (2017) concludes 'progress in coverage has only partially been driven by government's investments in infrastructure and utilities, and (that) other (private, informal) service providers may have played a critical role, too.'

Urban self-supply is not just due to limitations in municipal and utility finances, but also to poor planning or unregulated settlement. It is increasingly common in Nigeria, for instance, for new housing estates to be built with autonomous water supplies (see Photo 4.2) for blocks of 200 houses (Ikpeh et al., 2017 and personal communication 2019), because the utilities cannot extend reliable supplies to peripheral areas. As these estates expand in an unregulated way some of these mini-water schemes are run initially by government, but as the estates expand and management weakens, and tariff payments become more erratic, supplies become unreliable and people begin to take over management or to develop their own boreholes. There is a strong

Photo 4.2 Typical peri-urban development with its own water supply, Lafia, Nassawara State, Nigeria
Source: Photo A. Healy

belief in many areas of intermittent public supply that having your own well is preferable in terms of quantity and quality. Even when theoretically served by a piped supply, if water does not reach your house or is rarely available, investment in a private well or borehole is high on the list of household priorities. Some develop a supply primarily for their own use, but may start sharing or selling water to neighbours, and then expanding to become a small water company (see Preface).

Healy et al. (2018a) found a widespread belief among sector profes-sionals in sub-Saharan Africa that with peri-urban areas growing fast, the increase in private boreholes would equal or exceed that of piped water supply expansion in the next 10 years and that this results from a greater confidence in and preference for a supply over which the owner/consumer has direct control.

Interrelationship between urban public and self-supply systems

Self-supply offers additional sources of water, methods of payment, and reliability which relate to asset management at the lowest level. On the other hand, private supplies usually also offer higher levels of risk to health and may undermine the viability of commercial utilities that have the capacity to provide a reliable supply. For most, the decision to invest is strongly influenced by a desire for household security in water supply (Healy et al., 2018b). If such security can be provided by public supply few will regard self-supply as a worthwhile investment. The presence of self-supply is an indicator of inadequate public systems and is a symptom rather than the disease.

The development of self-supply in a town may relieve the pressure on an overloaded public supply system or become a competitive service which weakens it (Alam and Foster, 2019). Each town or city, municipality or utility will offer a different perspective; some recognize a need for additional sources of water, others will prohibit them whether they are needed or not. For instance, in the main area of piped water supply in Abeokuta, Nigeria, self-supply systems are prohibited, yet here water reaches households on average once every week, or once every two weeks in the driest periods (Oluwasanya et al., 2011). Households must therefore invest heavily in storage capacity and limit water use to survive. At the peripheries where public supplies do not reach at all, the ban is not imposed, and self-supply is widespread with over 2,300 private wells and boreholes serving at least 45 per cent of the urban population. Meanwhile in Tamatave, Madagascar, it is felt (Maccarthy, 2014) that the local utility cannot supply sufficient water and many households have a belt and braces approach with access to both. There is an acknowledgement that they are not competing services but complement each other. In neither case, however, does recognition stretch to regulation or to utilities offering advisory services to bring self-supply to a higher, safer level.

Flexibility of use and payment

Urban dwellers tend to be more flexible in choice of supply than rural populations. More options within walking distance result in a marked tendency to use multiple sources (Neville, 2017), with self-supply very often a key ingredient. Such flexibility is especially useful for households with an insecure or varying income. Salaried households can more easily make regular payments for water piped into the house without the threat of disconnection.

Urban groundwater in various forms reduces the burden of looking each day for affordable water within a convenient distance. It is often provided free and so is an essential element for the poorest who will use it before any other supply, while for many it is the cheapest water provided by vendors. Kano (Nigeria) even has a quarter said to have the highest concentration of private wells and boreholes in the continent, called 'water vendor's world' (Ahmad, 2016). In all regions it is the poorest who most use unimproved wells and surface water (JMP 2019 data). There is a patchwork of formal and informal supplies, reflecting not just varying availability of improved water supply with differing sources of finance. Choice of supply reflects in part the challenges presented by lump-sum payments for connection, and day to day costs in cash and time (queuing), which have forced many to depend on lower level supplies or to provide their own.

Self-supply forms one of several urban service delivery options, including public/municipal provision, small and medium-sized enterprises (SMEs), CBOs/NGOs (group self-supply), and household self-supply. Vendors who may be regarded as SMEs but fall between all these categories and are dependent on them, are common throughout urban Africa. They form a human pipeline which extends the service area and reliability of reticulated and point water supplies. Private suppliers and vendors may provide more expensive water than utilities but they do not impose large up-front connection charges.

Small frequent payments suit many poorer families better, and they can modify their demand and the supply quality they access, depending on their financial situation from day to day. The poorest urban dwellers find that buying water from vendors, accessing free water from private wells, or developing their own supply (and selling it on) better suits the flexible provision they require. Utilities are also more reluctant to sell to the poorest because of the areas they live in and the difficulties of maintaining services and collecting money. The poorest people are unlikely to be able to afford the higher rents charged for houses with their own piped connections or easy access to safely managed supplies. With large squatter populations there is considerable debate as to whether commercial utilities and market forces are appropriate or sustainable systems.

Differing risks and need for behavioural change

Individual self-supply in urban areas is generally not a recognized service delivery model and indeed is often condemned because of the risks of poor water quality and stress on aquifers. High densities of pit latrines and poorly maintained septic tanks and/or sewer systems mean that many parts of urban aquifers may already be highly contaminated (as with the karstic aquifer underlying much of Lusaka, Zambia, and the very shallow aquifer in Monrovia, Liberia). Others may not yet exhibit high levels, with relatively recent urban growth, but breakthrough from existing contaminant loads present a real future risk (Lapworth et al., 2017) in high density housing areas. Deeper boreholes may avoid these risks, but shallow wells generally will not. Nevertheless local groundwater can provide cheap or free supply for bulk (non-potable) uses for which piped water is expensive. The latter may then be retained for drinking and cooking purposes. The key is generally to look for conjunctive use and greater awareness of the potential and the risks, rather than dismissing a still valuable asset which is vital in the day-to-day reality for many urban dwellers (see Photo 4.3). As with the supply itself, the relationship between formal and informal systems and the groundwater resources they depend on is complex, and specific not just to each city but to individual areas within cities.

Studies in Ethiopia (Neville, 2017) and Zambia (Liddle et al., 2014) suggest that it is normal for households to understand the risks of different supplies, but not necessarily to turn knowledge into practice. The risks of urban self-supply may not be resolved through extension of over-stretched reticulation systems bringing their own quality and reliability issues at the peripheries. More effective approaches to behavioural change may be

Photo 4.3 Household (improved or unimproved?) self-supply well used for washing and family laundry business in Freetown, Sierra Leone

preferable, in terms of site hygiene and supply protection, greater use of household water treatment, and separate sources for drinking/cooking and for other domestic purposes.

Healy (2018a) noted widespread concern over available water resources and lack of effective monitoring or regulation. Only 10 per cent of respondents from 25 sub-Saharan countries felt their governments were monitoring the situation well and most felt that government had no control over, or knowledge of, the growth in private supplies. This situation reflects the large gap between the aspirations and realities of households and the perspectives of sector professionals. The implied level of dependence on urban self-supply suggests that it needs much better evidence and understanding, and greater recognition of the magnitude of the contribution of improved informal supplies to the urban scene.

Middle-income urban self-supply: the shape of things to come?

Trends and policies

South Asia is the region with the highest prevalence of urban self-supply, partly because of the difficulty for utilities to keep up with urban growth and partly because of the increasing stress on local water resources (see Box 4.2). The growth of African cities suggests that the problems being faced in countries such as India are the shape of things to come and to prepare for. As an example, urban India had reached a population of 450 million by 2017 (slightly more than in urban sub-Saharan Africa), of which approximately a quarter live in slums (slightly less than in sub-Saharan Africa) (World Bank, 2018), which are largely unserved by city services such as piped supply. Of these considerably fewer (India 5 million as opposed to 25 million in sub-Saharan Africa) still use unimproved groundwater (IIPS, 2017) and 135 million use some type of improved self-supply (rainwater harvesting or improved well/borehole) of their own. This is far higher than the present proportion in sub-Saharan Africa, but levels of growth are unparalleled (Alam and Foster, 2019). At present non-piped water supply is growing faster than piped in both according to JMP 2017 figures (WHO/UNICEF, 2019).

These developments in India are prompted by the challenges of piped systems which are unreliable because of the gap between supply and demand, but also because of big water losses from the system and environmental threats to water availability and quality. Government is acutely aware of these threats and has introduced regulations to make some types of self-supply compulsory (see Box 4.2).

Urban rainwater harvesting: an essential development

Development of additional water sources such as urban rainwater harvesting is increasingly regarded in a positive light as public supply capacities are outstripped by demand. In many countries it is still more a question of

---

Box 4.2 Indian government support to self-supply

The Government of India has developed strategies to ease pressures on urban water resources. Chennai (population now 10 million) depended to a large extent on fast declining groundwater resources and was one of the first to respond. In 1994 it made it mandatory for all new houses to be designed with rainwater harvesting (RWH) systems to recharge to the local aquifers. By 2003 this regulation was extended to all existing houses, with a penalty of disconnection from sewerage for defaulters. In other big cities like Bengaluru (2015; Rao, 2018) and Mumbai (2018) legislation is being established so that up to 50 per cent of rainwater can be recharged from house roofs and the rest be put into groundwater storage tanks for later use by the household.

In Bengaluru (Bangalore) the requirement for rainwater harvesting and recharge is combined with resuscitation of old self-supply systems of wells and boreholes throughout the city. These include over 105,500 private water points and an estimated further 200,000 which are unregistered as well as 172,000 public supplies. While non-compliance remains high, provision of loans and subsidies is encouraging home-owners to bring their old self-supply systems back into action and expand their use from just abstraction to abstraction plus recharge. Dependence on self-supply groundwater sources is particularly high in smaller towns where it is regarded as cheaper and more regularly accessible than public supplies (Wankhade et al., 2014).

Most people dream of house connections to public supply but fewer than half achieve them because of reluctance to pay connection fees for an uncertain supply in terms of quality and quantity, and they continue to depend on other sources. This reflects the awkward transition towards all piped supply, when utilities are under-resourced to provide a 24/7 supply.

Self-provision in squatter settlements does not have to mean unimproved supplies. The model city of Bhubaneswara (Odisha state) has a population of over 900,000. This includes some 140,000 in squatter settlements (Misra, 2014) whose inhabitants depend almost totally on informal supplies of group and individually owned wells and boreholes even though they have no legal land tenure. They have been so successful and well-organized that the municipality regards the area as covered and does not plan any further public supply development.

Self-supply can also turn commercial. Several larger cities, including Hyderabad (Prakash, 2010) have augmented their over-stretched public supply based on surface water, by buying water from peri-urban private wells and boreholes. Some of these are private domestic supplies and some are farm wells whose owners find they can make more money selling water to public utilities than by irrigation.

---

defining its potential on paper rather than execution on the ground. In India, despite increasing government emphasis, only 0.1 per cent of urban houses undertake RWH as a main source of drinking water (IIPS, 2017). A variety of reasons lead to low uptake in a number of countries:

- Unless stored rainwater can reach the house taps under gravity it is more expensive than municipal water because of the additional energy cost of pumping.
- Most households have limited space for rainwater storage and/or are rented. In a higher income context, in Australia in the more confined urban environment only 2 per cent of houses use RWH as a major source of drinking water, while in the greater rural expanses, 22 per cent do so (JMP, 2019).

- Hard mandates requiring all households to include RWH (e.g. India) suffer from the cost of policing legislation without adequate fines or funding, so are effectively not applied and harvesting facilities are not necessarily efficiently used (Wankhade et al., 2014).
- Soft legislation such as incorporation into building regulations for new offices and houses (e.g. Australia) seems to work better but takes a long time to achieve change, even with consistent enforcement.

The Indian government is beginning to recognize the role self-supply is playing and has played in the past but it is still developing coherent policies to maximize the contribution and safety of systems about which so little is known. As with boreholes, rainwater harvesting at levels which significantly reduce demand on piped supply is still very much the province of the rich.

Higher economy country triggers to conducive 'cosmetic' self-supply

Despite being fully covered by safely managed supplies, household investment in water supply also occurs even in urban areas of high-income countries. Here public supplies may be reliable and adequate but the desire to improve them is still triggered by various factors and nurtured by effective marketing (see Box 4.3). The reasons may be physical, where water hardness reduces the effect of washing powders and clogs pipes, or financial, where water becomes more expensive or rationed, but other factors are also relevant relating to different domestic water uses. Psychology plays a part in what people regard

---

Box 4.3 Triggers to self-supply, examples in high-income urban environments

1. In Perth, Western Australia in the late 1970s a restructuring of tariffs, designed to reduce high water usage, led to an enormous rise in the drilling of boreholes for garden watering. By the early 1980s over a quarter of households had their own borehole, leading to a major fall in revenue for the local water company. This led to fears of saline intrusion, lack of funds to invest in future surface storage capacity, constraints on groundwater development, and ultimately to enormous investment in desalination, monitoring, and regulation. From 2003 when desalination had become the main source of drinking water, drilling was again encouraged for garden watering (Rinaudo et al., 2015), supported by a rebate, to reduce unnecessary use of expensive treated water. By 2010, 167,000 private boreholes were in operation. Over-abstraction is again now leading to regulation of use.
2. In Canada over half of all households treat their water (Statistics Canada, 2017), often to reduce levels of chlorine before consumption. This may be a cosmetic rather than an essential change.
3. In Ireland in 2015 the government instituted water rates. Previously Ireland had been the only OECD country with free water. The change in policy led to a big surge in demand for private boreholes. This demand quickly evaporated when water rates were hurriedly abolished because of public outcry.
4. In the UK in 2018 a drought caused several water companies to introduce hose-pipe bans stopping direct garden watering and car washing off the mains. Sales of water butts (rainwater storage containers) increased threefold in a couple of months.

as desirable or good practice, even where the need may be regarded as purely cosmetic. Thus, some element of home investment in water supply may continue even when the highest level of service is reached, as consumers identify a gap between supply delivery and their expectations. Entrepreneurs can create markets where none exist.

These examples indicate certain human traits that are relevant to self-supply universally:

- The yardsticks of sector professionals are not necessarily those of consumers.
- In solving a problem or filling a gap many households prefer one-off known capital costs to a commitment to a lower regular payment whose rate of increase is beyond the consumer's control.
- On achieving a certain level of service people are very reluctant to give up the advantages they have achieved.
- Water may be a communal asset but it has very personal benefits, viewed differently by each household. A communal system provides an affordable common denominator; it rarely satisfies everyone.
- Self-supply can benefit individual families but where pressure on resources and scale of abstraction become too great, it needs to be controlled.
- The Perth experience (see Box 4.3). illustrates how water pricing and policies can have complex side effects.

Conclusion

While the formal water supply sector is generally well-regulated and documented, the urban informal element in water supply tends to be unrecorded. Worldwide, the mosaic of urban supply is poorly defined, and the interrelationship of private and public facilities is poorly understood and yet self-financed supplies cover at least 20–30 per cent of people in low economy countries. The role is largely different from that in rural areas since it is seldom the only option for a household. Most have some level of access to formal supplies and are more driven to develop alternatives for back-up because of their unreliability.

The formal and the informal often sit uncomfortably side by side because neither seems to understand the other. Commercial utilities see potential customers going elsewhere and may try to get household wells and water vendors outlawed, yet often do not have capacity to provide an adequate service. Self-suppliers are reluctant to give up their autonomy and their own relatively reliable supply until they can be guaranteed something better and vendors may oppose extensions to reticulation which take away their business. Liddle et al. (2014) describe the situation as 'institutional bricolage' which varies in the mix of elements in each urban area and each quarter within an urban area. Indications are that in the urban context private supplies play a major part, but there is much debate on whether more emphasis should be put on 1) improving individual supplies and promoting household water treatment systems; 2) linking private/group supplies to make regulated community supplies; 3) extending piped supplies to all areas to improve service delivery; or 4) building up more public/private partnerships of CBOs and utilities (Adams et al., 2018).

In urban environments self-supply faces a lack of professional interest (or outright dismissal) but constitutes a practical necessity for many. The lack of adequate data hinders the inclusion of self-supply into problem-solving and planning. The indications of the limitations of public supply and the sizeable contribution of private investment in guaranteeing at least some access to water suggest that it must continue to play a part, but how, is seldom defined. Certainly there is scope for public utilities to begin to understand informal water supplies better, the reasons they have grown up, how both can coexist where additional water is necessary, and what advisory or regulatory roles can be played by government and utilities. In urban and in rural areas self-supply is an established fact. If it is ignored the risks it brings will grow and will impact on the wider 'served' population. It must therefore be better understood and better quantified and better incorporated into the mosaic of supply options as urban supplies evolve.

Actions being taken in India show some ways forward for sub-Saharan Africa, preparing for stress on groundwater resources from increased demand and climate change, and planning for conjunctive use. Informal supplies can form a vital asset for filling gaps and augmenting inadequate public supplies. In the largest cities rainwater harvesting may be encouraged to help restore local groundwater resources as well as providing household supply. It can then reduce pressures on the natural resource by augmenting supply and reducing demand on it. Self-supply in the urban environment can be regarded as presenting unwelcome competition, or unacceptable risk, or it may be regarded as an integral part of composite services to provide adequate supply. For most urban areas it is essential to include self-supply as one of four elements, alongside public or private sector utilities, and community water supplies in planning for universal and convenient access, at least in the short and medium term in lower income countries. Everyone dreams of piped water in their house, but the dream includes being able to rely on it every day. And that is still a dream for much of the urban world.

References

Adams, E., Sambu, D. and Smiley, S. (2018) 'Urban water supply in Sub-Saharan Africa: historical and emerging policies and institutional arrangements', *International Journal of Water Resources Development* 35(2): 240–63 <https://doi.org/10.1080/07900627.2017.1423282>.

Ahmad, T.M. (2016) 'The role of water vendors in water service delivery in developing countries: a case of Dala local government, Kano, Nigeria', *Applied Water Science* 7(3): 1191–201 <https://doi.org/10.1007/s13201-016-0507-z>.

Alam, F. and Foster, S. (2019) 'Policy priorities for the boom in urban private wells', *The Source, Magazine of the International Water Association* November 2019 [online] <https://www.thesourcemagazine.org/policy-priorities-for-the-boom-in-urban-private-wells/> [accessed July 2019].

Ayelew, M., Chenoweth, J., Malcolm, R., Mulugetta, Y., Okotto, L. and Pedley, S. (2014) 'Small independent water providers: their position in the regulatory framework for the supply of water in Kenya and Ethiopia', *Journal of Environmental Law* 26(1): 105–28 <https://doi.org/10.1093/jel/eqt028>.

Capstick, S., Whitmarsh, L., Healy, A. and Bristow, G. (2017) *Resilience in Groundwater Supply Systems: Findings from a Survey of Private Households in Lagos, Nigeria*, RIGSS working paper, Cardiff University, UK.

Ezenwaji, E., Anyaeze, E. and Nwafor, A. (2018) 'Improving self-supply of urban water and sanitation projects through microfinancing in Nigeria', *Journal of Geoscience and Environment Protection* 6: 20–33 <https://doi.org/10.4236/gep.2018.62002>.

Foster, S., Bousquet, A. and Furey, S. (2018) 'Urban groundwater use in Tropical Africa – a key factor in enhancing water security?' *Water Policy* 20(5): 982–94 <https://doi.org/10.2166/wp.2018.056>.

Groenwall, J. and Oduro-Kwarteng, S. (2017) 'Groundwater as a strategic resource for improved resilience: a case study in peri-urban Accra', *Environmental Earth Sciences* 77 <http://dx.doi.org/10.1007/s12665-017-7181-9>.

Groenwall, J., Mulenga, M. and McGranahan, G. (2010) *Groundwater, Self-Supply and Poor Urban Dwellers: A Review with Case Studies of Bangalore and Lusaka* [online], IIED Human Settlements Working Paper, Water and Sanitation no. 26 <https://pubs.iied.org/10584IIED/> [accessed June 2020].

Healy, A., Danert, K., Bristow, G. and Theis, S. (2018a) *Perceptions of Trends in the Development of Private Boreholes for Household Water Consumption: Findings from a Survey of Water Professionals in Africa*, RIGSS Working Paper, Cardiff University, UK.

Healy, A., Upton, K., Bristow, G., Allan, S., Bukar, Y., Capstick, S., Danert, K., Furey, S., Goni, I., MacDonald, A., Theis, S., Tijani, M.N. and Whitmarsh, L. (2018b) *Resilience in Groundwater Supply Systems: Integrating Resource Based Approaches with Agency, Behaviour and Choice* [pdf], RIGSS Working Paper, Cardiff University, UK <http://orca.cf.ac.uk/119098/1/2018%20Resilience%20in%20Groundwater%20Supply%20Systems.pdf> [accessed 20 May 2020].

IIPS (International Institute for Population Sciences) (2017) 'National Family Health Survey NFHS-4, 2015-16: India', IIPS, Mumbai.

Ikpeh, I.J., Soetanto, R., Anvuur, A. and Smout, I. (2017) 'Adjusting institutional arrangements: towards improved governance of self-supply water systems in Uyo, Nigeria', *40th WEDC International Conference*, Loughborough, UK, Paper 2836.

Lapworth, D.J., Stuart, M.E., Pedley, S., Nkhuwa, D.C.W. and Tijani, M.N. (2017) *A Review of Urban Groundwater Use and Water Quality Challenges in Sub-Saharan Africa*, British Geological Survey, Nottingham, UK (OR/17/056) <http://nora.nerc.ac.uk/id/eprint/520718/> [accessed July 2019].

Liddle, E.S., Mager, S. and Nel, E. (2014) 'The importance of community-based informal water supply systems in the developing world and the need for formal sector support', *The Geographical Journal* 182(1): 85–96 <http://dx.doi.org/10.1111/geoj.12117>.

Maccarthy, M. (2014) *Low-Cost Household Groundwater Supply Systems for Developing Communities*, PhD dissertation [website] <http://scholarcommons.usf.edu/etd/5261> [accessed 10 March 2019].

Misra (2014) 'From formal-informal to emergent formalisation: fluidities in the production of urban waterscapes', *Water Alternatives* 7(1): 15–34 <https://www.researchgate.net/publication/280879164>.

Mosello, B. (2017) *How to Reduce Inequalities in Access to WASH: Urban Water in Ghana* [pdf], ODI/WaterAid report, November 2017 <https://www.odi.org/sites/odi.org.uk/files/resource-documents/11606.pdf> [accessed July 2019].

Neville, G. (2017) *Situating Everyday Water Realities: Low-Income Access, Informal Provision and Domestic Strategies in Urban Ethiopia*, PhD thesis, Department of Geography Royal Holloway, University of London <https://pure.royalholloway.ac.uk/portal/en/persons/george-neville(9932b955-6899-402f-9306-b2782296b726)/publications.html> [accessed 10 March 2019].

Oluwasanya, G. (2009) *Better Safe than Sorry: Towards Appropriate Water Safety Plans for Urban Self Supply Systems* [website], PhD dissertation, Cranfield University <https://dspace.lib.cranfield.ac.uk/bitstream/handle/1826/4453/Grace_Oluwasanya_Thesis_2009.pdf;jsessionid=8377553FBCD62168DD45B8D3C314E52D?sequence=1> [accessed May 2020].

Oluwasanya, G., Smith, J. and Carter, R. (2011) 'Self supply systems: urban dug wells in Abeokuta, Nigeria', *Water Science and Technology: Water Supply* 11(2): 172–8 <https://doi.org/10.2166/ws.2011.026>.

Peloso, M. and Morinville, C. (2014) 'Chasing for water: everyday practices of water access in peri-urban Ashaiman, Ghana', *Water Alternatives* 7(1): 121–39.

Prakash, A. (2010) 'The peri-urban water security problem: a case study of Hyderabad in South India', *Water security in peri-urban South Asia*, Discussion paper 04.

Rao (2018) 'As Bengaluru stares a water crisis in the face, residents turn to open wells', *The Hindu Newspaper*, 15 July 2018.

Rinaudo, J., Montginoul, M. and Desprats, J.-F. (2015) 'The development of private bore-wells as independent water supplies: challenges for water utilities in France and Australia', in Q. Grafton, K. Daniell, C. Nauges, J.-D. Rinaudo, and N. Chan (eds), *Understanding and Managing Urban Water in Transition'*, pp. 155–74, Springer, Netherlands.

Statistics Canada (2017) *Treatment of Drinking Water by Canadian Households, 2015 Environment, Energy and Transportation Statistics Division* [online] <https://www150.statcan.gc.ca/n1/en/pub/16-508-x/16-508-x2017001-eng.pdf?st=x42iBPXq> [accessed June 2020].

UNICEF/WHO (2019) *Progress on Household Drinking Water, Sanitation and Hygiene 2000–2017: Special Focus on Inequalities*, UNICEF, New York; WHO, Geneva.

Wankhade, K., Balakrishnan, K. and Vishnu, M.J. (2014) *Urban Water Supply & Sanitation in India* [pdf], Indian Institute for Human Settlement (IIHS) Paper on Water and Sanitation, Bangalore, India <http://iihs.co.in/knowledge-gateway/wp-content/uploads/2015/08/RF-WATSAN_reduced_sized.pdf> [accessed 20 May 2020].

WHO/UNICEF JMP (2019) *Estimates on the Use of Water, Sanitation and Hygiene in India*, updated July 2019 <https://washdata.org/data/downloads#IND> [accessed 12 August 2019].

World Bank (2018) *United Nations Population Division. World Urbanization Prospects: 2018 Rev.* [website] <https://data.worldbank.org/indicator/EN.POP.SLUM.UR.ZS?locations=IN&view=chart> [accessed 20 May 2020].

CHAPTER 5

Ownership and investment in self-supply in sub-Saharan Africa

This chapter looks at the natural development of self-supply in a variety of sub-Saharan countries, based mainly on field survey findings. The main driving force is the (usually individual) compulsion to improve the quality of life for oneself and one's family and maybe that of the wider community, along with the psychological power of ownership, which strengthen the desire to create and maintain the value of a family asset. Questions arise as to whether self-supply is only for the rich and well-educated, but investor profiles suggest that this is not the case. Convenience is the dominant justification for investing in water supply within an already stretched household budget. Cultural custom also requires that water should be a shared resource. Productive use follows on satisfaction of domestic demand. The assumption that people do not have the means to make changes to an aspect as fundamental as water supply or sanitation is challenged by looking at the sources of funding which may be available within social systems, and the barriers they face in effective investment. It is these barriers that self-supply acceleration is designed to overcome.

Keywords: self-supply, ownership, productive use, financing, equity, incremental change

Key messages

1. Ownership is a powerful driver which is weakened where some elements of responsibility are removed from users.
2. Most supplies which are not government/donor-financed are privately owned. Sharing may take different forms but is widespread and leads to self-financed water supplies acting as mini-community supplies in terms of service delivery, spreading the benefit to less advantaged households.
3. Most well-owners are from the poorer and less educated groups, but the richer and better educated are over-represented in well-ownership.
4. Most private wells are initially constructed for domestic purposes, with a small proportion being also for productive use.
5. Convenience is the greatest incentive for family well construction and has many spin-off advantages for quality of life, beyond just time and energy saving.

http://dx.doi.org/10.3362/9781780448190.005

6. Productive use increases food security significantly and moves families out of subsistence relatively quickly. Cost recovery may be completed within 1–2 years with investment bringing clear profit thereafter.
7. Sources of funding include traditional savings schemes, personal savings (in the house or translated into livestock), and remittances from family members, can extend the range of affordable options.
8. Remittances are a sizeable contribution to national economies, but are not targeted to play a part in water supply investment.
9. Traditional savings schemes and modern cooperatives offer potential ways to finance household investments
10. Barriers to investment include lack of technical and financial knowledge for choosing options and planning implementation. Poverty is seldom cited as the major constraint.

Supply ownership and sharing

Although self-supply is a global and persistent phenomenon, the lack of official value ascribed to it means there is little research on the social and financial arrangements that can help it grow and prosper. However there is valuable information from raw data obtained from baseline surveys and piloting in which the authors have been involved over the past two decades, which cover over 5,000 households. Reports discussing survey context and some findings include Zambia (Sutton, 2002; Roche, 2006; Zulu Burrow, 2008; Madavine, 2008; Olschewski et al., 2016a), Ethiopia (Sutton et al., 2011; Mekonta, 2011), Zimbabwe (Olschewski et al., 2016b), Malawi (PumpAid, 2015), and Sierra Leone (Gelhard, 2014). To these can be added the lessons learned from reconnaissance visits to Liberia, Ghana, Niger, Senegal, Angola, Mozambique, and Tanzania.

Elements of ownership in self-supply

While community water supply models have to generate feelings of ownership, for self-supply that is the starting point – a personal response to a perceived problem. The psychological sense of ownership starts from a feeling of need or unmet demand, and builds into a series of interrelated responsibilities (see Figure 5.1). The fewer responsibilities that are included in the relationship between the user and the supplier of water, the weaker the feeling of ownership. A family which does not feel a need for the supply or is not involved in the planning or does not invest significantly will not have the same feeling of ownership as a family which is involved in all the elements of self-supply. The sense of ownership leads to a higher feeling of value (Heshmat, 2015) and so to a desire to hold onto the asset and ensure its functionality. Ownership also implies control – of being the one who sets the rules and the one who decides when and what changes are needed, including when to maintain and how to upgrade.

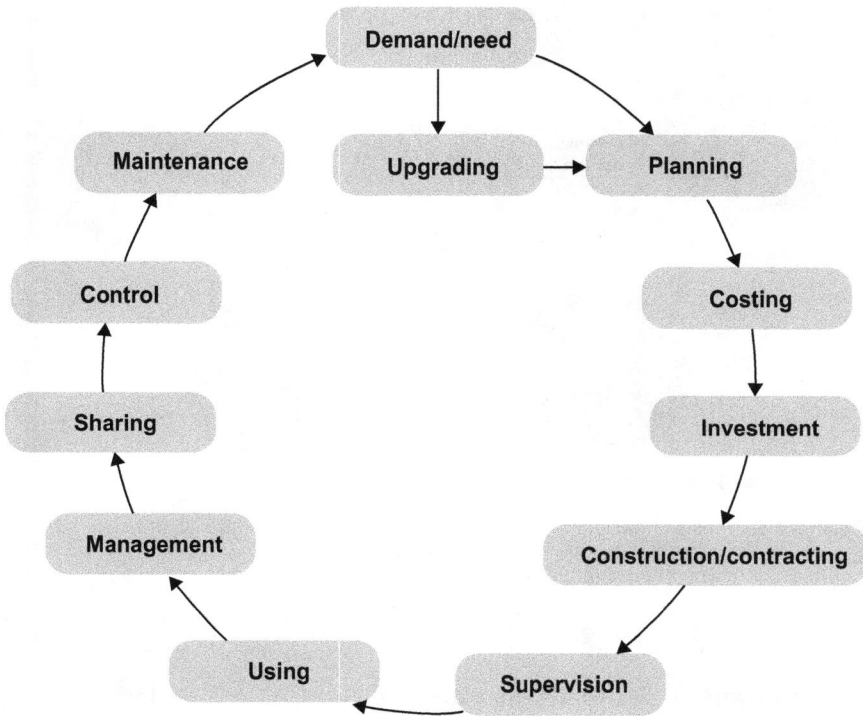

Figure 5.1 Water supply ownership responsibilities

Where all these functions are invested in one family or individual, rather than partly in a committee, in government, or NGOs, the feeling of ownership is at its most intense. Marks et al. (2013) note that the highest sense of ownership in community water supplies comes when contributions are not just 'token' amounts, and is strongest, in the case of higher service delivery models, with individual piped connections. In self-supply it is not a case of 'contribution', but the major part (if not all) is paid by an individual, family, or community group who then have a feeling of possessing a supply.

Wells are usually privately owned (see Figure 5.2) but most serve a group of houses. The relationship between owner and sharer may vary but management is still usually retained at the lowest level, that of the instigator and prime investor, except in truly communal/cooperative situations. Communal self-supply is rarer in Zambia and Ethiopia, and in Mali (Koulikoro region) 85 per cent of traditional wells were found to be privately owned. Individual family ownership rarely excludes other families unless almost every house has its own well, or the well-owning household is far from other houses which then use another closer waterpoint. Barring neighbours from drawing water is commonest if the well is going dry but may also happen if payment or manual help has been requested and refused, or as a result of a family or village feud.

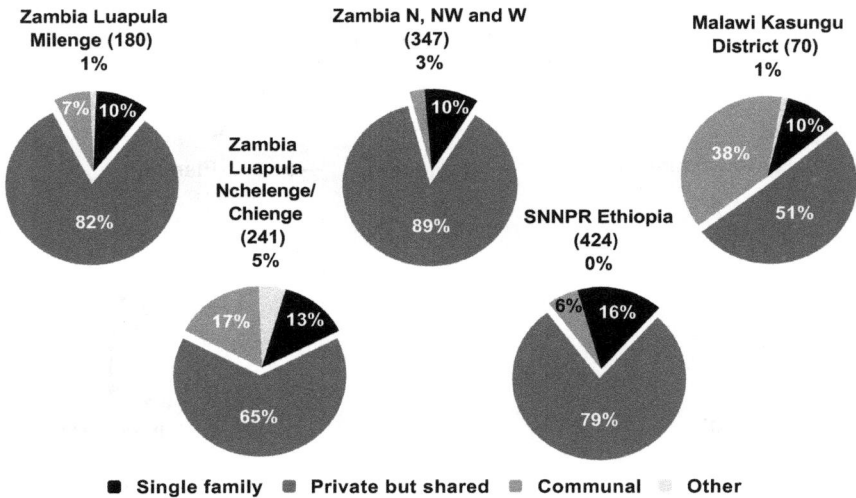

Figure 5.2 Examples of ownership patterns of traditional water supplies
Source: Raw data related to Zulu Burrow, 2008; Madavine, 2008; Sutton, 2002;
Sutton et al., 2011; PumpAid, 2015

Sharing

A supply owner will generally share the supply with others (see Box 5.1), since water is not viewed as a commodity, but by almost all as a god-given asset. Such a responsibility to neighbours is an additional incentive to keep the system operating as there is both a sense of social obligation and also a pride in being able to help others and show perhaps a superior ability to cope and provide for one's family and others. A well is not just a valued and convenient asset to family life, whose advantages can be shared with others, but a visible sign of status.

The main difference between owner and sharer is that sharers generally only have a right to water for domestic purposes, while the one who invests has the right to use the water to generate income, which may help to pay for the investment. Cooperative garden wells also provide water for productive uses but are usually constructed with this as the primary purpose.

The psycho-social balance between sharer and owner is not always straightforward. The owner wants to retain full control of his or her asset, but there is social pressure to share it, and the greater the number of users the greater the wear and tear and danger of the source going dry. There are cost implications in sharing, which are not often passed on, for fear of weakening ownership.

Relationships between owner and sharer are much influenced by culture and by the level of technology. For instance, the obligation of prospective sharers to contribute to maintenance is marked in the Oromia region of Ethiopia, where almost a half of well-owners with diesel pumps demand

Box 5.1 Cultural aspects of traditional water supply

Beliefs and practices relating to water use may affect ownership, sharing, and siting. For instance in the Western Province of Zambia, in the coastal Inhambane Province of Mozambique, and widely among Muslim communities in East and West Africa, it is common for householders to put their own well close to their house but at the edge of their property to make it easy for others to use. For some this is a neighbourly obligation linked to religion, for others an insurance against anyone 'poisoning' the well by cursing it or actually poisoning it as it is obviously being used by more than just the one household. Such shared wells are more likely to be chlorinated and looked after as owners do not want anyone to blame them for illness in neighbouring houses.

Photo 5.1 Household well in Bo, Sierra Leone, sited for use by neighbouring houses and passers-by

payment for access to their supply since it is the most popular for ease of water lifting and perceived water quality. For rope and bucket or rope pump abstraction charging is less common (less than 10 per cent). In Oromia 20 per cent of those drinking water from a well with a diesel pump actually have their own rope and bucket well (Mekonta, 2011), but (correctly) regard the pumped well as providing safer water.

Where groundwater is difficult to access and making a well is expensive or time consuming or requires expensive lining, the cost may be beyond the capacity of any one individual. In these cases, it is more likely that the community will get together (often instigated by the headman) to dig or contribute and that the resulting facility is communally owned.

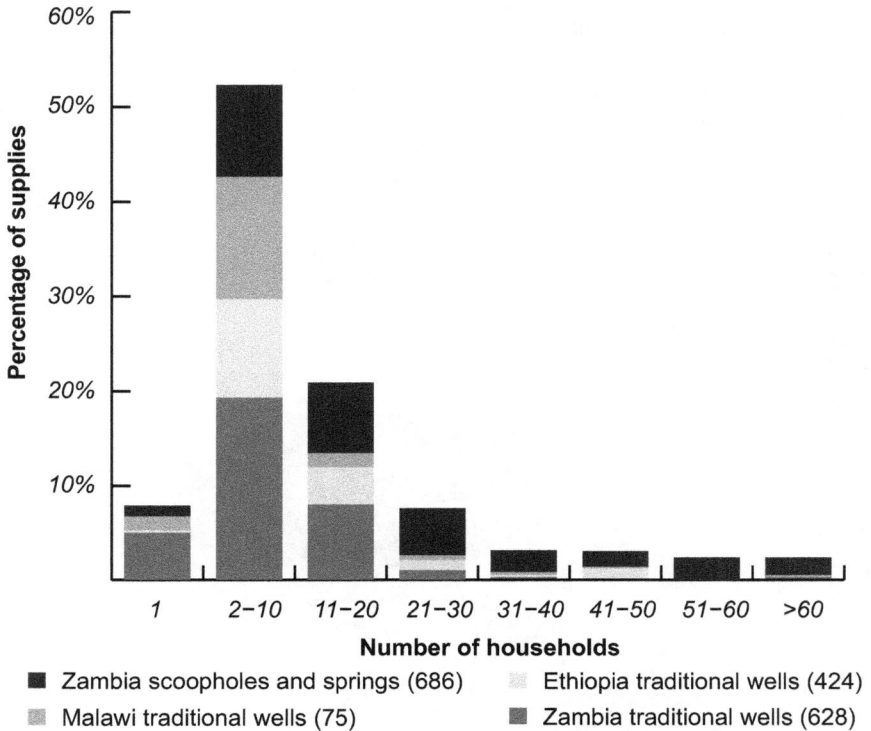

Figure 5.3 Numbers of households sharing traditional supply
Source: Data from 1,800 supplies in Ethiopia, Zambia, and Malawi

Where groundwater reaches the surface as a spring or scoophole, providing water freely for generations, it is usually regarded as a communal asset, even if it is on an individual's land.

Although traditional wells are widely regarded as privately owned (see Figure 5.2) most are shared by a group of 2–20 households (see Figure 5.3), mostly extended family and neighbours. Only in Malawi (of the selected countries), are a significant proportion of traditional supplies communally owned.

This may be because the high coverage with community supplies has led to remaining communities making more efforts to solve their own problems or paradoxically that having provided their own supply, they are being given lower priority by government. Generally it seems that the stronger hierarchical structure of societies (District/Traditional Area/Senior chiefs, village headman) plays a large part in galvanizing the whole community into action, in a similar fashion to the larger cooperatives in Kenya and Ghana (see Chapter 3, 'Improved group supplies').

A programme for self-financed improvement of scoopholes and traditional wells in Zambia (Sutton, 2002) was built on community rather than household

---

Box 5.2 The experience of Zambian research into improving traditional sources

In the three years to 2001 more than 200 supplies were improved communally by users at their own cost in three provinces of Zambia. However a major conclusion of action research carried out with the Ministries of Health and Water and Energy, with DFID funding, was that since most supplies were privately owned it was more logical and cost effective to enable private investment rather than more cumbersome community-managed efforts. There is significant suppressed demand which, once awakened, is a powerful force for change, but needs continuity of support for long enough to get supporting strategies embedded in government, and services sustainably developed in the private sector. This can take as much as five years or more (see Chapter 9).

A follow-on programme by UNICEF and WaterAid (2012–14) built on the results and focused on private ownership, strengthening private sector support services in one of the poorest and most remote districts in Zambia. Over two years more than 80 per cent of well-owners started improvements and were planning to continue with incremental changes. The results of both projects underline how building up an enabling environment for accelerating self-supply cannot be a short-term solution and establishing support services is effective only if viewed as a long-term service delivery model not a 'quick fix'. There is widespread grass roots demand which takes time to dissociate from innate donor dependency, but such pilot projects suggest demand can be awakened and built upon (see Chapter 6) if business models are provided with long-term but diminishing support until sustainable.

Source: Sutton, 2002 and Hillyard, 2014; see Part 2, Case study 6 for more details

---

initiatives and so led to higher user numbers per supply (average 20–25 as opposed to 10–15) (see Box 5.2). In Malawi, 10 per cent of PumpAid works on well construction and deepening were commissioned by communities where no individual was able to raise sufficient cash. However demand from individuals or families is generally the major part of the market as individual initiative is easier to stimulate than communal.

Issues of equity: who invests?

Investment and education

Levels of investment required to own a well are substantial. It might therefore seem to be the province only of the elite, the richest, and best educated. Analysis of wealth and levels of education among owners and sharers suggest that low or no education is not a barrier to household investment in water supply but does reduce the opportunity to own a well. An illiterate or lower educated well-owner is as likely as one with full primary, secondary, or higher education. In Ethiopia SNNP regional figures (DHS, 2016) show that some 10 per cent of males have secondary education or above. In the RiPPLE survey of 340 households in SNNPR, Ethiopia (see Figure 5.4) a third of all well-owners fall into this category, so that those with greater education are over-represented in well-ownership. The probability of owning a well increases with level of education, but in numerical terms a well-owner is equally likely to be someone with no or with higher education.

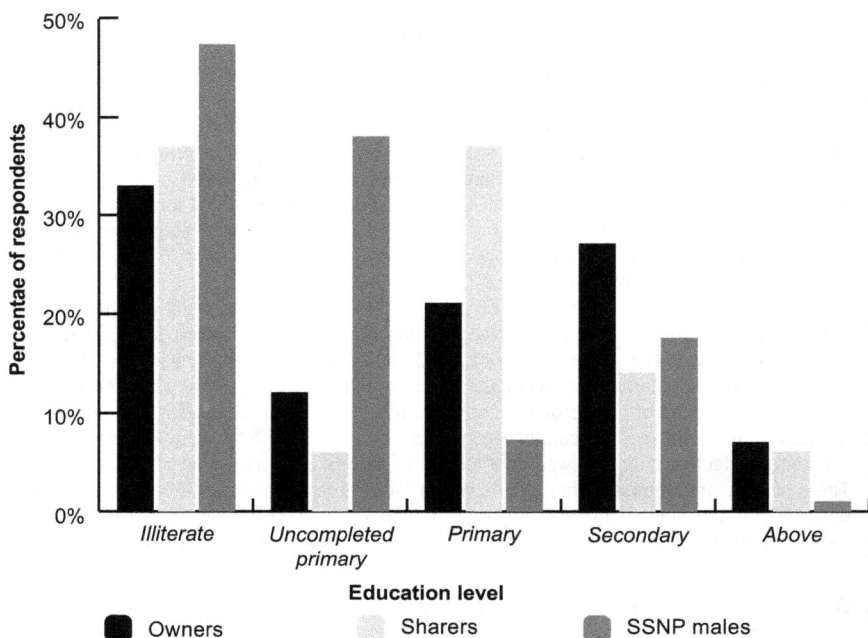

Figure 5.4 Level of education and well-ownership and sharing in SNNP region of Ethiopia
Source: Data from Sutton et al., 2011 and DHS, 2016

Table 5.1 Well-ownership and national education level, population percentages with secondary or higher education

Country/district	More than primary education (regional statistics)	Well-owners with more than primary education (field survey)	Data sources – regional
Ethiopia SNNPR 2012	7% (2016)	34%	DHS Ethiopia 2016 (SNNPR)
Malawi Kasungu District 2015	20% (2006)	23%	Kasungu District council data 2006
Zambia Milenge District 2012	27% (2015)	36%	Zambia DHS 2015 (Luapula)

Table 5.1 shows that the greatest discrepancy between education levels of surveyed well-owners and the general population is in Ethiopia, with less-educated groups most underrepresented in well-ownership. Even so, a third of surveyed well-owners were illiterate.

Investment and wealth

Baseline surveys dealing mainly with those on low incomes who often trade in kind rather than cash, found it difficult to get any accurate information on annual income from respondent families (e.g. Zulu Burrow, 2008).

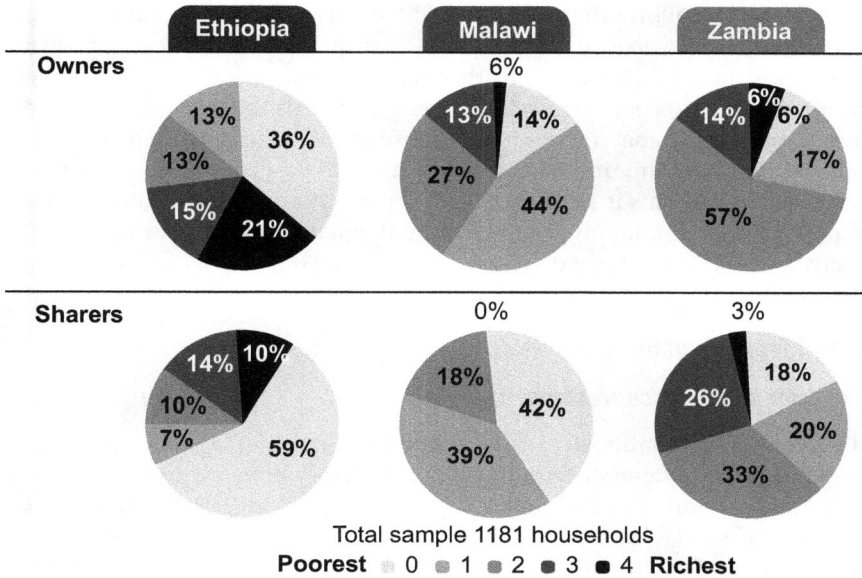

Figure 5.5 Wealth characteristics of well-owners and sharers
Source: Raw data from surveys by RiPPLE 2010, PumpAid 2014, and UNICEF 2015

Wealth has therefore been defined by easily identifiable assets, and households divided into one of five categories on this basis. Assets (mainly ownership of livestock, land, radio/TV, concrete floor, or metal roof) were selected in discussion with communities to be locally relevant and are therefore not directly comparable between countries. Wealth scoring is based on the number of assets owned. Those selected by communities in Zambia tended to put more people in the middle range than in Ethiopia and Malawi, perhaps reflecting its higher per capita gross national income or the nature of the indicators chosen.

In terms of wealth, in the Ethiopian SNNPR study 36 per cent of well-owners fell in the poorest group (see Figure 5.5) and put water above other home comforts such as a secure metal sheet roof over their heads or ownership of cattle as a priority for investment. In all three countries poorer households were more likely to be sharers than owners so the use of a neighbour's well seems to act as an important leveller in terms of access to water, especially for those who do not own land on which to put a well. In Malawi and Ethiopia it appears that those who are sharing are largely in the poorest group, while in Zambia over 50 per cent were in the middle wealth levels, which also constituted most owners. In Malawi for the group of surveyed wells, those in the two richest groups were all owners (19% of owners) and none was found among the sharers.

As with education, it appears that at least in the sample areas of these three countries there is consistent evidence that being poorer or less educated does reduce the probability that a family will have its own well by around 20 per cent, but does not preclude it. In Ethiopia many who fall into these categories have constructed their own wells through their own labour or with the help of others. Having your own well also generally leads to significant economic advantages which may mean that owners have already moved into a higher income group by the time of the survey, masking their situation at the time of construction. This is a 'chicken and egg' situation, where creating a water supply is easier if a family is better off, but equally having your own supply tends to make one better off.

Why invest in water supply?

The importance of 'convenience'

'Convenience' is almost always named by families as the paramount reason for supply construction and the greatest perceived benefit from it. It is the primary motive for digging a well, or investing in rainwater harvesting and forms a powerful driver in marketing. As the 'on-premises' indicator for Sustainable Development Goal (SDG) 6.1 suggests, having water 'on the doorstep' is valued by sector professionals and households alike. A survey in Mali by UNICEF (Sutton et al., 2006) shows that almost all (93 per cent) households were within 100 metres of the traditional source they use and over two-thirds within 20 metres. At this distance collecting water for an average family of six at 20 litres/head/day takes only about half an hour.

Translating convenience into time saving is identified (Hutton and Haller, 2004) as the main contributor to the benefits of better access to water and sanitation facilities. Cairncross (see Chapter 1, 'The significance of "on-premises" supply') puts the impact on health of close access to greater volumes of water and associated improved hygiene as a major benefit. Regression analysis by Pickering and Davis (2012) on data from 200,000 demographic and health surveys in 26 countries associates a 15-minute reduction in time to the water source with a 41 per cent reduction in under 5 diarrhoeal disease and 11 per cent relative reduction in mortality. This is independent of the type of supply/quality of water, linking impact therefore more to changes in hygiene behaviour, and showing the highest reduction where the household also has sanitation facilities. Both they and Cairncross conclude that improving water supply that is not close to the home is unlikely to have a major impact on health, even for under 5s. Evans et al. (2013) have also shown that positive benefits accrue from on-plot water supplies, but there is a need for further research to quantify the various benefits (especially health) and identify any confounding effects of water quality.

Households identify a set of interdependent benefits in reducing distance to the supply which tie up well with the academic view. Figure 5.6

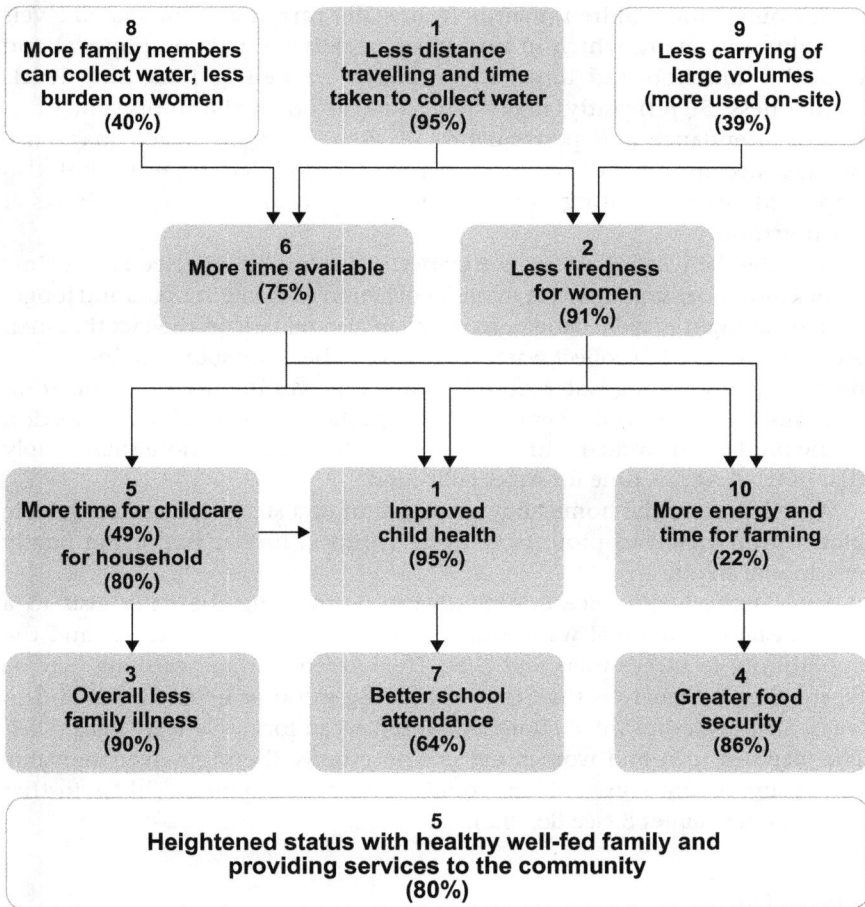

Figure 5.6 Top 12 perceived benefits of water supply close to the house
Note: Numbers are ranking obtained from percentage responses to open-ended questions
from 120 households
Source: Results from UNICEF Zambia study, 2015

summarizes the 'Top 12' impacts identified by well-owning households in a subsistence farming area of Zambia. The un-shaded elements are benefits particular to the owners and the shaded ones are the benefits to owners and sharers alike. The two main outcomes from travelling a smaller distance to collect water, according to almost all householders, were improved child/family health and less tiredness among women. The impact on child health is not just improved hygiene but also reduction in energy expenditure. Porter et al. (2013) note that water is commonly carried by children (Malawi: 70 per cent of girls and 30 per cent of boys; Ghana: 75 per cent of children). They link under-nourishment combined with high energy expenditure in both women and children (mainly from water carrying) to increased levels of malnourishment, which in turn has a negative impact on physical and cognitive function and impaired immunity as well as increasing levels of tiredness. Significantly, many families also noted the improvement in school attendance and performance of their children, which may arise not just because of the reduction in time spent collecting water but also improved health resulting from less load carrying and associated effects of malnutrition.

A further benefit is that, for the owner, water can be collected at any time while communal supplies tend to limit collection to daylight hours and longer walking at night may be dangerous. Women also remark on the fact that men are more prepared to collect water themselves where the source is close to the house. Equally having water close to home removes the need for women to carry small children with them to avoid them being left alone. The reduction of the burden on women with self- supply is therefore far more than simply that of needing less time for water collection.

A well close to the home allows cultivation of a small domestic vegetable plot, within view and protectable from livestock, further improving family nutritional status.

Some women do voice one disadvantage: forgoing the daily visit to a more distant communal water source cuts down social interaction and the opportunity to meet others and chat. The burden of water carrying may be regarded as less onerous than that of carrying wood or hoeing fields and so is not always an unwanted chore, but at times can form relatively light relief. The views of men and women are not necessarily the same over the value of self-supply and conventional community water supplies. This is further explored in Chapter 8 (see Box 8.2).

Potential use

The most fundamental question is the purpose of investment, and therefore what type of supply to consider and where to site it. The daily burden of collecting water at a distance from the house means that most wells are still principally constructed for domestic use (see Table 5.2) and often among larger households which require more water.

Domestic use is a less prominent reason for well-ownership once farmers have moved beyond purely subsistence production and are producing surplus for sale, as well as where it is culturally more usual to invest in livestock. For example, 85 per cent of traditional wells surveyed in SNNPR (Ethiopia) which are used in part at least for domestic purposes, provided water for animal watering, and 30 per cent were used for irrigation, with a few others providing water only for productive purposes.

In contrast, in Milenge district in Zambia, where cattle are rare and few families have achieved more than subsistence levels of existence, no well-owner uses water for more than domestic purposes, which may include

Table 5.2 Proportion of households using water from self-financed wells for domestic and productive use in three countries

Well uses	Drinking (%)	Cooking (%)	Washing clothes (%)	Bathing (%)	Watering animals (%)	Irrigation (%)
Malawi traditional wells (335)	88	90	88	84	31	18
Zambia 1999 (1,531)	93	95	86	87	24	17
Zambia 2015 (Milenge, 206)	99	100	99	98	0	0
Ethiopia						
SNNPR traditional wells (345)	99	99	90	86	85	30
SNNPR Rope pumps (35)	92	97	70	49	54	43
Oromia Ilu, Ad'a (220)	100	–	–	–	25	8

a household vegetable plot but no produce for sale. Most are perhaps unaware of the potential which the investment offers or are limited by the lack of a market. Here, only 1 per cent of respondents mentioned more than domestic use as a reason for investing in a well. A wider survey of Zambian traditional sources in 1999 (Sutton, 2002) and in Malawi in 2014 (PumpAid, 2015) covered more prosperous districts and reflect higher use for productive purposes. Nevertheless, only a quarter of well-owning households watered animals and fewer irrigated beyond very small-scale vegetable gardening or flowers around the house. Again, enhancing quality of life in the home, rather than looking for an economic return seems to be the primary reason for investing in supply.

It is when families move to higher technologies such as rope or motorized pumps that they look for a more tangible return for their investment. They are more likely to have already moved into small-scale cash crop irrigation which has provided them with greater means to invest. As primary demand is for domestic water, any efforts to promote the full economic potential of self-supply need to look not just at how to wean people off donor dependency but also how to encourage them out of a subsistence mindset and into productive farming which can transform their lives. Neither is a quick process.

Productive use

Having control over a water source and being able to site it for productive as well as domestic use is a major benefit of ownership (see Photos 5.2–5.4 and Box 5.3) but one little studied, and one not available to most people using

Photo 5.2 Household well with cattle trough and cow-shed; domestic and productive uses from on-premises self-supply well, Mali

Photo 5.3 Women's cooperative in South Africa, watering vegetables from their own well
Source: Photo MUS group 2003

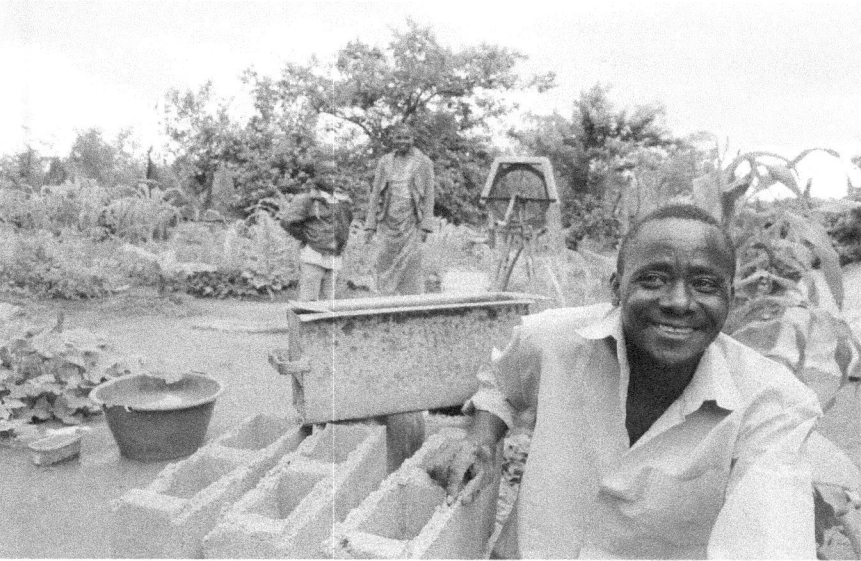

Photo 5.4 Brick-making in Zambia
Source: Photo R. Haanen, Jacana

community-owned supplies. Those private well-owners keeping livestock remark on increased milk production and improved breeding or healthy body weight of cattle, while small-scale irrigation for vegetables, pre-rainy season production of seedlings, or cash crops such as *khat*, tobacco, or peppers (Ethiopia) allows greater resilience to variations in rainfall. Jacana farmers in Zambia and Mali remarked in interviews with the author that they gain increased income from bee-keeping, livestock farming, or crop processing (e.g. cassava and shea nut), and beer and brick-making (Photo 5.4) are also common income generators. More peri-urban householders may use water for car-washing, hairdressing, or sale.

A study in Tanzania of the impact of rope pumps on income (Rosendahl, 2015) was confined mostly to peri-urban households and suggested a saving in expenditure over buying water from vendors or through income from the sale of water or products. Rosendahl concluded that there was an average increase in household income of 35 per cent as a direct result of rope pump use for agricultural production in rural settings, or from water selling, or a saving in water charges in peri-urban ones. This equates to an increase in income of some US$180 per year and is in line with the opinion of well-owners in Malawi, who invested in protected headworks and a rope pump (cost $160–180) and reckoned on a positive return from their investment on average within one or at most two years (author interviews, 2014–15). Data from Zimbabwe suggests that investing in a rope pump rather than a rope and bucket can mean a farmer can increase his or her irrigated area and income eightfold (Robinson et al., 2004).

Box 5.3 Changes in food security with investment in a well or a pump

To get some measure of the effect on food security, a small qualitative survey of 420 well-owners and sharing families was undertaken in Ethiopia, Zambia, and Malawi during years of average rainfall. Those who had constructed a well in the last five years were asked to think back to the time before having a well of their own to visualize their situation with regard to food production and then after answering, to do the same for the last year or more since having their own well. Those with a pump were asked to visualize the situation pre-pump installation and then to do the same for their situation afterwards. The aim was to minimize respondent bias by the sequence of questions. The survey does not provide any exact measure but reflects the perception of well-owners and why they might encourage others to follow their example.

In all cases (see Table 5.3) there is a very significant perceived shift towards having sufficient food for the whole year on having their own well, and a smaller shift towards having surplus to sell, partly dependent on the available market. Those who moved on to a motorized pump had the highest levels of food security and the greatest increase in selling produce. This change is only found after 1–3 years since early changes are partly constrained by lack of resources to buy seed and fertilizer so soon after paying for the well or pump. Increased productivity saves families from falling into debt from buying food for the 'lean' months and means they can pay back debts in kind as well as cash.

Table 5.3 Changing food security in 420 well-owning households (Oromia motorized pumps is before and after pump installation)

Household situation	Sufficient food for all the year		Excess for sale	
Survey area	Before (%)	After (%)	Before (%)	After (%)
Ethiopia, SNNPR wells	6	98	3	6
Ethiopia, motorized pumps, Oromia	61	100	20	51
Malawi, Kasungu	57	82	6	27
Zambia, Milenge	11	97	0	10

Source: Data from RiPPLE survey, 2010; PumpAid survey, 2015; UNICEF survey, 2015

Levels of investment and sources of finance

Basic costs and affordability

While a well can be excavated by a family and so have minimal cash implications, it is normal to employ at least unskilled labour and often also an experienced well-digger. To embark on a shallow well (5 m) with no lining may cost as little as $20–30 but for a deeper well requiring more skill, costs approach $100–300 or more. A supply with good wellhead protection requires at a minimum investment of $80–100 and adding on a rope pump another $100–150. Starting with a hand-drilled borehole costs a minimum of $200 for those in well clubs but at least $500 on the open market. A diesel/electric pump costs at least a further $150. Lining a well with bricks may cost only $30–50 but if concrete rings are needed the cost may be five to ten times more. Affordability is achieved by tackling levels of investment in manageable steps rather than trying to reach the ultimate goal of the safest, most reliable supply in one step, which almost none could achieve.

These steps can be compared with the way people build their houses, seldom able to achieve the final product in one go but progressing gradually. Windows may be bricked up until glass is affordable and roofs thatched until metal sheets or tiles are attainable. Looking at the amount paid for their roof provides a good basic indicator of the level of expenditure a household can afford for improvement to their quality of life. Not all roofing sheets may be bought at one time, but the capacity to save and store assets and/or obtain credit gives an indication of the resources available to a home owner. An increasing number of households are spending an average of around $150 on roofing sheets reflecting changing rural economies and product availability. Such steps of around $150–200 are affordable to increasing numbers. Levels of investment require an understanding both of the limitations that householders face but also the channels which they develop to increase affordability of something they really want. Apart from their own resources and those of friends and family, these channels include remittances from family members outside the country and a wide variety of savings schemes and micro-financial organizations, and to a very limited extent, banks.

Remittances

Remittances may be from within the country, for instance by a salaried civil servant sending money back to family in his home village. Several of the early self-supply adopters in Malawi and Zambia were retired civil servants or with family overseas. By far the largest element of remitted funds, however, is that of emigrants sending money back home from overseas. Migration is increasingly within Africa but historically was more to Europe and North America. Migrants beyond the region now exceed 33 million (IFAD, 2017). Remittances to sub-Saharan Africa are now officially approaching $40bn to which must be added probably as much again in money sent back by informal channels such as emigrants bringing cash when they visit home. Official remittances now approximately equal overseas development aid (official development assistance, ODA), so are valuable sources of funds, which are gradually growing (see Figure 5.7). Remittances may be small amounts, individually raised to augment the weekly household budget (food, school fees) or more substantial amounts coming from individuals earning higher incomes, which can be used for larger investment such as house purchase or building, land or infrastructure. Large amounts are also sent back, particularly from migrant associations which consolidate many small contributions, to a specific village or project. According to IFAD (2017) most remittances (as with ODA) go to urban areas as many migrants moved first to urban areas and then left the country, but some 30 per cent reach rural areas.

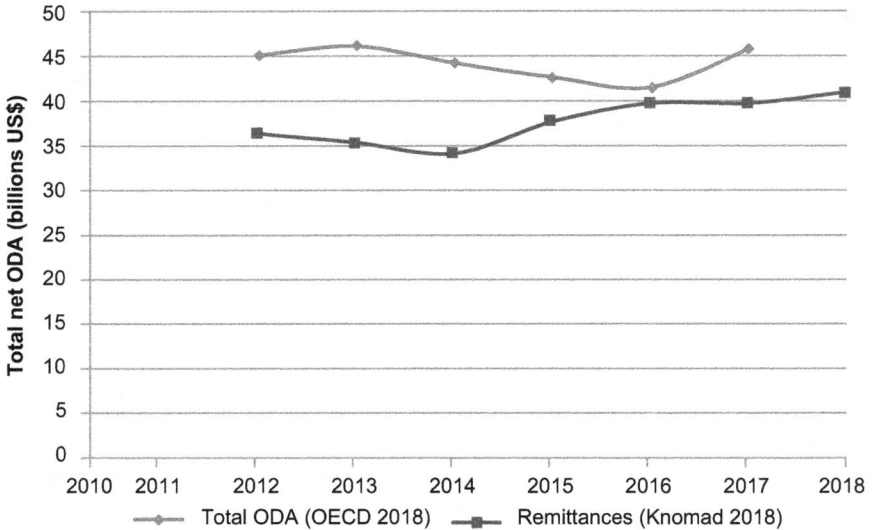

Figure 5.7 Annual official development assistance and official remittances to sub-Saharan Africa, 2012–2018
Source: ODA: OECD, 2018; remittances: KNOMAD, 2018

While 4 per cent of ODA is spent on the WASH sector it is thought that little remittance funding is spent on WASH. The potential is there though since total remittances to rural areas are over 5 times the ODA to the WASH sector. Nigeria (over $20bn total per annum), Ghana, Senegal, and Kenya (over $2bn) are the greatest recipients (KNOMAD/World Bank, 2018) of remittances and Liberia and Gambia receive over 20 per cent of their national income from this source. As the IFAD report points out, the thing that matters most is not the size of the overall movement of money so much as the effect it has on individual families. An annual amount of $200–300 may double a family's income and allow them to make their own personal SDGs. Globally IFAD estimate that 60 per cent of families obtain a significant part of their income from remittances. From several perspectives these therefore offer a sizeable source of funding so far little accessed for water supply.

Traditional savings schemes

Despite the scarcity of cash and subsistence levels of living for most rural people there is a long tradition of saving, mostly in rotating savings and credit associations (ROSCAs). Some are already used to support water supply investment but for many the advantageous link between the two has yet to be made.

The widespread nature of informal savings schemes is highlighted by the different names and types of traditional savings circles all over Africa (see Table 5.4).

Table 5.4 Examples of the widespread tradition of savings schemes in sub-Saharan Africa

Country	Fund name	Comment
Angola	Kixikilas	Move by NGOs to develop flexibility in access to funds
Senegal	Tontine	Popular, used by a third of the population, with moves to make it more phone-based
Ghana, Sierra Leone, Liberia	Susu/osusu	Being formalized in Ghana with Susu Collectors Association, so merging into more formal finance (Gugerty, 2005). Elsewhere still largely traditional
Kenya	Chama	Often run by women, even if illiterate. Over 1 million groups
Mozambique	Xtique	Greater participation from households receiving remittances
Tanzania	Upata	Usually small amounts for family investment (Brown et al., 2015)
Tanzania	Kuzikana	Community insurance/social funds
Rwanda	Tontines	Large proportion of national savings, estimates $16–20m in informal savings used by 56% of adults (Uwanziga, 2017)
Ethiopia	Equb/Ikkub	Generally not a fixed cycle in advance, but dependent on casting lots. Can be sizeable funds used for business development
Ethiopia	Iddr	Community insurance policy, for emergencies (e.g. funerals, house fires) so often banked formally and borrowed from with interest
Cameroon	Djanggi	A more flexible system that permeates many aspects of rural life
Zambia	Chilimba	As with others no long-term loans but cycle accumulation only

These systems are embedded in society, particularly among women, and offer several benefits. They:

- offer a framework which encourages a commitment to saving;
- present the opportunity to invest in something more than can be achieved if saving alone (Gugerty, 2005);
- create a group which socializes regularly and may form a structure for self-help activities;
- may provide a safety net in times of trouble;
- give women some autonomy to invest in their own priorities.

Such saving and credit circles mostly act like a 'tontine' initially, with members paying in a fixed (often monthly) amount, and then receiving the accumulated saved amount on a rotational basis. If there are 12 members, each receives the subscription of 11 other people once a year. The scale of payments in and out varies with the economic status of members. In a rural village the pay-out may be around $10, but in cities it may be hundreds or even thousands. According to Gugerty (2005) groups have developed more as a psychological prop to saving rather than as a defence against predation on cash by family and friends. They are perhaps the financial equivalent of Weight Watchers in that they use the commitment to the group and shame of not keeping to jointly agreed goals, as well as the shared joy of reaching a target (and being recipient of the month) to motivate people to join and to keep to the rules. It is effectively a widespread self-supply banking system, accessible to women and sometimes forming the basis for collaborative activities.

In Kenya, ROSCAs play an important role for small-scale entrepreneurs and women in particular, with alternatives becoming increasingly phone-based. Over a quarter of the adult population use ROSCAs, and as a group, Kenya, Uganda, and Tanzania provide 40 per cent of all group savings and credit products of the whole region (Barclays Bank et al., 2016). In WASH terms at one end of the scale they are sufficient for buying a latrine slab, a sack of cement, a bucket or simple household water treatment or storage system. In the middle of the scale they may be sufficient to get a well dug, or a higher-grade latrine constructed, and at the upper end a borehole drilled. They offer an opportunity to consolidate small amounts of money into larger ones where pressures on household finance and human nature combine to make saving for specific items or for 'rainy day' unexpected emergencies otherwise almost impossible. WaterAid encouraged households in Mali to use their savings circle to purchase safe water storage containers. In Ethiopia some communities used *iddr* funds to raise the community contribution for a well (the fund being paid back over time). While individuals may be poor, ROSCAs give them choices and purchasing power they cannot achieve alone (see Box 5.4).

Box 5.4 Savings circles and self-supply

The savings circle (ROSCA) principle is ideal for enabling all members in a group (especially women) to access a specific item they could not otherwise afford, such as rainwater harvesting tanks. Since the 1990s the combination of savings circle principles and self-supply has been promoted in Uganda, spreading from Kenya, to cover many of the water-stressed areas where groundwater alternatives are not feasible. The Ugandan Appropriate Technology Centre, founded by the Ministry of Water and the Environment actively promotes rainwater harvesting through revolving funds (Hartung and Rwabambari, 2007) as does the Muslim Rural Development Association (UMURDA) (Sulaiman, 2016). The cost of a household storage tank for one house is paid back into a group fund by the home-owner and then made available to the next. Rainwater harvesting is especially suitable for this approach since it is a family-level supply and can be upgraded over time with additional linked storage. Government policy is to promote it for areas with saline groundwater, but also over time to introduce piped water where possible with the funds available. Systems can operate conjunctively to reduce demands on piped systems so they can be extended to more communities.

A similar approach has been adopted for household groundwater supply through organizations such as Water For All, pioneered by Terry Waller, which facilitate the drilling of household boreholes (Westra, 2009). This is a form of supported self-supply but maximizes the contribution and management by families themselves. It is based on forming a club of 10 households with much the same principles as traditional savings clubs, each family benefiting in rotation and each with an obligation to the others. In this way weaker households are supported by the stronger, and all end up with their own supply. It has proved a successful approach in Bolivia, Nicaragua, and Ethiopia, among other countries.

Members tend to be the more progressive members of the community and so most open to new ideas. The degree to which ROSCAs have already been used for self-supply needs more research as do ways of realizing their potential within self-supply and making fund-holders more aware of the options open to them in WASH investment.

Microfinance services

ROSCAs and accumulating savings and credit associations (ASCAs) form the base of a pyramid in savings. There is a progression through informal to formal systems and the efforts of NGOs and the growth of mobile phone banking is moving groups slowly into more formalized ways of saving which do more to guarantee the integrity of funds and increase the flexibility of their use. This progression can be summarized as in Table 5.5, starting with the most regulated.

The SHIPO SMART centre in Tanzania has employed savings and credit cooperative societies (SACCOs) for investment in water supply with mixed success (see Part 2, Case study 5): one out of three working well. The experience leads to the belief that with multi-stakeholder guarantees workable models can be developed.

Village savings and loan schemes (VSLAs) and above tend to be counted more as formal loans and appear to be rarely accessed for investment in water supply at present. This arises partly from high interest rates and the prevalence of pre-existing loans for direct income generation, such as purchase of fertilizer, a plough, or seeds and a prohibition or reluctance to take out more than one loan at a time. Few microfinance institutions (MFIs) include water supply, especially domestic supply, within their investment portfolio, not recognizing its impact on family income, but they could play a greater part especially in group level self-supply.

Table 5.5 Progression (bottom to top) in financing mechanisms for savings and loans

Acronym	Name	Characteristics	Regulation
Bank	Formal commercial institutions	Centralized, often foreign investment	Fully regulated compliance with financial legislation
MFI	Microfinance institutions e.g. BRAC, Finca	Some NGO supported; some not for profit (NFP) organizations	Regulated as NFP companies
SACCO	Savings and credit cooperative society	Financial cooperatives	Legal entities with registration
VSLA	Village savings and loan schemes	Semi-formal, often NGO generated	Fixed term lending pass-books and shared balance
ROSCA/ ASCA	Accumulating savings and credit associations	Informal traditional systems based on community cohesion and trust	Generally unregulated, so not always dependable

Household resources

There is a significant difference between the spending capacity of families with a salaried or pensioned member and those depending solely on agricultural produce. The former can make longer-term plans than the latter, who still largely depend on rain-fed (and therefore unpredictable) crops and livestock.

Those with regular monthly income may be relatively few in rural areas but include an important and growing group of government retirees who, returning to their home village, wish to invest in some of the creature comforts they enjoyed when working in national, provincial, or district capitals. Among these, water close to the home is a high priority (as is a solar panel and television). Those depending solely on rain-fed agriculture are less able to commit to larger investments and loans but can achieve smaller steps using the resources within their control, along with ROSCAs and remittances from family members. Their own resources (see Box 5.5) include returns from crops grown, livestock, small-scale processing of natural produce (shea nuts, honey, bees wax, mushrooms, etc.), crafts, and their own labour. For landless families, working on the fields of a well-owner or on the well itself, generally gives them the right to draw water from the well and can be seen as their form of investment in a convenient domestic water supply.

Especially where farming is at subsistence level, fewer households sell food crops as a source of funds as few have any surplus (see Figure 5.8). Selling to raise funds in this common situation would require buying more expensively later in the year, leading to debt or hunger. Most money is raised from selling small livestock (chickens and goats) or comes from gifts from other members of the family plus savings, both of which are likely to have an element of remittance and ROSCA cash. As a result, in piloting self-financed upgrading, the demand for loans in Zambia (with scarce livestock) was higher than in the Ethiopian and Malawian contexts. In Malawi farmers are able to access a form of community development fund which helps a wider range of people to undertake upgrading.

Overall the result is that it appears possible for those with differing levels of wealth or education to see what others have done in constructing and upgrading water supplies and replicate it in bigger or smaller steps according to their own means and their access to a range of mostly informal funds.

Barriers to investment

Surprisingly, in essentially poor rural communities the reasons given for not investing in water supply are not first and foremost related to poverty. Typical responses are those from Milenge District in Luapula Province, Zambia, which is one of the poorest and most remote districts in the country where the greatest concern is lack of technical knowledge and so lack of confidence to invest. The advice needed is not just about what technologies to use but also where to find people with adequate skills.

Box 5.5 How households paid for their well or its upgrading in SNNP Region, Ethiopia

The RiPPLE baseline survey of 100 well-owning households in SNNP Region of Ethiopia showed that approximately half financed the well through their savings and half through the sale of their crops, and/or chickens, sheep, goats, and in one case a cow. Livestock is here regarded as another type of banking in that it is not just kept for eggs, or milk, meat, and breeding but as a way of retaining or increasing cash value which can be converted into money when needed. Most savings were kept as cash in the house, but 16 per cent of households were members of a ROSCA. Only one house had access to a bank account.

Photo 5.5 Ethiopian family well with investment in wellhead protection

Loans were available but mainly from the MFIs, or more rarely farming cooperatives and NGOs. Those who had successfully applied for a loan had done so with a local MFI, but since rates of interest are high (20–25 per cent) they were linked more directly to items for income generation such as farming equipment, seeds, or fertilizer. MFIs did not, at the time, lend for water supply alone, but moves were being made to change this by showing that owning a convenient water supply tended to increase income sufficiently to cover interest due. Loans ranged from as little as $25 up to $200. Household investment was augmented by relatives (60 per cent) and neighbours (35 per cent) contributing labour, materials, or food for the work, which would tend to make it easier subsequently for them to be granted access to take water from the well when the work was completed. Cash was seldom contributed and in very few cases (three) did the community as a whole contribute in any way. Knowledge of the availability of conventional loans was limited (35 per cent) and money lenders do not seem to be a much-recognized source of funds.

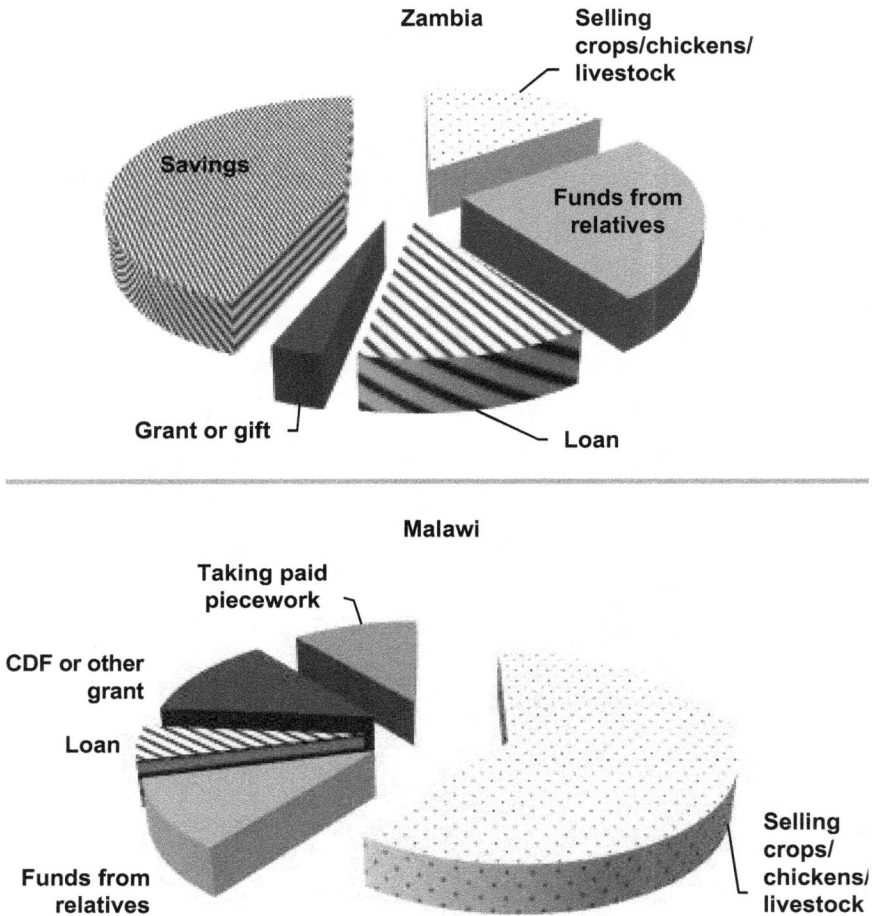

Figure 5.8 Sources of funds for self-supply well-construction in Zambia and Malawi
Note: CDF: community development fund

Financial considerations come far down the list with less than a quarter of families interested in loans or grants to purchase materials or carry out work they want to do. While loans and particularly grants may be welcomed in the long term, they are not the immediate concern and far fewer households regard them as being as important as obtaining technical and financial advice. Seasonality and variability in farming outputs makes it difficult for farmers to commit to major expenditure but they are mostly keener to do this or to undertake all the labour themselves than to depend on outside finance for community supplies which is almost equally variable and unpredictable, and over which they have even less control. Of surveys in 10 districts of Ethiopia, Malawi, Sierra Leone, Zimbabwe, and Zambia, only in one, in Sierra Leone, did households put outside financial assistance as the greatest need for future improvements to their own water supplies. The others were much more concerned over lack of technical knowledge.

Lack of land ownership and house rental are two major barriers to self-supply. Over 30 per cent of Malawi tobacco growers are tenant farmers and in many sub-Saharan countries there are moves to create larger farming units and estates, leaving small-scale farmers with the poorest land and least chance of improving productivity (UEA, 2016). Even though richer households are disproportionately more likely to own a well, they form overall a small proportion of the total population and the total of well-owners. Access to water for many of the more vulnerable may be achieved through the investment of others, some of whom may have fewer financial resources but perhaps more initiative and land ownership.

Conclusion

Water is not a normal economic or social commodity, but ownership and access are woven into the fabric of rural communities, linking also to traditional beliefs and village history. The psychological and social/anthropological aspects of water supply can play a major part in their success or failure (explored further in relation to community and private supplies in Chapter 8) and in the maintenance of community cohesion. Owning a well is a statement of status and some families put much effort and resources into it, generally not with productive use being the primary aim.

The answer to uptake lies not simply in economics, but equally in the psychology relating to a variety of aspects. These include ownership, attitude to risk taking, and priorities in household advancement/survival and moving from rain-dependent subsistence to groundwater-augmented production. Poverty and lack of education in themselves do not seem to be insurmountable barriers to self-supply. It appears that a sense of initiative and will for betterment in quality of life can override these disadvantages and significant numbers of people are achieving this. The question may be how to kindle this spirit of 'Yes we can' where it does not exist (e.g. PHAST manual *Encouraging Change* by Sutton and Nkoloma, 2011) and provide support services to aid investment and achievement where it already does.

Although people are undoubtedly poor, their poverty is more in terms of opportunity than simply in terms of resources. Many have access to a variety of funds and sources of labour and materials but there is a lack of linkage of such funds to WASH investment and a lack of advisory services which could facilitate the fulfilment of their demand for convenient water and then increasingly its safety. The question is how to leverage such funds and encourage their cost-effective use, especially where public supplies are still woefully inadequate or non-existent. Building up capacity for increased and better quality self-supply investment is not an instant fix, but an investment for the future and one of several catalysts for rural development.

References

Barclays Bank PLC, CARE International (UK), and Plan UK (2016) *The State of Linkage Report* [pdf] <https://insights.careinternational.org.uk/media/k2/attachments/The-State-of-Linkage-Report-2016.pdf> [accessed 15 September 2019].

Brown, A., Mackie, P., Smith, A. and Msoka, C. (2015) *Financial Inclusion and Microfinance in Tanzania: Inclusive Growth: Tanzania Country Report* [pdf], School of Geography and Planning, Cardiff University <https://www.cardiff.ac.uk/__data/assets/pdf_file/0010/592129/Tanzania-Feb-2015-FINAL.pdf > [accessed 12 October 2019].

DHS (2015) *Zambia Demographic and Health Survey 2013–14* [pdf], Central Statistical Office, Rockville, MD <https://www.dhsprogram.com/pubs/pdf/FR304/FR304.pdf> [accessed 22 September 2019].

DHS (2016) *Ethiopia Demographic and Health Survey 2016* [online], CSA, Addis Ababa, Ethiopia; ICF, Rockville, MD <https://dhsprogram.com/publications/publication-fr328-dhs-final-reports.cfm> [accessed 22 September 2019].

Evans, B., Bartram, J., Hunter, P., Williams, A.R., Geere, J., Majuru, B., Bates, L., Fisher, M., Overbo, A. and Schmidt, W-P. (2013) *Public health and social benefits of at-house water supplies*, Final Report, June 2013, University of Leeds.

Gelhard, M. (2014) *WASH Self-Supply in Sierra Leone: Perspectives and Options* [online], Welthungerhilfe and WaterAid <https://www.ircwash.org/resources/wash-self-supply-sierra-leone-perspectives-and-options> [accessed 23 April 2019].

Gugerty, M. (2005) *You Can't Save Alone: Commitment in Rotating Savings and Credit Associations in Kenya* [pdf], Daniel J. Evans School of Public Affairs, University of Washington <http://cega.berkeley.edu/assets/miscellaneous_files/wgape/2_Gugerty.pdf> [accessed January 2019].

Hartung, H. and Rwabambari, C. (2007) 'Financing mechanisms for roof-water harvesting: an example from Uganda' in A.C.T. Barton (ed.), *Rainwater and Urban Design*, pp. 348–245, Engineers Australia <https://search.informit.com.au/documentSummary;dn=889676720404624;res=IELENG> [accessed 03 September 2019].

Heshmat, S. (2015) 'How the ownership of something increases our valuations', 30 June 2015 [blog], Psychology Today <https://www.psychologytoday.com/us/blog/science-choice/201506/how-the-ownership-something-increases-our-valuations> [accessed March 2019].

Hillyard, D. (2014) *Stone Family Foundation projects -Year 3 report Milenge East Self-supply Project and Luapula WASH Programme October 2013-September 2014*, report submitted by WaterAid to Stone Family Foundation, London.

Hutton, G. and Haller, L. (2004) *Evaluation of the Costs and Benefits of Water and Sanitation Improvements at the Global Level* [online, World Health Organization <https://apps.who.int/iris/bitstream/handle/10665/68568/WHO_SDE_WSH_04.04.pdf?sequence=1&isAllowed=y> [accessed March 2019].

IFAD (2017) *Sending Money Home: Contributing to the SDGs, One Family at a Time* [online], IFAD, Rome, Italy <https://www.ifad.org/documents/38714170/39135645/Sending+Money+Home+-+Contributing+to+the+SDGs%2C+one+family+at+a+time.pdf/c207b5f1-9fef-4877-9315-75463fccfaa7> [accessed March 2019].

KNOMAD/World Bank (2018) *Migration and Remittances: Recent Developments and Outlook* [pdf], Migration and Development Brief <https://www.knomad.org/sites/default/files/2018-04/Migration%20and%20Development%20Brief%2029.pdf> [accessed 15 March 2019].

Madavine, T. (2008) *Zambia: Report on Baseline Survey of Household Waterpoints: Nchelenge and Chienge Districts* [online], UNICEF Zambia, Engineers Without Borders Canada/DAPP <https://www.rural-water-supply.net/en/resources/details/284> [accessed 16 September 2019].

Marks, S., Onda, K. and Davis, J. (2013) 'Does sense of ownership matter for rural water system sustainability? Evidence from Kenya', *Journal of Water, Sanitation and Hygiene for Development* 3(2):122–33 <https://dx.doi.org/10.2166/washdev.2013.098>.

Mekonta, L. (2011) *Self-supply: the potential and upper ladder household investment – the case of Haramaya and Kombolcha woredas (Oromia)*, RiPPLE Report, Addis Ababa, Ethiopia.

OECD (2018) *Geographical Distribution of Financial Flows to Developing Countries: Disbursement, Commitments, Country Indicators* [online], OECD Publishing, Paris, France <https://dx.doi.org/10.1787/fin_flows_dev-2018-en-fr>.

Olschewski, A., Sutton, S. and Ngoma, M. (2016a) *Review of Self-Financed Water Supply in Milenge District, Zambia* [online], UNICEF East and Southern Africa Regional Office <http://www.rural-water-supply.net/en/resources/details/754> [accessed 25 February 2019].

Olschewski, A., Matimati, R. and Waterkeyn, A. (2016b) *Review of Upgraded Family Well Programme in Makoni & Buhera districts, Manicaland Province, Zimbabwe* [pdf], UNICEF East and Southern Africa Regional Office <http://www.rural-water-supply.net/en/resources/details/755> [accessed February 2019].

Pickering, A. and Davis, J. (2012) 'Freshwater availability and water fetching distance affect child health in sub-Saharan Africa', *Environmental Science and Technology* 26: 2391–7 <http://dx.doi.org/10.1021/es203177v>.

Porter, G., Hampshire, K., Dunn, C., Hall, R., Levesley, M., Burton, K., Robson, S., Abane, A., Blell, M. and Panther, J. (2013) 'Health impacts of pedestrian head-loading: a review of the evidence with particular reference to women and children in sub-Saharan Africa', *Social Science & Medicine* 88: 90–7 <https://doi.org/10.1016/j.socscimed.2013.04.010>.

PumpAid (2015) *'Self-supply potential in Kasungu District'* Context Report for UNICEF Lilongwe, Malawi <https://www.pumpaid.org/wp-content/uploads/2020/06/Self-Supply-Potential-in-Kasungu-District-Malawi.-Pump-Aid-Context-Report.-June-2015.pdf> [accessed June 2020].

Robinson, P., Mathew, B. and Proudfoot, D. (2004) 'Productive water strategies for poverty reduction in Zimbabwe', in P. Moriarty, J. Butterworth, and B. van Koppen (eds), *Beyond Domestic: Case Studies on Poverty and Productive Uses of Water at the Household Level* [online], IRC Technical Paper Series 41 <https://www.ircwash.org/resources/beyond-domestic-case-studies-poverty-and-productive-uses-water-household-level> [accessed 15 February 2019].

Roche, N. (2006) *Study of the potential of self supply for rural drinking water provision in Zambia*, draft report, UNICEF Lusaka, December 2006.

Rosendahl, R. (2015) *The Impact of Rope Pumps on Household Income in Mzuzu, Malawi*, BSc thesis, Wageningen University, The Netherlands.

Sulaiman, K. (2016) 'Using the revolving fund approach to scale up rainwater harvesting in Uganda', in *Proceedings of the 7th RWSN Forum 'Water for Everyone', Abidjan, Côte d'Ivoire* <https://rwsnforum7.files.wordpress.com/2016/11/full_paper_0079_submitter_0064_walugendokyesa_sulaiman.pdf> [accessed June 2020].

Sutton, S. (2002) *Community Led Improvements of Rural Drinking Water Supplies* [online], DFID KAR Report 7128 <http://www.rural-water-supply.net/en/resources/details/249> [accessed 21 January 2019].

Sutton, S. and Nkoloma, H. (2011) *Encouraging Change: Sustainable Steps in Water Supply Sanitation and Hygiene*, 2nd edn, Practical Action Publishing, Rugby, UK.

Sutton, S., Maiga, B. and Maiga, H. (2006) *Improving Household Water Supply (Self-Supply) – The Potential in Mali* [online], WaterAid and UNICEF <http://www.rural-water-supply.net/fr/ressources/details/258> [accessed 20 January 2019].

Sutton, S., Mamo, E., Butterworth, J. and Dimtse, D. (2011) *Towards the Ethiopian Goal of Universal Access: Understanding the Potential Contribution of Self-Supply*, RiPPLE Working Paper 23 <https://assets.publishing.service.gov.uk/media/57a08aef40f0b652dd0009b6/working-paper-23.pdf> [accessed 29 January 2019].

UEA (University of East Anglia) (2016) *Agricultural policies in Africa could be harming the poorest* [online], University of East Anglia <https://phys.org/news/2016-02-agricultural-policies-africa-poorest.html> [accessed 1 April 2019].

Uwanziga, A. (2017) 'Rwanda: how informal women savings groups are changing lives in Huye', *The New Times*, 1 May 2017, AllAfrica Global Media, Kigali, Rwanda.

Westra, M. (2009) *Baptist drilling: affordable boreholes made by drilling clubs* [blog], Akvo <https://akvo.org/blog/baptist-drilling-affordable-boreholes-made-by-drilling-clubs/> [accessed 16 February 2019].

Zulu Burrow (2008) *Baseline Survey for Self-Supply in Luapula Province* [online], UNICEF, Lusaka, Zambia <http://www.rural-water-supply.net/fr/ressources/details/248> [accessed 23 February 2019].

CHAPTER 6
Early stage self-supply technologies

This chapter outlines starter technology options most suitable for early household-level investment and for low density or remote populations in sub-Saharan Africa and elsewhere, and reviews their relative merits and disadvantages. Facilitating their uptake forms a foundation for rural development and family well-being and the basis of support for households to progress towards a basic supply and on to safely managed options. A condition for successful self-supply is that in the early stages, technologies can be obtained through small, progressive steps, are easy to repair, and can be locally produced. This also makes them suitable for use in remote areas and those with low density population, but also then requires them to be officially accepted as a level of service for subsidy among poorer households. Early investment in lower steps facilitates greater productivity to fund higher technology options. Details within the chapter are limited but full references are given to manuals and training centres where more information can be gained.

Keywords: starter technology, hand-dug wells, manually drilled wells, rainwater harvesting, pumps

Key messages

1. The more basic the technology, the more limited are the conditions in which it may be applied, but the more affordable and sustainable it may be. However, 'simple does not mean easy' and introducing new technologies, however simple, is a complex and long-term process.
2. Hand-dug wells, protected springs, and rainwater harvesting are options which can most easily be developed incrementally with lowest cost initial steps onto the ladder.
3. The lack of a tradition of well-lining limits areas where wells can be hand-dug and where they are not prone to collapse. Introduction of reduced cost lining options would significantly expand the potential and sustainability of hand-dug wells.
4. Hand-drilling extends the areas over which groundwater can be exploited and extends the period of the year when new supplies can be created.
5. Most affordable technologies are aimed at providing options for the household market, but spring capture, stream diversion, and ram pumps plus surface water intakes in particular have potential for community self-supply.

http://dx.doi.org/10.3362/9781780448190.006

6. The growing availability of PVC/ABS pipes and fittings has facilitated the establishment of low-cost pump production and affordable household plumbing.
7. EMAS offers a package of cost-effective technologies aimed specifically at household investors. They have enormous potential in sub-Saharan Africa, but markets are slow to develop.
8. Rural development is a slow process, but big changes can be achieved over time where simple technologies build on existing skills and liberate supressed demand, as the Zimbabwe family well upgrading and Tanzanian SMART Centre examples show (see Part 2, Case studies 4 and 5).
9. Rural on- and off-grid electrification offers parallels to water supply and opportunities for investment in higher technologies and safer water.
10. Affordable technologies require official recognition as service levels to become eligible for subsidies, government training programmes, and social marketing. To achieve recognition robust local evidence on their performance needs to be made available.

Introduction

Household investment lies principally in a range of starter technologies for groundwater abstraction and rainwater harvesting to which this section is an introduction. Full technical details are available from a variety of sources to which reference is given. More expensive options open to group investment and families as they reach higher levels of income enter the realms of household plumbing and small piped supplies which are not covered in this book. Progress can be made incrementally (see Figure 2.1; Sutton, 2004; Morgan, 2016) in steps which may be affordable to a single family, starting with the most basic collection of water dripping off a roof, or a hand-dug well with little or no protection. These technologies offer an alternative route to safely managed water supplies (see Table 6.1), the target of Sustainable Development Goal (SDG) 6.1, for isolated households or small remote communities which cannot, in the near future or perhaps ever, be served by centralized piped water. Higher level economies have shown starter technologies to stimulate rural development, enhancing family income and enabling further owner investment which can eventually lead to in-house piped supply (see Chapter 3, 'The scale of rural self-supply in higher income countries'). They have also shown that in urban and many rural areas self-supply water points will ultimately be superseded by or absorbed into public services.

The use of private investment leaves families with a choice of water supply technology which can be tailored to their own means and needs. Much of the support needed is in providing good information and skilled services to make these options more accessible. Most remote supplies in high income countries started off at the starter level of basic rope and bucket technology and progressed as convenient well water played its part in raising family incomes and rural economies.

Table 6.1 Progressive steps towards a self-financed, safely managed groundwater supply

Attribute	Supply characteristic	Steps	SDG safely managed supply standard
1. Nearer	Supply outlet shared with smaller numbers	Increasing the number of water points. The ultimate aim is for supply to reach each house individually	Supply on premises
2. Safer	Better protected	1. Parapet and top lining to stop surface water inflow 2. Apron and drainage to avoid infiltration of spillage 3. Cover to stop air-borne debris 4. Pump to reduce hand-water contact 5. Microbial contamination removal 6. Chemical contaminant removal if necessary	Zero faecal coliform, free from priority chemical contamination
3. Easier to use	Less human energy expended, reduced hand-water contact, easier for the disabled	1. Rope and bucket 2. Lifting by windlass/pulley 3. Manual pump 4. Motorized pump	Piped into the house
	Gravity fed system	1. Pumped ground storage/elevated storage	
	In-house piped supply	1. Tap in house 2. Fully plumbed in supply including toilet	
4. Less down-time	Not drought affected	1. Deep enough not to go dry 2. Artificial recharge	24/7/365 reliable supply, available when needed
	Fewer breakdowns	1. Simple solutions until support services in place 2. Locally available repairs and spares 3. Improved quality products	
	Quicker repair	1. User knowledge of basic maintenance 2. Growth of private sector services including phone-based response	
5. More water	A combination of all the above	Increasing amounts reaching consumers for all purposes	Adequate supply for all domestic purposes

Rainwater harvesting and well starter technologies are those which can be improved or added to in stages, initially costing around US$150 or less, and which require the least complicated maintenance. They can readily be kept in operation by users themselves, with back-up from those who constructed or installed them. They therefore also offer a cost-effective option for small community supplies which are sustainable in remote areas where centralized support services are usually lacking.

Accessing groundwater

Groundwater resources

Using groundwater rather than surface or rainwater provides greater protection from climate change. While not equally accessible everywhere, it is more widely available and usually less contaminated than surface water. For almost two-thirds of rural populations of sub-Saharan Africa, shallow groundwater is obtainable within 25 metres of the surface (Bonsor and MacDonald, 2011). Being the product of many years' rainfall some of the year-to-year variation is ironed out, reducing problems for rain-fed crops and livestock. It is vulnerable to long-term variations which may lead to falling water levels. The modelling done by Thompson et al. (2019) in catchments in Tanzania and Ethiopia indicate that levels of groundwater abstraction from self-supply for domestic and garden or livestock use should have minimal impact on groundwater resources. MacDonald et al. (undated) estimate that 10 mm recharge across Africa would support community water supplies every 500 metres, indicating an overall potential far greater than demand, in the absence of large irrigation schemes.

Hand-dug wells

The most basic form of household self-supply is the hand-dug well, which requires little equipment (Watt and Woods, 1998; Collins, 2000) and usually taps the shallowest aquifer, which may be prone to contamination. Hand-dug wells are commonly 5–20 metres deep in sub-Saharan Africa, but in Sahelian and desert areas they may reach depths of over 100 metres. The narrower the well shaft, the less material that is removed, the more stable the walls, and the lower the cost (see Photo 6.1). Private hand-dug wells number several million (Chapter 3) and are increasing in sub-Saharan Africa, despite the major growth in community supplies (see Figure 6.1). For householders the problem is that neither standard community wells nor conventional mechanically drilled boreholes are usually affordable and they need to look for alternatives which have lower unit costs in the early stages.

Status as an 'improved' well in *Joint Monitoring Programme* (JMP) terms (synonymous with 'protected') is defined by the headworks to the well as being:

> protected from runoff water by a well lining or casing that is raised above ground level to form a headwall and an apron that diverts spilled water away from the well. A protected well is also covered so that contaminated materials (including bird droppings and small animals) cannot enter the well. Water is delivered through a pump or manual lifting device (WHO/UNICEF, 2018; see Photos 6.2, 6.3, and 6.4).

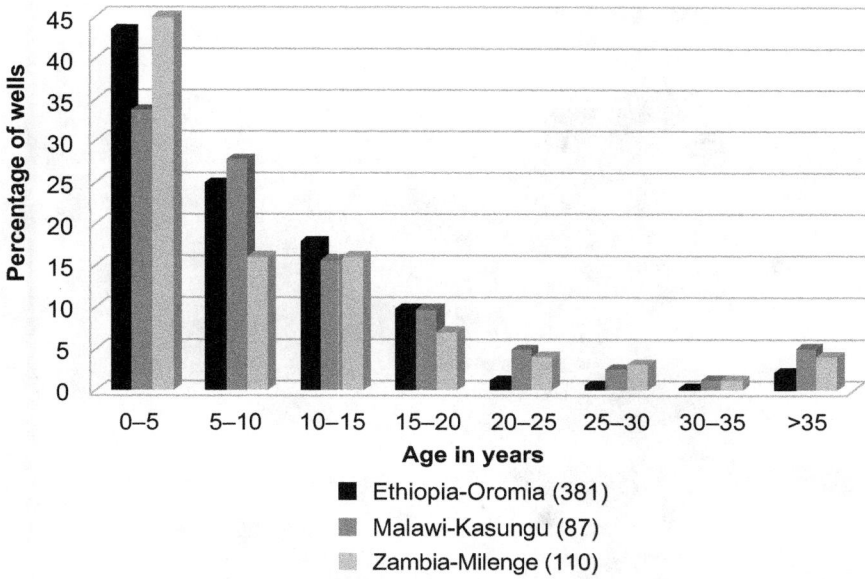

Figure 6.1 Growth in well-construction rates in parts of three sub-Saharan countries

Photo 6.1 Small diameter well-digging and underlining for additional shaft support
Source: Photo H. Holtslag

Photo 6.2 Unprotected well, Meskan woreda, Ethiopia

Photo 6.3 Protected? A household well in Luapula Province, Zambia

Photo 6.4 Protected self-supplied well in Ziguinchor, Senegal

The JMP makes it clear that even if a well is fitted with a lifting device (for example motorized pumps, hand pumps, rope pumps, and windlasses with buckets) if it lacks a cover then it should be classified as 'unprotected'. The different elements required make it possible to move towards an improved supply in affordable stages (see Morgan, 2016). If a reliable shallow well has good wellhead protection and water is lifted with a windlass or pulley it counts as a basic supply for the owner and neighbours and has the potential to become a safely managed supply for the owner's family. What is less clear in the definition is whether the many wells with a rope and bucket, where the rope and bucket are stored within the well or hanging from a post (see Photo 6.3) should also qualify, since the handling of the rope and bucket which enter the water is no more than for a pulley or windlass. The hundreds of thousands of poorly or un-protected wells where the rope is left lying on the ground would not qualify but highlight the fact that for all supplies many of the risks of contamination are behavioural rather than purely technical, with low-cost implications for improvement.

The well-digging season, without de-watering equipment (which very few local artisans can afford), seldom lasts more than three or four months of the year. Wells are usually dug towards the end of the dry season,

Photo 6.5 Brick lining for well and drainage channel (part completed) with foundation for top slab, Northern Province, Zambia
Source: Photo E. Kelly

when water levels are lowest, and are traditionally re-deepened or cleaned out by the owner in successive years as water levels fall or debris accumulates. At present, in the absence of a common tradition of well-lining, hand-dug wells are largely limited to areas with moderately consolidated formations, hard enough to stand unsupported but soft enough to be excavated by shovel or hammer and chisel. There is some stabilizing of topsoil with wood, bricks, or stones in sub-Saharan Africa but the introduction of low-cost full lining and excavation methods in unconsolidated formations could have far-reaching effects. Introduction of brick-lining (see Photo 6.5) in Zimbabwe in the 1980s has led to major growth of self-supply wells and their spread into new areas.

Community wells constructed using outside finance are lined with concrete rings but these are usually too expensive an option for families, unless done at small (0.8 m) diameter (see Photo 6.6) and with low-cement concrete mixes (Sutton, 2004). In very soft ground, brick or concrete rings are sunk by undermining them (caisson method) which enables the sides of the well to be supported during excavation. Wells can sometimes be effectively deepened by hand-drilling or jetting through the base of the shaft (see next section). This is advantageous where there is a lower confined aquifer, combining the depth of a borehole and the storage or a larger diameter well. Such low-cost options for households are not widely available or officially recognized. There is scope for the development of and training in household-level standards to enable official recognition, promotion, and even subsidy of technical options affordable at household level.

Photo 6.6 Concrete well rings for traditional family well improvement (well in background) Luapula Province, Zambia

The advantages and drawbacks of this low-technology option are summarized in Table 6.2.

Table 6.2 Main advantages and disadvantages of hand-dug wells

Advantages	Disadvantages
Cheap ($25–300 depending on depth and ground conditions)	Difficult to seal from surface contamination
Functions even in lower permeability aquifer	Shallow penetration of the aquifer
Simplest lifting device (bucket) doesn't break down	Shallow aquifer more prone to contamination (poor site hygiene, pesticides, latrines)
Can be developed into basic supply in stages	Limited areas of suitability
Traditional skills already exist	Risks of collapse
Usually simple to deepen	Limited (4 month) season suitable for digging
Easily replicable	

Hand drilled wells

Manual or hand drilling of boreholes (also called tubewells) refers to drilling using human force, sometimes combined with a motorized pump to circulate water or drilling fluid. Various methods of hand-drilling have limitations but

Table 6.3 Comparative features of low-cost drilling and well-digging

Advantages of hand drilling over digging	Disadvantages	In common
Quicker than hand-digging	Small water storage	Local labour and skills
Easier well construction in soft ground	Needs mechanical lifting device (pump or bucket pump) requiring regular maintenance	Low investment to set up business
Easier to seal against contamination	Very difficult to deepen	Can operate in difficult to access areas
Easier to penetrate beyond perched aquifer	Needs development (cleaning caked mud of walls to maximize water inflow)	Operate with simple supply chain
Can usually reach as deep or deeper than hand-digging	Head driller needs bespoke or on-the-job training	

also advantages over hand-digging (see Table 6.3) allowing low-cost expansion of wells into new areas. As hand-drilling is as much as two-thirds cheaper than mechanical drilling, this offers a more affordable option for boreholes which are less than 50 metres deep or 150 mm (6 inches) diameter, and in areas without too many boulders or very hard fissured rock. As such it is a long-term investment, but a starter technology in terms of providing household water supply on premises with the potential for incremental improvements in lifting devices and storage ultimately bringing water into the house.

Although hand drilling is a long-established practice, its growth in the region is accelerating. There are many thousands of hand-drilled boreholes (Danert, 2015) in Africa especially in Senegal, Niger, Chad, Madagascar, Ghana, Tanzania, and Nigeria and much has been done by RWSN and UNICEF and many NGOs (e.g. Practica, SMART centres, Water For All International, WaterAid, World Vision) to spread the technologies more widely. Hand-drilling is also widespread in Latin America, promoted in particular by EMAS training (Mobile Training Centre for Water and Sanitation, Bolivia). The largest and fastest-growing market is that of Southern Asia served by an established, but largely unregulated private sector (Dave, 2018).

The objective in choosing a type of drilling is to use the least expensive method that can successfully reach the necessary depth for a reliable source of groundwater. Five primary hand-drilling techniques for penetrating the ground and lifting out the cuttings are augering (see Photo 6.7), bailing, percussion, sludging (see Photo 6.8), and jetting, some of which may be combined. RWSN has produced a range of publications which cover fieldnotes on technologies and country uptake (e.g. Adekile and Olabode, 2009; Maccarthy et al., 2013) and include the comprehensive RWSN Hand Drilling Directory and Compendium (Danert, 2009, 2015, with a more recent update Danert et al., 2019). The SMART Centre group also offers a range of training manuals and videos (SMART Centre, 2017) as does EMAS (2010).

Photo 6.7 Hand-augering in Senegal

Photo 6.8 SHIPO drilling in Tanzania
Source: Photo H. Holtslag

Table 6.4 Drilling methods and their basic characteristics

Technology	*	Cost drill set US$	Max depth + geology	Ease of operation/ water detection	Wells drilled (2019)	Country examples
Mzuzu Combined auger, bailer, percussion	L	200–300	25 m Soft and stony layers	Easy/easy	300	Malawi, Zambia, Mozambique, Ethiopia www.smartcentregroup.com
EMAS Drilling with fluid circulation	L	200–400	80 m Soft	Difficult/ difficult	25,000	(Bolivia), Sierra Leone https://vimeo.com/50990902
Baptist Sludging bottom valve	L	300–500	80 m Clay Soft	Difficult/ difficult	4,000	(Bolivia), Uganda, Ethiopia www.waterforall international.org/
SHIPO Sludging, top valve with fluid circulation	L	500– 1,000	50 m Soft and stony layers	Difficult/ difficult	4,000	Tanzania, Malawi, Zambia Mozambique www.smartcentregroup.com
Rotary jetting	I	1,000– 3,000	25 m Soft	Difficult/ difficult	>100,000	Nigeria, Niger, Ethiopia www.practica.org
Jetting/water boring	L L	1,000 200	20 m Soft 10 m Sand	Easy/ difficult	>600– >10,000	Madagascar, Zambia, Senegal www.bushproof.com/products/boreholes/

Note: Where equipment is made I = imported; L = produced with local materials
Source: information from H. Holtslag, 2019

Table 6.4 summarizes the technologies used in sub-Saharan Africa with an indication of whether equipment can be produced locally or must be imported, cost of a drill set, depth it can drill and soil types, and the estimated number of wells drilled with the technology. The ease or difficulty of operation and detecting when water is reached reflect the length and intensity of training needed. Use of simple phone-based geophysics packages can be added to improve success rates.

Using simple equipment small businesses can be established relatively cheaply (see Table 6.4 and Box 6.1). Costs can further be reduced by training groups to drill or dig their own wells as a club with each member household drilling or digging a well with the aid of the other members. This method of spreading hand-drilling is used by NGOs such as Water for all International and H2O in Ethiopia, Uganda, and Gambia, among other countries. The NGO trains the families to drill one or two wells and then the families drill for the rest of the group to reduce the costs and develop expertise. Over 4,000 wells have been drilled this way in Bolivia and Africa, even to depths of 60 m or

Box 6.1 Making drilling into a business – a Tanzanian success story

In 2005 Laban Kaduma was trained for one month by the Southern Highlands Participatory Organization (SHIPO) Tanzania, now a SMART centre, in hand-drilling and rope pump manufacture (see part 2 case study 5). Over the years since then he has drilled over 4,000 boreholes and expanded his business from being leader of one team into being manager for six. These drill more than 300 new boreholes a year and improve over 100 hand-dug wells, repairing headworks and installing rope pumps. With advisory back-up from SHIPO, he has set up a limited company (UVINO) with its own metal workshop, making pumps and repairing drilling equipment. His business is now well-established and actively spreads the technologies to other parts of the country. On the strength of his growing experience and reputation he now also acts as an international trainer in Malawi, Mozambique, and Zambia.

Photo 6.9 Laban Kaduma demonstrating the principles of the rope pump to trainees in Tanzania
Source: Photo H. Holtslag

more at a cost of $5–10 per cased metre or as little as $200 in total. Costs vary per country and ground conditions. In Zambia the cost of hand-drilled boreholes starts at about $500.

The challenge for hand-drilling is to ensure a level of professionalization and official acceptance without over-regulation. Registration is becoming a more common requirement but needs to differentiate between big companies with large mechanical rigs and small hand-drilling enterprises. Regulation needs to cover its costs, but not drive small enterprises out of business or increase drilling costs above levels affordable to self-financing customers.

Conventional rotary and down-the-hole hammer percussion drilling

While conventional mechanical drilling (Sterrett, 2007; Danert and Gesti Canuto, 2016) is too expensive for most households, some households or groups in urban areas or large production farmers may be able to afford deeper and more productive boreholes. In large cities with unreliable supplies or limited pipe networks a big market for mechanically drilled boreholes has developed, as in Lusaka or Dar-es-Salaam, in the search for deeper, less contaminated water. In low income countries it is very rarely an affordable self-supply option for rural families, starting at around $5,000 including mobilization.

Spring protection

Groundwater naturally reaches the surface in springs and scoopholes, which form the simplest sources. Left open, they can easily be contaminated by surface water inflow and poor water collection practices. Capturing the water in a spring box before it reaches the surface and capping the cistern in which it collects, improves quality and ease of collection (Morgan, 1990) (see Photo 6.10). Community rules are needed to protect the catchment area closest to the well and exclude livestock and contaminating activities such as open defecation or corralling of animals.

Photo 6.10 Community self-supply spring protection, Northern Province, Zambia

The simple masonry works (Muehli and Wehrle, 2001) needed make it an ideal community self-supply endeavour, not least because the spring is usually already regarded as a community asset, but also because technical solutions can be tailored to available funds. In hilly/mountainous areas this can mean a gravity system bringing piped water into each house or to standpipes. Where elevation of the source above houses is insufficient, simple protection as in Photo 6.10 can be achieved for as little as $150.

Low-cost lifting devices

Rope and bucket

At its most basic, water is scooped from springs and scoopholes or lifted by rope and bucket directly or aided by a pulley, windlass, or pump (see Photos 6.11 and 6.12). Risks of contamination and cost are inversely related; the cheapest methods of water lifting present the greatest risks of contamination. Users have their preferences but need to be made aware of good practice when making their choices, to reduce risks of contaminating both the source and the water abstracted.

A rope and bucket are high risk since the bucket and rope are in contact with dirty hands and sometimes in contact with the ground. The risk from lying in the dirt can be avoided by using a windlass or reduced by using a pulley,

Photo 6.11 Drawing water by pulley, Senegal

Photo 6.12 Locally made handpump on a household well in Niger

hanging the rope and bucket inside the well, hanging them on a pole or taking the bucket home when not in use. Ease of lifting is greater with a windlass or pulley especially if water is more than 5 metres below ground level.

Costs of a rope and bucket are minimized by using cast-off materials such as old cooking oil containers, inner tubes, and strips of tyre. Windlass and pulleys can be made from wood or manufactured more expensively in metal. The simplicity of rope and bucket means that the supply is as reliable as the water in the well and is seldom affected by technical breakdown.

Low-cost pumps for household investment

While the concept of low-cost pumps is an imported one in the sub-Saharan region, the cheapest for domestic use are those which can be locally produced, such as the primed suction Pitcher Pump, EMAS or rope pump. Recent progress has been made, but each is still largely confined to relatively small areas and linked to project approaches rather than to government or private sector scaling up. The Ethiopian government is something of an exception with the rope pump but has still to roll-out a market-based approach. Starter pumps are chiefly made with locally available materials and are easy to repair using skills available in car or bicycle repair workshops. The spread of PVC pipes and their low cost has encouraged the development of affordable pumps. The cost of pumps generally rises for those which can

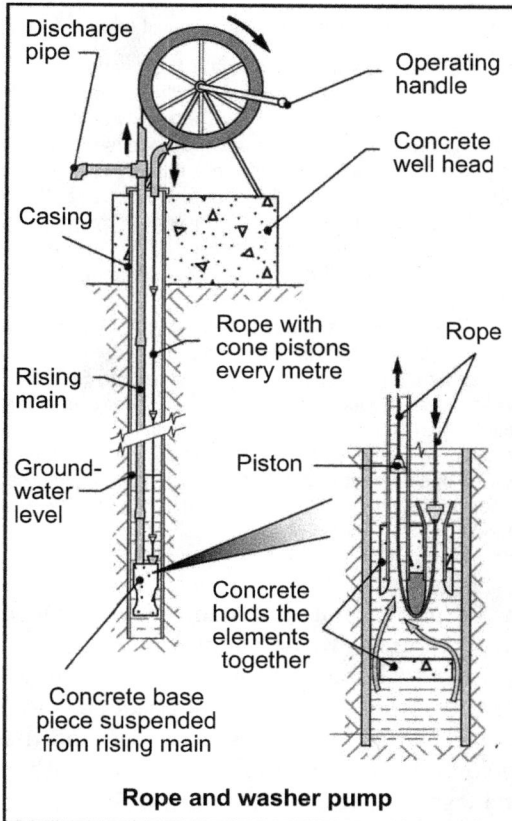

Figure 6.2 Schematic diagram of a rope pump
Source: Shaw, 2019

be best sealed off from the environment and lift water the highest, but the EMAS pump is an exception, being cheap, sealed, and also able to lift water as much as 40 metres in total.

Rope pump (see cover and Figure 6.2). The rope pump is attractive for self-supply since it is simple, has a high flow rate, and is relatively low-cost. It can be produced locally with materials that are available in any country: for example, PVC pipes, galvanized pipes, or used car tyres. Based on well-tested ancient Chinese pump technology, it is a very effective lifting device that can easily lift water 35 metres, and over 60 metres with modifications.

This pump technology was introduced in Nicaragua (see Box 6.2) around 1985 and its success is explained by its acceptance by government as a national standard pump for rural water supply (Government of Nicaragua, 2001) and its ability to pump water from depth. Another key reason for success was its manufacture by small private companies rather than NGOs. The initial market

---

Box 6.2 Economic impact of the rope pump in Nicaragua and beyond

The economic impact of rope pumps in Nicaragua has been considerable. By the year 2010 there were an estimated 70,000 pumps of which some 50,000 were installed at family level, either 100 per cent paid for by the family or donated by an NGO with the condition that the family invested in the well. An extensive study in 2000 of 5,025 families indicated that a family with a rope pump had on average $225 a year higher income than families without a pump (Alberts and van der Zee, 2003). This makes it possible for a family to recover the cost within a year and then reap the benefits of the increased income. Similar effects on increased family income due to self-supply investment in rope pumps were found in Malawi (Rosendahl, 2015) and in Tanzania (Maltha and Veldman, 2015).

Over the past 10 years there have been many attempts to spread the technology, initially from Nicaragua, and by 2018 there were an estimated 40,000 rope pumps installed in Africa (Haanen and Holtslag, 2016). In Tanzania, SHIPO have trained pump producers who have sold over 11,000 rope pumps. Over 60 per cent of these are self-supply investments, mainly for peri-urban families but increasingly for rural ones. The growth of copycat pump producers in Ethiopia and Tanzania is a tribute to the strength of demand but also brings a threat of sub-standard products which can damage the reputation of the technology. Promotion of the rope pump for domestic use in Ethiopia has largely been subsidized by the government.

---

development was for private households and only expanded to community models once its reputation was well-established.

Transference of the technology to Africa, starting in 2004, has shown mixed success (Sutton and Gomme, 2009; Haanen and Holtslag, 2016) partly because it was first introduced as a cheaper (and therefore regarded as 'second-best') community handpump, combined with all the problems of community management and quality control. While easier to repair, the higher frequency of breakdown than for conventional piston pumps puts a strain on community management of the supply. Kamanga et al. (2018) found 75 per cent of 127 six-year-old rope pumps working in Malawi and recommended they be promoted more for household rather than community ownership. Appraisal of the technology is available using the Technology Applicability Framework (TAF) (NETWAS and WaterAid, 2013) applied to Uganda.

EMAS pump. The EMAS pump was developed by the Bolivian Mobile Training Centre for Water & Sanitation (EMAS) specifically as a household level water supply. It is a direct-action pump (see Photo 6.13) which can lift water a total of 35 to 40 metres including height above the pump, which makes it fit for households that want to pump water to elevated storage in order to have running water in the kitchen or bathroom or to irrigate by hose or sprinkler. It has a major advantage in that it can be made without the need for electricity (Carpenter, 2014). It is a sealed pump, which reduces risks of contamination, compared with the rope pump, and is cheaper ($50 vs. $80–150 for depths of 15 metres) but also less robust. At the normal riser pipe diameter of 20 mm the rope pump and EMAS pumps

Photo 6.13 EMAS pumps for demonstration in Sierra Leone

discharge approximately equal amounts of water when pumping from 20 metres (Maccarthy et al., 2013), but at lesser depths rope pump yields are significantly higher. Appraisal of the technology is available using the TAF (Gelhard, 2015) in Sierra Leone.

In 2014 EMAS started transferring their technologies for self-supply from Bolivia to Africa; firstly in Sierra Leone with Welthungerhilfe (WHH) (see Box 6.3) and later in Zambia with Jacana. Maccarthy et al. (2013) found that 62 per cent of households had purchased their pumps without subsidy in Bolivia and the rest partially with loans, illustrating its suitability for self-financed acquisition.

Pitcher pump. The Pitcher pump is a low lift cast iron suction pump which follows the design of the several millions sold in the United States towards the end of the 19th century and subsequently superseded by windmills and then electric submersibles. In sub-Saharan Africa the main pocket of Pitcher pumps is in Madagascar, where they are manufactured locally. Maccarthy (2014) estimated that there are 9,000 Pitcher pumps in Tamatave city alone. The market is unsubsidized and has grown up purely through local demand. The pumps are prone to contamination, especially if they have to be primed. Pump owners recognize the risks and some 75 per cent boil or chlorinate their drinking water. These pumps are only able to operate in areas of shallow groundwater but provide a rare example to date

---

Box 6.3 EMAS technologies and self-supply in Sierra Leone

Welthungerhilfe and EMAS have trained 80 master technicians who are now organized in small business units (micro enterprises) and who offer a range of WASH services to NGO and private customers (Y. Kargbo, Welthungerhilfe, personal communication, 2019). Services offered include manual drilling, self-made hand pumps, micro irrigation systems, storage tanks, shower cubicles, kitchen sinks, rainwater harvesting systems (rain capture, sediment removal, and storage), and low-cost VIP latrines (see Figure 6.3).

In July 2016, the government of Sierra Leone formally launched a 15 year (2016 to 2030) National Rural Water Programme that focuses on addressing WASH in rural settlements, communities, and towns. WASH self-supply and a formal recognition of service delivery to household WASH especially for rural areas is now a key government programme.

The national WASH inventory (Ministry of Water Resources Sierra Leone, 2019) states that the Rural Water Supply and Small towns Strategy Paper lists self-supply as one strategic option to improve access to water and sanitation in rural areas of Sierra Leone. 'As the biggest share of the population lives in villages with a population of less than 150 people these areas will not be served by subsidized conventional water supplies in the near future. Self-supply is the only realistic supply option for thousands of households living in rural areas in Sierra Leone.' EMAS technologies are a key element of this.

Figure 6.3 EMAS promotional material showing basic household water and sanitation technologies: rainwater harvesting with underground water storage tank; a manual pump to lift water to a small elevated tank for a shower and washing sink; and a ventilated latrine
Source: J. Buchner, EMAS, 2010

Photo 6.14 Kickstart treadle pump
Source: Photo Kickstart

of a sizeable market for a 'home-grown' pump technology which operates totally without subsidy, and for which owners are prepared to pay for a replacement when necessary.

Treadle pump. The treadle pump is a large discharge suction pump, using pedal power (see Photo 6.14). It was introduced in Bangladesh for rice irrigation and helped over a million small famers out of poverty. In Africa over 350,000 pumps have been sold mostly for irrigation (Kickstart, 2019) often sited out in the fields. It is not sold primarily for domestic use, as it operates on open wells and requires priming, and is very open to contamination. However, it forms an ideal household investment in moving upwards from subsistence farming which can enable families to improve their domestic supply.

The four pump types – rope, EMAS, Pitcher, and treadle – are low-cost, locally manufactured, and have distinguishing features (see Table 6.5), which suit each to particular situations. Each represents a starter-level pump from which owners can progress to mechanized ones (see Box 6.4).

The EMAS is most versatile for domestic use, the rope pump provides largest volumes for irrigation with low gravity storage, while the treadle pump can provide a good volume of water for sprinkler and hosepipe irrigation under pressure. The rope and treadle pumps form entry-level investments to move

Table 6.5 Summary of starter level handpump design characteristics affecting customer choice

Characteristic	Rope pump	EMAS pump	Pitcher pump	Treadle pump
Height of water lift	>30 metres	>30 metres	7 metres	7 metres
Flow	High <20 metres lift	Moderate	Moderate	High
Forwards water under pressure	No	Yes	No	Yes
Sealed	Partially[1]	Yes	Partially[1]	No
Robustness	High	Moderate	High	High
Cost (US$)	80–150	30–45	35–100	70–170
Main extent for household use in sub-Saharan Africa	Ethiopia, Tanzania, Malawi, Zambia, Senegal, Niger	Sierra Leone, Zambia	Madagascar	Kenya, Zambia, Senegal, Mali, Nigeria, Niger, Burkina Faso etc.
Cost information source	Maccarthy, 2014	Maccarthy, 2014	Maccarthy, 2014	Kickstart, 2019

Note: [1] Dependent on the quality of the headworks, and need to prime or repair

---

Box 6.4 Moving up the ladder

In 2012 the owner of this household well in South Gonder, Ethiopia, lifted water with a rope and bucket. In 2013 he bought a rope pump for ETB 2,300 ($68) and watered his cattle and his garden and did well in business. In 2017 he sold his rope pump for ETB 2,500 ($74) to a neighbour and on advice bought an Afridev (Photo 6.15), a strong pump for community use but an expensive one with little advantage for family use. He constructed a shower (Photo 6.16) and wanted to further modernize his house. Motorized or EMAS pumps were not available and there was no connection to electricity, so his options were limited. He is now looking for information on a more suitable next step, such as solar pumping which could bring water (and electricity) into his house and lessen the burden of hand pumping and water carrying. Local entrepreneurs, government offices, and NGOs have so far not been able to provide information.

Photo 6.15 Household Afridev with animal watering tank, Ethiopia

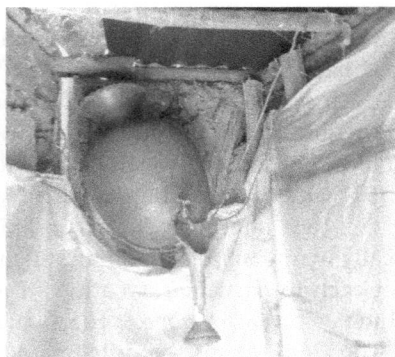

Photo 6.16 Homemade shower using storage pot and watering can rose, Ethiopia

to larger-scale irrigation, often replaced by motorized pumps as income grows. Other low-cost pumps are being installed mainly for domestic use, by specific projects in sub-Saharan Africa (e.g. Baptist pump in Ethiopia and Uganda; Water for all International, and H2O pumps for water clubs in Senegal and Gambia).

One of the major challenges is that EMAS and rope pumps have been introduced largely through NGOs and the technologies are not often recognized as an official level of service, excluding them from promotion through government services, and from subsidies and inclusion in national inventories.

Note that standard commercially made community handpumps such as the India Mk 2 and Afridev are generally unsuitable as household level pumps because they are over-specified for small user numbers and equally or more expensive than basic motorized pumps which avoid the labour of hand-pumping.

Moving on up

The technologies outlined above are compatible with modest levels of household investment. Further steps involve larger costs (see Table 6.6) but build on assets that have already been shown to bring economic benefits, which may allow bigger investment. All can lift or forward a wide range of water volume to varying heights depending on the pump specification and therefore cost.

Ram pumps are particularly suitable for households or villages in hilly terrain with perennial streams (see Watt, 1975 for details) and can be locally made for $50–500. They can bring piped water into the house and are manufactured locally in Tanzania, Kenya, and Sierra Leone. Higher cost imported pumps are also available (Practical Action, 2014). As with spring protection, these pumps are ideal for group (community) self-supply allowing incremental expansion of piped supply.

The spread of rural electrification offers great potential for expanding the market in motorized pumps, as does the continued cost reduction and

Table 6.6 Summary of higher level pump types for household and group supply

Pump type	Ram pump	Engine pumps (suction/ centrifugal)	Electric submersible/ turbine	Solar pumps
Sealed source	No, surface water	Variable	On boreholes	On boreholes
Robustness	High	Dependent on cost		Moderate
Cost (US$)	50–500	80–500	50–5,000	400–5,000
Main extent for household use in sub-Saharan Africa	Sierra Leone, Malawi, Kenya, Tanzania	All countries	All countries	Mainly NGO initiated in most countries. Markets developing

Source: Cost information from Holtslag, 2019

fast changing developments in solar power. There are major efforts being made by some NGOs (e.g. IDE, SMART centres, EMAS) as well as commercial businesses to develop and market lower cost solar water lifting. These may combine self-supply electricity generation and water lifting, filling the gap in rural services which are off-grid or where both services have weak supply (Demarco and Annejohn, 2018). The potential is enormous, and costs are falling, but not yet reaching the levels affordable to most rural households. The main barriers to market expansion in all sorts of pumps are lack of knowledge of products, high initial cost, lack of access to microcredit, and distrust of product quality as Khare and Economu (2019) concluded with solar pumps in mind. Technical and business support are needed to make higher level technologies more available especially in rural areas.

Rainwater harvesting

Domestic rainwater harvesting and water storage

The pressure of demand on urban supplies provides a particular stimulus for households to adopt rainwater harvesting. Some 40 per cent of Africa averages over 750 mm rainfall a year which can theoretically provide a household's annual needs if the water can be captured at household level, with the added advantage of reducing demand on centralized systems. Harvesting roof water is increasing as sheet metal roofs become more common but is traditionally practised only to provide small quantities of water for immediate use (see Photos 6.17 and 2.1). In sub-Saharan Africa it is rarely the sole source of domestic supply, since the cost of storage capacity for year-round use is high. Despite NGOs and governments promoting rainwater harvesting where access to groundwater is problematic (e.g. Uganda and South Africa) uptake is still generally low, averaging 1.2 per cent of households in most rural areas according to JMP (WHO/ UNICEF JMP, 2019).

There are many manuals on domestic rainwater harvesting design (e.g. CAWST, 2011; Morgan, 2015) which illustrate a ladder of progression in water quantity and quality (Martinson, 2007). The main elements after the roof are guttering, flush diversion, storage, and access from storage, with storage being the most expensive component. As in the case of groundwater, the technology ladder provides choices about where one steps onto the ladder and what further investments can be made. This can involve upgrading to bigger tanks or replicating smaller units for the same purpose (see Photo 6.18). Smaller storage is needed where dry months are fewest (generally where there are two rainy seasons in the year) but few can afford adequate storage for more than drinking water. While underground water storage is cheaper and can accommodate bigger volumes, above ground storage is generally preferred by households for ease of construction, abstraction, cleaning out, and monitoring leakage.

Photo 6.17 Basic roof water collection jars, Ghana

Photo 6.18 High cost expansion of rainwater in-series storage, Ghana

Photo 6.19 Constructing domestic wired-brick rainwater storage with cement lining, Malawi
Source: Photo R. Veldman, SMART Centre Group

Large elevated storage tanks can only be justified economically in combination with year-round input supply but are sold in larger urban areas in a range of sizes in glass fibre or plastic.

Payback times for rainwater storage may be short in urban areas, through savings in cost of piped and tankered water (Amos et al., 2016), but the high initial cost is a barrier where no credit systems or subsidies are in place. The provision of year-round supply is not usually an option for low- income households without subsidy, but small capacity systems (see Photos 2.1, 2.2, and 6.19) can temporarily free up valuable water collecting time for other purposes during the rainy season when crops need most attention and may then also provide better quality drinking water than other sources.

Artificial recharge with rainwater

Much larger volumes of rainwater can be stored in the ground. Increasing the efficiency of local recharge may compensate to some degree for abstraction, and on a larger scale for the negative impacts of climate change or incursions of saline water. The proportion of rainfall infiltrating, and of the recharged water which is recoverable depend on the recharge mechanism, hydrogeology, and time since recharge. Recharge may be by diversion of rainwater off a roof directly into a pit or well, with or without a tubewell (see Knoop et al., 2012), or by de-silted surface flow from a larger area (using a stilling pond).

The technology is there, with isolated examples of success, but research on cost-benefit or effect on water quality in different hydrogeological environments is needed, and then also guidelines of good practice.

Water use technologies

EMAS produces a range of domestic low-cost plumbed in showers, water flush latrines, and water storage (Buchner, 2006) linked to the ability of EMAS pumps to forward water under pressure, above ground level. The growth in availability of PVC/ABS pipe fittings, in low and high income countries alike, has replaced metal pipework and significantly reduced costs of bringing water into the home.

For productive use IDE, among others, began promoting low-cost, low-pressure trickle irrigation kits suitable for use with slightly elevated storage from the end of the millennium (Polak et al., 1997). Commercially produced systems cost nearly £1,000 per hectare, but with cheaper emitters or punched holes the cost can be reduced by 50–90 per cent (see Photo 6.20).

Photo 6.20 Low-cost trickle irrigation, Ethiopia

Trickle irrigation increases water use efficiency, yields, and the number of harvests and reduces weed growth and labour requirements. Affordability, willingness to pay, and reliability of supplies are all common issues challenging development as IDE has found in Burkina Faso (Krizan, 2015). Sprinklers may be used with treadle pumps, but most farmers in the region are still using watering cans, hose pipes, or channel irrigation which are more labour intensive and less water-use efficient. However unless water resources are limited and value of agricultural produce and/or farmers' time is high, there is little reason to make larger investments in higher cost options.

Introducing and marketing new technologies

The technologies discussed above may not be complicated, but they are not simple and are not mostly indigenous to sub-Saharan Africa. Successful introduction of new technologies takes time and demands investment, to develop, test, pilot, and provide training in production and maintenance as well as devising marketing strategies. This has been the role of SMART and EMAS centres (see Box 6.5) as well as more localized initiatives by many NGOs.

The TAF can assist in the evaluation of the conditions under which piloted technologies can be taken to scale (SKAT Foundation, 2013) and highlights blockages to scalability and sustainability. Affordable technology solutions abound, but markets are still undeveloped and technology transfer encounters many obstacles; the 'Valley of Death' between piloting and mainstream production engulfs many on the way (see Figure 6.4). The framework provides a participatory and systematic way to unravel the

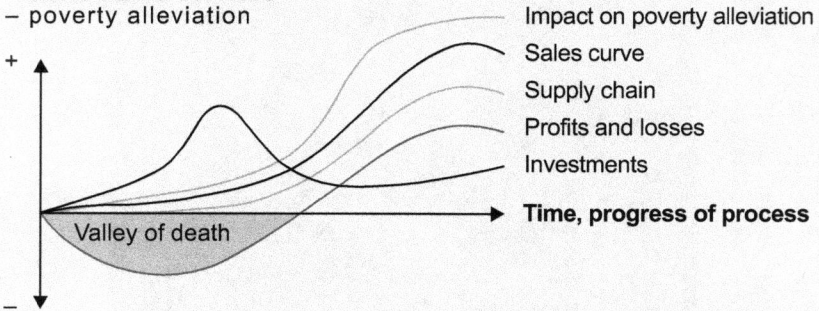

Impact on market and services
- sales
- profits
- supply chain
- sustainable services
- poverty alleviation

Impact on poverty alleviation
Sales curve
Supply chain
Profits and losses
Investments

Time, progress of process

Valley of death

Figure 6.4 Trends in uptake, costs, and impact relating to technology introduction
Source: Olschewski, 2013

Box 6.5 SMART and EMAS centres

There is an important role in technology introduction for local or national centres which provide expertise in research, design, training, monitoring, and business skills development. The SMART Centre Group (http://smartcentregroup.com/) is a major resource in sub-Saharan Africa, encouraging collaboration between the member centres in Tanzania (SHIPO), Mozambique (Grupo de Saneamento de Bilibiza (GSB)), Malawi (CCAP Smart Centre), Zambia (Jacana – see also Part 2, Case studies 5 and 6), and Ethiopia (Ethiopian Water Technology Institute), with a further centre in Nicaragua (WaterAid) and links to EMAS (Mobile School for Water and Sanitation) technologies with centres in Bolivia (https://www.emas-international.de/de/; Maccarthy et al., 2013) and elsewhere in Latin America. Further centres are being formed in Niger, South Sudan, and Kenya. Welthungerhilfe and EMAS have established a WASH technology training centre in Sierra Leone and EMAS and SMART centres have recently started to collaborate. Similar centres may be found in many countries, often linked to NGO or CBO projects (e.g. the SELAM technical and vocational centre in Ethiopia, Aqua Clara, and the Kaguru Agricultural Training centre in Kenya).

Photo 6.21 SMART Centre in Mzuzu, Malawi
Source: Photo R. Veldman

Centres build up local entrepreneurial capacity for sustainable supply chains to provide services and products for affordable and easily repairable WASH household technologies. These centres provide demonstrations of technology types and also have expertise in training of trainers, innovation, monitoring outputs, and advocacy to government on new technologies. The SMART centre in Ethiopia is part of the Ethiopian Water Technology Institute and so is ideally placed to help the growth of policy and donor support to self-supply, as well as to build relevant curricula and capacities in government technical training centres (TVETs) throughout the country.

---

potential and barriers to the uptake of a given technology and to monitor progress after introduction. It has been applied to a wide variety of WASH technologies in 13 countries and considers first the demand and applicability of the technology. If both are positive it continues with assessment of the matrix of relevant social, economic, environmental, organizational, skills and know-how, and technology issues from the perspective of three groups. These are the user/buyer, the producer/provider, and the regulator/facilitator, who then help to provide scores for each issue and identify enabling and limiting factors.

While this framework forms a good foundation for assessing the potential of a technology for scaling up, there is no silver bullet for technology introduction, and design of the process is context specific. The Technology Introduction Process (Olschewski, 2013) gives some guidelines of what aspects need to be considered in both unsubsidized and subsidized models and the tasks and roles to be fulfilled.

Conclusions

At the bottom end of the ladder, simple technologies use locally available materials and skills in order to be affordable. Despite their simplicity, apart from well-digging, they are mostly foreign imports in concept, and the mixed success and time taken to establish the technologies in Africa highlight the care needed in introducing new ideas, the continuing challenges, and the lessons learned, which also largely apply to the introduction of self-supply itself (see Chapter 9). The potential lies in the suppressed demand discovered when a range of technologies have been put in place, the widening choice of options available, and the creation of business opportunities in rural areas in which they have largely been lacking. In this light, hand-drilling businesses seem to be spreading the fastest, taken up by government, NGOs, and private markets. Official recognition of the value of affordable technologies is rare but needs to grow if SDG targets are to be achieved, especially for the hard to reach.

The range of technologies allows an entry level of access to water of an unprotected well which a family can dig themselves for free or employ a well-digger. Wells can be dug in stages and wellhead improvements constructed in small steps (see Table 6.1) to suit available household funds. In the early stages, groundwater or rainwater supplies costing less than $150 may not conform to accepted standards, but they are a prerequisite for those of limited means, usually costing less than $150. The case is similar for basic rainwater harvesting. Larger initial investments are needed for hand-drilled boreholes but a similar progression can be followed. As higher levels of service are reached, the cost steps can be bigger as household income increases with easier access to water. Moving to motorized pumps or storage (5,000 litres) will add at least $300–1,000 for each step.

Personal investment in technologies for water abstraction and water use needs a change in thinking to achieve financial returns from production rather than subsistence, and changes in microfinance to bridge the transition. The potential is enormous, but so is the effort needed to achieve uptake. An increasing range of affordable technologies is available but reaching a 'take-off' point where the spread is achieved solely through market forces seems a long way off.

References

Adekile, D. and Olabode, O. (2009) *Hand Drilling in Nigeria: Why Kill an Ant with a Sledge Hammer?* RWSN Field Note 2009-1, RWSN/UNICEF, St Gallen, Switzerland.

Alberts, J.H. and van der Zee, J.J. (2003) 'A multi-sectoral approach to sustainable rural water supply: the role of the rope handpump in Nicaragua', *Proceedings of the International Symposium on Water, Poverty and Productive Uses of Water at the Household Level, 21–23 January 2003, Muldersdrift, South Africa* [online] <https://www.semanticscholar.org/paper/Multi-sectoral-approach-to-sustainable-rural-water-Alberts-Zee/388102fa23e33c92b79d92 7452b817e0a615eba4> [accessed November 2019].

Amos, C., Rahman, A. and Gathenya, J. (2016) 'Economic analysis and feasibility of rainwater harvesting systems in urban and peri-urban environments: a review of the global situation with a special focus on Australia and Kenya', *Water* 8(4): 149 <https://doi.org/10.3390/w8040149>.

Bonsor, H. and MacDonald, A. (2011) *An initial estimate of depth to groundwater across Africa*, British Geological Survey Open Report, OR/11/066 <http://nora.nerc.ac.uk/id/eprint/17907/1/OR11067.pdf> [accessed June 2020].

Buchner, W. (2006) *Water for Everybody: A Selection of Appropriate Technologies to be Used for Drinkable Water*, EMAS, Bolivia (translated by Dublin Institute of Technology) <https://www.emas-international.de/images/technik/2006_v5_Water_for_Everybody_lowQuality.pdf> [accessed November 2019].

Carpenter, J. (2014) *An Assessment of the EMAS Pump and its Potential for Use in Household Water Systems in Uganda* [online], Master's thesis, University of South Florida <https://scholarcommons.usf.edu/etd/4996> [accessed November 2019]

CAWST (2011) *Introduction to Household Rainwater Harvesting* [pdf], Manual CAWST Calgary, Canada <https://wedc-knowledge.lboro.ac.uk/resources/pubs/CAWSTRWH_Manual_2011-11_en.pdf> [accessed November 2019].

Collins, S. (2000) *Hand-dug Shallow Wells* [pdf], Series of Manuals on Drinking Water Supply, Volume 5, SKAT, Switzerland <http://skat.ch/wp-content/uploads/2017/01/Handbook_Volume5.pdf> [accessed November 2019].

Danert, K. (2009) *Hand Drilling Directory: Cost Effective Boreholes*, RWSN, St Gallen, Switzerland <https://www.rural-water-supply.net/en/resources/details/156> [accessed November 2019].

Dave, S. (2014) 'Manual drilling in India'/Forage manuel en Inde, in K. Danert, *2nd UNICEF -RWSN Webinar on Manual Drilling, 18 February 2014* [online] <http://www.rural-water-supply.net/en/resources/details/565> [accessed November 2019].

Danert, K. (2015) *Manual Drilling Compendium 2015*, RWSN Publication 2015-2, SKAT, St Gallen, Switzerland <https://www.rural-water-supply.net/en/resources/details/653> [accessed November 2019].

Danert, K. and Gesti Canuto, J. (2016) *Professional Water Well Drilling: A UNICEF Guidance Note*, UNICEF, New York; Skat Foundation, St Gallen, Switzerland <http://dx.doi.org/10.13140/RG.2.2.21914.64964> [accessed June 2020].

Danert, K., Abuuru, D., Adekile, D., Diene, M., Fussi, F., Gesti, J., Kane, C., Martinez-Santos, P., Museteka, L., O'Dochairtaigh, B. and Tindimugaya, C. (2019) *The Role of Manual Drilling for Universal Access to Drinking Water:*

Sharing Experiences and Ideas in Madrid, April 2019 <https://www.rural-water-supply.net/en/resources/details/848> [accessed November 2019].

Demarco, J. and Annejohn, N. (2018) 'Simple, low-cost solar pumping is now a reality', in Shaw, R.J. (ed.), *Transformation towards Sustainable and Resilient WASH Services, Proceedings of the 41st WEDC International Conference, Nakuru, Kenya, 9–13 July 2018* [online], paper 3018 <https://repository.lboro.ac.uk/articles/Simple_low-cost_solar_pumping_is_now_a_reality/9593366> [accessed November 2019].

EMAS (2010) *Summary of EMAS technologies and training videos* [video] <https://vimeo.com/channels/emas> [accessed June 2020].

Gelhard, M. (2015*) WASH Self-supply in Sierra Leone: Perspectives and Options*, Welthungerhilfe/WaterAid, Bonn, Germany <https://www.rural-water-supply.net/en/resources/details/596> [accessed November 2019].

Government of Nicaragua (2001) *Estrategia Reforzada de Crecimiento Económico y Reducción de Pobreza* [pdf], Gobierno de Nicaragua, Julio 2001 <http://www.codeni.org.ni/contenido/instrumentos_juridicos/educacion/decretos/ercerp.pdf> [accessed November 2019].

Haanen, R. and Holtslag, H. (2016) '130.000 Rope pumps worldwide: 25 years experiences from Nicaragua, Ethiopia, Tanzania and six other countries', *7th Rural Water Supply Network Forum 2016, Cote d'Ivoire* [pdf] <http://smartcentregroup.com/wp-content/uploads/2017/06/RWSN-130.000-Rope-pumps.-R.H.-Paper.pdf> [accessed November 2019].

Kamanga, A., Mhango, J. and Veldman, R. (2018) 'Assessment of the functionality of rope pumps for sustainable water supply in rural areas of Malawi', *Proceedings of the 41st WEDC International Conference, Nakuru, Kenya, 9–13 July 2018* [online] <https://repository.lboro.ac.uk/articles/Assessment_of_the_functionality_of_rope_pumps_for_sustainable_water_supply_in_rural_areas_of_Malawi/9592499> [accessed November 2019].

Khare, A. and Economu, N. (2019) *Solar Water Pump: Technology Roadmap* [pdf], Efficiency for Access Coalition, UKAID <https://assets.publishing.service.gov.uk/media/5d31c9e4ed915d2fefd0bdea/Solar-Water-Pump-Technology-Roadmap.pdf> [accessed November 2019].

Kickstart International (2019) *Impact: by the numbers* [website] <http://kickstart.org/impact/#by-the-numbers> [accessed October 2019].

Knoop, L., Sambalino, F. and Van Steenbergen, F. (2012) *Securing Water and Land in the Tana Basin: A Resource Book for Water Managers and Practitioners* [pdf], 3R Water Secretariat, Wageningen, The Netherlands <http://metameta.nl/wp-content/uploads/2010/05/FINAL_tana_manual_digital_LQ.pdf> [accessed November 2019].

Krizan, A. (2015) *Hurdles in Scaling Up Drip Irrigation in Burkina Faso* [pdf], MSD Consulting, Switzerland (for IDE) <https://s3.amazonaws.com/www.dripplus.org/Burkina+Study+AK+*19082015*.pdf> [accessed November 2019].

Maccarthy, M. (2014) *Low Cost Household Groundwater Supply Systems for Developing Countries* [online], PhD dissertation, University of South Florida <http://scholarcommons.usf.edu/etd/5261> [Accessed November 2019]

Maccarthy, M., Buckingham, J. and Mihelcic, J. (2013) *EMAS Household Water Supply Technologies in Bolivia* [pdf], RWSN Fieldnote 2013-4, SKAT,

Switzerland <https://www.rural-water-supply.net/_ressources/documents/default/1-518-3-1375685563.pdf> [accessed November 2019].

MacDonald, A., Davies, J. and Callow, R. (no date) *African hydrogeology and rural water supply* [online] <http://nora.nerc.ac.uk/id/eprint/5107/1/rural_water_NORA.pdf> [accessed November 2019].

Maltha, A. and Veldman, R. (2016) 'A market-based approach to scale up sustainable rural water supply: experiences from Tanzania', , Briefing paper 2439, in R.J. Shaw (ed.), *Ensuring Availability and Sustainable Management of Water and Sanitation for All, Proceedings of the 39th WEDC International Conference, Kumasi, Ghana, 11–15 July 2016.*

Martinson, D. (2007) *Improving the Viability of Roof-Water Harvesting in Low Income Countries* [pdf], PhD thesis in Engineering, University of Warwick <https://warwick.ac.uk/fac/sci/eng/research/grouplist/structural/dtu/pubs/reviewed/rwh/dbm_thesis/dbm_thesis.pdf> [accessed November 2019].

Ministry of Water Resources Sierra Leone (2019) 'Water point management' [website] <https://washdata-sl.org/water-point-data/water-point-management/> [accessed November 2019].

Morgan, P. (1990) *Rural Water Supplies and Sanitation: A Text from Zimbabwe's Blair Research Institute*, MacMillan Publishers, London.

Morgan, P. (2015) *Rainwater Harvesting in the Homestead* [online], Aquamor, Zimbabwe <https://www.rural-water-supply.net/en/resources/details/666> [accessed October 2019].

Morgan, P. (2016) *The Upgradeable Upgraded Family Well* [pdf], Aquamor Pvt. Research and Development <://aquamor.info/uploads/3/4/2/5/34257237/the_upgradeable_upgraded_family_well._april.2016.pdf> [accessed November 2019].

Muehli, C. and Wehrle, K. (2001) *Spring Catchment* [pdf], Series of Manuals on Drinking Water Supply, Volume 4, SKAT, Switzerland <http://skat.ch/wp-content/uploads/2017/01/Handbook_Volume4.pdf> [accessed November 2019].

NETWAS and WaterAid Uganda (2013) *Recommendations for the sustainability and scalability of the rope pump in Iganga, Mayuge and Mpigi districts, Uganda* [website], Technology Applicability Framework (TAF) <https://technologyapplicability.wordpress.com/2013/10/01/rope-pump-in-iganga-mayuga-and-mpigi-districts-uganda/> [accessed November 2019].

Olschewski, A. (2013) *Framework for Technology Introduction Process – The TIP Guide* [online], SKAT Foundation, Switzerland <https://www.rural-water-supply.net/en/resources/details/546> [accessed November 2019].

Polak, P., Nanes, B. and Adhikari, D. (1997) 'A low cost drip irrigation system for small farmers in developing countries', *Journal of the American Water Resources Association* 33(1): 119–24 <https://dx.doi.org/10.1111/j.1752-1688.1997.tb04088.x>.

Practical Action (2014) *Hydraulic ram pumps* [online], Technical brief, Practical Action, Rugby, UK <https://answers.practicalaction.org/our-resources/item/hydraulic-ram-pumps> [accessed November 2019].

Rosendahl, R. (2015) *The Impact of Rope Pumps on Household Income in Mzuzu, Malawi* [pdf], Water Resource Management Group, Wageningen, Wageningen University <http://www.smartcentremalawi.com/wp-content/uploads/2015/08/BSc-Thesis-Rosendahl-2014-How-do-Rope-Pumps-Impact-Household-Income-in-Mzuzu-2.pdf> [accessed November 2019].

Shaw, R. (2019) *Pumps* [online], Loughborough University Collection <https://doi.org/10.17028/rd.lboro.c.4413785> [accessed June 2020].

SKAT Foundation (2013) *Technology Applicability Framework Manual* [online], SKAT Foundation, Switzerland <https://technologyapplicability.wordpress.com/> [accessed June 2020].

SMART Centre Group (2017) *SMARTech Catalogue: Water and Sanitation Technologies for Rural Communal Supply & Self-supply* [pdf], The SMART Centre Group, The Netherlands <http://smartcentregroup.com/wp-content/uploads/2018/02/SMARTech-Catalogue.pdf> [accessed November 2019].

Sterrett, R. (2007) *Groundwater and Wells*, 3rd edn, Johnson Screens, St Paul, MN.

Sutton, S. (2004), *Low Cost Water Source Improvements: Practical Guidelines for Fieldworkers* [website], Health Books International, St Albans, UK <https://healthbooksinternational.org/product/low-cost-water-source-improvements-2004/> [accessed 25 May 2020].

Sutton, S. and Gomme, J. (2009) 'Transferring the rope pump to Africa: A long and winding road?' *Waterlines 28(2)*: 144–60 <https://doi.org/10.3362/1756-3488.2009.015>.

Thompson, J., Bellwood-Howard, I., Gebregziabher, G., Shamsudduha, M., Taylor, R., Kilave, D., Tarimo, A. and Kashaigili, J. (2019) *Six pathways identified for sustainable groundwater futures in Africa* [blog], Steps Centre <https://steps-centre.org/blog/six-pathways-identified-for-sustainable-groundwater-futures-> [accessed November 2019].

Watt, S. (1975) *A Manual on the Hydraulic Ram for Pumping Water* [online], Practical Action Publishing <https://doi.org/10.3362/9781780441603.001> [accessed November 2019].

Watt, S. and Woods, W. (1998) *Hand Dug Wells*, Intermediate Technology Publications, London, UK.

WHO/UNICEF (2018) *Core Questions on Drinking-Water and Sanitation for Household Surveys,* World Health Organization and UNICEF, Geneva, Switzerland <https://washdata.org/monitoring/methods/core-questions> [accessed June 2020].

WHO/UNICEF JMP (2019) 'Global household database 2017 update' [online] <https://washdata.org/data/household> [accessed June 2020].

CHAPTER 7
Self-supply and well water quality

With lower levels of protection, self-supply wells are more at risk of contamination than other types of supply. Water quality can however be improved to some degree with enhanced wellhead protection, pumps, and better hygiene practices around the source. Nevertheless, sanitary inspection scores and water quality cannot yet be tied to any specific features where there are so many variables. Contaminant risks at the source and during water collection and storage indicate that household water treatment should be a fundamental element of self-supply investment, not just for household wells but for most water not piped into the house.

Keywords: faecal coliform, well protection, household water treatment, point of consumption water quality

Key messages

1. The line between protected and unprotected shallow wells is blurred. The need and scope for improvements appear almost equally large for both, based on current definitions and performance. It seems illogical for sector strategies to consider improvements only for underperforming communal protected wells and to ignore the potential of self-funded ones.

2. Shallower groundwater generally seems more of a risk, but improvement to headworks suggests this is not necessarily through wholesale aquifer contamination, but more due to the shorter pathway between surface contaminants and poorly sealed wells or boreholes. Lack of correlation between sanitary survey scores and water quality in traditionally constructed wells suggest more research on risks is needed.

3. Small improvements to wellhead protection can be effective especially if combined with behavioural change that encourages greater family focus on hygiene in water collection practices and use.

4. There are substantial risks of contamination, but rejecting protected shallow wells as an improved source would reduce numbers of improved point water sources in sub-Saharan Africa by more than half.

5. Contamination *en route* to consumption often negates the considerable investments made in providing improved sources. The detailed causes still seem unclear as not all households face the same problems, or not all the time.

6. The risk that almost all households will contaminate non-piped and off-premises water before consumption at some stage whatever the source,

http://dx.doi.org/10.3362/9781780448190.007

means that household water treatment is an essential step in water safety planning, unless contaminating practices are better understood.

7. Faecal coliform loads in food far exceed those in water, so households need to include both water and food safety planning if either is to be effective.

8. The poorest are the most vulnerable and most exposed to contaminated water, so financing strategies for water quality improvements through source protection and/or water treatment are needed if they are not to be left behind. On a large scale this can include funding through carbon credits if water boiling can then be reduced.

9. In the long term, household filters are most likely to provide consistent, improved micro-biological improvement for water consumption. However, despite concerted efforts by health authorities and many NGOs over many years, adoption rates for household water treatment are still less than 20 per cent in sub-Saharan Africa and do not appear to be growing.

10. Improving well-protection, hygienic practices around the source, water collection and storage, and promoting household water treatment are all necessary parts of water safety planning and progressive improvement, as is a better understanding of contaminating practices. Water quality should not be viewed in isolation but balanced with the benefits of convenience.

Self-supply technologies and microbial water quality

Water quality tends to be a major challenge for self-supplied sources of water in high- and low-income countries alike. The image of family wells with little or no protection and poor site hygiene has been a major reason for government and donor water sector organizations to disregard self-supply as a service delivery model in lower income countries. The alternative is to consider the potential for improvement and progressive health risk reduction, as most health ministries do through primary healthcare promotion of water supply protection and good practice including household water treatment. The water sector has focused on more expensive technologies such as machine drilled boreholes, protected wells, and imported pump technology, all prohibitively expensive to most small investors. New evidence is challenging the assumptions made 20 years ago about the performance of these technologies when Millennium Development Goal (MDG) indicators were set. It also highlights how water quality is generally of greater concern to sector professionals than it is to users and is subject to greater complexities of supply characteristics than perhaps originally appreciated.

Faecal coliform in protected and unprotected sources

Faecal contamination is of concern due to its role in diarrhoeal diseases, but also for its indication of risks in epidemic diseases such as cholera. Of particular relevance at individual sites is whether contamination is associated with the

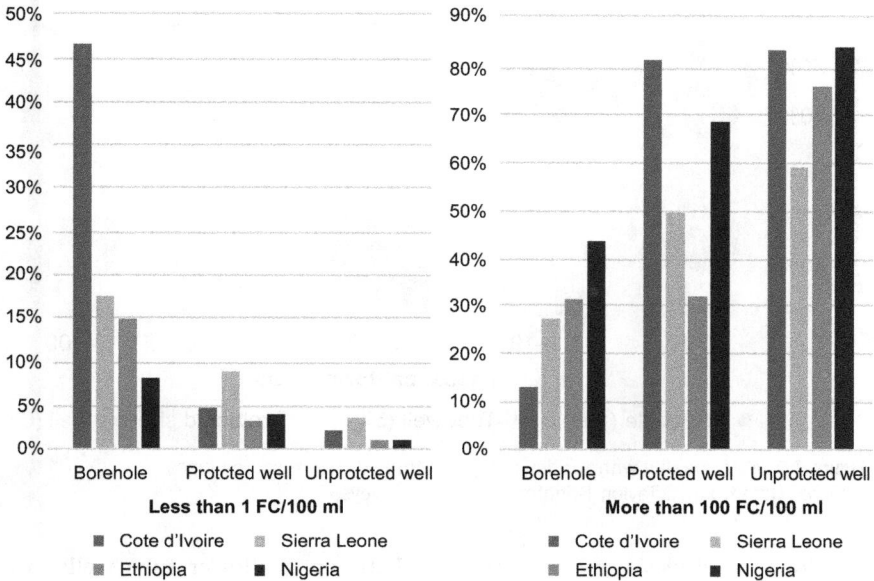

Figure 7.1 (a) Low and (b) high levels of contamination in different source types in four sub-Saharan countries
Source: Data source MICS country surveys Côte d'Ivoire 2016, Sierra Leone 2017, Nigeria 2016–2017, and CSA Ethiopia 2017

aquifer and wider environmental factors, or just with the well or borehole and its environs. Poor construction standards are leading to increased concerns about the latter – hence the differentiation between protected and unprotected sources. In water quality terms however, 'protected' does not mean safe, and indeed the difference between the two may be relatively small in some countries (see Figure 7.1) especially in urban hand-dug and tube-wells.

Risks of faecal contamination are proving much higher for all improved water supply technologies than perhaps was assumed in the original separation of protected and unprotected supplies, but particularly for shallow wells and springs. Using MICS data from countries constituting just over a third of the sub-Saharan population (Figure 7.1), water from a combination of deep and shallow, rural and urban boreholes has consistently lower levels of faecal contamination than that from protected or unprotected hand dug wells. This should be expected given their depth and easier sealing, but they still exhibit a significant probability of contamination. There are large variations between countries: 47 per cent of boreholes in Côte d'Ivoire but only 8 per cent in Nigeria were found with no detectable faecal coliform. Around 10 per cent of boreholes are commonly highly contaminated (>100 faecal coliform/100 ml) in Côte d'Ivoire; in Nigeria this is more than 40 per cent. Some of the difference may be due to different standards of siting, construction, and completion and some, mainly in urban settings, due to aquifer contamination.

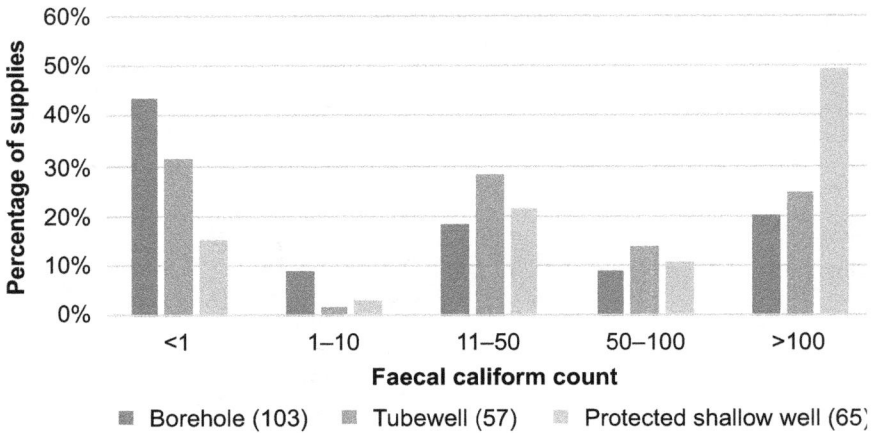

Figure 7.2 Water quality with Afridev pumps on three different source types
Source: Data from H. Taylor, Brighton University surveys

When boreholes were differentiated between shallower tube wells and deeper mechanically drilled boreholes in a small study in Malawi (Figure 7.2), rural tube wells appeared more vulnerable to contamination than mechanically drilled boreholes but less vulnerable than protected wells (data from Taylor et al., 2012).

How much is due to quality of seal against very localized infiltration or to more widespread vulnerability of shallower aquifer layers is not always clear. Aquifer contamination is indicated by fairly constant year-round elevated levels of faecal coliform with no period without detectable coliform. It is linked to localized sources of pollution (e.g. latrines, sewers, *kraals*, manure spreading) and depends on factors such as vertical separation between contaminant source and water table, formation type and vertical and horizontal transmissivity, rates of abstraction/drawdown, and age of contaminant source. Among scattered housing, aquifer (as opposed to source) contamination appears to be relatively rare, increasing in frequency in denser housing. Recommended distances between latrines and wells or boreholes vary widely (10–75 metres) based on studies in different hydrogeological conditions and on whether source of contamination was confirmed by water chemistry (Graham and Polizotto, 2013).

The overall low performance of 'improved' sources, especially protected wells, revealed by the MICS surveys indicates a need to find ways to improve performance for all these water points, not just for unimproved supplies. The Ugandan Ministry of Water and Environment recently placed a moratorium on the construction of new protected dug wells due to water quality concerns. This raises the question – should policy makers choose only the safest and highest cost technologies and so reach fewer people? Or would greater benefits be gained by incrementally improving the performance of all common technologies, since not even treated piped supplies can be

guaranteed to provide safe water? Such decision-making has crucial consequences for self-supply. Water quality associated with self-supply will always
tend to be less good than public supply (see Chapter 3, 'Growing awareness
of the higher risks of self-supply') but can often be improved at low cost.
The greater water quality risks need to be weighed against other advantages
and aspects of performance (see Chapter 9).

Incremental improvement/progressive risk reduction

Where contamination is local to the water source, incremental improvements
to wellhead construction and behaviour change appear to significantly reduce
health risks. Monitoring in Zimbabwe, Zambia, and Ethiopia has shown how
low-cost modifications to wells and site hygiene can lead to overall water
quality improvements in the rural environment (Morgan, 1990; Sutton, 2002;
Sutton et al., 2011, 2012).

The initial step to improve water quality in traditional wells is small and
without cost: stopping surface water and spillage being able to flow back
directly into the well by raising the mouth of the well above ground level
using the spoil dug out of the shaft (Sutton, 2002, 2011). Then, at low cost,
it is possible to increase the height of an impermeable parapet (e.g. oil drum,
concrete ring, or stone or brick lining) and its depth below ground level to
cut-off seepage back into the well. After this the addition of cover, apron, and
drainage leads to a better sealed system, improved further by a low-cost pump
installed in a top slab, replacing the cover.

The impact of such small protective steps is illustrated (Figure 7.3) from
cross-sectional surveys in Ethiopia, a country with relatively dense human and

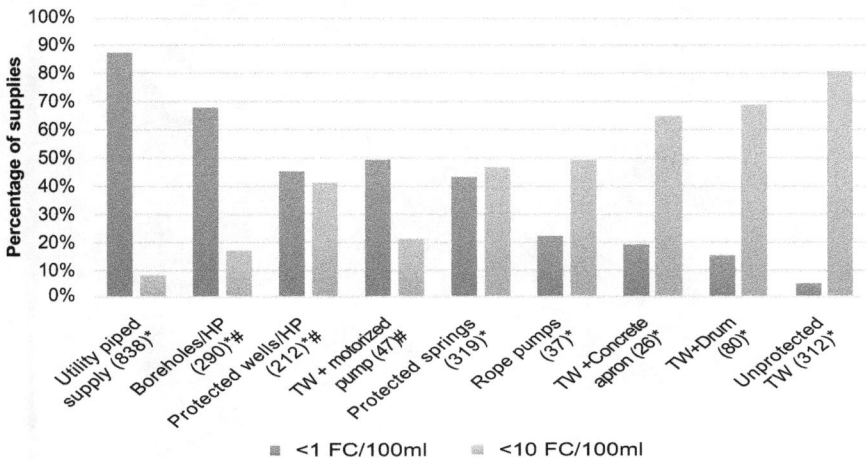

Figure 7.3 Progressive improvement in quality with higher technology in Ethiopia from
RADWQ 2010* and RiPPLE results#
Note: TW = traditional well; HP = conventional piston hand pump (Afridev)
Source: Sutton et al., 2012

livestock populations. Rope pump performance was constrained by particularly low standards of installation. Reaching a level of mechanised pumps on poorly protected wells in Oromia provided households with water as safe as a conventional handpump on a protected well

Promoting wellhead improvements and raising issues of site hygiene and good water collection practice may lead to significant improvements in quality of water at the source. Sanitary inspection scores were not so consistent in correctly predicting microbial water quality in traditional wells as in conventional community wells constructed to specific designs, highlighting the complexity of variables involved. Westberg (2011) found that a cover on a well had no significant effect on water quality and that other elements may have opposite effects in dry and wet seasons. Efforts in Ethiopia to expand sanitary inspection elements and link with water safety planning and user satisfaction (Sutton et al., 2012) concluded that much further research is needed for sources of no fixed design.

Unprotected traditional wells (such as those depicted in Photos 7.1, 7.2, and 7.3) in Zambia were first monitored as part of the WHO/UNEP projects testing the relevance of *WHO Guidelines for Drinking Water Quality Volume III* (Utkilen and Sutton, 1989) and then monitored as part of the

Photo 7.1 Unimproved household well in Mbala district, Zambia

Photo 7.2 Unimproved wellhead, Luapula province, Zambia

Photo 7.3 Household well covered but with no other protection, Luapula Province, Zambia

Photo 7.4 The well in photo 7.1 improved by the household, but still lacking a cover or drainage

Photo 7.5 The well in Photo 7.2 with basic improvements including a pole for hanging up the rope and bucket

Photo 7.6 The well in Photo 7.3 with basic improvements including lockable cover

NORAD- and later DFID-funded research on traditional source improvement (see also Part 2, Case study 6). The results for a larger number of sites (80) of which 70 were subsequently improved, showed that the proportion of newly improved wells without detectable faecal coliform (49 per cent) was lower than for conventionally protected shallow wells, but very much higher than before the improvements (see Figure 7.4). At moderate or more severe contamination levels (more than 10 faecal coliform per 100 ml) the newly improved wells actually presented a lower risk than wells costing 10 times as much. Improvements in water quality continued even a year or more after improvements (see 'Main Findings' in Sutton, 2002). Health centre staff not only advised on simple supply protection (see Photos 7.4, 7.5, and 7.6) but also focused community or family attention on the supplies, leading to the emergence of stronger management and clearer rules on norms of behaviour. Site hygiene measures included exclusion of animals and clothes washing and reducing water spillage and water ponding near the well, plus the more hygienic use and storage of rope and bucket, inside the well or on a pole.

Water quality and low-cost lifting devices

Even the simplest pumps may lead to improved quality of water in the source, since they remove hand contact with water while drawing and contamination

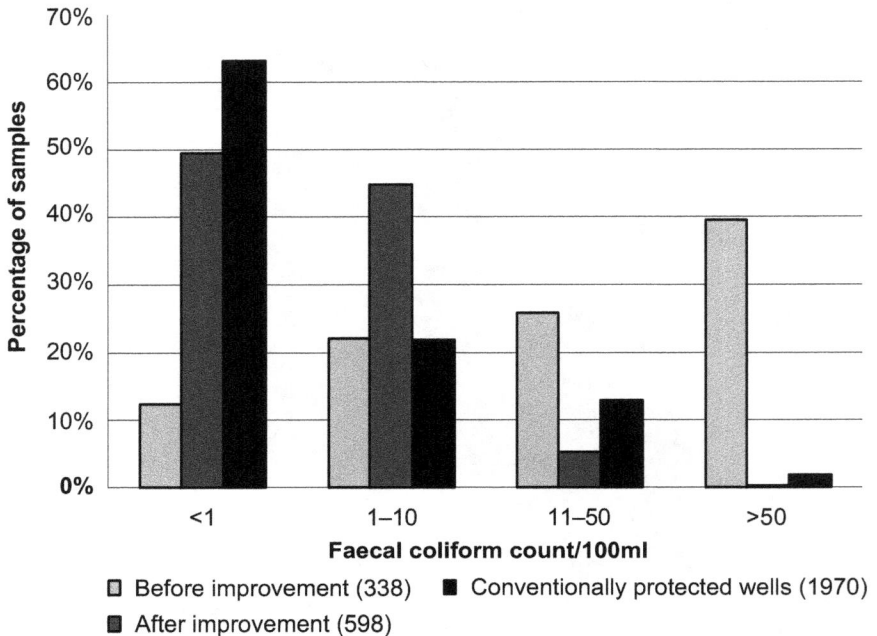

Figure 7.4 Water quality in traditional wells before and after improvement, compared with fully protected wells (larger diameter, fully concrete lined, metre-wide apron, drainage, cover, windlass, chain and bucket) (Figures in parentheses = number of samples)

from ropes left in the dirt. For example, Gorter et al. (1995) in Nicaragua and the RiPPLE study in the SNNP region of Ethiopia (Sutton et al., 2011) found rope pumps improved water quality over rope and bucket wells with or without a concrete plinth for the pump. In Nicaragua there was a 62 per cent improvement (geometric mean).

Several studies have looked at the quality of water pumped by different types of handpumps. More robust and more expensive imported hand pumps such as the Afridev, Indian MK or NIRA pumps (often on tubewells/boreholes) have been compared with cheaper, locally produced, low cost pumps like EMAS or rope pumps (for example Harvey and Drouin, 2006; Coloru et al., 2012; Sutton et al., 2012) mounted on shallow wells. Studies by Coloru and Sutton indicate better performance by the more expensive pumps, and Harvey and Drouin postulate no difference. So far studies appear inconclusive in the effect of pump type alone; results seem to be much influenced by the characteristics of the water source which could not be separated from the effects of the pump type in these studies.

Larger capacity pumps or ones that can pump more continuously (diesel, electric, and solar pumps) may offer greater safety through the rapid turnover of stored water in the well. Sampling of 47 unprotected wells with diesel pumps used for irrigation and drinking water supply in Oromia, Ethiopia (Sutton et al., 2012) showed that, despite the lack of protection, such wells provide water that is equally as safe as that from community handpumps on protected wells. With careful management all pumps can operate without contaminating the source, but the standard of headworks and human behaviour in water collection and around the site often affects the outcome. Water quality can also be affected during repairs and with greater frequency of repairs of rope pumps, source chlorination after re-installation becomes especially important.

Water quality at the point of consumption

Water from water points has to be carried to the house for consumption. Contamination of water in collection, transport, and storage (Trevett et al., 2004) challenges a main assumption driving rural water policy in recent decades: that an 'improved' communal water point will improve health (see Chapter 1 'The significance of "on-premises" supply'). The Trevett et al. study found widespread contamination in transit, but no consistent patterns.

The biggest deterioration in quality from source to consumption in three countries with most recent MICS data (Sierra Leone, Nigeria, and Côte d'Ivoire), was between handpump/borehole supplies and the home, with a 90–95 per cent increase in samples with detectable faecal coliform. In the end the difference in quality of water consumed from boreholes and unprotected sources was small. Sierra Leone is an example where contamination after abstraction greatly reduced any advantage from taking drinking water from better protected sources. Only sachet water almost retained its original quality (see Figure 7. 5). In terms of providing safe water at the point of consumption, these surveys illustrate the need for safe transport and storage and that investment in costly hand pumps and boreholes can be largely wasted if there is no awareness and action to avoid further contamination before consumption. The results also call into question the main reason for neglecting self-supply: the assumed much poorer quality of water at point of consumption. Another consideration is that if contamination of water is so widespread, then contamination of food is likely to be even more common

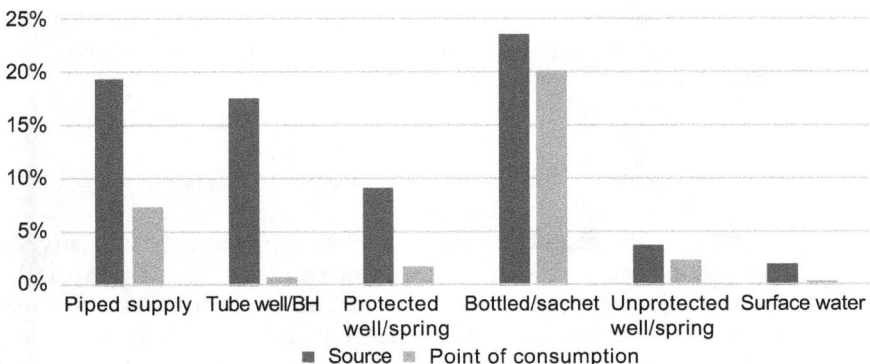

Figure 7.5 Proportion of water samples without detectable faecal coliform at source and at point of consumption in Sierra Leone

Water quality difference	Mali	Zambia	Mozambique	Ethiopia
A. Water quality in traditional sources (FCC/100 ml)				

B. Point of consumption water quality comparative to traditional source			
Level of change	Mali	Zambia	Mozambique	Ethiopia
Far worse (>100 FC/100 ml increase)	2%	3%	17%	21%
Moderate increase	3%	14%	38%	26%
(10–100 FC/100 ml)				
Slight increase	8%	18%	14%	15%
(1–10 FC/100 ml)				
No change	77%	36%	22%	26%
Better (1–50 FC/100 ml reduction)	8%	22%	9%	12%
Number of samples	130	224	70	155
Source of raw data/year of data collection	WaterAid/ Ministry of Health/2007	Department of Water Affairs/2000	WaterAid/2011	IRC RiPPLE surveys/2011
All water quality analysis personnel trained and supervised by Ministry of Health central laboratories.				

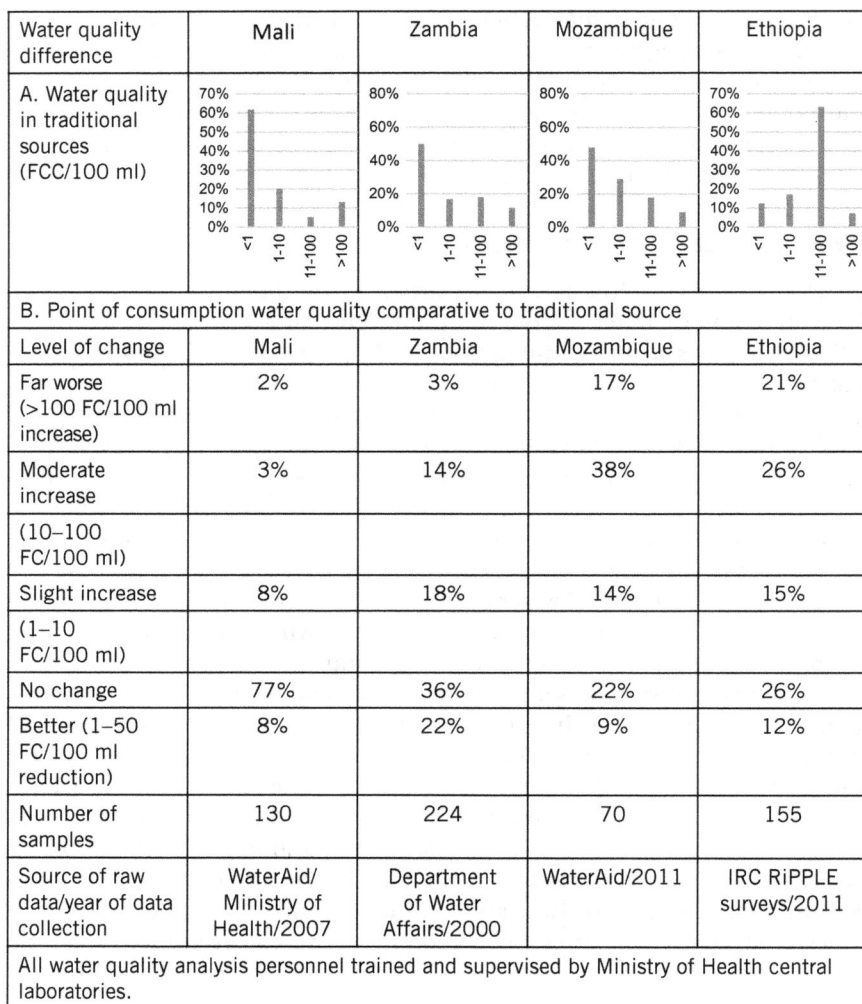

Figure 7.6 Point of consumption water quality relative to source water in four countries
Note: Top graphic section shows distribution of water quality in source water. The table below shows changes at point of consumption.

and with higher faecal coliform loads. Water safety plans and food safety plans need to go hand-in-hand for optimal impact.

MICS summary data combines rural and urban supplies, but other surveys comparing water quality at source and point of consumption in sparsely populated rural areas alone, in different cultures, and with or without sizeable livestock populations show that in 30–85 per cent of 579 sampled households water quality improved or remained the same (see Figure 7.6). Source water quality (see top section of Figure 7.6) can be carried through to point of consumption, but contamination in transit and storage is complicated, and not easily predictable or consistent.

These results suggest a major need for research into differences in practice and behaviour of households that do and don't sustain water quality consistently or sporadically. The MICS data also shows that the poor are consistently more exposed to bad quality water than the better-off, and they are also less likely to be able to afford to treat their drinking water. Identifying and promoting effective changes in behaviour therefore becomes doubly important.

While behavioural changes and improved construction practices may play a part, results from protected and unprotected sources and from point of consumption suggest that almost all water carried to the home risks being contaminated at some time and that therefore in the long term household water treatment is essential if safe water is to be achieved.

Water treatment and safe storage for self-supply[1]

Impacts of household water treatment

In addition to improving the protection and management of self-supply facilities, household water treatment offers a means for households to invest in water quality improvements at the point of consumption. Sources of more detailed information include:

- International Network on Household Water Treatment and Safe Storage, initiated by WHO/UNICEF, with updated information on technologies and best practice (WHO, 2019a).
- Centre for Affordable Water and Sanitation Technologies (CAWST) database on products and technologies (CAWST, 2019).
- Swiss Federal Institute of Aquatic Science and Technology (Eawag) and École Polytechnique Fédérale de Lausanne (EPFL), comprehensive online course on household water treatment and safe storage (HWTS) (Eawag/EPFL, 2019).

To guide technology selection and certification, the WHO has established an international scheme that evaluates the microbial performance of different technologies and identifies products failing to meet the scheme's minimum standard (WHO, 2016, 2019b). Those deemed adequate household treatment options relevant in the context of self-supply can be grouped into four categories: boiling, chemical disinfection, household water filters, and solar disinfection. Overall, the use of household water treatment technologies is relatively low, especially in sub-Saharan Africa where less than 20 per cent of households report regularly and adequately treating drinking water. Boiling is the most common adequate method, followed by chemical disinfection, filtration, and solar disinfection (Figure 7.7). Uptake so far tends to show that for many families, household water treatment is not affordable or not a priority.

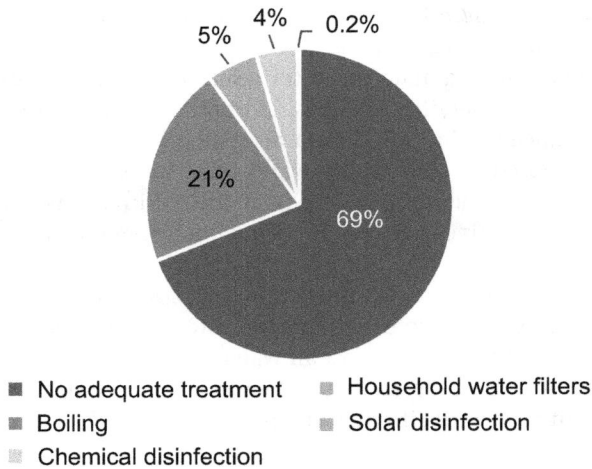

Figure 7.7 Estimated use of household water treatment
Source: Global figures based on 67 national surveys (Rosa and Clasen, 2010); sub-Saharan figures based on national surveys (MICS/DHS 2009-2017) of 75 per cent of the regional population

The Cochrane review on the impact of household water treatment methods (Clasen et al., 2015), based on a meta-analysis of 55 studies, concluded that household water treatment interventions are likely to reduce the prevalence of diarrhoea in adults and children (results summarized in Table 7.1), but there is ongoing debate about effectiveness because most included trials were not blinded, and those that were did not find a statistically significant health effect (see also Wolf et al., 2018). In order to reduce the prevalence of diarrhoea, treatment options have to be used consistently and correctly and need to be effective in removing pathogens. Larger health effects are reported for treatment products that include a safe storage container (WHO, 2011; Brown and Clasen, 2012; Clasen et al., 2015). Likely reasons for the limited health impact in some interventions are low adherence (e.g. consumption of untreated water outside household-setting, water treatment only performed when someone is sick), technologies that are ineffective or incorrectly used (e.g. inadequate dosing), or pathogen pathways other than drinking water (particularly food) that diminish the potential health effects in certain settings.

Treatment methods

Overall, household water filters are the most promising technology group, especially if chlorination at the point of delivery for a bigger number of households is not feasible. Water filters have been shown to be effective in reducing diarrhoea and are usually preferred by end users due to the ease of use. Some 10 million people are using a household water filter in sub-Saharan Africa, but there is no indication from MICS/DHS surveys that this number has

Table 7.1 Selected HWTS technologies and products (boiling water was not included in the review)

Method	Product group/Local availability[1]	Price range[2]	Treatment efficiency - WHO testing scheme[3] (WHO, 2016, 2019b)	Health impact - Cochrane review (Clasen et al., 2015)
Household water filters	Ceramic candle filters and ceramic pot filters (L/I)	**Product costs:** US$15 to 40 for one filter **Operating costs:** $8 per HH per year	Targeted protection, limited performance for virus removal (SPOUTS Water Purifaaya Filter, Nazava Water Filters and Tulip Table Top Water Filter)	Reduce diarrhoea by around half
	Membrane filters (I)	**Product costs:** $40 to 100 for one filter **Operating costs:** $20 per HH per year	Comprehensive protection (Lifestraw filters); targeted protection with limited performance for virus removal (Uzima filter UZ-1)	
	Biosand filters (L)	**Product costs:** $25 to 50 for one filter **Operating costs:** $5 per HH per year	Variable and limited performance for bacteria and virus removal (WHO, 2011). Not assessed by WHO scheme	
Chemical disinfection (point-of-use)	Liquid chlorine (L/I)	**Product costs:** $0.10 to 0.30 to treat 1,000 L water **Operating costs:** $4 per HH per year	Targeted protection, limited performance for protozoa removal (H2gO Purifier and WATA-Standard™)	Reduce diarrhoea by around one-quarter
	Chlorine tablets (I)	**Product costs:** $1.50 to 3.00 to treat 1,000 L water **Operating costs:** $10 per HH per year	Targeted protection, limited performance for protozoa removal (Aquatabs® and Oasis Water Purification Tablets)	
	Chlorine powder combined with coagulant (I)	**Product costs:** $5 to 10 to treat 1,000 L water **Operating costs:** $57 per HH per year	Comprehensive protection (Aquasure Tab10 and P&G™ Purifier of Water)	
Chemical disinfection (point-of-collection)	Chlorine dispenser (L/I)	**Product costs:** $50 to 100 for dispenser hardware **Operating costs:** $3 per HH per year[4]	Targeted protection for liquid chlorine, limited performance for protozoa removal. Based on performance of liquid chlorine	Insufficient evidence to determine impact on reducing diarrhoea

(Continued)

Table 7.1 Continued

Method	Product group/Local availability[1]	Price range[2]	Treatment efficiency - WHO testing scheme[3] (WHO, 2016, 2019b)	Health impact - Cochrane review (Clasen et al., 2015)
	Water tank with in-line chlorination (L/I)	**Product costs:** various **Operating costs:** $3 per HH per year[4]	Targeted protection, limited performance for protozoa removal (Aquatabs Flo)	
Solar disinfection	SODIS (L)	**Product costs:** $0 **Operating costs:** $1 per HH per year	Targeted protection, limited performance for virus removal. Based on performance of WADI	Reduce diarrhoea by around a third
	SODIS/ WADI (L/I)	**Product costs:** $15 to 25 **Operating costs:** $3 per HH per year	Targeted protection, limited performance for virus removal (WADI)	

[1] L = Usually locally manufactured, L/I = usually some spare parts or consumables imported, I = Usually imported.
[2] 'Product costs' indicate typical retail prices for products (providing safe storage) in the African market. 'Operating costs' indicate average annual costs per household (c. 20 litres of drinking water per day) over 10 years.
[3] Protection refers to the specific tested product (indicated in brackets) and may not apply to all similar products.
[4] Assumed to be used by 25 households.

increased significantly in the 10 years to 2016. Interventions largely remain project based. Nevertheless, there is an increasing and promising trend towards commercial approaches led by private sector actors and by those organizations using carbon credits to fund water treatment methods to replace boiling and so reduce carbon emissions (Summers et al., 2015).

Boiling water remains the most popular method of treating water globally and within the sub-Saharan region. It is less recommended because of the serious health impacts from indoor air pollution if water is boiled inside the house using solid fuels, the absence of protection from recontamination, and the negative environmental impacts. Solar disinfection is more environmentally friendly and has been promoted for more than three decades but interventions largely remain at project level and further proof is needed that it can be scaled up to play an effective and more important role.

Chlorine products and bleach are widely promoted by governments and distributed for free in emergencies to treat water (e.g. during a cholera outbreak) both for chlorination of sources and use in the household. However, consistent use in non-emergency situations remains low despite relatively wide availability. Chlorination at the point of delivery developed for communal water supply is one of the lowest cost treatment methods and recent evidence suggests that it can achieve high uptake and reduce diarrhoea (Pickering et al., 2019), but requires efficient management. Modifications are needed for self-supply to a small number of households and its effectiveness is dependent on low turbidity, which is not available from some unlined wells or those with little depth of water.

Upscaling has been challenged by a number of factors. In many locations clear water is considered safe and so not in need of treatment. Relatively high capital costs (e.g. household water filters) can deter households but free distribution can undermine the development of sustainable markets. Another challenge is the establishment of sustainable distribution channels, especially to remote rural areas: some products are difficult to transport (e.g. biosand filters), some include breakable spare parts (e.g. ceramic pot filters), and others have a limited shelf life (e.g. liquid chlorine). The importation of goods can be challenging due to a lack of foreign currency and thus products that can (partly) be manufactured locally become more favourable.

Water treatment recommendations

The right combination of self-supply and water treatment technologies can provide safe water and eliminate drinking water as a potential pathway for pathogens. However, emphasis needs to be given to effective treatment options, high adherence, reliable supply, and suitable financing models. Behaviour change needs to be triggered to sustain consistent and correct use of household water treatment technologies. Commercial approaches might be promoted to ensure reliable supply of replacement products and spare parts. Locally adapted financing models that allow low-income households to purchase treatment products might be based on revolving funds, phased payments or smart subsidies for the most vulnerable. To complement self-financed water supplies, governments and development partners are encouraged to facilitate private sector marketing of household water filters. In community supplies, low-cost chlorination systems at point of delivery are recommended. To allow assessment and improvements, sample surveys of microbiological water quality at point of use are recommended as part of any water supply intervention (WHO, 2012).

Conclusion

The aim of Sustainable Development Goal (SDG) 6.1 is to provide safe water for all. However, it seems that the vulnerability of systems requires consumers to have the same priorities as sector professionals for water quality, but even though knowledge of water quality issues is high, practice tends to relate more to aspects of convenience of access and cost. With differing consumer and professional perspectives, the difference in microbiological quality of water from protected and unprotected hand-dug wells at the point of consumption does not seem to justify the two or three orders of magnitude difference in cost implied between a community-protected lined well and a traditional protected well, or it suggests that definitions are inadequate to indicate the relative risk. Should protected shallow wells therefore continue to count as an improved supply for SDG 6.1? If yes, should not funding for protection of unimproved wells be regarded in the same light as funding for new shallow wells? If no, this has big implications for improved water supply coverage, since improved shallow hand-dug wells constitute almost half (47 per cent of 88,000) of all 'improved' community water points with handpumps (WPDex, 2019). A significant proportion of self-supplied groundwater sources (56 per cent in rural areas and 86 per cent in urban areas) qualify as improved in MICS surveys (see Tables 3.1 and 4.1). Removing all these protected shallow wells from the 'improved' category would very significantly reduce stated coverage with at least basic water supplies.

Studies on small improvements to well protection and site hygiene suggest that water quality can be improved where contamination is site specific, not widespread within the aquifer itself. It may also be possible for behavioural change to reduce contamination during collection and transport of water, but risk factors are at present little understood. Contamination may be sporadic but it is a constant risk, so household water treatment is the only way to ensure safe water. Its adoption by households on a regular basis is still, at a low level (<20 per cent) and appears not to be rising despite many attempts to promote it. Household water filters offer the best option, with chlorination for emergency back-up. Belt and braces approaches are still needed in aiming for safe water for all.

Note

1. This section was written by Lars Osterwalder, water quality consultant for IRC.

References

Brown, J. and Clasen, T. (2012) 'High adherence is necessary to realize health gains from water quality interventions', *PLoS One* 7(5): e36735 <http://dx.doi.org/10.1371/journal.pone.0036735>.

CAWST (2019) 'HWTS Products and technology database' [online], CAWST <https://www.hwts.info/products-technologies> [accessed 12 November 2019].

Clasen, T., Alexander, K., Sinclair, D., Boisson, S., Peletz, R., Chang, H., Majorin, F. and Cairncross, S. (2015) 'Interventions to improve water quality for preventing diarrhoea', *Cochrane Database of Systematic Reviews* 10: CD004794 <http://dx.doi.org/10.1002/14651857.CD004794.pub3>.

Coloru, B., Magaya, S. and Pozzi Taubert, R. (2012) *Appropriate Technologies for Rural Water Supply*, Report of Fondazione Acra, Milan, Italy.

Eawag/EPFL (2019) *Introduction to household water treatment and safe storage* [online], Coursera <https://www.coursera.org/learn/water-treatment> [accessed 12 November 2019].

Gorter, A., Alberts, J., Gago, J. and Sandiford, P. (1995) 'A randomized trial of the impact of rope pumps on water quality', *Journal of Tropical Medicine and Hygiene* 98: 247–55.

Graham, J. and Polizotto, M. (2013) 'Pit latrines and their impact on groundwater quality: a systematic review', *Environmental Health Perspectives* 121(5) <http://dx.doi.org/10.1289/ehp.1206028>.

Harvey, P. and Drouin, T. (2006) 'The case for the rope pump in Africa', *Journal of Water and Health* 04(4): 499–510 <https://doi.org/10.2166/wh.2006.0033>.

Morgan, P. (1990) *Rural Water Supplies and Sanitation*, MacMillan Publishers, London.

Pickering, A., Crider, Y., Sultana, S., Swarthout, J., Goddard, F., Islam, S., Sen, S., Ayyagari, R. and Luby, S. (2019) 'Effect of in-line drinking water chlorination at the point of collection on child diarrhoea in urban Bangladesh: a double-blind, cluster-randomised controlled trial', *Lancet Global Health* 7: e1247–56 <https://doi.org/10.1016/S2214-109X(19)30315-8> [accessed 12 November 2019].

Rosa, G. and Clasen, T. (2010) 'Estimating the scope of household water treatment in low-and medium-income countries', *American Journal of Tropical Medicine and Hygiene* 82(2): 289–300 <http://dx.doi.org/10.4269/ajtmh.2010.09-0382>.

Summers, S., Rainey, R., Kaur, M. and Graham, J.P. (2015) 'CO2 and H2O: understanding different stakeholder perspectives on the use of carbon credits to finance household water treatment projects', *PloS One* 10(4): e0122894 <http://dx.doi.org/10.1371/journal.pone.0122894>.

Sutton, S. (2002) *Community Led Improvements of Rural Drinking Water Supplies* [online], DFID KAR Report 7128 <http://www.rural-water-supply.net/en/resources/details/249> [accessed 21 November 2019].

Sutton, S. and Nkoloma, H. (2011) *Encouraging Change: Sustainable Steps in Water Supply, Hygiene and Sanitation* [online], 2nd edn, Health Books International/Practical Action Publishing, Rugby, UK <https://healthbooksinternational.org/product/encouraging-change-sustainable-steps-in-water-supply-sanitation-and-hygiene-2nd-edition/> [accessed 29 May 2020].

Sutton, S., Mamo, E., Butterworth, J. and Dimtse, D. (2011) *Towards the Ethiopian Goal of Universal Access to Rural Water: Understanding the Potential Contribution of Self-Supply* [online], RiPPLE Working Papers no. 23, RiPPLE Office, Addis Ababa <https://www.gov.uk/dfid-research-outputs/working-paper-23-towards-the-ethiopian-goal-of-universal-access-to-rural-water-understanding-the-potential-contribution-of-self-supply> [accessed 13 November 2019].

Sutton, S., Butterworth, J. and Mekonta, L. (2012) *A Hidden Resource: Household-led Rural Water Supply in Ethiopia*, IRC International Water and Sanitation Centre, The Netherlands <https://www.ircwash.org/resources/hidden-resource-household-led-rural-water-supply-ethiopia> [accessed 13 November 2019].

Taylor, H., Ebdon, J., Phillips, R., Chavula, G. and Kapudzama, O. (2012) *Assessment of Drinking Water Quality for Low-Cost Water Options in Rural Malawi*, UNICEF Report, University of Brighton, Brighton.

Trevett, A., Carter, R. and Tyrell, S. (2004) 'Water quality deterioration: a study of household drinking water quality in rural Honduras', *International Journal of Environmental Health Research* 14(4): 273–83 <http://dx.doi.org/10.1080/09603120410001725612>.

Utkilen, H. and Sutton, S. (1989) 'Experience and results from a water quality project in Zambia', *Waterlines* 7(3): 6–8.

Westberg, J. (2011) *Evaluation of the Potential, Benefits and Risks of Self Supply Water*, MPhil thesis, Department of Engineering, University of Cambridge.

WHO (2011) *Evaluating Household Water Treatment Options: Health-based Targets and Microbiological Performance Specifications* [online], World Health Organization, Geneva <https://www.who.int/water_sanitation_health/publications/2011/household_water/en/> [accessed 14 November 2019].

WHO (2012) *A Toolkit for Monitoring and Evaluating Household Water Treatment and Safe Storage Programmes* [online], World Health Organization, Geneva <https://www.who.int/water_sanitation_health/publications/toolkit_monitoring_evaluating/en/> [accessed 15 November 2019].

WHO (2016) *International Scheme to Evaluate Household Water Treatment Technologies: Results of Round I*, World Health Organization, Geneva <https://www.who.int/water_sanitation_health/publications/household-water-treatment-report-round-1/en/> [accessed 12 November 2019].

WHO (2019a) 'HWTS network resources' [website] <https://www.who.int/water_sanitation_health/water-quality/household/hwtnetwork-resources/en/> [accessed 15 November 2019].

WHO (2019b) *Results of Round II of the WHO Household Water Treatment Evaluation Scheme*, World Health Organization, Geneva <https://www.who.int/water_sanitation_health/publications/results-round-2-scheme-to-evaluate-houshold-water-treatment-tech/en/> [accessed 15 November 2019].

Wolf, J., Hunter, P., Freeman, M., Cumming, O., Clasen, T., Bartram, J., Higgins, T., Johnston, R., Medlicott, K., Boisson, S. and Prüss-Ustün, A. (2018) 'Impact of drinking water, sanitation and handwashing with soap on childhood diarrhoeal disease: updated meta-analysis and meta-regression', *Tropical Medicine & International Health* 23(5): 508–25 <http://dx.doi.org/10.1111/tmi.13051>.

WPDEx (2019) *Abstraction of data on water sources with handpumps from WPDEx database* [online] <https://www.waterpointdata.org/water-point-data> [accessed June 2020].

CHAPTER 8

Community and self-financed supplies: complementary services in sustainability

This chapter looks at the intrinsic differences between group and individual thinking and the factors which affect sustainability of supplies expressed through customer satisfaction. These factors include convenience, functionality, affordability, and organization. Understanding sustainability in terms of customer satisfaction accentuates the need to listen to the priorities and concerns of users for long-lasting change. The symbiosis of donor/government-funded community water supply and self-financed household supplies indicates that each has a part to play and that support to self-supply services does not offer a threat to community supplies so much as a way to reduce the numbers of those being left behind. Ultimately multiple service delivery models are needed in the quest for universal coverage.

Keywords: psychology, performance, functionality, customer satisfaction, gender

Key messages

1. There are complementary strengths and weaknesses to the way people think as individuals or as members of a group. These differences have a strong influence on sense of ownership and management effectiveness and ultimately on sustainability of water supplies.
2. Functionality is greatly affected by type of ownership; at the local level in sub-Saharan Africa it is highest in privately owned and self financed supplies.
3. The speed with which supplies are brought back into operation following a breakdown depends to a large degree on the complexity of management, not just the technology.
4. Community water supply requires organizational skills and post-construction support to a greater extent than self-supply.
5. Adequacy of supply depends much on user numbers: rural systems should be designed to allow for population growth and with an eye also to availability of alternative sources during breakdown.
6. There is an inequity in large subsidies to community water supply users and none for those forced or electing to pay for their own supply. However, subsidies can distort naturally developing markets so need to be 'smart' and carefully targeted.
7. Self-supply offers an alternative in which women can more easily play an active part in decision-making, and one where on-premises supplies can become a reality for vulnerable households.

http://dx.doi.org/10.3362/9781780448190.008

8. Community water supplies offer a cost-effective service to large groups, and has a yet- unrealized potential to be developed or upgraded cooperatively by users to provide a higher level of service.

9. Much remains to be clarified as to the psycho-social characteristics of both management models, if the strengths of each are to be knitted into rural water strategies. Research is needed, starting with field studies of communities in which there is an interaction between both private and community supplies.

10. Reluctance to give up existing investments means that community water supply and self-supply systems naturally and necessarily coexist: policies need to recognize the value given to existing on-premises supply and to traditional sources.

Introduction

Self-supply almost always precedes other water supply provision, and different forms of supply often coexist in both rural and urban environments. How they relate to each other depends on the degree to which each satisfies the demands of users, and so it is important to see how they fit together and what each brings to the mix of service delivery models. This chapter looks at factors in their coexistence and sustainability.

Communal and individual interaction

Differences in thinking as a group member and as an individual

Community water supply and self-supply may appear as just technically different approaches to bigger or smaller groups. Community water supply starts with demand from a community leading to response from outside agencies providing approved technologies not affordable to the community on its own. In self-supply the demand and response are both from a household or group of households which then have to decide what technology they can afford with their own funds. The differences in the psychology of acting as an individual or as a member of a community are fundamental to the performance and the long-term sustainability of the assets created.

These differences can affect the speed with which new ideas are taken up. For instance personal enthusiasm is more effective in acquisition or implementation, but communal motivation can achieve more, and through peer pressure be a stronger force in behavioural change. Table 8.1 summarizes some of the pluses and minuses of both levels of thinking, based on observations of group and individual mentality, which should be considered for effective self-supply support and community water supply sustainability.

There is always a fear that individual interests may introduce inequality and greed, implying private ownership may not serve the community well. The special non-market value given to domestic water in almost all cultures minimizes this risk with a vision of water as a common good necessary for

Table 8.1 Some differences in communal and individual thinking relevant to WASH sustainability

	Driving forces/strengths	Drawbacks/weaknesses
Personal/ individual	• Personal optimization – doing the best possible for oneself • The urge to control personally and derive the major benefit oneself • A clear goal of what is wanted in return for one's investment • Power to distribute favours to affect one's position in a group • Pride in one's own achievement • Ease of motivation/reduced time needed to respond	• Inequality – the most capable/ resourced will do best • Greed – may sacrifice common good for own gain • Limitations of what one can achieve on one's own • Insecurity in acting on one's own
Communal	• Perceived scale achievable with pooled resources • The power of teamwork • Sharing responsibility • Feeling of community cohesion/ solidarity with others • Swiss Cheese (plywood) principle that the weaknesses in one person are compensated by the strengths of another • Establishing social norms/peer pressure for behavioural change	• The ephemeral nature of altruism/voluntarism • Less care of assets, more wastage • Reduced efforts when working communally rather than as individuals • Social conscience versus selfish impulses – the latter usually win • Groups copy bad habits more easily than good • Complex relationships dependent on personalities • Variable group-wide motivation over time • Protracted time taken to reach community consensus • Individual reluctance to invest in communal assets

Source: based on work by Hardin, 2001; Latane et al., 1979; Baumeister and Bushman, 2017; Sedikides et al., 2011

survival. However, the same vision tends also to reduce community willingness to pay for it.

The best-known difference between group and individual thinking is the concept of the 'Tragedy of the Commons' introduced by Hardin (2001) in which individual self-interest predominates in collective action. As a result, lesser care is taken of communal assets, and resources are more likely to be squandered or not used in an optimal or advantageous way. It may be summed up as 'what belongs to everyone belongs to nobody' – a common phenomenon with far-reaching effects on asset management and sustainability.

Cultural norms of 'self-help' teamwork as a community, such as *harambee* in Kenya, are a valuable asset, seldom used elsewhere in the region for WASH. Building on traditions of shared effort for communal gain offers potential to expand self-supply in new directions such as higher-level supplies for larger communities. In the context of community management there are strong reasons for using the power of teamwork and social conscience to initiate cooperative projects but then to find ways to avoid the complexities of community ownership and decision-making in day-to-day running. Community contracts that devolve responsibility to an individual or individuals, whose livelihood depends on keeping the system running, play to the strengths of both.

Both group and individual thinking bring their own risks and strengths, with neither offering overwhelming advantage, suggesting that neither should be excluded, and it may be possible to combine their strengths in both community supply management and acceleration of self-financed supplies.

The intersection between community and individual interests

In the case of individually owned water supply, communal and individual interests converge where use of the supply as a personal asset is shared with the wider community. The driving forces presented in Table 8.1 make the creation of a supply by an individual easier than by a community but are counterbalanced by the complexities of cultural rights of others to share it. Conflict can arise if too many people take advantage of their perceived right (Box 8.1) to share in a well-owner's water, and there is no social mechanism in place to reduce numbers without causing offence and social disruption.

In management, community ownership has become established as the cost-effective norm to deal with group assets in sizeable villages. However, as group sizes diminish, household level management structures may be more efficient. The labelling of anything as 'community' suggests a level of social cohesion despite being the product of many disparate views and interests (see Box 8.2) but strength in numbers can be a great advantage if the numbers exhibit a degree of solidarity and competent management.

Box 8.1 Binta Koli in Ziguinchor Senegal: individual or communal responsibility?

Binta Koli shared a well at her house freely with a few neighbours in peri-urban Ziguinchor, the regional capital of Casamance in Senegal. Wanting to reduce the burden of water collection for her family, she bought a rope pump and paid for its installation. When word got around the number of neighbours coming to draw water from the well increased from 15 households to 50 as even families from further away preferred her safer and better-tasting water to their own rope-and-bucket wells. This led to queues and quarrels, disruption of her household, increased breakdowns, and a level of community unease. The situation made her almost wish she had not installed the pump. But how could she ask some of these relatives or acquaintances not to use her well without causing offence? One solution might be for Binta Koli to institute payment for the water, which could be used to help buy a pump on another well; but again, how can she ask her relatives and neighbours to pay? This requires consultation with a higher authority such as a community development group or traditional management to get their support and shift the burden of decision from the individual to the communal. The wish to benefit others is strong as is the social obligation to share water. It is easier to exclude someone who does not pay their dues or does not keep to the rules of a communal facility than to do the same at a private well.

Box 8.2 Mali: a typical tale of public and private supplies

The psychology of water ownership and sharing is complex but has enormous effects on sustainability and sharing of resources. Mali has over 170,000 private traditional family wells (see Figure 8.1 and Photo 8.1). Komi is a large village with some 80 such wells and six communally owned handpumps that were planned with the community and implemented with their contribution of materials and some labour. When visited, none of the handpumps were working. The women who were trained to repair the pumps were getting tired of doing so, since they cannot see who is causing the frequent breakdowns and have difficulty in raising funds for spares. They would prefer to improve their own wells in their courtyards where they can regulate their use, reduce water carrying, and draw water at any time. The men, however, regard the pumps as a communal asset and something to be cherished through community solidarity, but do not appear to have much understanding of the costs, often just waiting until some outside organization (NGO or government) includes them in a rehabilitation programme. Paying for water as a communal asset is not well accepted here, and the views of men and women in the community are not necessarily harmonized. Yet the cost of private ownership is accepted and regarded as affordable, so families may invest hundreds of dollars in private supplies when they appear unable, as part of the community, to raise even three dollars for pump repairs. The problem partly arises from applying the same community water supply model to communities with scarce or no water sources and to those that have already developed their own as household assets with community access. It is also partly a function of differing gender-related views and private and communal values.

Number of hand-dug wells

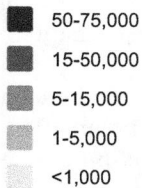

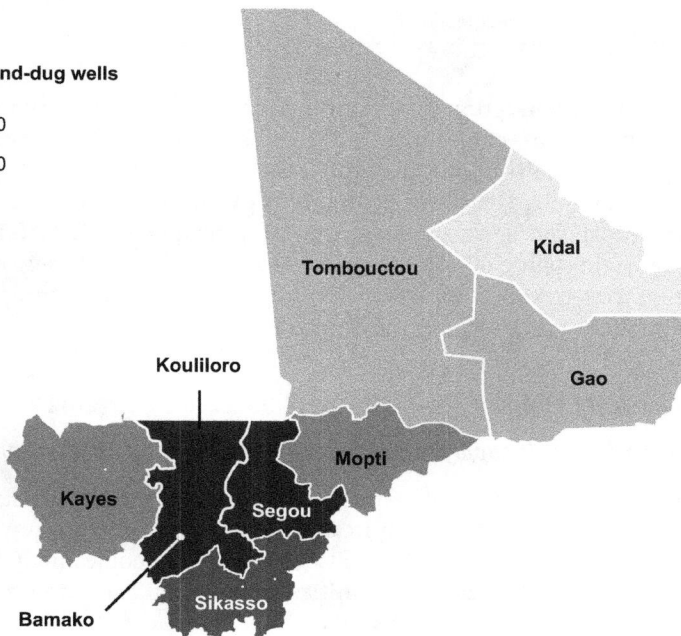

- 50-75,000
- 15-50,000
- 5-15,000
- 1-5,000
- <1,000

Figure 8.1 Numbers of wells per region
Source: DNH, 2004

(Continued)

Box 8.2 Continued

Photo 8.1 A traditional Malian family well

It is the intersection between household and community interests which is harnessed in community-led total sanitation (CLTS) (see Chapter 2, 'Supporting self-supply in sanitation' and Chapter 9) to bring about behavioural change. It has proved effective in motivation for rapid changes but not always long-lasting ones. How people think is fundamental to the sustainability of supplies and means that each system is unique and influenced by their thoughts as individuals and as a group, and by the cultural context in which they operate.

Community and self-financed supplies working together

Moving from self-supply to community supply – not a simple step

All households have some level of access to water (generally surface water or traditional wells) before the introduction of community supply. A community supply can provide safer water to larger groups of people and if the new source is much closer, it offers opportunities to save significant time and energy and to obtain better quality water. For those with access to other sources which are nearer (or not significantly further away) and with which they are more familiar or have stronger feelings of ownership, the choice is less clear cut and changes may be more gradual or may not happen at all.

Box 8.3 Household decisions on water source

Kumamaru et al.'s (2011) small-scale observations mirror something of the larger-scale trends in surface and groundwater use reflected in the JMP figures for the region which imply that the strength of feeling of ownership and convenience greatly affects the speed of transition to a new community supply. He found:

- 90 per cent of those who changed to a community water supply over three years originally collected surface water, for which there was much less feeling of ownership;
- the other 10 per cent had previously shared someone else's traditional well;
- no one who owned a traditional well moved to use a community water supply;
- four households that had used the community water supply changed to use a new traditional well of their own for its convenience;
- surface water users largely chose convenience over safety in moving from surface water to household or community supply.

Users have to make mental and behavioural adjustments to a new supply, including sharing with a usually larger and/or different group of people, being subject to management and rules, altering times of water collection, and paying for supply usage. The relationship between new and historic source use is the product of convenience, personal cost, relative perceived benefits, and habit or tradition. For well-owners it may also mean a loss of social control or status as those with whom they shared their supply move to a new source.

Most national surveys capture patterns of water use at one particular time and do not compare changes over time in individual household behaviour. Kumamaru et al. (2011) studied the history of water supply for 330 rural households in northern Zambia (Luapula Province) and the main reasons why people changed their supply (see Box 8.3 and Figure 8.2). The households were those presently using community handpumps or traditional wells in an area of relatively easy groundwater access (within 10–15 metres of the surface). Convenience was the main factor for changing supply and ownership the main reason for not moving.

Conjunctive use

Self-financed water supply is frequently used together with community supply. The combination was found in the Ethiopian rural survey data to resemble the patterns found in urban areas where alternative supplies are more common. Time, energy, and cost saving for bulk water needs from traditional wells are combined with better quality water from community supplies for the smaller volumes required for drinking or cooking. Surveys in Ghana show a continuing role for the informal supplies that preceded community supplies. Whittington et al. (2008) found that 38 per cent of Ghanaian households in two regions continued to use their own informal sources alongside the public ones for cooking and drinking, and WASHCost studies (Moriarty et al., 2012) in another region found that despite almost universal coverage, 48–80 per cent of households were getting at least part of their supply from unimproved

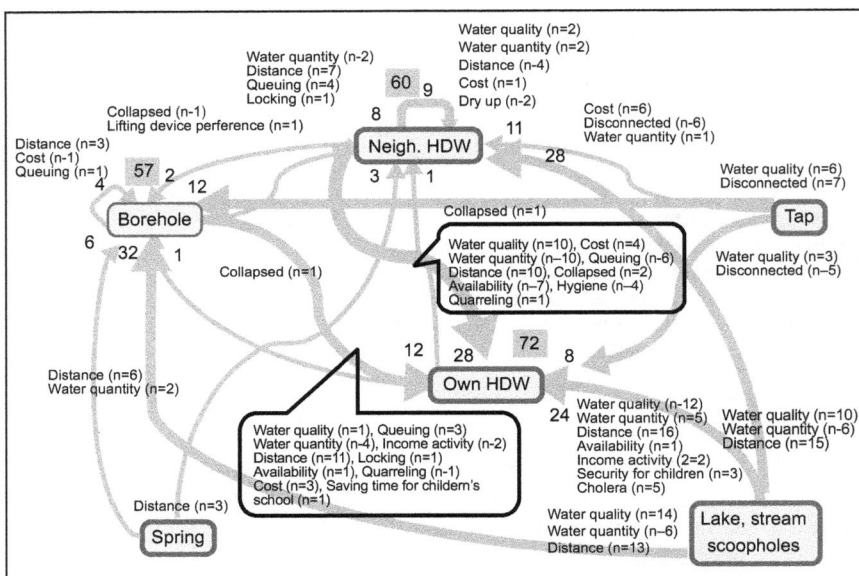

Figure 8.2 Motivating factors for changing household primary water source, Milenge District, Zambia
Source: Kumamaru et al., 2011

sources. In both studies overcrowding (manifested as excess queuing time) was the chief cause of conjunctive use or of moving to a different source whose management was better controlled. Whittington et al. (2008) made the point that while excess capacity is usually designed into urban water supply systems, the same is seldom done for rural water supplies. They found that user satisfaction is inversely related to user numbers and that informal self-supply forms an essential insurance policy for continuity of supply among most community water supply users, where 18 days is the average down time before repairs.

Informal (self-supply) sources act as a 'belt and braces' insurance over most of the sub-continent. In Ethiopia, Malawi, and Zambia approximately half of households were found to use such sources when their communal supply was interrupted. The rest had another conventional improved supply within reach. Of households using informal supplies, 50 per cent turned to other informal supplies when theirs dried up and the rest moved to community water supply. There is therefore a reciprocity in one type of supply providing back-up when the other is out of action.

Unless the traditional source is considerably further away than the community water supply for all houses, it is seldom a case of 'either/or' but an integration of the two into village life. Patterns of water use are not constantly the same but may vary from day to day. Self-supply wells offer flexibility for additional non-domestic productive use, as well as the feeling of direct ownership, so they are seldom abandoned completely.

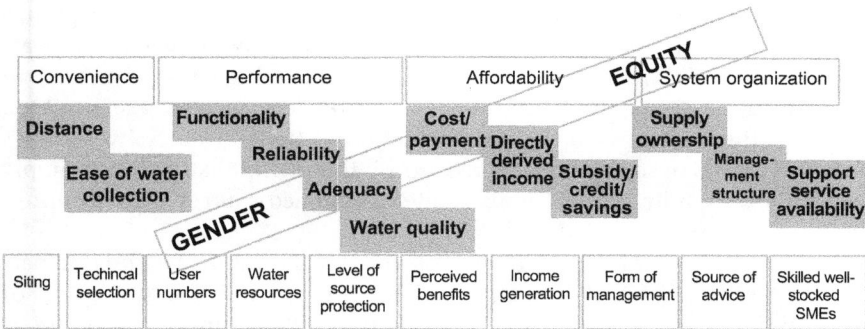

Figure 8.3 Factors affecting user satisfaction

Supply sustainability

The key elements for user satisfaction

Sustainability embraces an enormous complexity of interdependent factors which include technical, financial, environmental, social, and psychological elements. This is often summed up in terms of continued system functionality of handpumps (Harvey and Reed, 2004; Carter and Ross, 2016) or sustainable investment and professionalization in small piped supplies (Gia and Fugelsnes, 2010). Functionality is a key factor, but if a working supply is unaffordable, or too far away relative to other options, or if management is weak and lacking in support from users and professional public and private sectors, the supply may be functioning with low user satisfaction and high long-term risk of failure. From the user perspective, convenience, affordability, and ownership/management (see Figure 8.3) are interdependent and equally important elements affecting technology choice and long-term reliability of small community supplies. Ultimately if the user is not satisfied, motivation to keep the system running will be compromised. Equally, high user satisfaction is a driver to seek solutions to any problems which arise.

This user-focused measure of sustainability emphasizes the value of listening to consumers before, during, and after the formulation and implementation of solutions. It also highlights the interdependence of most of the factors identified and the dominant linkage to users' perception rather than to the aims and options of outside agencies. Sustainability is discussed in the rest of this chapter with this user-oriented framework in mind, with cross-cutting issues of gender and equity.

Convenience

The easiest element for which to devise indicators and to quantify is convenience, which has been found to dominate choice of supply. Community water supply usually offers the advantage of water at a distance which is a common denominator for all households. It improves access for large groups of households, particularly where the only available supply is further away. National standards for community water supply planning tend to be based on a service area of 0.5–1.5 kilometres radius, being reduced as coverage increases. Those at the margins of a 'served' population at these distances will always consider partial or sole use of closer sources if they are available. Public supply generally only fully replaces household self-supplied sources when it brings water reliably into the house.

Convenience in access and ease of use (see Box 8.4) depends in part on the degree to which users can choose the technology and siting of their supply. Greatest satisfaction is achieved where supply is as close as possible, and users feel they have a technology which suits their needs and their capacity to maintain it.

Box 8.4 Convenience in water lifting in Niger

Convenience is not only a question of distance but is related to effort required to lift water. The value put on easy water lifting increases dramatically with depth. Lifting shallow water by bucket is not much more onerous than by handpump, but over 20 metres requires increased effort and time. At over 50 metres, as is common in Niger, the time to lift 20 litres can reach more than 3 minutes with a hand or footpump and 30–45 minutes by bucket and rope (see Photo 8.2). As the water table is frequently below 50 metres, a few entrepreneurs have combined community and individual interests by linking a hammer mill to a turbine pump on a communal borehole and generating income from both water and grain milling (e.g. Bamo, Maradi region). The community willingly handed over ownership of their borehole to an individual and paid for water to avoid hand-pumping from depth.

Photo 8.2 Drawing water by hand from 80 metres down, Maradi, Niger

---

Performance

Functionality

Whether a water supply is working at the time of observation is the most basic indicator of sustainability. It is also linked to reliability over time (the amount of down-time in a year), adequacy (do all users get as much water as they want?), and water quality. One question is whether type of ownership (communal or private) has any effect on the probability that a supply will be working. A second is whether the coexistence of alternative supplies influences the likelihood of a community supply being in operation.

Studies of functionality tend to concentrate on community water supplies and what factors affect their performance. Comparable studies of private, communal or government managed supplies which include the same technologies for different management models are relatively rare, because few households invest in a piston handpump and few public supplies consist of a rope and bucket. Table 8.2 summarizes data from five sub-Saharan countries showing that while community supplies are generally more likely to be functioning than institutional/government-owned facilities, they both tend to under-perform compared with privately owned ones. Self-financed facilities appear consistently to exceed the functionality of others of the same technology, except in Ghana, where privately and communally owned handpumps perform about equally. This pattern suggests that management type generally overrides technical and physical factors in functionality.

Table 8.2 The influence of type of supply ownership on functionality

Country	Supply type	Proportion of each supply type still functioning			Number	Data source
		Institutional (%)	Community (%)	Private (%)		
Kenya	Rope and bucket	n/a	60	84	1,770	1
Sierra Leone	Rope and bucket	55	57	92	7,331	2
Kenya	Handpump	59	76	84	1,326	1
Ghana	Handpump	54	76	74	19,926	1
Sierra Leone	Handpump	62	57	85	11,976	2
	Submersible	37	78	90	489	2
	Hydram	52	48	90	636	2
Malawi	Rope pump	n/a	64	87	127	3
Tanzania	Various	10–41		96	702	4

Sources: [1] WPDx data export April 2019
[2] Ministry of Water Resources Sierra Leone, 2019 WASH data portal download April 2019
[3] Kamanga et al., 2018
[4] SNV, 2010

The second question on functionality is whether it is affected by other sources being available. Fisher et al. (2015) found that if there were more than seven alternative sources in a community there was a higher probability of any one being out of action but also a higher probability that at least one would remain in service. Using Bayesian analysis, the effect on functionality became less pronounced, and other studies such as Foster's analysis of supplies in Liberia, Sierra Leone, and Uganda (Foster, 2013) did not identify availability of alternative sources as a significant factor. Indications are that coexistence of community and self-financed water supplies may not threaten the sustainability of one or the other, at least in the situations studied, but existence of alternative supplies should anyway be considered when planning new ones because of their necessary interaction.

Reliability

Reliability depends partly on water resources and partly on rates of breakdown and the speed with which non-functioning supplies are brought back into operation for different technologies. The advantages of greater depth of community wells and boreholes are partly counterbalanced by the greater simplicity of technology for most self-supply in terms of reliability of access to water (see Figure 8.4). A handpump on a borehole only gives water while the handpump is working, even if there is water in the borehole. A rope and bucket can provide water as long as there is water in the well.

Reliability of self-supply shallow wells varies with fluctuations in water levels. In surveys of over 700 such wells in the Ethiopian Oromia region,

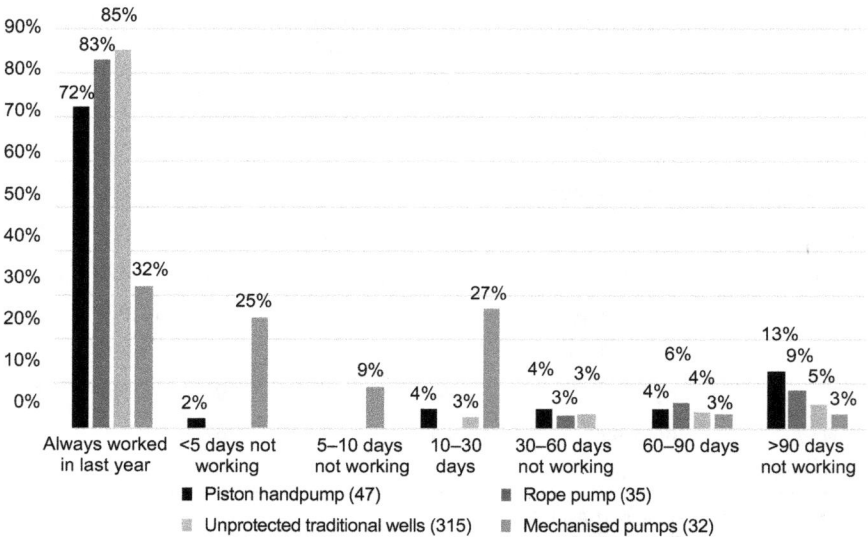

Figure 8.4 Reliability of different supply technologies in Ethiopia
Source: RiPPLE data 2010

reliability over five years varied from 42 per cent in Elu *woreda* to 97 per cent in Ada'a. The lower dependence that could be put on wells in Elu did not deter people from digging them, as reduced distance to collect water even for part of the year (especially during the busiest time in the farming calendar) was regarded as sufficient incentive for investment. In those areas, the larger the number of wells, the greater the probability of some having a perennial supply. Unreliable wells were mostly re-deepened and over half did not dry again after deepening. In Zambia a powerful motivation for households to invest in concrete rings was to eliminate the annual cost of cleaning out or re-deepening.

The much better construction of communal shallow wells allows greater penetration of the aquifer and so greater reliability but for those that go dry, re-deepening can only be done with outside support. Conversely those practising self-supply can arrange deepening and repairs with their own already proven resources and with artisans they have previously contracted.

The Sierra Leone WASH portal data gives a good picture of the differences in reliability linked to type of ownership. Private open wells and handpumps are almost twice as likely to have never broken down or to be repaired within a week, compared with community or institutional supplies. As for virtual abandonment, a private well-owner is five times less likely to write off his investment, by leaving a supply out of action for a year or more. With even greater investment in a borehole and submersible pump, the chances it will be abandoned by a private owner are ten times less than for community or state-owned units. Investing a significant sum in a supply and being the main beneficiary are powerful motivators to keep a system running and the more that is spent by the owner/user the greater the effort that is made to keep it working.

Adequacy

Adequacy of supply depends in part on the available water resource especially among users of traditional unlined wells and scoopholes, which are more prone to seasonal reductions in yield. Pressure of numbers is seldom a challenge, with user numbers averaging 50–100 per self-financed supply (see Chapter 5) and with some capacity to replicate systems if user numbers become inconvenient. In community water supply with generally higher construction standards, yields tend to be less of a problem than the greater number of users (see Figure 8.5) and consequent queuing which can reduce the amount of water collected. An average family needs six trips a day to collect 20 litres/head/day, so time added in queuing and the associated stress (Stevenson et al., 2012) can rapidly force a change in supply if others are available.

A borehole or well installed with a handpump in 2000 for a design population of 250 will, at a typical rural population growth rate at the time averaging 2 per cent (World Bank, 2019), be serving a population of around

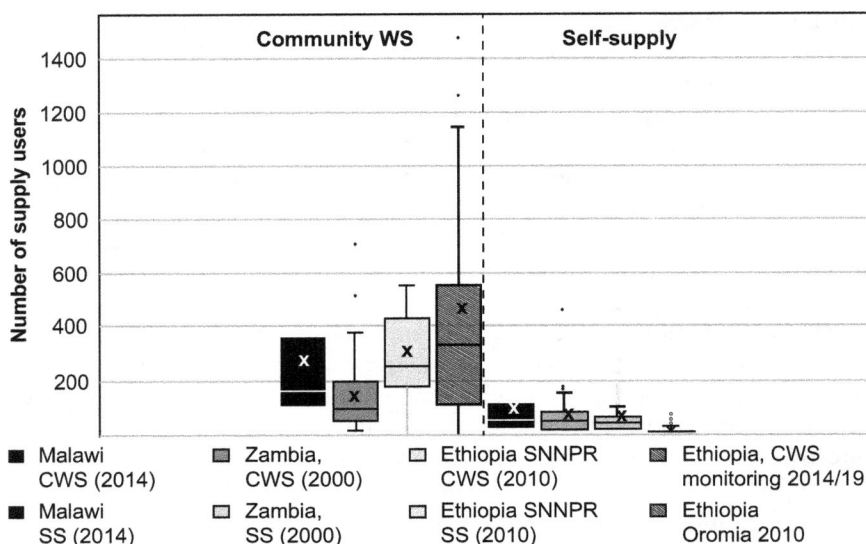

Figure 8.5 Examples of distribution of community water supply and self-supply water point user numbers

340 fifteen years later. Estimates from the Water Point Data Exchange (WPDx, abstracted 2019) show that for five selected countries with adequate data, some 39 per cent of over 89,000 point water sources (boreholes with handpumps and protected hand-dug wells) are already over 15 years old. As the design of community water supply does not generally start with excess capacity, growth in user numbers is putting more systems under stress. Thompson et al. (2001) in *Drawers of Water II* noted a big shift over 30 years from the dominant practice of using a single source to using additional sources in rural water supply in Kenya, Uganda, and Tanzania. This was partly attributed by them to the reduction in water available from the primary source because of increased user numbers and higher breakdown rates as well as the larger number of options available.

Elements of performance and user number trends mean a constant oscillation between service delivery types, each being a safety net for the other.

Longer queues and more frequent handpump breakdowns will continue to drive households to look for other solutions. Unless government can respond with provision of new boreholes or wells, these solutions will *de facto* only be ones which households or communities can afford, such as rainwater harvesting or hand-dug or hand-drilled wells. Where possible, by their own efforts, households are likely to supplement over-used community water supply, to reduce water-drawing time. This is rarely through a community effort, partly because the standard donor-dependent model of community water supply provision has tended to change community solidarity from an active process which traditionally undertook works on its own, to a more passive one which lobbies for outside intervention. Most supplements to community water supplies are therefore at present by individuals rather than groups, but there is scope for self-supply cooperative upgrading of community water points, with some support, to relieve the pressure of demand.

Water quality (bacteriological) and overall performance

Smaller (especially self-financed) systems tend to offer poorer water quality than more conventional public systems (see Chapter 7). This is seldom a result of aquifer contamination, except in dense urban housing, but much more commonly as a result of environmental site contamination. The same is true for a smaller proportion of community supplies which are performing less well than their designed levels of protection would suggest. Measures to improve protection of community supplies are seldom carried out by users because of the cost and materials needed so they await government or NGO intervention. Self-supply repairs can be carried out by owners but are seldom done without motivation from health extension workers or others. The potential to change the situation is there, but the software mechanisms (and in the case of community supplies also the financial resources) are not.

In the Ethiopian context, greatest satisfaction with water quality was expressed by those using diesel pumps, and these did indeed perform best (see Table 8.3). In this table, water quality refers to the proportion of supplies delivering water with undetectable faecal contamination, reliability to those providing year-round water over the previous year, and adequacy to those which users said provided sufficient water for their needs. Total score is the sum of percentage points as integers. The poorer water quality in unprotected wells in the wet season suggests that improved levels of protection against inflowing surface water and seepage would improve performance and user satisfaction, and indeed most well owners put improvements to infrastructure (protection) highest on their 'to do' list.

There appears to be little difference here between community handpumps, private rope pumps, and dry season performance of unimproved traditional

Table 8.3 User satisfaction and supply performance, an example from Ethiopia

Supply type	User satisfaction (%)	Water quality (%)	Reliability (%)	Adequacy (%)	Total score (max 400)
Motorized pumps	98	82	88	90	358
Conventional handpumps	91	72	72	70	305
Rope pumps	100	43	83	78	304
Unprotected family wells (dry season)	82	53	87	75	297
Unprotected family wells (wet season)	82	19	87	75	263

wells, none of which were performing ideally. The better water quality of community handpumps over traditional self-supply wells is counterbalanced by lesser reliability and adequacy of supply.

Affordability

Water supply capital costs must be affordable to a combination of the user, government, or non-government provider. For community water supply it is government and NGOs for whom capital costs must largely be affordable. As handpumps are regarded as 'low-cost options', a critical assumption has previously been made that recurrent costs are therefore affordable to users. For self-supply it is largely the owner, and more rarely the user, who bears the cost, removing capital cost from state responsibility. Affordability to the private investor depends partly on ability to cover capital costs, but also on the balance of the outgoings of cost against the perceived benefits derived from their water supply, plus any subsidy available (Figure 8.3). In both cases willingness to pay depends specifically on the perceived benefits from the supply.

Such user willingness will depend on the perceived return to be gained in both social and economic capital, the allied elements of functionality, convenience, and feeling of ownership. The contrasts in these link to the differences in ways of thinking with the gap between affordability and willingness to pay seemingly greater in community supplies, with consequent effects on functionality.

Costs

Within community water supply unit capital costs are high (ranging from US$5,000–15,000 for a shallow well or borehole with a handpump). As these costs are beyond the reach of most individual investors they are largely borne by the state or NGOs (see Table 8.4) who then have a major decision-making part to play in the chosen solution. In self-supply all the costs are normally borne by the individual or group financing the supply directly through their payment to contractors/artisans. The solutions therefore reflect the investors' priorities as well as their means.

Indirect CapEx consists largely of state/NGO indirect subsidies in training and social marketing, in much the same way as for CLTS or sanitation marketing. The lack of any public support services to self-supply creates major inequity among those effectively undertaking the responsibility of the state, either as individuals or as cooperative groups.

Except in rare cases such as the Ethiopian Community Managed Projects (CMP) model (CoWASH, 2016), where the community manage the finance and construction of their supply (see Box 8.5), community water supply divorces the user from the financing and contracting and users are rarely aware of the true capital cost, let alone the level of life-cycle recurrent costs to which they have been committed.

Table 8.4 Stakeholder contribution to life-cycle costs (for detailed definition of costs see Fonseca et al., 2011)

Type of cost	Community water supply	Self-supply	Accelerated self-supply
Capital hardware cost Social marketing/ training (Total CapEx)	95–100% public sector/NGO 100% public sector/ NGO	100% owner/ user 100% private sector	100% owner/user unless subsidy available 80% public sector/NGO 20% private sector
Regular operation and maintenance costs (OpEx)	Theoretically 100% user, in practice often deferred	100% owner/ user	100% owner/user
Capital maintenance costs (CapManEx)	Theoretically 100% user, but increasingly paid by public sector/NGO	100% owner/ user	100% owner/user
Expenditure on direct support (ExpDS) (support to local level stakeholders)	100% public sector/ NGO (in practice also largely deferred or absent)	n/a	Shared with community water supply
Expenditure on indirect support (ExpIDS) (macro level support to build the sector)	100% public sector/ NGO	n/a at present, not policy	Shared with community water supply
Cost of capital (CoC)	100% public sector/ NGO	n/a	Cost to user but rarely using loans

Note: n/a = not applicable

Box 8.5 CMP approach in Ethiopia

The Community Managed Projects (CMP) approach developed in Ethiopia puts control of WASH construction (wells, protected springs, and latrines) in the hands of the community and is being taken to scale as a government strategy. Each community plans and handles the finances, contracts, and implementation of their own WASH projects. As a result, the sense of ownership, connections with contractors, and awareness of costs (which are the chief advantages of self-supply in sustainability of services) are all built up in the community. CMP also creates job opportunities and trains small local artisans as investments for the future and to provide continuity of private sector support services.

Working in 76 rural districts in Ethiopia, more than 15,000 communities have organized their own water supply construction, serving more than 3.1 million people. CMP has also built up the empowerment of women and trained more than 16,000 people in disability inclusion. The devolution of responsibilities to community level has largely been achieved within government training capacity and funding and has resulted in non-functioning supplies falling from 27 per cent to 6.7 per cent (OneWASH, 2019). It is an approach which builds up capacities relevant to smaller groups and so can offer a bridge between community water supply and self-supply and improved sustainability for both.

(See also www.cmpethiopia.org)

Table 8.5 Proportion of users paying for rural supply regularly or on breakdown

Country	Water supply owned and managed by:				
	Government (%)	Institution (%)	Community (%)	Private (%)	Total number
Sierra Leone	2	9	1	11	16,015
Ghana	53	33	56	29	19,688
Kenya	14		45	26	1,197
Tanzania	27				8,542
Liberia	28				6,200

Source: Data from WPDx 2019 download

For most who are subsidized, the technology is very seldom chosen by the users on the basis of what they feel they can afford but starts at a technology level defined by international standards, and government policy requiring only a very low payment of 0–5 per cent of capital cost – deemed to be affordable. Payment at this level is important for the development of community management capacity to raise cash, but the community contribution is widely commuted into its equivalent in labour and materials, leaving many communities untested in their ability to raise cash. The result is that covering recurrent costs is often problematic as cash payment systems appear difficult to establish (see Table 8.5) and much affected by seasonality of income.

Maintenance and replacement costs for community water supply remain the main threat to supply sustainability. Almost all systems were designed assuming community-based management and maintenance, with autonomy in OpEx (see Table 8.4), and little or no support for longer-term replacement and major repairs. This assumption is now being addressed through pilot initiatives such as FundiFix (Dahmm, 2018) in Kenya and Whave in Uganda (Harvey, 2019), but these pilots are yet to scale up and are likely to need substantial subsidies to do so. Water has traditionally been regarded as a non-market commodity, so instigating any, let alone adequate, user payments has been a major challenge, but one Ghana and Kenya are addressing with some success in community managed supplies.

The present 100 per cent dependence on the owner for self-supply capital costs limits the capital investment possible at one time and so also operation and maintenance costs and the rate of progress up the technology ladder. On the other hand, the owner undertaking the work personally or negotiating costs with a local contractor/artisan is more aware of actual costs incurred and of costs to maintain or replicate. He or she has already proved willingness to pay the level of investment necessary during the construction and to accept all or a part of recurrent costs and often further investment costs. Technology choice is therefore tailored to affordability of capital and recurrent costs, the private sector capacity to maintain, and the owner's ability to manage and pay, in a way that community water supply is usually not. The CMP system to some degree marries the advantages of the two service delivery models of community water supply and self-supply, leading to higher levels of sustainability.

Return on investment. In community water supply, user investment is minimal relative to the actual capital cost but returns in time saving may be significant. It is rare for community domestic water supply to be linked to productive use, because of difficulties with land holding, and division of labour and outputs, plus the number of supplies which are already suffering from long queues. Return on investment tends to be a theoretical one (time commuted to potential productivity/health cost savings) as opposed to the less measurable but more easily user-perceived benefits summarized in Figure 5.6 for self-supply. Fundamentally, if sufficient value is attached to a supply by all it will be kept functioning. Hammer mills and bicycles are not discarded, and nor are most private supplies. The problem for the standard model of community water supply at present is more to do with the weakness in community management and perception of the value of supply in terms of measurable benefit than to do with the nuts and bolts of maintenance.

Most self-supply wells are primarily for domestic use, but watering livestock and garden vegetables are common and visible benefits (see Table 5.2). Personal ownership of a supply, combined with land holding, offers the potential and flexibility for increasing income generation related to water. Jacana, an enterprise building NGO in Zambia (www.smartcentrezambia.com/), is training entrepreneurs to invest in self-supply, using water-related businesses to create sustainable water points, shared with neighbours. The majority of rural families who own a well notice a marked improvement in food security and those irrigating cash crops can repay investment in a low-cost pump within a year (see Chapter 5, 'Productive use').

Subsidy

Subsidies reduce the cost of a service to the consumer. The capital cost of all community water supply hardware is subsidized directly (see Table 8.4) and the supply is further subsidized by provision of planning, promotion, training, and monitoring services. The subsidy depends on the total cost per unit and number of people served but averages between $20 and $60 per capita according to WashCost (2011 figures). A more recent study (Eskandari-Torbaghan and Burrow, 2019) suggests subsidy is now generally nearer $40–80 for a borehole and handpump. Subsidies per supply depend on government policy, local costs, and the technologies offered.

To date subsidy to self-supply is largely lacking, leading to significant inequity between the two delivery models and specifically among those who are already generally more disadvantaged in being in smaller, poorer rural communities or in poor, marginalized urban communities. While direct subsidy is generally not the biggest preoccupation of rural households, the support services which indirect subsidy could fund are seen by them to be needed but lacking. Subsidies are therefore discussed further in the next chapter on supporting self-supply.

Management capacity and ownership

Management capacity depends in part on management structure but also on ownership (engendering a feeling of obligation to care for the asset) and the back-up available from the private sector for advice and maintenance and from umbrella organizations and government/NGO providing post-construction support. Functioning, reliability, and adequacy are outputs of management and indicators of its effectiveness.

Sense of ownership

A sense of ownership is the most powerful driver motivating care for an asset and is strongest at a personal level and weaker at a community level. A 'natural leader' can stimulate group feelings of ownership in a community but they may be dependent on the continued presence and interest of the leader and the cohesion of the group.

Management structure

In areas where groundwater is accessible with traditional construction, providing a new community water supply designed for 200–300 people either means an amalgamation of groups who are used to being autonomous or providing a supply to smaller groups and so increasing per capita costs. Previously, groundwater sources (often managed by women) would have a single family in ownership or would be owned and managed by the traditional hierarchy. The shift to broader community ownership and management may alter the whole dynamics of the community, in so far as it revolves around a new water supply with a new committee structure (see Figure 8.6). Within this structure new organizational tasks and skills are needed, and decisions need to be made through consensus, which can be time consuming and cumbersome.

Supply management poses perhaps the major challenge to community water supply, shifting responsibility from traditional structures to committees. The standard format is to establish a management committee elected by the community (for example McCommon et al., 1990), with advice that women should be (almost) equally represented as members, for example 40 per cent in the case of community water supply in Ghana (Community Water and Sanitation Agency, 2014). In this way, community water supply is often used not just as a vehicle to provide water, but as a way of introducing new forms of democracy, asset management, equity, and gender balance. Developing the

- Accounting
- Tariff setting
- Revenue collection
- Banking revenue
- Transparency

- Interfacing with local government
- Setting rules
- Planning and decision making
- Liaising with community

Finance

Coordination

Organization

Logistics

- Motivating
- Scheduling meetings
- Setting and enforcing rules
- Settling disputes
- Updating committee expertise

- Contracting repairs
- Purchasing spares
- Cleaning rotas
- Monitoring supplycondition

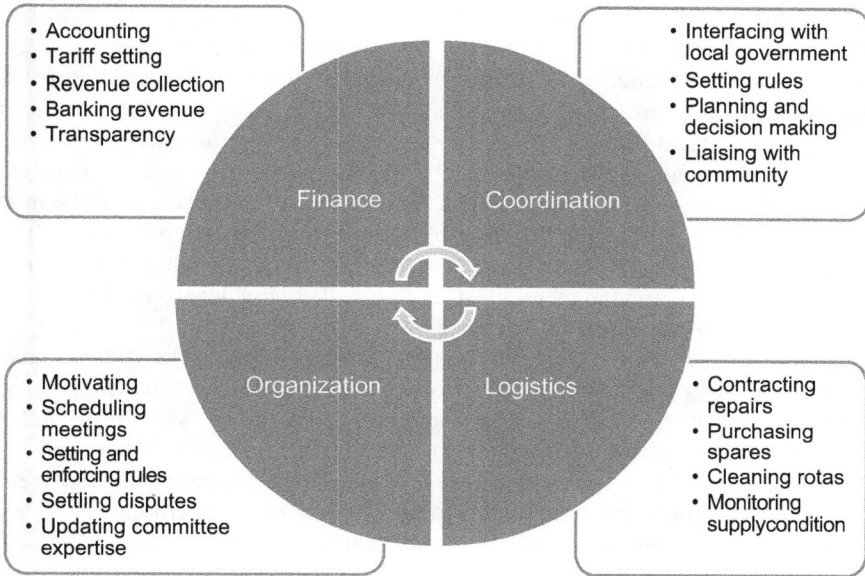

Figure 8.6 Committee management responsibilities in community water supply

necessary attitude changes and feeling of ownership and transparency for all these needs both time and support, if they are not to threaten supply sustainability and use.

Post-construction support to management is vital, yet still to be consistently built into district budgets. If support is only available for one or two years it does not provide a long-term solution unless voluntarism can be replaced by an existing well-established traditional system, or one where the individuals who manage it derive an income only while the system continues to function, which is the case for self-supply. At present the introduction of community water supply does not usually consider the different situations into which it is being inserted, in terms of existing sources, community dynamics, management structure, and experience. As Whaley and Cleaver (2017) suggest, there is a need for more context-specific solutions, which take account of local governance and of the technical/management interface in which communities seldom have a choice.

Individually self-financed supplies have the advantage of a clear management structure within the family. The functions in Figure 8.6 are much simplified since organizational aspects which require time-consuming consensus building are avoided and transparency and financial control are not an issue since the owning family is solely responsible. The women of the household will normally either organize supply functioning themselves, or where purchase of goods or services must be made outside the village or higher technologies are involved, the men of the household or relatives may also be involved. Loss of convenience or loss of water for animals and vegetable gardens are powerful stimuli to ensure the continuing functioning of the well, and within family finances it can be given priority in the same ways as for the original construction.

The rarer group-financed systems, such as in Kenya, are constituted with a board management structure which may have moved on to contracted management as in many European cooperatives or be prone to the same fatigue as many community water supply committees. In matters of ownership and finance they are perhaps hybrids between community water supply and self-supply both in management structure and, being legal entities, often using centralized funds as well as their own.

In Sierra Leone and Mali the most reliable privately owned wells have sometimes been upgraded by NGOs to provide rapid increase in community coverage without the cost of constructing new wells (see Photo 8.3). The shift in responsibility tends to produce only short-term benefits as it loses the ownership advantage of self-supply and creates confusion between the imposed committee and the original owners. Consequent problems in maintenance, management, and sharing sometimes result in abandonment of previously well-functioning facilities.

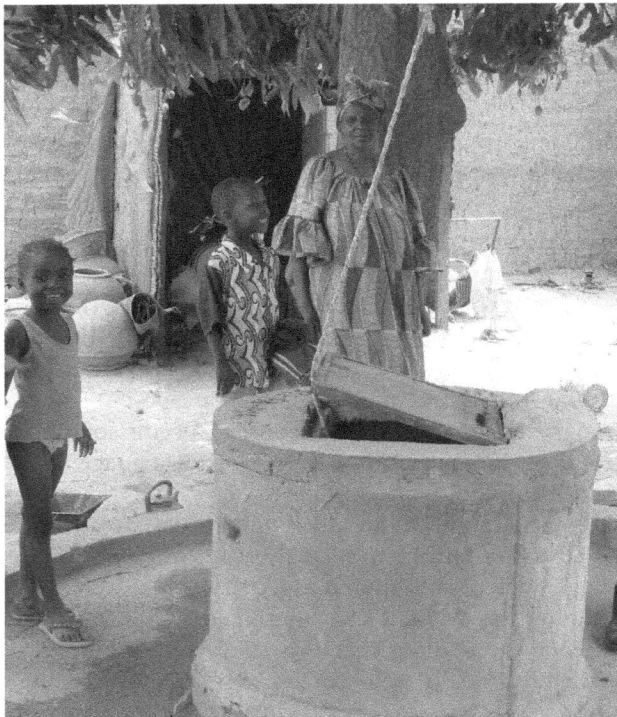

Photo 8.3 Household well upgrading financed by an NGO in Niono, Mali

Support services: public sector

Effective long-term management requires bodies providing support to those managing the facility. In community water supply, support is provided in part by government (advice, contract management, funding, monitoring, training). Group water supply schemes in Kenya, as in Europe, can call upon the Water Services Board for advice, finance, planning, and assurance of credit-worthiness to apply for loans. Increasingly, government or NGO services are also needed to rejuvenate defunct committees or provide refresher training. Management committees require maintenance just as much as the supplies they manage, because of natural wastage (ageing and declining enthusiasm) and population mobility, such as drift to towns of the most proactive, often committee members or technicians.

Governments or NGOs may set up 'umbrella' organizations researching and providing training and advice to private sector support services. These include water user associations (more common in irrigation), borehole drillers associations (e.g. Nigeria), rainwater harvesting associations (Malawi, Uganda, Senegal, etc.), and handpump mechanics associations (Uganda).

Self-supply systems receive no support from government except in some instances where government has recognized them as a service delivery model (Uganda, Sierra Leone, Ethiopia, Zimbabwe). Assistance then may include incentive-level funding or hardware, but mainly provides information on request for technical options, costs, and sometimes a directory of artisans/SMEs who can offer quality services. Here services to support community water supply and self-supply merge (see Chapter 9) when self-supply is recognized as a level of service.

Support service: private sector

The private sector provides both construction and maintenance services for all levels of service, since sector reforms have generally removed imple-menting roles from governments. For community water supply and group self-supply, government tends to provide a regulatory framework which safeguards quality control of products and services and may assist in bulk purchase of equipment or spares. Even at community supply level, however, supervision or inspection is sporadic at best and while some countries are beginning to require accreditation for smaller contractors, it is doubtful that standards can be guaranteed for either type of client. Contracts for work and purchase of pumps are not the responsibility of user communities, except in CMP-Ethiopia-type approaches and group-managed self-supply. Established contractual relationships of client (government/NGO) and contractor (driller, well-digger, pump stockist/producer/installer) are therefore a major barrier preventing community water supply users from forming a working rapport with members of the private sector on whom they will in future depend for repair, maintenance, and replacement services. Area mechanics form a vital link between community water supply and centralized services, and a useful (but rarely yet exploited) resource for self-supply support too. Malawi provides a case where trained area mechanics also install and repair privately owned rope pumps (PumpAid, 2016).

Community supplies are constructed with local government supervision which may provide some level of quality control. There is no ethos of warranty or assured performance in most of rural sub-Saharan Africa, and no expectation of being able to hold a producer or contractor to task for sub-standard works. Self-supply investors depend much on the goodwill and traditional values of shame in the community to hold local entrepreneurs to account. Hand-drillers and pump producers may belong to local chambers of commerce or local trade associations but without government support, small-scale investors or businesses have no technical advisory body or umbrella organization to call upon for advice or adjudication on work poorly performed, or spare parts not available.

The strengths of community water supply and of private water supply need to be merged to improve the sustainability of both. This cannot be done until governments recognize self-supply as a service delivery model which fills gaps they cannot fill at present and which needs their support (see Chapter 9).

Cross-cutting issues: gender and vulnerability

Issues of gender cut across all aspects of WASH and self-supply. Women have a variety of productive, reproductive, societal, and care roles, all of which are affected by the time and effort they expend on water collection and on caring for those with water-borne diseases. Having water on-premises is therefore of special advantage to them, not only for ease of collection but also for household and personal hygiene, giving women an incentive to press for self-supply (see Box 8.6). As a result, they have been the main instigators in the development of group or individual self-supply in the recent past in countries such as Ireland, Finland, and Vietnam.

In many sub-Saharan countries, women are required by government to form part of community water supply management committees, but they are not necessarily a very influential part. When they suffer from the inconvenience of pump breakdowns their ability as part of a group to persuade the committee or the community to pay for repairs seems limited. It is generally easier for a woman to be heard in her own household or as part of a women's savings group. The urgency for repair or re-deepening is more likely to receive a positive response when the source is her own and perhaps is leading to problems for her neighbours. Decision-making in these cases is a simpler affair in terms of women having influence relative to that within the broader community context.

In western Zambia women managed their traditional water supply sources and asked men to assist with physical works they could not do on their own. They also remarked that supplies close to the house greatly increased the

---

Box 8.6 Integrating a perspective on gender and vulnerability in WASH in Uganda

In Uganda early rainwater harvesting (RWH) initiatives in the 1990s built on existing women's savings groups in the Oruchinga valley to organize construction of storage for each house in the group on a rotational basis, in the same way as for a savings scheme (see Chapter 5, Box 5.4). The success of this model spread to other districts, led to the formation of the umbrella rainwater harvesting association, and became part of rural water strategy which continues up to the present (Ministry of Water and Environment, 2017). It also played a part in the country's gender policies (Ministry of Water and Environment, 2010) in WASH 2010–2015 which included promotion of self-supply groundwater and rainwater harvesting. Rural Water Supply District Officers were required to provide advice, train artisans, develop affordable technologies, and support the private sector in order to reduce the time women took to collect water. Grants of 40 per cent were offered for rainwater harvesting, with consideration of higher grants for vulnerable households to make water available on-premises. The Water for Production Department also included gender guidelines for inclusion to guide local government and the private sector and training courses in leadership for women to be more active in Water User Committees. The WASH gender strategy 2018–2022 follows the African Ministers' Council on Water vision for mainstreaming gender in WASH (AMCOW, 2011), requiring all new waterpoints to have access ramps for the disabled and moving on to promotion of piped water into the home in rural areas.

---

degree to which men took day-to-day interest in the supply and were prepared to draw water.

While women have less access to formal credit and savings schemes, they may have more access to traditional ones. In Ghana for instance, twice as many women as men use savings and loans schemes, and three times as many used 'susu' saving schemes (ROSCA) (Ghana Living Standards survey 2017), giving them some flexibility to pay for those things to which they give priority.

Water supply may be the province of women, but management and maintenance require women's voices to be heard and responded to alongside the complementary roles of both men and women in household and community settings.

Constructing facilities at household level makes it possible to focus subsidies on the poorest and most vulnerable and particularly those households which have difficulty in accessing or transporting water to the house. These may be rainwater harvesting or groundwater solutions geared to disability as in Uganda (Box 8.6). To date the commonest response is that well-owners share their water for free with the most vulnerable even if they charge others (e.g. among many Muslim communities in peri-urban Dar es Salaam and Mali), but if support is given to self-supply the needs of the most vulnerable can be more specifically addressed.

Conclusions

There are almost as many combinations and permutations of communal, traditional, and self-supply water supplies as there are communities. Such varied conditions require flexibility in approach. All require time to get established sustainably and so need long-term post-construction support in the case of community supplies and medium-term support to the private sector in the case of self-supply.

Gaps exist in running effective community water supply, and considering self-supply/traditional organization may offer alternatives, especially among smaller communities. There is also scope for sharing of support services, and of adopting a hybrid approach such as the CMP in Ethiopia which plays to the strengths of both service delivery models.

Consideration of pre-existing social and technical conditions and the transition to community water supply indicate a range of elements for which time is needed for a new paradigm to reach sustainability or absorption into the fabric of each society. This time element conflicts strongly with global aims for universal access (see also Anderson et al., 2012), and even if it were recognized as fundamental, it tends to be sacrificed in the race to reach more measurable outputs rather than a long-term sustainable outcome.

The different strengths and weaknesses of the two approaches suggest that coexistence offers real opportunity to provide a more sustainable mosaic of rural water supplies which is inclusive of smaller groups, and one which other countries show to be an essential part of economic rural transformation (Chapter 3).

References

AMCOW (2011) *AMCOW Policy and Strategy for Mainstreaming Gender in the Water Sector in Africa* [pdf] <https://www.amcow-online.org/images/Resources/24%20June%20AMCOW%20Eng.pdf> [accessed November 2019].

Anderson, M., Brown, D. and Jean, I. (2012) *Time to Listen: Hearing People on the Receiving End of International Aid*, CDA Collaborative Learning Projects, Cambridge, MA.

Baumeister, R. and Bushman, B. (2017) *Social Psychology and Human Nature*, Brief, 4th edn, Cengage Learning, Boston, MA.

Carter, R.C. and Ross, I. (2016) 'Beyond "functionality" of handpump-supplied rural water services in developing countries', *Waterlines* 35(1): 94–110 <http://dx.doi.org/10.3362/1756-3488.2016.008>.

Community Water and Sanitation Agency (CWSA Ghana) (2014) *Project Implementation Manual* [pdf], Ministry of Water Resources Works and Housing Republic of Ghana <https://www.rural-water-supply.net/_ressources/documents/default/1-598-2-1407846958.pdf> [accessed November 2019].

COWASH (2016) *Assessment on the Implementation of CMP Approach in High Tech Water Supply Schemes in COWASH Regions* [online], Ministry of Water and Energy, Addis Ababa, Ethiopia <https://www.cmpethiopia.org/media/assessment_of_cmp_implementation_in_high_tech_full_report2> [accessed November 2019].

Dahmm, H. (2018) *Handpump Data Improves Water Access: Case Study by SDSN TReNDS* [pdf], UN Thematic Research Network on Data and Statistics

<https://static1.squarespace.com/static/5b4f63e14eddec374f416232/t/5bf f2aae562fa7887f89bc5d/1543449264692/CaseStudy_SmartHandpump_ Nov2018.pdf> [accessed November 2019].

Eskandari Torbaghan, M. and Burrow, M.P.N. (2019) *Small Town Water Supply Infrastructure Costs* [pdf], K4D Helpdesk Report, Institute of Development Studies, Brighton, UK <https://assets.publishing.service.gov.uk/media/5cd 99a52ed915d5c77c18a10/562_Urban_Water_Supply_Costs.pdf> [accessed November 2019].

Fisher, M., Shields, K., Chan, T., Christenson, E., Cronk, R., Leker, H., Samani, D., Apoya, P., Lutz, A. and Bartram, J. (2015) 'Understanding handpump sustainability: determinants of rural water source functionality in the Greater Afram Plains region of Ghana', *Water Resources Research* 51(10): 8431–49 <http:// dx.doi.org/10.1002/2014WR016770>.

Fonseca, C., Franceys, R., Batchelor, C., McIntyre, P., Klutse, A., Komives, K., Moriarty, P., Naafs, A., Nyarko, K., Pezon, C., Potter, A., Reddy, A. and Snehalatha, M. (2011) *Life-Cycle Costs Approach: Costing Sustainable Services*, WashCost Briefing Note 1a, IRC International Water and Sanitation Centre, the Hague, Netherlands <https://www.ircwash.org/sites/default/files/ briefing_note_1a_-_life-cycle_cost_approach.pdf> [accessed November 2019].

Foster, T. (2013) 'Predictors of sustainability for community-managed handpumps in sub-Saharan Africa: evidence from Liberia, Sierra Leone, and Uganda', *Environmental Science and Technology* 47(21): 12037–46 <https:// doi.org/10.1021/es402086n>.

Gia, L. and Fugelsnes, T. (2010) *Public-Private Partnerships for Small Piped Schemes: A Review of Progress in Seven African Countries* [pdf], WSP Field Note Oct 2010 <https://www.wsp.org/sites/wsp/files/publications/PPPs_for_ small_piped_water_schemes_English.pdf> [accessed May 2020].

Hardin, G. (2001) 'The Tragedy of the Commons', *American Association for the Advancement of Science* [reprint of 1968 paper] <https://www. garretthardinsociety.org/articles_pdf/tragedy_of_the_commons.pdf> [accessed October 2019].

Harvey, A. (2019) *Whave Solutions: information* [online] <https://www. rural-water-supply.net/en/member-organisations/details/68> [accessed November 2019].

Harvey, P. and Reed, B. (2004) *Rural Water Supply in Africa: Building Blocks for Handpump Sustainability* [pdf], WEDC, Loughborough University, UK <https://wedc-knowledge.lboro.ac.uk/resources/books/Rural_Water_ Supply_in_Africa_-_Complete.pdf> [accessed November 2019].

Kamanga, A., Mhango, J. and Veldman, R. (2018) 'Assessment of the functionality of rope pumps for sustainable water supply in rural areas of Malawi' in R.J. Shaw (ed.), *Transformation towards Sustainable and Resilient WASH Services, Proceedings of the 41st WEDC International Conference, Nakuru, Kenya*, paper 3041.

Kumamaru, K., Odhiambo, F. and Smout, I. (2011) 'Self supply dynamic mapping', in *Proceedings of the 6th RWSN Forum, Uganda* [pdf] <https:// rwsnforum.files.wordpress.com/2011/11/153-self-supply-dynamic-mapping.pdf> [accessed June 2020].

Latané, B., Williams, K. and Harkins, S. (1979) 'Many hands make light the work: the causes and consequences of social loafing', *Journal of Personality and Social Psychology* 37(6): 822–32 <https://doi.org/10.1037/0022-3514.37.6.822>.

McCommon, C., Warner, D. and Yohalem, D. (1990) *Community Management of Rural Water Supply and Sanitation Services* [pdf], IBRD, Washington, DC <http://documents.worldbank.org/curated/en/174491468780008395/pdf/multi-page.pdf> [accessed November 2019].

Ministry of Water and Environment, Uganda (2010) Water and Sanitation Sub-Sector Gender Strategy (2010–15) [pdf] <http://extwprlegs1.fao.org/docs/pdf/uga152829.pdf> [accessed November 2019].

Ministry of Water and Environment, Uganda (2017) *Sector Performance Report* [pdf] <https://www.mwe.go.ug/sites/default/files/library/SPR%20 2017%20Final.pdf> [accessed May 2020].

Ministry of Water Resources Sierra Leone (2019) *WASH data portal* [online] <https://washdata-sl.org/water-point-data/> [accessed April 2019].

Moriarty, P., Nyarko, K., Dwumfour-Asare, B., Obuobisa-Darko, A. and Appiah-Effah, E. (2012) *Life-cycle Costs in Ghana: Uses and Sources of Water in Rural Areas*, Briefing Note no 8, IRC International Water and Sanitation Centre, The Hague, the Netherlands <https://www.ircwash.org/sites/default/files/briefing_note_8_uses_and_sources_of_water_in_rural_areas.pdf> [accessed November 2019].

One WASH (2019) *Community Managed Programme Implementation Manual* [online], Federal Republic of Ethiopia <https://www.cmpethiopia.org/media/cmp_implementation_manual_in_cwa_march_2019> [accessed November 2019].

PumpAid (2016) *Innovative Community Water Supply Solutions in Malawi: Self-Supply*, Pump Aid, End of Pilot Research Project Report, UNICEF Malawi and UKAID <https://www.pumpaid.org/wp-content/uploads/2020/06/Pump-Aid-Self-Supply-Pilot-Project-Final-Report-May-2016-.pdf> [accessed June 2020].

Sedikides, C., Gaertner, L. and O'Mara, E. (2011) 'Individual self, relational self, collective self: hierarchical ordering of the tripartite self', *Psychological Studies* 56(1): 98–107 <http://dx.doi.org/10.1007/s12646-011-0059-0>.

SNV (2010) *Water Point Mapping: The Experience of SNV Tanzania*, SNV, Dar es Salaam <https://www.ircwash.org/sites/default/files/SNVTanzania-2010-Water.pdf> [accessed January 2020].

Stevenson, E., Greene, L., Maes, K., Ambelu, A., Alemu, Y., Rheingans, R. and Hadley, C. (2012) 'Water insecurity in 3 dimensions: an anthropological perspective on water and women's psychosocial distress in Ethiopia', *Social Science and Medicine* 75(2): 392–400 <http://dx.doi.org/10.1016/j.socscimed.2012.03.022>.

Thompson, J., Porras, I., Tumwine, J., Mujwahuzi, M., Katui-Katua, M., Johnstone, N. and Wood, E. (2001) *Drawers of Water II: 30 Years of Change in Domestic Water Use & Environmental Health in East Africa*, IIED, London <https://pubs.iied.org/pdfs/9049IIED.pdf> [accessed November 2019].

Whaley, L. and Cleaver, F. (2017) 'Can "functionality" save the community management model of rural water supply?' *Water Resources and Rural Development* 9: 56–66 <http://dx.doi.org/10.1016/j.wrr.2017.04.001>.

Whittington, D., Davis, J., Prokopy, L., Komives, K., Thorsten, R., Lukacs, H., Bakalian, A. and Wakeman, W. (2008) *How Well is the Demand-Driven, Community Management Model for Rural Water Supply Systems Doing? Evidence from Bolivia, Peru, and Ghana*, BWPI Working Paper 22, Brooks World Poverty Institute, Manchester, UK.

World Bank (2019) *Databank: Population estimates and projections* [online] <https://databank.worldbank.org/data/source/population-estimates-and-projections/Type/TABLE/preview/on#> [accessed November 2019].

WPDx (2019) *Water point data* [database] <https://www.waterpointdata.org/water-point-data> [accessed April 2019].

CHAPTER 9
Supporting self-supply acceleration

This chapter investigates the complex and varied interactions of government, development agencies, private sector, and households which evolve to support self-supply, and their respective strengths and weaknesses. It emphasizes that government has important roles as for any service delivery model. The chapter looks at the processes to introduce and scale up self-supply, the stage that different countries have reached, and the software costs of providing support. This is a cost-effective way for the state to support those in isolated households or in locations that are most difficult to reach and offers a range of services to enable others who invest for themselves to improve their level of service.

Keywords: private sector, human rights, piloting, service delivery model, institutional support

Key messages

1. Supporting self-supply is not a way to evade state obligations over water, but one of several routes to their progressive fulfilment. Local, national, and international champions are needed for significant and continued acceleration.
2. Recognition of self-supply as a service delivery model is essential if overall coverage is to reach the last 20 per cent of rural households.
3. There is significant saving to government if self-supply support is included in planning for dispersed households and small communities.
4. Design of self-supply support is country-specific depending on economic, political, and organizational frameworks. Designs to kick-start the process should be participatory, involving a range of stakeholders.
5. Those few countries that have gone to scale successfully engaged government early, alongside NGO support and private sector development.
6. NGO-led initiatives strengthening private sector capacity show relatively rapid local results and growing demand but are limited in their ability to scale up on their own and may not lead to sustainability.
7. NGOs have several roles, including lobbying governments for approval of a household level of service, developing and promoting affordable technologies, and early budgeting for software costs (e.g. social marketing, monitoring, and coordination).

http://dx.doi.org/10.3362/9781780448190.009

8. Support for self-supply may originate in one of several sectors but leadership ultimately needs to be within the water sector if it is to be integrated into government policy.
9. The time-scale is long but the end product empowers individual households, enhances local economies, and provides long-term returns on investments in support.
10. There is potential cost saving in promoting household-level self-supply alongside sanitation. New models need developing to see how they best fit within government extension services.

Objectives of supporting self-supply

There are two levels at which self-supply needs support. One is at the mega level where government through polices, strategies, and budgets sets an enabling environment for self-supply and sets agendas for improvement and quality standards and monitoring. The other is in the local availability of the practical necessities for households that are trying to improve their supplies. The technical options for the latter were outlined in Chapters 6 and 7 and basically provide the means to bring the water nearer, and ultimately into the home, to make it safer and better protected, to make it easier to lift the water (eventually with motorized pumping for elevated storage), and access repair services. When used in combination these lead to more water for the household which in turn impact not only on health but on livelihoods.

In particular the creation of an enabling environment means taking steps to build a responsive private sector that sustains itself because it provides what people will pay for to improve their supplies, using market forces for upward mobility. In most rural areas and poorer countries, the 'private sector' is a grand name for what is sometimes just a few artisans who lack good products and equipment. The purpose of training and financial support is to enable these businesses to grow and to stand on their own feet. This has been recognized in the sanitation sector through sanitation marts and the like but insufficiently supported to foster widespread water supply improvements. In this process we can say that the government and NGOs have a responsibility to drive these improvements while the private sector has the role and opportunity to provide the means of doing so.

As outlined in Chapter 2 ('Supporting self-supply: accelerating progress in sanitation and water' and Figure 2.4)) the emphasis is on helping individuals and communities to enjoy the right to safe water largely through their own efforts, where there is need or demand and public funds for adequate provision are inadequate. The vision is that a supported service delivery model would fill the gaps being left by other options, extending coverage, raising standards, and providing continued back-up, with monitoring and regulation to ease coexistence with other delivery models – community based management, direct local government, public utility, private sector.

The aim of full integration of self-supply support services into the private and public sector is to be achieved through:

- availability of and advice on a range of affordable technologies offered to all;
- a competent, appropriate, and sustainable private sector accessible to rural and peri-urban populations including dispersed and remote communities, providing well digging, drilling, and source protection, plus water lifting, storage, and treatment devices;
- a range of savings, affordable micro-financial and grant options suitable for a range of investors (households, groups, artisan/entrepreneurs);
- supported self-supply incorporated as an equal partner among service delivery models, giving access to government support, with clear policies on the transition from self-supply to other delivery models in various contexts.

The enabling environment does not consist of a stand-alone service specific to self-supply, but can largely be achieved by building capacities and expanding existing government duties with a new emphasis on kick-starting expansion of SME services into a range of household-level technical options. For some families self-supply may be an interim service but for a proportion of rural and isolated households it is an endpoint, albeit one which can be continually improved. Moving towards universal access requires knowledge and understanding of households in both categories.

Developing core support service capacity

Institutional functions

Government has distinctive roles at different levels. The national level sets the policy framework within which service delivery models function and coordinates the involvement of larger NGOs. Processes and guidelines are established for community/household level, with earmarked funding for district inputs.

Provincial and district level government, equivalent to service authority level in more institutionalized service delivery, primarily performs an advisory role. They may be involved in assessing SME capacity, in fitting coordinated self-supply support into the working schedules of officers in different sectors, and ensuring NGOs active in their areas follow the same strategies and fit in with district water supply plans. Major activities at this level include training service providers and social marketing, alongside coordination.

An example of how this may work in institutional terms is given by the Ugandan Ministry of Water and Energy, which, in 2014–15, developed a strategy for self-supply support along with functions among different administrative levels and stakeholders (see Figure 9.1).

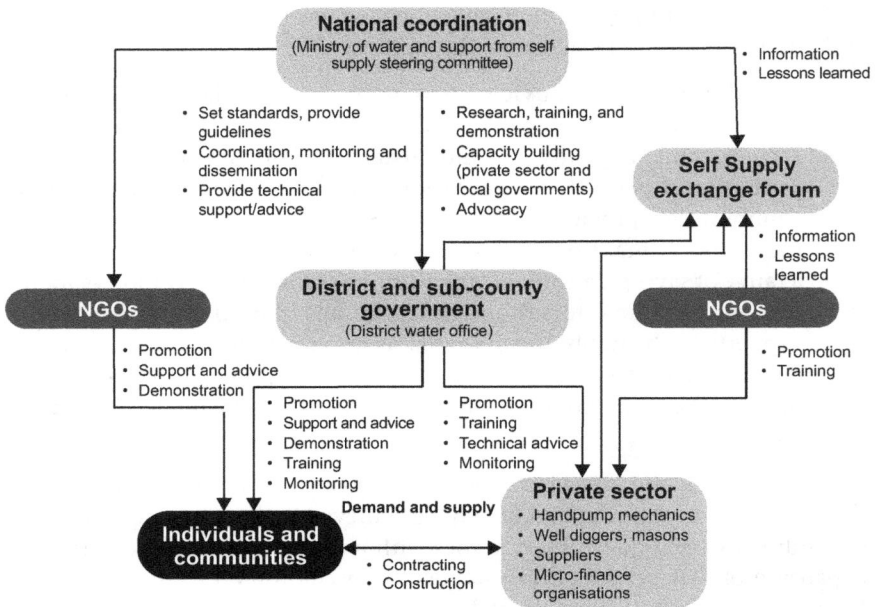

Figure 9.1 Roles and responsibilities developed by Ministry of Water and Energy Uganda for self-supply support in 2015
Source: Kiwanuka, 2015

Support service providers

Figure 9.2 shows the framework of support services and expertise needed for households to move more rapidly in improving their own supplies or being subsidized to do so. It is based on sub-Saharan institutions but with relevance to other developing regions of the world. The outer ring illustrates the range of services required to develop self-supply for rainwater and groundwater systems and the inner ring, a network of relevant service providers. The main role of government and NGOs is to develop links between households and support service providers, define the roles and extend the range and improve the quality of the essential services the latter should offer. Since many low-income rural areas lack support service providers with sufficient capacity, stimulation and training will be the main (and highest) cost. The aim is to raise awareness of self-supply needs and define locally relevant roles so that the range and skills of service providers is known to and used by households.

Developing support service delivery

Although the specifics vary with context, five elements particularly facilitate support service delivery: *training, market development, subsidies, monitoring/review*, and *regulation*.

The core requirements from support services can be provided by a variety of agents, with specific roles for government, particularly at policy level.

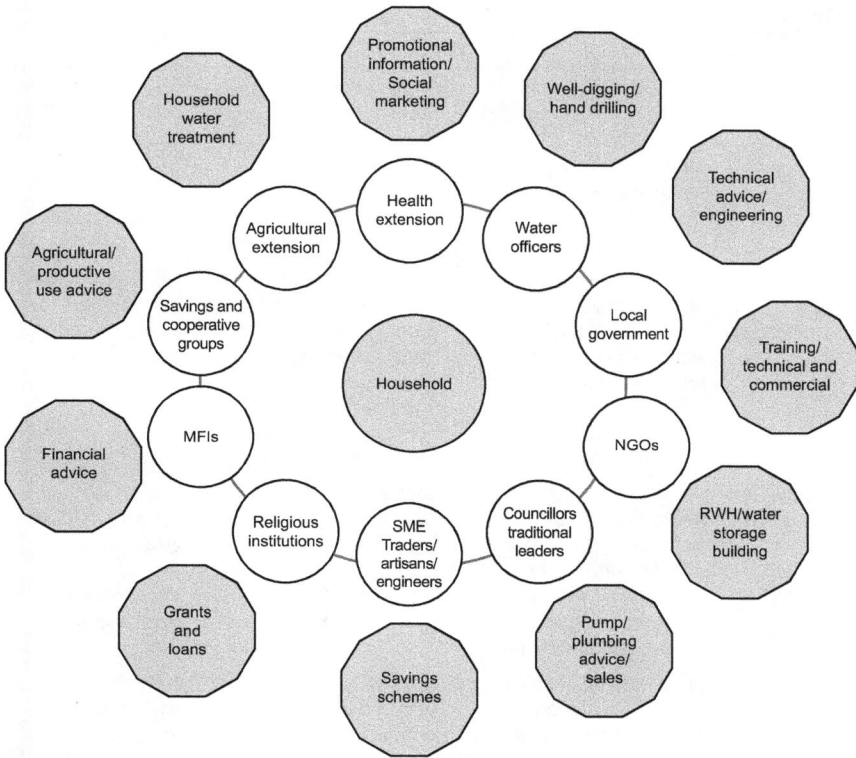

Figure 9.2 Local service providers and range of products required to support basic household supply investment

The indicators and service agents are summarized in Table 9.1. Key points are the need for multi-sectoral cooperation and coordination, and the important role that NGOs play in piloting, action research, and evidence gathering.

Training. Artisans have traditional skills but often lack skills in business development and marketing. Training is partly to change attitudes and partly to introduce new practices and technologies and higher quality products or services. Much of the training is initially provided by NGOs as part of the introduction of new technologies and skills to the private sector. Public sector officers have knowledge and respect for standard water supply technologies but usually a disregard for traditional ones or affordable technologies in which they see liability rather than potential. There is a need to encourage their appreciation of the value of self-supply both to achieve national targets and for the well-being of end-users. Training should include workshops where participants can air concerns, discuss evidence, and develop ideas. Training will over time be integrated into government college curricula for technicians, health workers, sociologists, and engineers and into continuous professional development.

Table 9.1 Core indicators for sustainable self-supply support

Core services	Objective	Indicator elements	Agents
Technical	Availability of, and advice and training on, a range of affordable good quality technologies	– Advisory services – Training capacity – Demonstrated products – Research and technical guidelines – Approved technologies	– Government – District officers and entrepreneurs – NGO inputs
Private sector	A competent, appropriate, and sustainable private sector accessible to rural and peri-urban populations including dispersed and remote communities	– Upskilled workforce – Effective marketing – Variety of supply construction methods and products – Customer base – Quality of business management	– NGOs, government training, extension officers, entrepreneurs
Financial options	A range of savings, affordable micro-financial and grant options suitable for a variety of investors (households, groups, artisan entrepreneurs)	– Savings schemes – Subsidies – Loans/credit – Remittances – Financial advice	– Traditional schemes/NGOs/ government (various), microfinance institutions
Policy	Supported self-supply incorporated as an equal partner among service delivery models, with appropriate finance, monitoring, and regulation	– Formalized household service delivery level – Regulation – Inter-departmental cooperation – Budgets for software – Monitoring and review	– National government with implementation of policy by local government

Market development. The challenge is to stimulate demand for unsubsidized water systems by promoting affordable technologies and services that can be supplied locally. However, the market is not a level playing field, since governments and NGOs provide subsidized water supplies to some but not all. Social marketing through participatory (PHAST) methods is a valuable element in introducing self-supply and changing attitudes, and a variety of modules on the process for WASH have been developed, tested, and widely used with the Ministry of Health in Zambia (see *Encouraging Change* by Sutton and Nkoloma, 2011).

National and local government services have strong capacity in a number of sectors to carry messages to the grass roots via extension workers and traditional networks of community leaders. A host of communications skills and networks already exist in agriculture, community development, health, water, tribal or local affairs, and education and these cascade down to traditional leaders, mayors and councillors, women's groups, religious institutions, youth groups, and village development and WASH committees. NGOs may have their own community mobilizers to liaise with district, community, and household levels and means to advertise on local radio, television, and public events such as agricultural shows or local celebrations. It takes some time before local entrepreneurs build up business enough to be able to bear these costs themselves.

As the market develops, more and more is achieved purely through copying what neighbours have done, at little or no cost. However in the early stages promotion is partly to provide information and increase familiarity with new products (see Box 9.1).

Box 9.1 Introducing new products

Introducing a new product requires people to see it before they will buy. Lack of options suppresses demand and demonstration models accelerate uptake. But subsidizing demonstrations also distorts the market and leads others to believe they too can get a 'free sample'. Early marketing strategies need to be carefully designed, and will vary depending on culture, economy, and previous knowledge. Sila Mumba in Luapula Province, Zambia shows the power of peer marketing.

> I drink from the stream because the well water is dirty. I plan to put in rings and stop collapse so I can drink it. I chlorinate my water when I can afford to, but the stream is cloudy in the rains. The well is much nearer my house.
>
> The artisans came and talked to the community about improving our wells. Before I did not have any idea what I could do. I asked the mason to come to my home and tell me what he could do.
>
> I was amazed after the first ring was made – so many people came to look. I think at least 15 out of the 20 nearest wells will make rings this year (quotes from Sila Mumba, March 2009).

Photo 9.1 Well-lining rings made by local artisans at Sila Mumba's house (Existing well head in the background)

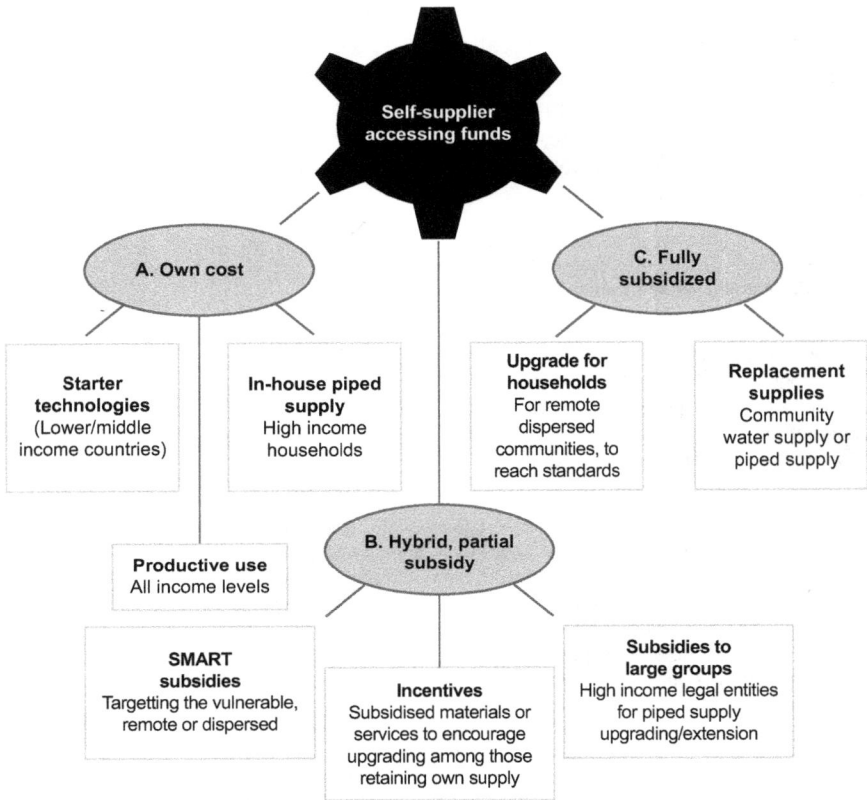

Figure 9.3 Funding types and purpose

Subsidies. Self-supply begins with the end user in the driving seat paying for their own improvements in supply but limited by what funds they can access. In some cases state assistance which provides indirect subsidies which ensure that relevant services are available and may offer some level of direct subsidy or access to funds through grants or loans to raise the level of supply. Such subsidies (see Figure 9.3) open up wider access for potential investors to the range of technical, private sector, and in some cases additional financial services that can support self-supply investment (see also Figure 2.3). They also may bring into play the regulatory and resource management parts of policy. Subsidies may target the vulnerable (as in the Brazilian One Million Rainwater Harvesting Programme; Noguiera, 2008) or as in the case of cooperative water schemes in Europe, Mali, and Kenya, allow piped extensions beyond those which members of a cooperative can afford on their own.

In some cases, government takes over technology choice and funding, covering the full cost of upgrading or replacing what households achieved for themselves, as in the replacement of self-supply by community water points or public piped supplies. Government agencies tend to be most comfortable with this approach, which reflects their experience as the main decision-makers and can predict their outputs for the financial year. However, this removes elements of ownership and may reduce sustainability.

Building up support services indirectly subsidizes everyone who makes use of them. Direct subsidies may be designed to achieve whatever targets a government or NGO sets, such as upgrading existing self-supply or new construction in unserved areas. They should, however, be designed to facilitate rather than drive the market and avoid distorting it by demotivating those who do not qualify for incentives or subsidies.

Monitoring and review. For district-wide sector plans it is vital that spatial distribution of self-supply wells and rainwater harvesting is known, and progress towards safe supply monitored. However there is a fear that self-supply offers too many water points to be effectively monitored by inclusion in water point inventories. There are several ways of monitoring, without large new surveys. Initially for piloting and policy making spot surveys of specific areas may be sufficient. Many health ministries already have their health information monitoring systems (HIMS) which feed household and community level data on household sanitation and water supply to district levels. Some irrigation or agriculture ministries (e.g. Ministry of Water, Irrigation and Electricity, Ethiopia) have detailed records of wells used for productive purposes. Secondary data collection may be adequate to feed into sector reviews and analysis of progress and bottlenecks.

Monitoring at household level has advantages for review of progress and for the positive effects of such visits on household behaviour (Hawthorne effect), even without other interventions (McCambridge et al., 2014). If it can lead to better maintenance of facilities, the additional cost of visiting more sites (necessary also to monitor sanitation) may be justifiable.

Regulation. A decision on whether or when regulation or registration is necessary is a critical element in the healthy evolution of self-supply. Registration of supplies and/or contractors may bring a welcome improvement in information on new wells. However registration systems will be challenging to keep updated, operational, and sustainable in regions where few local contractors or well-owners can afford to bear the costs. Registration and regulation introduce the twin risks of stifling private initiatives and of introducing opportunities for corruption. Regulation for self-supply in higher income countries has generally only been introduced if and when it affects water resources or public health, and only when the state can support people's endeavours through loans and grants (see Chapter 3 'Government roles in high income self-supply'), and when the national economy or fees can cover the costs of monitoring and regulation. Regulating small water supply development, without having alternatives or incentives to offer, runs the risk of holding back emergent rural economies.

The process of establishing supported self-supply

How can self-supply be supported to achieve a pathway which ends with all households having access to sustainable services which enable them to improve their water supply? A four-stage framework is presented here (see Figure 9.4) covering *introduction, piloting, policy/strategy development,* and *going to scale.* This is based on earlier models by Smits and Sutton (2012) and reflections on supported self-supply processes in several countries (e.g. Butterworth et al., 2014; Sutton, 2007). It is a long-term process which ensures that no gaps are left but might take five to ten years for full integration and sustainability shifting responsibilities away from NGOs and towards government and the private sector.

Stage 1: Introducing the supported self-supply approach

The first stage develops an understanding of what households and communities are doing for themselves, combined with a recognition of the contribution that self-supply support can make to national targets. Support is relevant where:

- countries or regions are unable to reach national targets for safe and reliable supply at past rates of progress with present service options;
- small groups and isolated households constitute many of the remaining unserved;
- self-supply already exists with below standard performance.

Assembling the data for country-specific situation analyses can be done as a low-cost preparatory exercise by NGOs or government, to provide evidence of need for additional solutions. This information provides a useful foundation for gaining government and donor interest. Desk studies followed by workshops and discussions in Uganda, Ethiopia, Zambia, Sierra Leone, and Mali led to positive responses from all the governments, and a wish to look more deeply, through piloting or policy development.

NGOs often have a key role to play. WaterAid started in 2004 to consider the relevance of self-supply for sub-Saharan countries (Sutton, 2004), and has since been active in Uganda, Zambia, Mali, and Sierra Leone in responding to government interest to explore its potential and to pilot options. UNICEF led early stages of the process in Ethiopia, Zambia, and Mali. The Water and Sanitation Program (World Bank) supported preliminary studies and promotion of the potential through the Rural Water Supply Network (RWSN) over eight years. RWSN plays a valuable role in fostering collaboration and information exchange between organizations and individuals working at different stages of piloting, implementing, researching, and policy development, with a specific self-supply theme. Its e-library has a large range of documents with background information on self-supply in various countries.

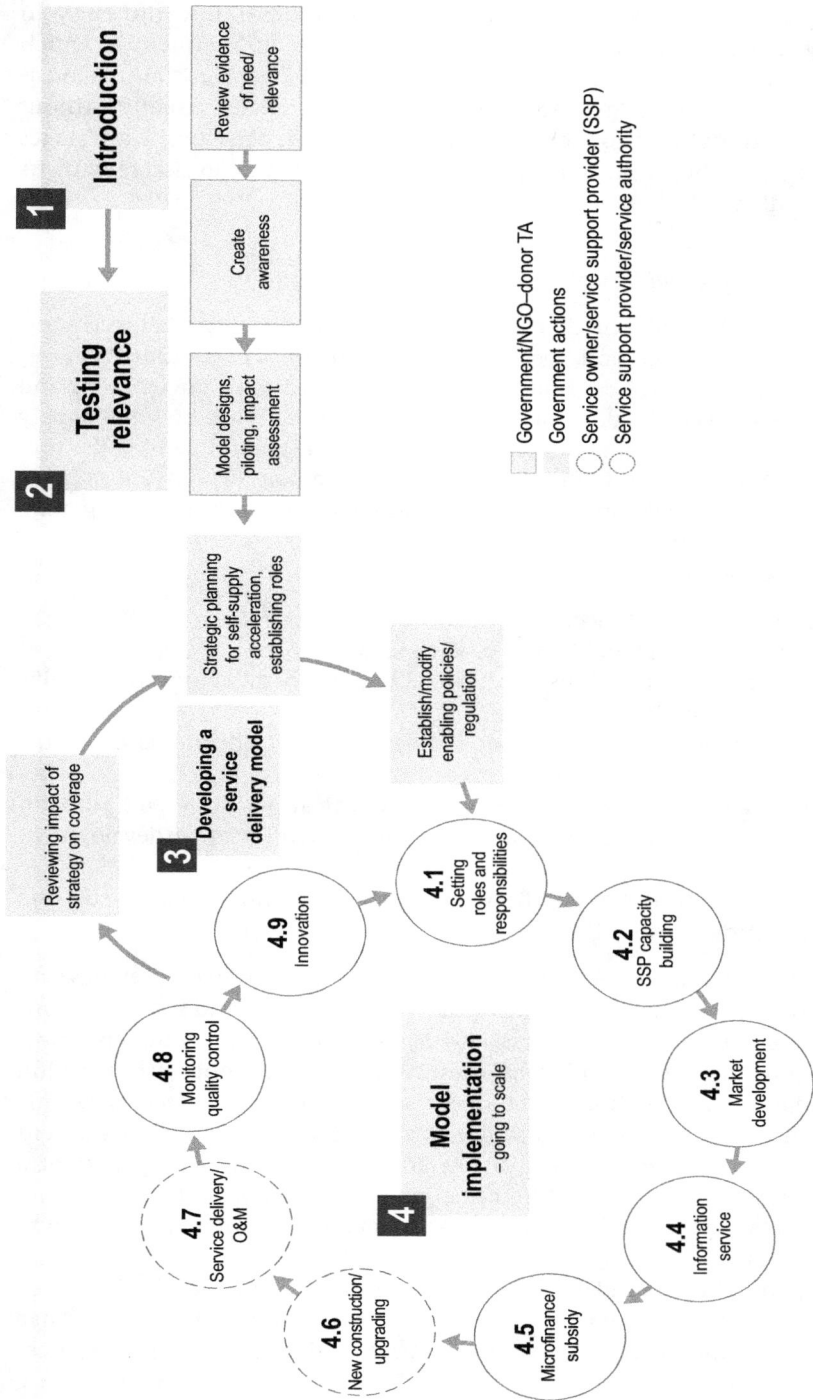

Figure 9.4 Stages in the process of establishing a self-supply service delivery model
Source: Modified from Smits and Sutton, 2012

Requests for NGO inputs arise where governments find difficulty in testing new ideas within organizational and procedural structures which focus only on established service delivery models. Funding is also a constraint since annual budgets are linked to existing policies, usually without the opportunity to introduce new, untested research activities. Early stages also require action research capacity which may not be available with its own funding.

Stage 2: Piloting and testing

The next step is to pilot models of support which can establish what works best in country-specific physical, social, economic, and policy environments.

Selection of pilot areas and models is developed with government and other relevant stakeholders. Details of the process of establishing self-supply can be found for Ethiopia (Butterworth et al., 2014) and for Zambia (Sutton, 2007). The SMART and EMAS training centres (see Box 6.5) provide valuable capacity for this stage in introduction and could also play important roles towards scaling up.

Piloting should:

- establish best practice;
- test the market and identify obstacles;
- provide demonstrations of what a technology or an approach looks like on the ground;
- train private and public sector and develop/test guidelines and training materials;
- gather evidence for marketing, communications strategies, and for government to assess whether to proceed towards strategy development and scaling up;
- clarify support roles and how these fit with existing private sector and government capacities.

The measure of success for pilot projects lies in the impact they have on policies, technology uptake, and business development, and the indications they give for cost effectiveness and sustainability. Unfortunately, most funding is simply tied to physical outputs, which tends not to show its full potential within the short timeframe of a pilot. Support services take time to reach a sustainable level and demand takes time to build. Investment in piloting is lost if it is seen as an end in itself rather than part of a larger process. Pilots should be undertaken to prove, disprove or modify hypotheses of what can work at a bigger scale, but few are brave enough to publicize failures.

In many pilots founder demand/markets are not sufficiently developed before support is withdrawn. In the case of a new approach, the challenge lies at the point where, even after a successful pilot, there are no resources for policy and strategy development, fund allocation, and scaling up.

Stage 3: Policy and strategy development

The next stage is to develop policies and strategies to go to scale and maintain sustainability. This may require more ground-testing but is a time for government to establish roles, identify the key strategic issues, and decide how to tackle them within existing policies or new ones. Technical assistance may be required to steer the process from piloting to scaling up. In both Ethiopia and Uganda a major player has been a national Self-supply Task Force or Steering Committee to push for change and coordinate efforts of different ministries. Task forces however, only survive and maintain influence if linked to government or international funding.

Issues to be addressed include:

- official recognition of a service delivery model where households take the lead;
- adoption of different service delivery standards for individual households or small groups;
- division of responsibilities for support between water, health, and other ministries;
- level of subsidy (none, partial, full provision) and conditionality (vulnerable households, un-served, all) in supply provision or upgrading;
- priority areas for early intervention;
- integration of mobilization and post-construction support with household sanitation and community water supply;
- integration into other existing service provision, changes to job descriptions;
- establishment of budget lines linked to organizational framework;
- identification of capacity building gaps and training needs;
- policies for relationship with other service delivery models.

Stage 4: Going to scale

Scaling up to national coverage implies that, by the end, support strategies are fully absorbed into policies and practice throughout the country. Supporting roles are embedded in job descriptions, budgets, sector-wide approach (SWAP) funding, annual plans, and national training schemes, and activities of NGOs in associated undertakings are coordinated and follow similar lines. Private sector capacity is expanded and upskilled by a mix of market forces and government/NGO facilitation. Supported self-supply is considered alongside other service delivery models in terms of funding, monitoring, and policy development. The cost to government is not then zero, but significantly less than during the period of initial stimulation of markets and building public and private sector capacities.

Government coordinates inputs of NGOs and different ministries, seeks funds from donors, monitors progress, and encourages upgrading through extension services, in conjunction with marketing and promotion from the private sector. As with sanitation, clear guidelines on subsidies are needed.

Country experiences

The processes detailed above have been carried through to different stages by a variety of countries (see Figure 9.5 and Table 9.2).

It can be seen that for more than half the countries, progress stopped after successful pilots. Progress has continued beyond piloting, when NGO and donor support and technical assistance has remained in place for long enough, and where government was involved early enough for government and the private sector to adopt the approach and/or technologies and promote affordable self-financed solutions alongside other delivery options. It is essential to have champions within government and donor communities who believe in the long-term need to support self-supply to reach SDG targets.

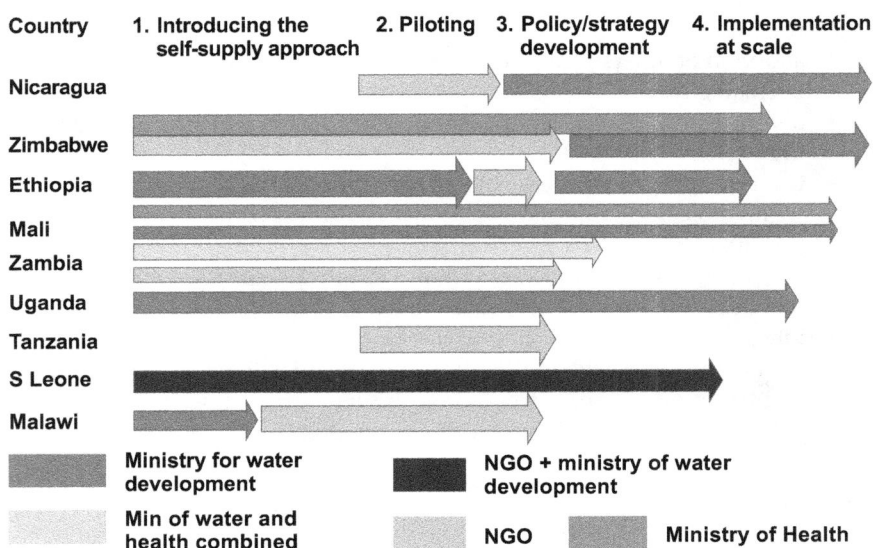

Figure 9.5 Progress in scaling-up supported self-supply in selected countries

Table 9.2 Situation summary for countries in Figure 9.5

Country	Situation analysis
Nicaragua	Support mainly through private sector capacity building by NGOs in early stages. After five years, taken up by regional government. Implementation reached a scale that central government adopted approach and technologies. Now government is funding individual self-supply upgrading to fill gaps at a higher service level.
Zimbabwe (see Part 2, Case study 4)	Initiated by Blair Institute (Min. of Health) and NGOs (WaterAid/Mvurumanzi) in the early 1990s. Incorporated into water policy and inventories. Self-supply forms the basic supply for at least 30% of rural population as an approved level of service, but despite this no longer appears in the rural water strategy.

(Continued)

Table 9.2 Continued

Country	Situation analysis
Ethiopia	Need quickly recognized regionally and nationally. Piloting came after, rather than before federal strategy development, resulting in some confusion on how to operationalize it. Current piloting may clarify.
Mali	The need for improvement of individual household supplies was recognized by the Ministry of Health and is promoted by health centre staff. Ministry responsible for water supply supports cooperative self-financed piped supplies especially in Kayes region.
Zambia (see Part 2, Case study 6)	Need for strategy for dispersed populations recognized since 1997, with piloting by Ministries of Health and of Water and Energy. Responsibility then shifted to local government. Subsequent piloting (UNICEF/WaterAid) uncovered high suppressed demand. Successful piloting with short-term funding has not carried over into policies, plans, and budgets NGOs WaterAid and Jacana continue introduction and advocacy.
Uganda	Ministry of Water and Environment recognized need for strategy for dispersed households in 2006. Supported piloting by NGOs (Carter et al., 2008) and subsequently developed strategy and district level training in 2010–11 for self-supply advisory services. However, a presidential decree in 2019 ruled out household level supplies including rainwater harvesting and shallow wells.
Tanzania (see Part 2, Case study 5)	NGO initiatives to develop private sector hand-drilling and rope pump production through SMART/SHIPO training centre. Over 11,000 installed so far without integration with government strategies.
Sierra Leone	NGO initiatives in 2014–2015 to strengthen private sector and government roles. Self-supply officially recognized in national rural water strategies as key to much rural coverage, but without a budget to support subsidy or training except through NGO (WHH). Privately financed water supplies included in the national inventory, many district officers and entrepreneurs trained.
Malawi	Need for supported self-supply recognized by government for some of the remaining 13% unserved, but not yet developed as policy. SMART centre providing support to entrepreneurs, but links to government still developing.

In CLTS, the donor community pushed for a largely unsubsidized software solution through concern over lack of progress. For water too this is an issue. It is very easy for the focus to become diverted to high-profile, capital-intensive programmes which bypass the interests of those being left behind.

Why governments should get involved

While self-supply is recognized by some in the sector as a service delivery model when supported by government (World Bank, 2017), it very rarely features alongside other models (community-based management, direct local government, public utility, private sector) in sector analyses and certainly not in its widespread unsupported form. The question arises: since it occurs naturally and without assistance, why interfere? The answer is partly that most self-supply systems perform below accepted standards and the risks they present will only be reduced by intervention along the lines outlined in Chapter 2 ('Supporting self-supply: accelerating progress in sanitation and water') and in this chapter. Unsupported self-supply continues to grow in most under-served areas, alongside conventional service delivery models on which millions of dollars are being spent. The interaction between them is critical in their effectiveness as service delivery models and for the well-being of end-users. Omitting self-supply leaves an unbalanced equation and an incomplete picture.

As with the initial devolution of responsibilities for village-level operation and maintenance, it might be assumed that including self-supply as a service delivery model removes responsibility from government, putting it on end-users. An opposite view is that government has full responsibility for water supply provision and the end-user has none. The responsibility in human rights terms lies somewhere between the two. The obligation of the state to fulfil the right requires it to 'facilitate, promote and provide', in that order (see Box 9.2), acknowledging that resource limitations may

---

Box 9.2 Background to the human rights fulfilment for water and sanitation

The International Covenant on Economic, Social and Cultural Rights (adopted 1966 by the UN) sets the basis of state responsibility (UNHCHR, 1976). It requires the state to take the necessary steps towards the progressive achievement of the right to everyone to an adequate standard of living, including housing. It was subsequently clarified by Comment 15 of the Economic and Social Council of the UN (UNHCHR, 2003) that housing included water supply.

Fact Sheet 33 (UNHCHR, 2008)
Page 11:

> In order to clarify the meaning of States' obligations, they are sometimes put under three headings: to **respect** (refrain from interfering with the enjoyment of the right), to **protect** (prevent others from interfering with the enjoyment of the right) and to **fulfil** (adopt appropriate measures towards the full realization of) economic, social and cultural rights.

Page 13:

> The obligation to achieve progressively the full realization is a central aspect of States' obligations in connection with economic, social and cultural rights under international human rights treaties. At its core is the obligation to take appropriate measures towards the full realization of economic, social and cultural rights to the maximum of their available resources.

Clause 25 UN General comment 15 Obligations to fulfil the human right to water 2002:

> The obligation to fulfil can be disaggregated into the obligations to facilitate, promote and provide. The obligation to **facilitate** requires the State to take positive measures to assist individuals and communities to enjoy the right. The obligation to **promote** obliges the State party to take steps to ensure that there is appropriate education concerning the hygienic use of water, protection of water sources and methods to minimize water wastage. States parties are also obliged to **fulfil** (provide) the right when individuals or a group are unable, for reasons beyond their control, to realize that right themselves by the means at their disposal.

dictate progressive realization rather than instant universal provision (Heller, 2015).

Grönwall and Danert (2020) argue that 'If State Parties are only obliged to providing drinking water (services and facilities) as a last resort solution when right-holders are unable to, "for reasons beyond their control", self-provision becomes a norm in realizing the right to water'. This suggests that self-supply, facilitation, and promotion may be a norm which merits expenditure if it can lead to cost-effective solutions where funds are insufficient for the state to fulfil the right in full. At present this element is widely omitted from policies.

Integrating with sanitation

Similar processes to those used in aspects of CLTS and sanitation marketing are employed to encourage improvements in water through self-supply, so there is a lot to learn and share across these WASH sub-sectors. Supported self-supply water services (Figure 9.2 and Figure 2.3) have households at their core, and similarly mix public sector promotion and social marketing with local private sector entrepreneurship. The shame element is not usually a necessary trigger for water supply as demand is already there for more convenient supply; the trigger is enabling actions which have been suppressed through lack of support services or lack of awareness of perceived opportunity. There is a concept in common of households moving up a technology ladder over time associated with strong feelings of ownership and many of the same debates on the justification for subsidies and need for long-term support to avoid slippage and monitoring at household level to track progress. For both there is the challenge of sub-standard installations in need of upgrading and how to effect post-construction support. For both there is a need to provide similar entrepreneur training in masonry, basic plumbing, and business management, and to monitor progress at household level. Combining water and sanitation in training and monitoring (see Box 9.3), the two most expensive elements of support, can reduce service provision costs. It is easiest where the two elements of WASH fall under the same government ministry.

Box 9.3 Combined water and sanitation programmes

WaterAid's 'Community-based total sanitation' project in Zambia was expanded to include support to self-supply and training of 14 local artisans (see Photo 9.2). These 14 sold their services successfully to 62 per cent of the 117 traditional well owners in the pilot area in the first 18 months and were contracted to dig and protect five new ones. In Mali the Ministry of Health's (DNS) Risk Reduction Programme employed the dynamics generated for CLTS also for water supply on the basis that this might prolong community interest and reduce rates of slippage. Water-related preventive healthcare packages with four WASH elements (source protection, household water treatment, hand washing, and sanitation) were promoted through rural health centres.

(Continued)

Box 9.3 Continued

Photo 9.2 Artisans trained by WaterAid in techniques for self-supply water and sanitation, Luapula province, Zambia

Government, non-government, and private sector as stakeholders

Complementary responsibilities

Government and the private sector play the main roles in supporting self supply – with a catalytic role for NGOs. In an entrepreneurial model the private sector is supported (usually by an NGO) to build a market-based service, providing hardware and operating where it can do so commercially because there are households which can afford it. In the public sector model the government is engaged in the growth of local private sector services which are incorporated into a national service delivery model with an aim to leave no one behind. The government needs the private sector for implementation. The private sector sphere can develop locally but seldom goes to scale on its own across a country. The overlapping roles are strengthened where both stakeholders are involved, as illustrated in Figure 9.6. NGOs often play a critical role in the development of the private sector and a catalytic role in introducing technologies and in getting models of best practice tested and refined, building public and private sector capacity, and in providing evidence of performance, sustainability, and cost. They can be a key factor in getting self-supply recognized and its support normalized within government policy, where government does not have the capacity or the information to do so on its own.

**Enterprise
private sector**

**Government
public sector**

Business
management

Enabling
policies

Product/service
development

Research

Marketing/
promotion

Coordination and
communication

Well/borehole
construction

Credit/funding
systems

Sales of services,
pumps, and water
treatment

Technical
advisory
services

Subsidies   Planning

Regulation

Maintenance/
replacement
services

Training

Monitoring/
progress review

NGO support where necessary

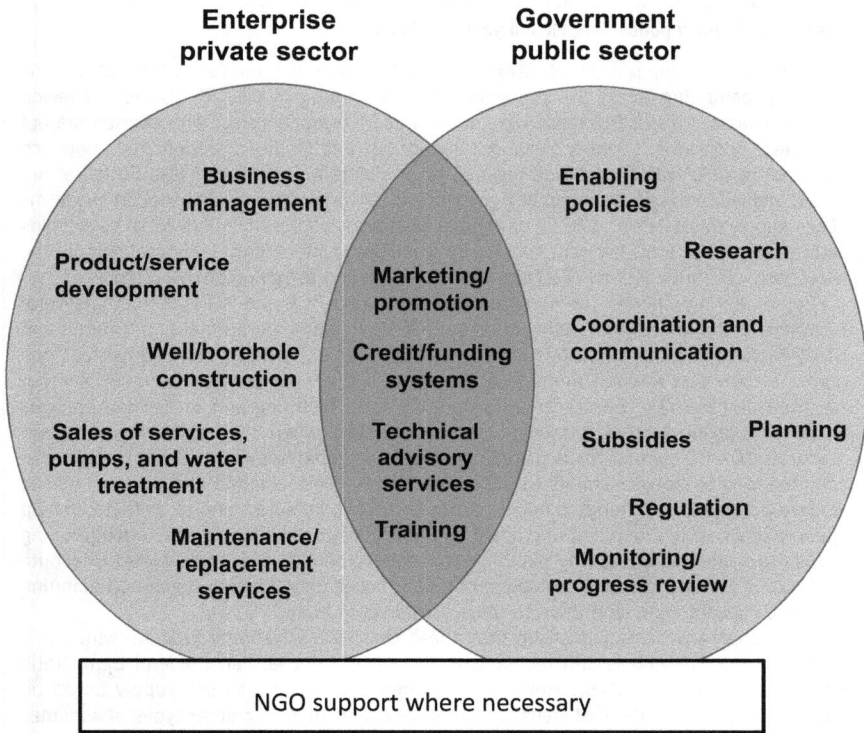

Figure 9.6 Complementary public and private sector roles in self-supply support

Experience of support through government

The degree to which government intervenes will depend to some degree on the political nature of the government and the roles it wishes to take in dealing with household-owned facilities. In Zimbabwe (see Part 2, Case Study 4) the government with NGOs and local government provided incentive-level (20 per cent of cost) subsidies which encouraged increasing numbers of households to construct or improve their supplies. The concept continued even after subsidies ceased. As a result, more than 150,000 household wells have been constructed and improved through government advisory and subsidy support and NGO implementation.

In Ethiopia self-supply forms part of the national water supply programme (see Box 9.4) with a subsidy for small-group self-supplies, similar to the policies in some Latin American countries with subsidies for upgrading individual supplies (see Chapter 3, 'Examples in Latin America'), providing handpumps to small groups with a protected well.

For individual households in Ethiopia there is a 'no subsidy policy'; but in both cases there has so far been little investment in building services to facilitate more, or better quality, construction or upgrade self-supply. The policy

---

Box 9.4 Self-supply policy, targets and gaps in Ethiopia

The Family Well Campaign (2004–2006) was a major government initiative that led to many new wells being dug across the Ethiopian highlands, reportedly over 86,000 in one region alone (Mekassa, 2006). But these were not counted towards coverage and efforts were not sustained. Soon after, a series of national workshops and studies were initiated. Evidence gathered together with federal and regional governments was published (see Sutton et al., 2012) and led to the development of a government policy to recognize and support two forms of self-supply (MoWE et al., 2012), one with a no-subsidy approach for individual households and the other with a 50 per cent subsidy for small-groups of at least 10 households. In the latter case, government or an NGO provided the pump and the group provided the well.

Some piloting followed through projects initiated by JICA and NGOs including several members of the Millennium Water Alliance (MWA). Regional governments in Oromia and SNNPR planned more ambitious scaling (Mekonta et al., 2015). JICA supported rope pump introduction through multiple efforts including a pilot programme in SNNP that ran from 2013–2016. Efforts to build up local manufacturing and to develop linkages between households and producers were challenged when the regional government procured 10,000 pumps for distribution to achieve rapid scale-up. This highlighted a common tension between pilots to build systems and best practice and direct action to achieve scale and get things done. In Amhara, MWA piloted an approach that built up support services and included upgrading and new construction through the strengthening of local artisans, supported by planning and engagement at the *woreda* level (Mekonta et al., 2017). This included development of plans based on guidelines to support planning by *woreda* governments and their partners (Butterworth et al., 2014).

Self-supply was included in the first phase One WASH National Program which was launched in 2013 and is still included in the second phase plan (Federal Democratic Republic of Ethiopia, 2018). However, government seeks to plan self-supply based on targeted outputs (numbers of wells) in the same way it plans for other types of schemes when an alternative approach may be needed. There are no targets or activities for strengthening private sector capacity to support self-supply, so there is a lack of advice or promotion of guidelines or training of artisans. No plans are mentioned for upgrading of self-supply which is already very widespread in these regions. Planning self-supply seems to be equated with numbers of new rope pumps. On the plus side, there are new plans for *kebele* level water extension workers for all *woredas*, with support for self-supply a key aspect of their job alongside community-managed systems and monitoring. A budget of US$15m (3 per cent of the total for capacity building) is also included for self-supply technical assistance but this has so far not attracted interested donors.

Despite government and NGO interest, self-supply largely remains unsupported across Ethiopia. The activities of a self-supply working group at national level brought together interested government and non-government individuals over recent years but has failed to attract substantial financing. Linkages with the household irrigation programme under the Ministry of Agriculture also offer potential – with some form of package added on to improve wells and reduce risks in drinking – but these have not yet materialized given the limited incentives for cross-sectoral collaboration.

---

is there but the means to carry it out is largely lacking. With over 23 million rural Ethiopians using unimproved springs and wells and some 2 million more having made some improvement to their own supply, the potential recognized by government is not given priority alongside other service delivery models.

Others have worked to build support services through government: for example WaterAid Uganda (Carter et al., 2008), DFID funding in Zambia

---

Box 9.5 Government role in group water supply in Meru County, Kenya

There is a history of community self-help water supply in Kenya, following government support to such initiatives in the 1990s onwards (see also Chapter 3 'Improved group supplies'). In Meru County at the turn of the millennium there were more community self-financed schemes than government ones. New self-financed schemes (mainly gravity fed piped supplies) are still being constructed, largely without treatment, and the process is much the same as that found in Irish group water supplies (see Chapter 3, Box 3.4).

   Initially a few householders, who may or may not have their own supply get together and brainstorm over the need for piped water supply to the house and how it could be achieved. They form a committee (group executives), composed of both men and women, who spearhead the process and start registration of those willing to become members. The executive group develops group bylaws and with advice from the social service development officers, registers as a development group and becomes a legal entity which can hold a bank account. The group then registers with the water resources management authority (WARMA) as a water user group. WARMA provides advice on how the group may get technical advice and help in drawing up plans and bills of quantities, and employ consultants for design and environmental impact assessment. The intake is constructed by a trained mason (at a fee) but less skilled work such as trench-digging and pipe-laying is done by the members on a weekly rota, to keep costs as low as possible. Each household buys their own pipes to connect to the mains. A supervisory committee ensures work is done to avoid leakage and wastage and oversee repairs. A monthly maintenance fee ($0.5–1) is paid by each member household to keep the system operating and the system covers its own operation and maintenance. Government in the form of social services and water authorities provide essential advice and monitor performance but the state provides less than 10 per cent of the capital costs.

Source: Information kindly provided by Paul K. Kininya, Principal of Kaguru Agricultural Training Centre, Meru County, Kenya

---

(Sutton, 2002), and UNICEF funding in Mali (Osbert and Sutton, 2009). It is difficult for government to define its own role: changing with sector reform from implementer to funder, supervisor, and contract manager has been a hard-enough step; moving to being simply a facilitator is even harder. This is especially true for sector professionals trained in engineering solutions who are used to working with large contracts and planned, measurable outputs.

   Government roles in higher technology self-supply options prove less problematic, as they do not require new thinking and are officially recognized service delivery systems. In Mali (Maizama, 2015) and in Kenya (see Box 9.5), for example, piped supplies may be financed by users, with government advice on design, tariff setting, access to additional funds, and how to set up and operate as legal entities.

Experience of the entrepreneurial approach

The entrepreneurial approach is a common NGO starting point, and one employed by SMART and EMAS centres (see Boxes 6.5 and 9.6). Building

---

Box 9.6 The Tanzanian experience (see also Part 2, Case Study 5)

In Tanzania, there have been substantial NGO efforts to promote self-supply at grassroots level with a focus on technology introduction, training, and business development. Around the town of Njombe, for example, self-supply has developed in response to the town's population growth, the inability of the utility to supply services to all, the availability of shallow groundwater, and opportunities to use water productively in a range of enterprises (see Part 2, Case study 5). The NGO SHIPO (later a SMART centre) has worked to improve and introduce a wide range of technologies in the area, including upgraded dug wells, manual well drilling, rope pumps, water storage, aquifer recharge systems, water filters, and hand washing devices. As a result, more than 60 local businesses have been established, and by 2015 at least 3,000 wells had been constructed with project support and 6,000 further wells through household investment. At least another 2,000 have been upgraded. The challenge here is how to scale up further without national government commitment and support. Self-supply is not recognized in national policies. New regulations for drilling companies seem more likely to hamper than support the growth of self-supply, unless small artisan drillers can be differentiated from large national or international drilling companies.

---

localized water service businesses is a popular entry point because it can provide measurable outputs (trained personnel) quickly and cheaply once a centre is established. It is similar in form to sanitation marketing, being essentially business-led.

In building up services through business development rather than by installing hardware, the first challenge is in tracking what happens to trainees and their businesses, and how the training increases supply coverage. The second major challenge is to maintain sufficiently constant funding to allow continuity of support until resultant businesses are self-sustaining. The third challenge is to move from training to liaising with government and being in a position to influence policy. These three challenges are more easily addressed where innovation involves government from the start. If government does not see additional approaches as essential it will take substantial grassroots demand to convince them of its value and that takes time to develop. With early government involvement it took five years in Nicaragua (see Box 9.7) and Zimbabwe (Part 2, Case study 4) for the approach to be accepted and promoted by the state. In Tanzania with more than 10 years' private sector capacity building without government involvement, the same result remains to be achieved. Local markets are well-developed and there is much evidence of the acceptability and performance of affordable technologies but they are yet to be officially approved in policy as a household-level option.

NGOs and technical assistance may be needed to introduce the concept of self-supply support and to start the process of capacity building. Countries such as Ethiopia, Uganda, and Rwanda, recognizing the need for additional strategies and the potential of self-supply, have in the past encouraged NGO pilots to circumvent the difficulties of building private sector capacity within government protocols.

Box 9.7 Self-supply progress in Nicaragua

Support to self-supply in Nicaragua started with the introduction of the rope pump in the mid-1980s (IRC, 1995). In the early stages The Nicaraguan Centre for Appropriate Technology introduced it with small local businesses for domestic and farm use later supported by SNV. In 1988 the Directorate of Rural Water Supply became interested in improving designs and by 1990 was giving credit and advice for their installation in a limited area. By 1995 the rope pump became an integral part of rural water supply programmes implemented by NGOs and government agencies at family and community level. By 2000 rural water supply coverage doubled, to reach 55 per cent with almost all (85 per cent) of the growth due to rope pumps, which were largely privately owned (Alberts and van der Zee, 2004). Early uptake by government, popularity with families, and buy-in from donors all led to successful upscaling of self-supply support services over much of the country. By 2000 the estimated addition to the rural economy from rope pump production alone was some $7.5m over five years.

In Sierra Leone DFID initially funded one NGO to develop the private sector (WHH) and another (WaterAid) to liaise more closely with government (Gelhard, 2014), providing a system which embraced both spheres in Figure 9.6. The two-pronged approach led to government integrating the concept into policy in only three years. The two approaches each have advantages and drawbacks (see Table 9.3). More rapid, localized results may come from concentrating on the entrepreneurial approach but combining the two lays the foundation for scaling-up nationwide within national policies.

The aim from the start must be to devise an exit strategy which devolves NGO key roles to government and the private sector as the initial emphasis on capacity building gives way to lower level monitoring, review, and, when necessary, regulation. Devolution of NGO roles could, for example, consist of:

- moving training on affordable technologies and social marketing fully into government training curricula and institutions;
- quality control taken over by water officers or artisan guilds/guarantees;
- subsidies adopted by local government/development funds;
- umbrella organizations such as drillers cooperatives self-managing or adopted by chambers of commerce/water departments;
- monitoring of upgrading included in water point inventories or health information systems;
- training certification and artisan accreditation undertaken by government;
- transition of locally employed personnel into not for profit companies or own NGOs.

Which approach to introduce support to self-supply works best?

There are three key players in introducing support services. Each has its strengths and weaknesses (see Table 9.3) and as the history of Zimbabwe and Nicaragua,

Table 9.3 Summary of merits and drawbacks of introducing a new concept through commercial, government, and NGO channels

Sector	Strengths	Weaknesses
Government -led self-supply	• Provides long-term support and well-established dissemination networks. • Inclusion in policies allows access to public funding/subsidies. • Offers cost-effective options for remote and dispersed communities reducing need for public sector funding to cover the last 10–20%. • Results can be monitored within government systems, including health sector. • Permanent institutional framework. • Local authority planning can integrate a range of service delivery models.	• Public policy may not favour supporting the private sector on which sustainability depends. • Big capital-intensive programmes may well divert official interest away from the initially smaller achievements in supporting self-supply. • Market dynamics and ownership may be distorted if government provides the hardware. • Vulnerable to changes in policy and personnel due to changes in government and staff turnover. • Political and regulatory procedures may slow down progress. • Politicians and government personnel tend to favour high technologies as signs of progress – even if unaffordable. • Emphasis will always be on outputs which are easy to measure and contract out, rather than service provision.
NGO-led self-supply	• Easier to try out options outside government policy framework. • Provides capacity and flexibility to develop and adjust new approaches as further evidence emerges. • Intersectoral inputs more easily achieved.	• Time bound, inputs often limited by funding. • Spatially limited by project areas. • NGO may not coordinate and communicate sufficiently with government. • May be more influenced by NGO policy than host government ones. • May be reluctant to phase out.
Private sector-led self-supply	• Can move more rapidly unencumbered by political considerations or budget releases. • Can develop through clear market dynamics.	• Technologies affordable to produce locally are seldom accepted by government with gaps in capacities in approval and regulatory systems. • If not officially approved, they cannot be subsidized or promoted in state systems, nor included in strategies for remote/dispersed communities.

(Continued)

Table 9.3 Continued

Sector	Strengths	Weaknesses
	• Provides direct relationships between client and service provider. • Once well-established it can grow without further outside funding. • Provides additional funding source, investing in supply chains and production, and sometimes credit for customers.	• No monitoring of development or assessment of bottlenecks. • Mostly confined to area of activity of supporting NGOs. • Needs time to become sustainable. • Perception of government that private sector is profiteering.

and to a lesser extent Sierra Leone, have shown, it is by combining them all that supported self-supply has the greatest chance of becoming firmly established and an officially recognized service delivery model. Who leads in the beginning can depend on early government commitment, but in the end it must be government that absorbs the approach into the sector strategy and leads the way.

Who will lead in government?

Figure 9.5 shows that early government response may lie with health, local government, or water ministries. It is best if all the sectors have memoranda of understanding to work together, which allow some resources to be shared, sometimes through local government influence or management at district levels. The health sector is often quickest and best prepared to take up self-supply as they are used to looking at measures which incrementally reduce health risks through their primary health care programmes. Water professionals are more used to technical solutions designed (theoretically if not in reality) to provide instant safe water. Standard training for primary health extension staff usually includes sanitation options and well-head protection, household water treatment and safe water collection and storage, water testing, and advisory and facilitatory roles with communities/households. Health centre development funds suitable for small subsidies for items such as cement may be available, and communications networks are designed to cascade information from rural health centres to community health workers and individual families. Health personnel's 'listening' relationship with households means that they are therefore often well-placed and trained to help families or communities with problem-solving and to undertake participatory meetings which allow communities to reach their own decisions on WASH solutions.

The water sector can offer more expert advice on water resource management, technical quality of works, training of artisans, technical guidelines, and official endorsement of service delivery technologies. Where both can work together greatest progress can be made. In the case of Zimbabwe, the early works by the Blair Research Institute (Ministry of Health) were endorsed by the National Action Committee (responsible for rural water supply) within three years and taken up by NGOs as well as government extension officers.

Costs

The cost of facilitation

Supported self-supply implies costs to government or others providing the services, and to investing households. For government there are two considerations, how much does it cost and how much, if anything, does it save the public purse? The main costs are in training, social marketing, advisory support and problem solving, and post-construction monitoring. Setting up these support services is achieved in much the same way as for CLTS and community health clubs (Waterkeyn et al., 2019), for which there is more cost information (see Table 9.4). The training costs are for public and private sector understanding of the approach and providing advice, facilitation, and social marketing. In CLTS and self-supply support, additional training is given in technical improvements to skills and products, business management, and product or service promotion. Per capita costs are mostly programme costs divided by numbers of (responding) beneficiaries. These are much affected

Table 9.4 Per capita costs of facilitating sanitation and water self-supply

Country	Year 1 (US$/head)	Year 3 (US$/head)	Facilitation	Information source
Zambia ZSHP	8.3		Sanitation CLTS mobilization	Tillett, 2018
Zimbabwe	4.5		Community health clubs	Waterkeyn et al., 2019
Rwanda	13.3	10	Community health clubs	
Ghana	6.7		Plan CLTS with local NGO mobilizers	Crocker et al., 2017
	18		With natural leader training	
Tanzania	6		CLTS government facilitation	Briceno and Chase, 2015
	10		CLTS including hygiene	
Ethiopia	2.4		Plan CLTS using teachers	Crocker et al., 2017
	3.3		Plan CLTS with health extension staff	
Zambia	20	10	WaterAid self-supply project	Olschewski, 2016
	8	4	Zambia government self-supply implementation	Kumamaru, 2011

by country economics, Rwanda being much more expensive to operate in than Ethiopia, for instance. The degree of training influences per capita cost. The most expensive example is the Zambian WaterAid support because artisans were given almost two months training in masonry, plumbing, welding, marketing, and business management, and population density was extremely low (fewer than two houses/km²). Extensive natural leader training in Ghana also more than doubled the per capita cost in the short term. Facilitation may seem cheaper through government, but this is partly because salaries are not included.

Reducing per capita support costs and facility unit costs over time

In scaling up capacity building mostly constitutes one-off investments and low-level follow-up, which result in high per capita programme costs initially, but which reduce over time as more and more households respond to marketing messages without further project costs. On average the per capita software costs for facilitating community and household sanitation or water supply improvement appears to work out at less than US$10 in sub-Saharan Africa. Private sector marketing reduces costs as, after the initial technical and business training and any early promotion campaign, uptake comes from entrepreneurs selling their skills and products, reducing the software element of total per capita and unit cost. The same is true for supply costs in Cambodia, for example, costs per latrine in the IDE sanitation marketing programme decreased tenfold from their height of $328 to $35 (IDE Global, 2018). Figure 9.7 shows the front-loading of costs during intro-duction and piloting, which is then diluted as sales increase and market forces begin to drive uptake. Costs increase again with strategy development and further training and early marketing inputs for going to scale, and then

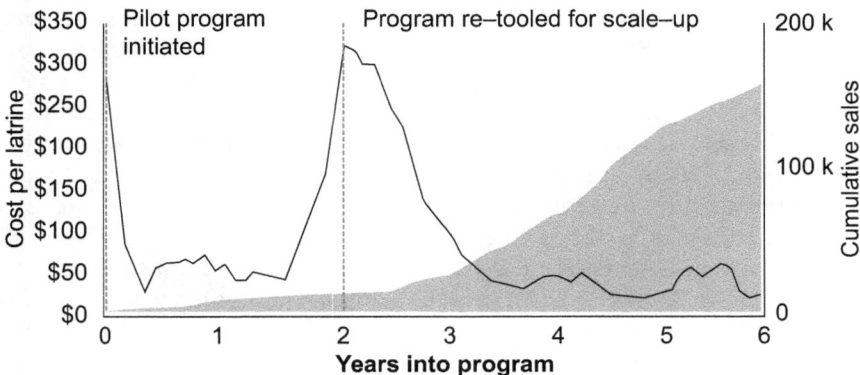

Figure 9.7 Variations in unit/uptake costs (including software costs) during piloting and scaling up. An example in Cambodia
Source: IDE Global, 2018

drop off again in the same fashion. If sufficient momentum has not been generated in the downhill period after the highest cost inputs of piloting, then, like a roller-coaster without enough power, momentum falls off and progress halts in the so-called Valley of Death. In scaling up, if the market is successfully established costs level off with small rises mainly for monitoring and evaluation and adjustments requiring additional training. Market forces can naturally lead to a progression towards higher levels of self-supply as economies improve.

Investment in the enabling environment provides mainly long-term gains with initial higher per capita costs of programme elements until the market takes off. Evaluation often takes place too soon after implementation to judge long-term cost-effectiveness of software interventions. Costs may slightly rise again later when easy-to-reach markets are saturated leaving only poorer households unserved.

Leveraging household resources and reducing costs to government

Promotion of self-supply to dispersed households in Zambia led to an average investment by households of more than $120 for upgrading and $180 for new wells. The software costs of $10–12 per head levered an average of $25 per head of household expenditure on water supply or 1:2–2.5 of programme costs to investment by the well-owning family. In contrast, studies suggest a ratio of two to six times of programme to hardware costs (2–6:1) in sanitation, especially where cheap local materials are used for latrine construction (Radin et al., 2019). Provision of community water supplies to the same Zambian households would have cost $100–300 per head with little or no contribution from households themselves. Software costs may rise in remoter areas with greater distance between households, and more difficulty to access support services.

There needs to be a blend of service delivery models for different settlement patterns to reach universal coverage, mixing small piped schemes, community water supplies and self-supply, with shared support services available to all, including options for rainwater harvesting where other potable water sources are not available. The software and hardware life cycle costs to government to achieve 95 per cent coverage for Zambia (Olschewski, 2016) are estimated at $700m. This assumes that 30 per cent of remaining unserved households are in communities of over 250 inhabitants, and a further 25 per cent are in smaller villages (average 120 inhabitants) and dispersed households, and that they are not in areas with shallow groundwater, both of which require community water supplies (mainly boreholes and handpumps). As Figure 9.8 shows, the largest cost in this case (Case A) is in providing supplies to the smallest communities in areas of shallow groundwater. In Case B, 55 per cent of the population are provided with community water supply, but 45 per cent are covered by self-supply, supported with indirect subsidies. The total cost to government

**All community
water supply**

A. Total cost $700 million

**Hybrid solutions with community water
supply and supported self-supply**

B. Total cost $360 million

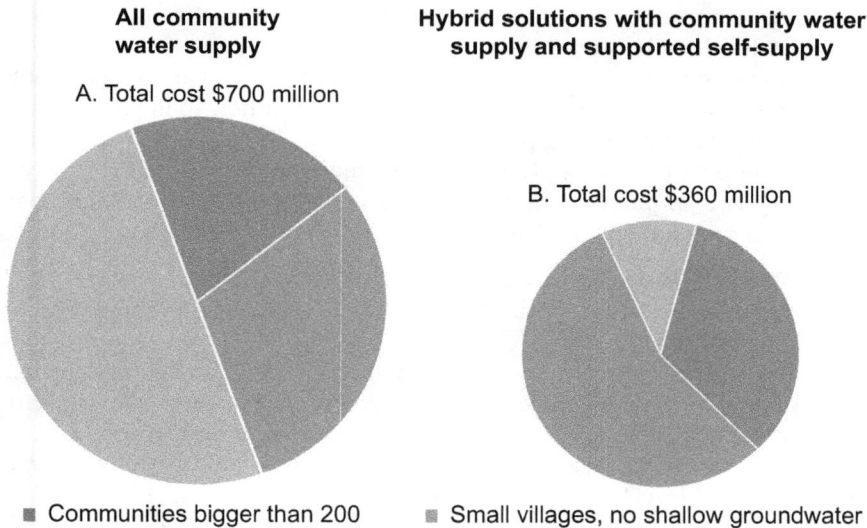

▪ Communities bigger than 200   ▪ Small villages, no shallow groundwater

Figure 9.8 The example of Zambia. Cost savings to government of including self-supply support as an option to reach the last 20 per cent

is halved. The proportion of cost to cover the 45 per cent of small/scattered communities falls to some 10 per cent of the total. Including self-supply as an option for groups averaging fewer than 15 households could reduce the cost to government by 46 per cent if all adopted it, and by 30 per cent if only half did so. The overall saving would be $230–330 m.

A similar exercise for Zimbabwe, with a history of upgraded family wells, suggests that such a blended approach (Olschewski, 2016) could save the state around $260 m with opportunity for subsidies to starter technologies for the most vulnerable.

Conclusion

National policies and strategies determine how resources are allocated, what is prioritized, and how success is measured. Self-supply needs government backing to be supported at scale, and that requires government recognition as a service delivery model. Where there is high dependence on development partners for support, it also requires their backing even when it may challenge existing practice of focus on community supplies as the only acceptable solution. A potential quick win of formal recognition is the contribution of self-supply to official estimates of coverage, since over half of self-supply in sub-Saharan Africa appears to qualify as an at least basic supply. But policies need to recognize the associated value of long-term support, the costs involved, and the likely capacities that will be required to stimulate movement towards safely managed supply. Supported self-supply demands comprehensive strategies involving multiple stakeholders at different levels to kick-start the process.

Piloting of support to self-supply suggests healthy demand at both grassroots and district levels, but there is still often confusion over how to implement it at national levels within existing policies.

How support to self-supply is implemented is country specific, or even district specific in piloting. Models will evolve over time but at the start may depend on such fundamental aspects as:

- Who and where are the champions?
- Which areas have the most potential and what are their settlement patterns?
- How is the rural economy and availability of strong local entrepreneurs?
- What government policies affect strengthening of private sector capacity or working with individual households in different ministries?
- Which are the most active, relevant, and interested ministries at national or district level?

Introduction and piloting may be easier through building up private sector capacity and/or through the health sector. Ultimately, however, in going to scale, coordinating responsibility will be with the ministry(ies) responsible for water and sanitation (rural) services for full integration into country-wide sector planning and equitable coverage with supportive policies and budgets. Self-supply can provide service delivery which is cost effective among marginalized populations and facilitate progressive realization of an 'at least basic' supply (or higher for some) for many millions more if included in a cohesive strategy covering all service delivery models.

References

Alberts, H. and van der Zee, J. (2004) 'A multi-sectoral approach to sustainable rural water supply: the role of the rope handpump in Nicaragua', in P. Moriarty, J. Butterworth, and B. van Koppen (eds.) *Beyond Domestic*, IRC Technical Paper Series 41, IRC, The Netherlands.

Briceno, B. and Chase, C. (2015) 'Cost-efficiency of rural sanitation promotion: activity-based costing and experimental evidence from Tanzania', *Journal of Development Effectiveness* 7: 423–34 <https://doi.org/10.1080/19439342.2015.1105848>.

Butterworth, J., Adank, M., Bakker-Kruijne, E., Mekonta, L. and Klaassen, I. (2014) *Guidelines for Developing a Self-Supply Acceleration Plan for Your Area* [online] <https://www.ircwash.org/resources/guidelines-developing-self-supply-acceleration-plan-your-area> [accessed February 2020].

Carter, R., Mpalanyi, J. and Kiwanuka, J. (2008) *The Uganda Self-Supply Pilot Project 2006–2008* [online], RWSN, Kampala, Uganda <https://www.rural-water-supply.net/fr/ressources/details/278> [accessed January 2020].

Crocker, J., Saywell, D., Shields, K., Kolsky, P. and Bartram, J. (2017) 'The true costs of participatory sanitation: evidence from community-led total sanitation studies in Ghana and Ethiopia', *Science of the Total Environment* <https://doi.org/10.1016/j.scitotenv.2017.05.279>,

Federal Democratic Republic of Ethiopia (2018) *One WASH National Programme: A Multi-Sectoral SWAP Programme* [pdf], PHASE II Programme Document <https://www.unicef.org/ethiopia/media/1111/file/OWNP%20 Phase%20II.pdf> [accessed March 2020].

Gelhard, M. (2014) *WASH Self-supply in Sierra Leone: Perspectives and Options* [online], Welthungerhilfe and WaterAid <https://www.rural-water-supply. net/en/resources/details/596> [accessed January 2020].

Grönwall, J. and Danert, K. (2020) 'Regarding Groundwater and Drinking Water Access through a Human Rights Lens: Self-Supply as a Norm', *Water* 12(2): 419 <https://doi.org/10.3390/w12020419>.

Heller, L. (2015) 'Self-supply and human rights', in *Human Rights and Self-Supply: Potential and Challenges* [online], RWSN Webinar 8, November 2015, RWSN SKAT, St Gallen, Switzerland <https://vimeo.com/147012798> [accessed June 2020].

IDE (2018) *Measuring WASH Cost Effectiveness: IDE's Sanitation Marketing Portfolio* [online] <https://cdn-ms.ideglobal.org/www/documents/iDE-Cost_ Effectiveness_Publication.pdf?mtime=20181228191819> [accessed March 2020].

IRC (1995) *Evaluation Report: Nicaraguan Experiences with the Rope Pump* [online], IRC, The Hague <https://www.ircwash.org/resources/evaluation-report-nicaraguan-experiences-rope-pump-final-report> [accessed March 2010].

Kiwanuka, J. (2015) 'The role of government in accelerating access to safe and reliable water through self-supply', presentation in *Does the Government Have a Role in Self-supply?* [webinar], March 2015, RWSN Secretariat, Switzerland <Vimeo.com/121332803> [accessed 29 May 2020].

Kumamaru, K. (2011) *A Comparative Assessment of Communal Water Supply and Self-Supply Models for Sustainable Rural Water Supplies: A Case Study of Luapula, Zambia* [online], Doctoral thesis, University of Loughborough <https:// repository.lboro.ac.uk/account/articles/9454874> [accessed 10 February 2019].

McCambridge, J., Witton, J. and Elbourne, D. (2014) 'Systematic review of the Hawthorne effect: new concepts are needed to study research participation effects', *Journal of Clinical Epidemiology* 67(3): 267–77 <https://doi. org/10.1016/j.jclinepi.2013.08.015>.

Maizama, D. (2015) 'Self water supply in Sahelian context', presentation in *Does the Government Have a Role in Self-supply?* [webinar], RWSN Secretariat, Switzerland <https://vimeo.com/121332803> [accessed March 2020].

Mekassa, M. (2006) 'Getting the people onto the first rung of the ladder', *Proceedings of the 5th RWSN Forum, Accra, Ghana* <https://www.rural-water-supply.net/_ressources/documents/default/180.pdf> [accessed March 2020].

Mekonta, L., Butterworth, J. and Holtslag, H. (2015) 'Great expectations: self-supply as a formal service delivery model for rural water in Ethiopia', *Proceedings of the 38th WEDC International Conference*, Loughborough University, UK <https://wedc-knowledge.lboro.ac.uk/resources/conference/38/Mekonta-2291.pdf> [accessed March 2020].

Mekonta, L., Ward, R. and Butterworth, J. (2017) *Self-Supply End Line Evaluation: Report of an End Line Evaluation for the Millennium Water Alliance-Ethiopia*

Programme Self-supply Acceleration Pilots [pdf], IRC WASH <https://www.ircwash.org/sites/default/files/mwa_self-supply_endline-final.pdf> [accessed February 2020].

MoWE (Ministry of Water and Energy, Ethiopia), Self-supply Working Group (SSWG), IRC, UNICEF, WHO, RiPPLE, and COWASH (2012) *National Policy Guidelines for Self-Supply: Guidelines to Support Contribution of Improved Self-Supply to Universal Access* [online], MOWE, Addis Ababa, Ethiopia <https://www.ircwash.org/resources/national-policy-guidelines-self-supply-guidelines-support-contribution-improved-self> [accessed June 2020].

Noguiera, D. (2008) 'Brazil: Rainwater harvesting in semi-arid region helps women' [online], Gender and Water Alliance <http://genderandwater.org/en/gwa-products/knowledge-on-gender-and-water/articles-in-source-bulletin/brazil-rainwater-harvesting-in-semi-arid-region-helps-women-1> [accessed March 2020].

Olschewski, A. (2016) *Review of Self-Supply and its Support Services in African Countries: Synthesis Report* [online], UNICEF, SKAT Foundation <https://www.rural-water-supply.net/en/resources/details/753> [accessed February 2020].

Osbert, N. and Sutton, S. (2009) 'Self supply in Mali: early steps towards an innovatory approach', *Proceedings of 34th WEDC International Conference, Addis Ababa, Ethiopia* [online] <https://www.rural-water-supply.net/en/resources/details/285> [accessed June 2020].

Radin, M., Jeuland, M., Wang, H. and Whittington, D. (2019) *Benefit-Cost Analysis of Community-Led Total Sanitation: Incorporating Results from Recent Evaluations* [pdf], prepared for the Benefit Cost Analysis Reference Case Guidance Project Funded by the Bill and Melinda Gates Foundation <https://cdn2.sph.harvard.edu/wp-content/uploads/sites/94/2017/01/Radin-Jeuland-Whittington-CLTS-2019.01.07.pdf> [accessed February 2020].

Smits, S. and Sutton, S. (2012) *Self-supply: The Case for Leveraging Greater Household Investment in Water Supply*, Triple S, Building blocks for sustainability, Briefing Note March 2015 (reprint), IRC, The Hague, Netherlands <https://www.ircwash.org/sites/default/files/084-201502triple-s_bn03defweb_1.pdf> [accessed 29 May 2020].

Sutton, S. (2002) *Community Led Improvements of Rural Drinking Water Supplies* [online], DFID KAR Report 7128 <http://www.rural-water-supply.net/en/resources/details/249> [accessed 21 January 2019].

Sutton, S. (2004) *Preliminary Desk Study of Potential for Self-supply in Sub-Saharan Africa* [online], RWSN/WaterAid <http://www.rural-water-supply.net/en/resources/details/264> [accessed January 2020].

Sutton, S. (2007) *Implementation Plan for Self-Supply Piloting in Luapula Province*, RWSN/UNICEF, Zambia <http://www.rural-water-supply.net/en/resources/details/877> [accessed January 2020].

Sutton, S. and Nkoloma, H. (2011) *Encouraging Change: Sustainable Steps in Water Supply, Hygiene and Sanitation*, 2nd edn, Health Books International/Practical Action Publishing, Rugby, UK <https://healthbooksinternational.org/product/encouraging-change-sustainable-steps-in-water-supply-sanitation-and-hygiene-2nd-edition/> [accessed 29 May 2020].

Sutton, S., Butterworth, J. and Mekonta, L. (2012) *A Hidden Resource: Household-Led Rural Water Supply in Ethiopia*, IRC International water and Sanitation Centre, The Netherlands <https://www.ircwash.org/resources/hidden-resource-household-led-rural-water-supply-ethiopia> [accessed March 2020].

Tillett, W. (2018) *Learning from a Review of One of Southern Africa's Largest Rural Sanitation Programmes*, Aguaconsult <https://www.aguaconsult.co.uk/aguaconsult-completes-a-review-of-one-of-southern-africas-largest-rural-sanitation-programmes/> [accessed 15 January 2020].

UNHCHR (1976) *International Covenant on Economic, Social and Cultural Rights* [online] <https://www.ohchr.org/en/professionalinterest/pages/cescr.aspx> [accessed January 2020].

UNHCHR (2003) *General Comment No. 15: The Right to Water (Arts. 11 and 12 of the Covenant)* [pdf] <https://www2.ohchr.org/english/issues/water/docs/CESCR_GC_15.pdf> [accessed January 2020].

UNHCHR (2008) *Frequently Asked Questions on Economic, Social and Cultural Rights* [pdf], Fact Sheet 33 <https://www.ohchr.org/Documents/Publications/FactSheet33en.pdf> [accessed January 2020].

Waterkeyn, J., Matamati, R., Muringaniza, A., Chigono, A., Ntakarutimana, A., Katabarwa, J., Bigirimana, Z., Pantoglou, J., Waterkeyn, A. and Cairncross, C. (2019) 'Comparative assessment of hygiene behaviour change and cost effectiveness of community health clubs in Rwanda and Zimbabwe', in U. Bacha (ed.), *Healthcare Access* [online], IntechOpen <https://www.intechopen.com/books/healthcare-access-regional-overviews/comparative-assessment-of-hygiene-behaviour-change-and-cost-effectiveness-of-community-health-clubs-> [accessed June 2020].

World Bank (2017) *Sustainability Assessment of Rural Water Service Delivery Models: Findings of a Multi-Country Review* [pdf], World Bank, Washington, DC <http://documents.worldbank.org/curated/en/271221503692975915/pdf/Sustainability-assessment-of-rural-water-service-delivery-models-findings-of-a-multi-country-review.pdf> [accessed February 2020].

CHAPTER 10

Conclusions and recommendations

This chapter summarizes what existing self-supply teaches us, especially in the rural environment of sub-Saharan Africa, and the potential it has if supported by governments and NGOs. The points made are also of relevance to other regions where the starting point may often be a bit higher, but the need and potential for improvements are still enormous. Many gaps in knowledge are identified in this book, which is the first on the subject, and actions to raise the profile of self-supply and reduce the 'known un-knowns' are proposed. It finishes with an exhortation, frequently voiced throughout, to give self-supply due recognition as an important element in water supply evolution and one which should no longer be ignored.

Keywords: sector perspective, self-financed, scale, potential, self-supply

A focus on the gaps

At the start of this book the gap between global targets and rates of progress in rural water supply construction was used as a justification for looking more closely at self-supply as a little explored additional option for water supply delivery. Analysis of the existing situation in subsequent chapters identified a set of interlinked gaps which need addressing if sections of the population are not still to be left behind in 2030.

The first of these other gaps is the need for a service delivery model suited for smaller communities that cannot sustain conventional community water supply. At present in most countries there is very seldom any policy to cover the many who live in small groups of fewer than 10–15 houses, or those dispersed in isolated houses. Even in the highest income economies any support is recent and, for most, local solutions to bring scattered households to safely managed or at least basic provision are still lacking.

Self-supply is happening almost everywhere as rural economies improve and is growing year by year. The second gap occurs where community water supply policies do not meet the expectations of rural households who feel they can do better for themselves in whole or in part. In attempting to fill this gap, they are creating a third, which is a gap between the standards governments would like to achieve and the ones families have the capacity to reach for themselves. Support is needed to ensure that those most at risk do not remain the least supported, and where necessary they are empowered to upgrade their own supplies to adequate standards over time. Different policies are needed for the different circumstances in which self-supply exists or is needed.

The gap in achieving standards in part links to a fourth, the gap in capacity of local SMEs in sparsely populated areas with weak rural economies.

http://dx.doi.org/10.3362/9781780448190.010

Here support is needed to kickstart capacity building and business development to provide services of quality which have the skills and products to serve both dispersed communities and those peripheral to public supplies in peri-urban and rural surroundings. It requires a major focus on training, the most expensive element of support, but also on coordinated efforts of government and NGOs to build up private sector capacities, and for them to support market development both as potential customers and as organizations with social marketing expertise and personnel.

A fifth and final gap is that of water being seen only as a social good, when it can also (where feasible) be a stepping-stone in rural development. Water supply so far has often been viewed as little more than a domestic necessity, siloed from its other values which can provide a return for household investors.

The first step in filling all these gaps is to recognize the part that self-supply is already playing in bringing water to millions of households, and to understand the forces that drive it. The second is to appreciate the potential of government, private sector, and NGO support to enable self-suppliers to move more rapidly beyond sub-standard supplies into the realms of safely managed facilities. The third is to turn the accumulated understanding into strategies and actions to become a part of the overall system of district-wide water supply planning in any region or district. Self-supply can then stand appropriately alongside other service delivery models.

Step One. Considering existing self-supply in the evolution of service delivery

Putting the user first

Self-supply is the ultimate in a demand responsive approach – where both demand and response are generated in the household. Sector service delivery on the other hand is driven by a professional perspective in terms of goals and performance standards especially in water quality. Supported self-supply acknowledges these differences (Figure 10.1) and offers opportunities to bring both perspectives together. The objective is to match available technologies with support to household preferences and resources, aiming progressively to converge with sector objectives for higher service delivery levels. Self-supply as a group or individual initiative and in a supported or unsupported form may be regarded as a household service delivery model, in that the household is the prime financer, and asset management is the by household(s) who also monitor performance and make decisions.

Self-supply brings management and ownership to the lowest level of decision-making, allowing the individual household or small group maximum opportunity to exercise their own choice in water supply solutions. For households, convenience is the highest priority and brings many associated benefits

which positively affect family members (especially women and children) and neighbours, stimulating further investment in many cases.

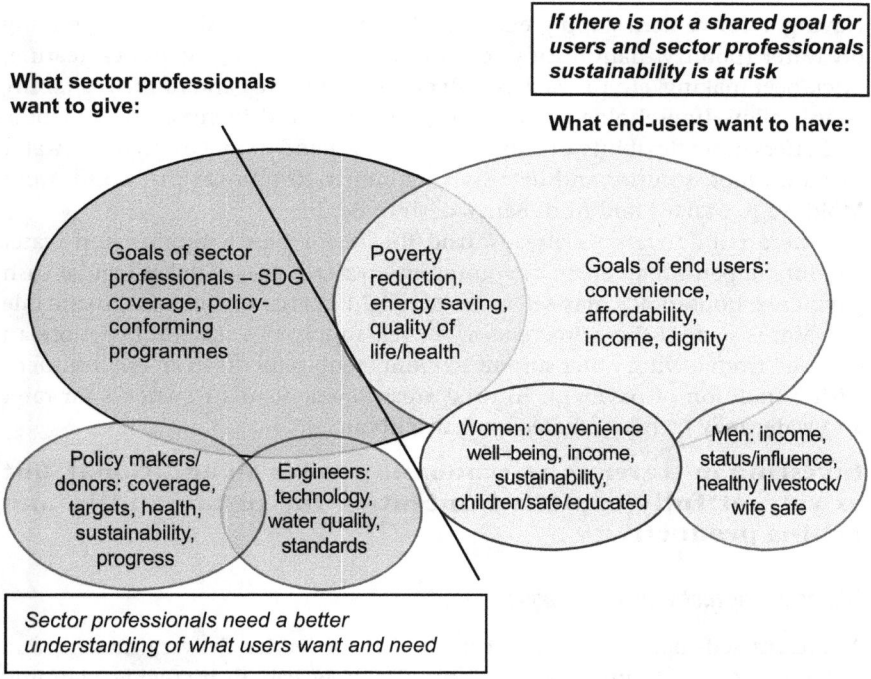

Figure 10.1 A generalization of the difference between the professional and household perspectives
Source: Modified from IRC, 2006

Recognizing self-financed supplies

Self-supply is the original form of water supply before any externally supported intervention. It precedes other forms of service delivery, interacts with them as they grow, and is left filling the gaps which remain at the end. How it is viewed and supported needs to change so that strategies can be developed in each country to improve the roles it can play in urban and rural contexts. The scale of self-supply across the world is huge, undervalued, and under-resourced. It is time to stop seeing it as a problem and start seeing it as an opportunity to help meet global goals and improve family well-being.

The SDG 6.1 puts high value on 'on-premises' sources. At present, self-supply, which globally delivers 'on-premises' supplies to many millions of households and is shared by many more, is mostly unrecognized in sector reviews or policies. In its improved forms it contributes to the SDG but is hidden from view (see Chapters 3 and 4).

Self-supply should be recognized as one of a set of valid service delivery models and become part of an integrated sector vision.

Enhancing livelihoods

Having a convenient supply enables investors to run businesses depending on water (poultry, hairdressing, car washing, beekeeping, livestock rearing, brick/beer making, etc.) as well as cash crops. Time saved and improved family health allow households to be more productive and increase their income and offers more flexibility of choice in what to spend it on. On-premises water increases food security and decreases malnutrition all over the world, from Moldova to Malawi and from Bangladesh to Benin.

Where public water is already paid for, as for piped supplies and water vending in peri-urban areas, or community water supply invokes regular cash payments, households may sell water to neighbours or to vendors. Private sale of water is seldom the prime reason for self-supply investment, but more an offshoot from having water surplus to family requirements in an environment with a tradition of payment. In rural areas payment to an owner is far rarer and water may be freely shared with neighbours.

Investing in water as an economic good is an additional, but as yet not fully exploited, incentive for sustainability and raising productivity.

Water is not just a physical asset

At present self-supply does not fit in the box of service delivery models, and certainly not in its unsupported form. Yet how can district-wide planning for universal access of safely managed supplies be achieved if half of what people already use in much of South Asia for instance, is not even acknowledged by the sector to exist? Ownership of water supply is a complex subject, because water is not just a commodity like a television or a car. For some it cannot be bought and sold, it can only be shared, for some it forms a bond of communal initiative, for some it is an asset which is difficult to abandon, and yet for many as a communal asset it is not as valued as it needs to be for long-term sustainability.

As a fundamental element of human survival, water is not just viewed by consumers as a commodity. Self-supply is the extreme in this, but non-functioning of community supplies and non-payment of tariffs to utilities also indicate the need for better understanding of how people think of water in different societies and at different levels if sustainability is to be achieved.

The scale of existing self-supply

Self-financed investment in water supply exists worldwide, in urban and rural and low- and high-income contexts, but mostly in rural areas. At the top service level, it provides piped water into over 40 per cent of rural households in North America, and to many more through cooperatives. At the bottom level, in rural areas worldwide 360 million people are using unimproved groundwater supplies (155 million of them in sub-Saharan Africa – a quarter of the population – as illustrated in Figure 10.2), offering potential for upgrading what are mostly privately owned supplies. In almost all countries for which data was obtained, self-financed household supplies comprise more improved than unimproved sources. This implies that owners are aware of the need for source protection and have already been prepared to invest in some upgrading their supplies. In sub-Saharan Africa 87 per cent of urban and 56 per cent of rural self-financed supplies are of improved standards providing an at least basic supply. In high income countries 100 per cent of self-supply consists of improved sources (Chapter 3) and it is perfectly clear that self-supply can provide a good level of service.

In rural sub-Saharan Africa, 70 million people are using their own on-premises groundwater supply that is either improved or unimproved (a further 8 million use rainwater harvesting, which is seldom shared). Assuming the same level of sharing for improved and unimproved groundwater supplies, a total of approximately 337 million people (55 per cent of the rural population) therefore may depend at least in part on some level of groundwater self-supply in the region. Many of these supplies have the potential for upgrading over time to at least basic standards and some to safely managed service levels.

The scale of self-supply is large and growing, especially in rural areas. It contributes significantly to at least basic level coverage through individual ownership and sharing, and chiefly in richer countries to safely managed supply through individual and cooperative ownership.

The scale of self-supply and the potential to contribute to SDG aims suggests that private efforts, especially in poorer economies, should be regarded more as assets with the capacity to reach at least basic service levels, rather than only as liabilities.

Rural and urban self-supply

Self-supply is depended upon in both rural and urban areas but differs to a degree in purpose and form. Ownership, levels of sharing, and availability of support services are not the same in all contexts. The relationship with other service delivery models and the potential for self-supply vary not just between urban and rural, but between different cities or rural areas within a country and even within different quarters within a city, or different wards within a district.

Self-supply comes in many guises and its variety means that government policies, forms of regulation or support need to be designed to cater for a range of local conditions.

The overall picture of existing supplies

Whatever service level a supply has reached, there is room for improvement, whether utility-operated or self-supply. Many households in lower- and

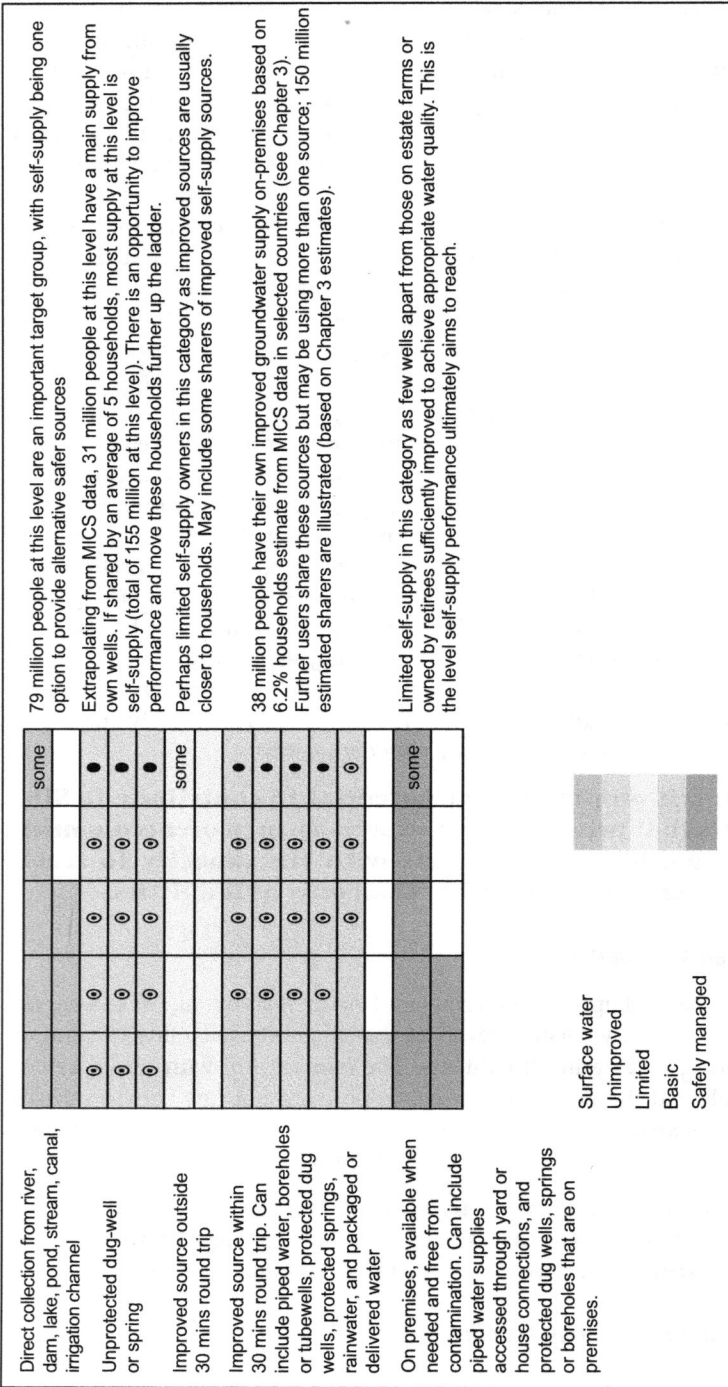

Main drinking water source	Surface water	Unimproved	Limited	Basic	Safely managed		Notes
Direct collection from river, dam, lake, pond, stream, canal, irrigation channel						some	79 million people at this level are an important target group, with self-supply being one option to provide alternative safer sources
Unprotected dug-well or spring	⊙	⊙	⊙	●	● ●		Extrapolating from MICS data, 31 million people at this level have a main supply from own wells. If shared by an average of 5 households, most supply at this level is self-supply (total of 155 million at this level). There is an opportunity to improve performance and move these households further up the ladder.
Improved source outside 30 mins round trip						some	Perhaps limited self-supply owners in this category as improved sources are usually closer to households. May include some sharers of improved self-supply sources.
Improved source within 30 mins round trip. Can include piped water, boreholes or tubewells, protected dug wells, protected springs, rainwater, and packaged or delivered water	⊙	⊙	⊙	●	●		38 million people have their own improved groundwater supply on-premises based on 6.2% households estimate from MICS data in selected countries (see Chapter 3). Further users share these sources but may be using more than one source; 150 million estimated sharers are illustrated (based on Chapter 3 estimates).
On premises, available when needed and free from contamination. Can include piped water supplies accessed through yard or house connections, and protected dug wells, springs or boreholes that are on premises.						some	Limited self-supply in this category as few wells apart from those on estate farms or owned by retirees sufficiently improved to achieve appropriate water quality. This is the level self-supply performance ultimately aims to reach.

Figure 10.2 Illustration of the scale of self-supply in rural sub-Saharan Africa (owners and sharers of self-supply sources) shown in comparison with levels on the JMP water supply ladder

Note: Each shaded cell represents 10 million people showing the main drinking water source for households as reported by JMP for 2017. Cells including ● reflect an estimate of the scale of well ownership based on results presented in Chapter 3 using MICS survey data. Cells with ⊙ illustrate the possible number of sharers of self-supply sources.

middle-income countries have developed supplies which are on the lower rungs of the technology ladder. Their number is not yet fully known nor is the level they have reached. User investment has tended to fill gaps and provide a convenient basic supply until public alternatives bring water into the home. It frequently reduces pressure of demand on over-stretched public supplies, and with over 300 million worldwide still depending on unimproved groundwater, and many more on their own or their neighbours' private supplies of varying standards, there is plenty of scope for movement up the service delivery ladder (see Figure 10.2). Remote households in Ireland, Bosnia Herzegovina, Australia, and the United States among others show how households have undertaken improvements to reach national standards, at first by their own efforts but often later with loans or grants. At the other extreme some of the poorest households in the remotest districts of sub-Saharan Africa have created and begun to improve their own supplies at their own cost. They are the most difficult and costly for governments to serve with conventional piped supply or community water points and for users to have access to or afford maintenance services. They remain largely unserved in developing countries and without strategies for the higher per capita costs entailed.

Self supply and public supply are rarely in competition. Indeed, in areas where there are few reliable water points, the existence of private and public sources raises the probability that there is a functioning source within convenient distance.

Self-supply and other paths to service delivery form part of a dynamic whole (see Figure 10.3). Evolution can involve moves between public and private models at the small scale of villages, just as much as it does in higher economies. State and private (commercial or not for profit) management are not static entities but often interrelated and with potential to be transformed from one to the other.

The evolution of high-quality self-supply in higher income countries can provide lessons for emerging economies – but we have to recognize appropriate starting points and progression in service levels and make this forgotten history better documented and understood.

Step Two. Developing support to self-supply acceleration

An appropriate and affordable response

Decision-makers should see support to self-supply and starter technologies as an appropriate and affordable response for households and small clusters in remote areas or those peripheral to existing supplies, especially when they recognize the limitations of available resources at district and sub-district levels. This can result in a wide variety of outcomes. Where there is already a tradition of community cooperation, mobilizing group efforts can lead to affordable solutions and higher levels of internal and

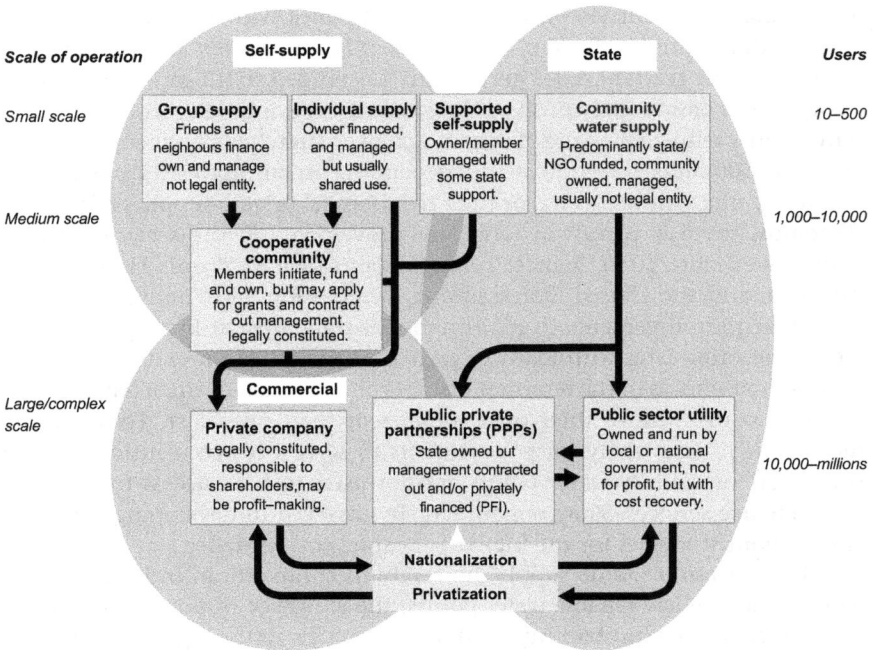

Scale of operation	Self-supply			State	Users
Small scale	**Group supply** Friends and neighbours finance own and manage not legal entity.	**Individual supply** Owner financed, and managed but usually shared use.	**Supported self-supply** Owner/member managed with some state support.	**Community water supply** Predominantly state/NGO funded, community owned, managed, usually not legal entity.	10–500
Medium scale		**Cooperative/community** Members initiate, fund and own, but may apply for grants and contract out management. legally constituted.			1,000–10,000
Large/complex scale	**Commercial** **Private company** Legally constituted, responsible to shareholders,may be profit–making.	**Public private partnerships (PPPs)** State owned but management contracted out and/or privately financed (PFI).		**Public sector utility** Owned and run by local or national government, not for profit, but with cost recovery.	10,000–millions
		Nationalization			
		Privatization			

Figure 10.3 The mix and fluidity of public, private, and commercial service delivery

external funding to finance cooperative piped supplies for many lower levels of improved supply or initially even unimproved ones. In other cases, rainwater harvesting may form a stand-alone partial solution where safe groundwater is not available.

The market for water supply services and products can grow, if a mentality develops to feed the household desire for a more convenient supply. It will be stifled if local and national government see self-supply as an inferior stopgap they should discourage. Sector professionals and politicians need to recognize and respect the right and capacity of households or groups of households to access water and the efforts they make for themselves and build them into a district-wide approach.

Self-financed facilities need to be identified, quantified, and included in monitoring, planning and budgeting as part of a coherent systems approach for district-wide coverage.

Cost reduction for government and new sources of funding

In reaching universal access, including support to self-supply as a service delivery option can reduce the call on public sector funding. Blending community water supply and self-supply support approaches on a countrywide basis not only speeds up progress but can reduce costs to government of universal access by as much as half (see Chapter 9), in reaching the last 10–20 per cent.

Supporting self-supply implies costs to government and/or NGOs. Most costs are indirect as in CLTS, since households pay the capital costs and government or NGOs focus more on building private sector capacity to satisfy demand. The costs of building up support services, social marketing, and short-term monitoring for lower cost technologies starts at around $20 per head without subsidy for hardware but falls to $4–8 as numbers using the services increase. In dispersed households, typical per capita costs for conventional borehole and handpump supplies are more than 15 times higher. With lower cost technologies and full subsidy, the costs to government or NGO remain less than a fifth as much. They are mainly front-loaded and aimed primarily at training and demonstration and market development. They reduce to a point where they mostly consist of monitoring performance, regulating, and providing advice, which are common to all service delivery models and should be shared between them.

Governments need to estimate and factor in potential financial savings from including self-supply approaches in rural water strategies, in terms of immediate construction and life cycle costs.

Targeting remote rural communities and dispersed households

Remote communities in lower income countries need technical options with capital and maintenance costs affordable to individuals or small groups, or partly covered by the state. Support services may promote more affordable self-supply starter technologies, and the state, if it can, may subsidize supplies. This makes sense because households are taking on the responsibility vested in the state to provide a safe water supply where government is unable to do so. High priority countries in sub-Saharan Africa include Ethiopia, Nigeria, Democratic Republic of the Congo, Tanzania, and Niger where almost 90 million people are still drinking from unprotected groundwater sources.

Clear policies and budget lines for targeted (smart) subsidy strategies are needed, including grants or loans for the poor and vulnerable plus adequate training for local government personnel and local artisans to provide long-term back-up for user-level construction and maintenance. These mirror support services for sanitation marketing and CLTS and can mostly be combined with them.

Governments need to establish guidelines, policies, budgets, and smart subsidies to ensure affordability among the poorest, even if this means considering lower service levels to start with for dispersed households and small communities.

Providing back-up for all whose own supply presents a risk

For almost all households, even those with piped water at the house, water quality improvements may be necessary, so the global scope for improvement through source protection, water treatment, and storage is large, but many have already taken the first steps. In lower-middle income countries (e.g. Pakistan, Bangladesh, Ukraine, Moldova), self-financed improved supply into the house is an increasing trend, while for low-income countries households are still mainly seeking to achieve a more convenient supply and then a basic level service with improved source protection and water lifting device.

The existence of so many on-premises supplies providing a basic or less than basic level of service delivery justifies universal support to bring them to higher standards, and for their (improved) replication where necessary. Upgrading at household level will be largely financed with household investment. The support role is in advice, research, training, marketing, and monitoring. Post-construction support services are increasingly provided for community and small piped water supplies; why should these advisory capacities and budgets not also be accessible to smaller groups and individual households?

The need for improvement is universal, but the form and technology options it takes vary with country and household economy. Water supply, saniation and household water treatment support services need to be accessible to all in the quest for universal provision, especially where public supplies are lacking or inadequate.

Self-supply in large urban areas

In lower income countries with high population growth rates urban self-supply remains an essential gap filler:

- for the urban poor and those needing to augment unreliable or unaffordable supply often in high-density unsewered housing areas;
- for those in new, low-density peri-urban housing beyond the limits of piped services.

If not already contaminated, the quality of groundwater may be expected to deteriorate over time, in higher density unsewered areas and wellhead protection may do little to reduce risks. In such areas, urban groundwater self-supply should generally be earmarked only for non-potable uses. For peri-urban supplies and low-density housing, groundwater is more likely to be safe if it is safely abstracted and stored, especially from deeper aquifers. Here self-supplied piped systems are rapidly increasing.

The demand for urban groundwater can become acute, and the quality may be poor, but rainwater harvesting remains a partial solution mostly only for the well-off with space to spare and money to invest. Self-supply can reduce demand for piped supply where utilities have difficulty in meeting demand as in many Asian and African cities. Utilities can play an important advisory role and plan coexistence or absorption of high-quality self-supply systems into their own over time. An objective view is needed of whether self-supply threatens the viability of a utility or is helping to ensure adequate, reliable services.

Concerns over water quality have often influenced attitudes to self-supply. However, self-financed supplies are increasing and the solution should turn towards promoting conjunctive use rather than dismissing what owners value, especially where the state cannot afford a guaranteed safe, reliable, and convenient supply.

Large urban areas present a complex range of supply types and interactions between them. Self-supply fits into this for specific groups and purposes, but is largely unacknowledged and optimizing its contribution and relationship to formal service delivery requires further development.

Group self-supply in smaller urban areas

Cooperative self-supply provides water to over 30 per cent of households in Canada, the United States, Denmark, and Austria. Amalgamations of individual and group supplies are evolving to improve standards, since larger groups can afford to pay for better management and move away from dependence on volunteers. Kenya, with a long tradition of group cooperation for self-help (*harambee*), Mali's remittance-dependent small piped supplies, and the Ethiopian Community Managed Project approach show that similar group initiatives could be promoted in many other small towns that are being left behind. Group self-help has formed an important step, alongside municipal systems in much of Europe, often forming legal entities to access additional public funds (see Figure 10.3). Group approaches offer another route for communities to upgrade to a higher level of service where limited or no outside funding is yet available. Many communities have had a community handpump supply for 15 to 20 years without any information on how to reach higher service levels.

Self-supply need not just be for individual families and small groups but should also be considered for larger groups, especially where there is already a tradition of community self-help.

Improving sustainability

Systems provided through private investment have been shown in Chapter 8 to be more likely to be repaired and looked after. Returns on investment in water supply enable families to re-invest in further improvements, and what one household does can be copied by a neighbour, especially as household water supplies are highly visible, and showing the world that you can care for your family is an important concept for many. The more the demand, the greater the private sector strength to respond.

Offering support and advice provides a route for households to take progressive and sustainable steps to improve supply reliability and adequacy through bite-sized investments.

Donor dependence and self-help.

In many cultures a history of self-help for water has stalled where people have been taught to be completely dependent on provision by government or NGOs. Awakening or re-awakening community confidence to look for solutions is part of what support services can offer, and also develop a new source of funding and sense of ownership.

Piloting self-supply services gradually awakens strong demand and this grows over time as people see what others are able to achieve (see Part 2, Case study 4). Demand is suppressed by lack of available information and services, if households are unaware of what they can do for themselves. The history of self-supply in Zimbabwe shows that small incentives can speed up responses but these may slow down again once incentives cease.

Speeding up self-supply to help meet SDG targets needs to be carefully balanced against any risks of jeopardizing longer-term sustainability when donor support is withdrawn.

A long-term approach

Water supply systems evolve gradually, typically over decades. While the process can be sped up to some degree, reaching a sustainable state is not a short-term process. For government to accept and value lower cost options and establish sustainable private sector capacity requires long term commitment. The inclusion of self-supply initially boosts the numbers of recognized improved supplies but building an enabling environment to support further progress takes longer. Experience from Nicaragua and Zimbabwe suggests that self-supply can become locally sustainable in five years or less but it takes a decade to be completely sustainable and embedded in government and private sectors.

The slippage in open defecation-free communities indicates the need for post-construction support for sanitation and the same is true for improvements in water self-supply. The sustainability of community water supplies has also required long-term post-construction commitment, and the need is still evolving as the limitations of village level operation and maintenance become increasingly apparent. Making shared support services available is a powerful stimulus and can help to maintain community dynamics and reduce slippage in all aspects of WASH.

Achieving sustainability in self-supply, as with community water supply, needs to be seen as a long-term process. Combining with sanitation programmes could strengthen both and maintain a focus on household level provision. Parallels between sanitation marketing/CLTS and promotion of household financing of water supply suggest that reductions in cost and improvements in efficacy may be achieved.

Resilience and cross-sector opportunities

Water supply is a multi-sectoral necessity and many stakeholders will benefit from support to self-supply (see Figure 10.4) which offers opportunities for accelerating change for the WASH sector, households, and rural economies.

Health and water sectors are particularly concerned with domestic supply and have services relevant to self-supply support. Health, agriculture, and community development communications networks usually reach household level while water personnel seldom operate below district level. The responsibilities of local government and its links to civil society are highly pertinent and will determine who takes the lead country by country. There is a clear need to develop cross-sectoral collaboration and clarity about the resources each can offer. For instance, health extension personnel and area mechanics can offer advisory and technical services, often within their existing skills and job descriptions, but not necessarily within their (public or

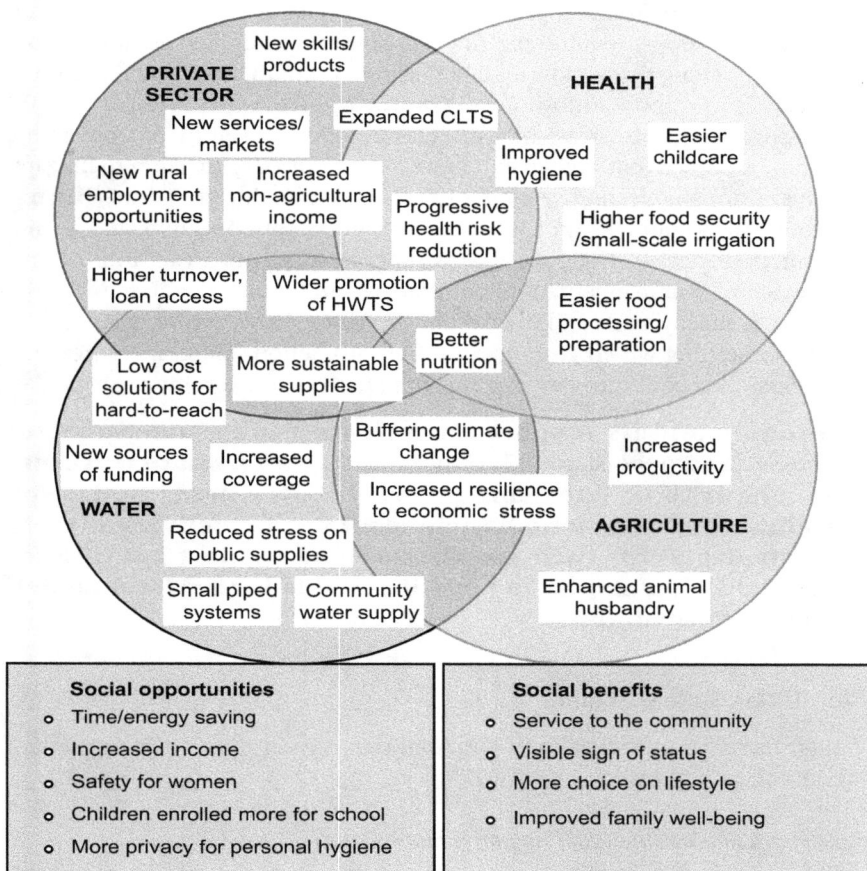

Figure 10.4 Multi-sectoral potential in supporting self-supply

private sector) budgets. Collaboration is easiest at district level through local government coordination, but ultimately requires national level policies to access budget lines, training curricula, monitoring, and research.

Cost-effective support could largely be provided through sharing existing resources if different sectors can identify advantages and ways to collaborate, and develop a strategy which employs combined capacities to increase resilience to climatic, economic, and social stresses.

Challenges

As with community water supply there are many but perhaps some different challenges to donor/government support and supply sustainability. Considering service delivery at household levels and more from the customer's point of view needs a similar shift in thinking to that brought about in the 1980s when emphasis changed from supply to demand-responsive approaches. The shift to include self-supply requires big changes in ways of thinking at all levels but particularly among those most used to dealing in certainty and the precision of engineering. 'Disruptive innovation' (Wahnbaeck, 2016) is a good way to describe it. The suggestion is to create new markets and look at realistic progress rather than only designed (but limited and more rarely realized) perfection to fill gaps. It moves from engineering systems to human plus engineering ones. The two are not exclusive but take time to develop a joint 'modus operandi' and are not without challenges. Self-supply and its support do not fit easily into normal service delivery implementation or financial and institutional frameworks. However, it already exists and there is not yet the capacity everywhere to replace it with something which gives greater user satisfaction. Much more needs to be understood about it to develop appropriate situation-specific strategies.

Self-supply and its support are awkward to include in sector processes and procedures, but even more awkward to leave out, if no one is to be left behind. Each country needs to develop sustainable systems which include all service delivery models, with strategies for their co-existence and support but also for their transition or phasing out if reliable higher-level models can be made available.

Step Three. Taking action

While challenges are numerous, potential is also great if the following action points can be addressed.

For donors and international financial institutions

Action is needed to ensure that self-supply is on the radar of high level donors and international finance institutions and is included in arrangements for a

---

Box 10.1 Recommended high-level actions for donors and international aid agencies

- Endorse self-supply and its support as a service delivery model to fill gaps which will otherwise remain untouched (e.g. AMCOW, World Bank, UNICEF).
- Recognize the degree of investment necessary for evidence gathering, private sector development, and public support mechanisms to provide a safer sustainable service in poorer economies.
- Champion service delivery rather than simply short-term numerical outputs, and allow extended funding windows for changing attitudes and building new long-term markets.
- Encourage governments to take account of self-supply achievements and challenges in their sector planning and budgeting.
- Invest in technical assistance to countries to develop strategies including self-supply support.
- Support better data collection, analysis, and learning (e.g. by UNICEF/ WHO JMP) to bring a level of knowledge and understanding to self-supply comparable to that of other service delivery models.

---

sector-wide approach. Donors should view it as a valued part of the armoury of rural water supply strategy (see Boxes 10.1).

If sector review procedures are based on infrastructure outputs rather than service delivery the role of self-supply in improving household access to water may be overlooked.

Investors in self-supply support must take a long view as uptake by households may start slowly and accelerate later.

For governments

Box 10.2 summarises what national governments can do to harness self-supply towards their objectives. Absorbing self-supply into rural water strategy at all levels of government is a gradual process, made easier where

---

Box 10.2 Recommended actions for governments

- Assess the prevalence of existing self-supply at improved and unimproved levels from household cluster surveys and trends in its contribution towards universal coverage.
- Identify priority areas for subsidized and unsubsidized self-supply.
- Recognize a level of service for individual households and for small groups which includes low-cost starter options, as for CLTS, where feasible.
- Include self-supply in rural water strategy as an alternative service delivery model with quality support services available to all.
- Develop rural water strategies which are flexible where there are many household water supplies already established.
- Create clear policies on subsidies for remote and dispersed and vulnerable households.
- Include unprotected and private water supplies in water service inventories and monitoring.
- Ensure quality of self-supply options through advisory services and training for public and private sector personnel.
- Create supportive regulations, accreditation systems, planning, and budget lines to accelerate self-supply and include equity and local water resource management.
- Clearly define roles at national, regional, and district levels, and where relevant at sub-district and community levels.

---

governments are involved in all steps from the start. This means assessing the need for alternative approaches and how to collect information on what already exists. Urban self-supply needs greater understanding in planning and needs coordinating with privately developed services.

For NGOs implementing WASH activities

NGOs play an essential role as catalysts for change, helping prepare the ground for new approaches. Their true success is demonstrated when they are no longer needed to play a part. A range of NGO actions can assist governments to develop a supported self-supply service delivery model (see Box 10.3).

Box 10.3 Recommended actions for NGOs

- Research and highlight the role self-supply plays and its potential in reaching SDGs.
- Integrate safe water at household level into CLTS and sanitation marketing.
- Work with government to pilot models for accelerating self-supply, and how to devolve NGO roles into government services.
- Assist in the development of training modules and materials on starter technologies for households and government training institutions/curricula.
- Research, test, and train public and private sector in new technologies.
- Collect information on self-supply and publicize the results internationally.

Research institutions – filling some of the gaps

This book sketches an outline of the prevalence and potential of self-supply but acknowledges that there are many 'known unknowns'. It breaks new ground but is written around enormous gaps in knowledge and may seem annoyingly incomplete. There should be many lessons from experiences of self-supply in India or Vietnam for instance, but apparently almost nothing has been published on them. Much further research is needed and some suggestions are provided in Box 10.4.

Box 10.4 Areas of missing research on self-supply

- The dynamics of community and household supplies where they coexist, especially in countries with most self-supply but little or no information on how they fit together (e.g. India, Pakistan, Vietnam, Cambodia, Bangladesh)
- The roles and forms of individual and group self-supply and of government support in the evolution of safely managed water supply services (e.g. United States, Ireland, Croatia, and parts of Latin America)
- The roles of health, water, agriculture and other sectors in supporting self-supply. Where is budget support most likely to be effective in bringing about change and what are the opportunities and barriers to a coordinated response to household demands?

(Continued)

Box 10.4 Continued

- Barriers and drivers to technology uptake, market research into how to be more effective in introducing new ideas. Can the technology introduction process (TIP) be modified for introducing an approach rather than a technology?
- Equity in self-supply; how inclusive is it compared with other service delivery models and how can it be extended towards hard-to-reach and vulnerable households?
- The cost effectiveness of local recharge from roof water and effects on groundwater quality
- Water quality changes between source and point of consumption – why do some households not contaminate their water or not all the time?
- The evolving roles of urban and peri-urban self-supply, differing health risks and how to minimize them and complement public supply provision
- Productive water-use in self-supply; its influence on individual and rural economy and on groundwater balance
- Predicting the use of multiple water sources, who will use what water source, when, how, and why?
- Lowering the cost of starter technologies and practical ways to make them more affordable
- The potential for accessing remittances for water supply.
- Use and potential of saving and credit schemes to support household investments in self-supply

---

When all this knowledge is accumulated, self-supply may really confirm its potential and its contribution to the mosaic of service options found globally.

Conclusion

Global targets to improve access to water require faster progress than has ever been achieved before. The pressure in the 2020s is enormous if the world is to get close to the aspirational SDG target for drinking water. Extending and improving the management of piped water supplies in rural as well as urban areas and expanding and strengthening community management of point sources like wells and boreholes will be essential. But these service delivery models will not reach everyone, and progress will be constrained by limited resources in the time available. A suite of overlapping service delivery models is the only way to reach everyone.

Self-supply – already employed at scale by many millions of households and supporting more than half the rural population in sub-Saharan Africa – offers a way to reach some households more cheaply than other forms of supply, principally in rural areas, and it offers a way to accelerate progress towards the SDG target. Self-supply can fill gaps in services, including in urban areas, until service utilities and providers improve over time and reach parts of the population that are at risk of being left behind. Examples throughout this book illustrate the contribution and potential of self-supply and show how it can be scaled up and progressively improved as a formal service delivery model to reach the last 10–20 per cent.

Removing our sector blindness to self-supply means adopting strategies to extend support and co-opting the efforts of many households that invest in their own supply with little or no assistance from government. It provides a means to tap household finances in areas where there are already willing investors and other sources of funding constrain progress. Understanding self-supply and the social network it serves is essential.

Self-supply is neither radical nor un-tested but it is not yet part of the mainstream policies and service delivery models promoted by governments and development partners. It has been part of the history of water supply in countries that have reached universal access and remains important everywhere where there are large rural populations. This book is a call for both investment in practical support to households that are, or could be, engaged in self-supply and investment in research to enhance the evidence of its potential. It is a call for self-supply and household facilities to be recognized as part of the conventional, mainstream, established approach to water supply delivery everywhere, especially in sub-Saharan Africa. The sector and its professionals must pay attention to a mass movement that households have already started.

References

IRC (2006) *Landscaping and Review of Approaches and Technologies for Water, Sanitation and Hygiene: Opportunities for Action* [pdf], Bill & Melinda Gates Foundation <https://www.ircwash.org/sites/default/files/IRC-2006-Landscaping.pdf> [accessed January 2018].

Wahnbaeck, T. (2016) 'Innovation is the answer to a simple question "Is there a better way?"' *The Guardian*, 4 November <https://www.theguardian.com/global-development-professionals-network/2016/nov/04/innovation-is-the-answer-to-a-simple-question-is-there-a-better-way> [accessed April 2020].

PART 2
Self-supply case studies

This section presents six case studies, three from upper- and middle-income economies (Scotland, the Danube basin, Thailand) and three from sub-Saharan Africa (Zimbabwe, Tanzania, and Zambia). In Scotland, Thailand, and Zimbabwe self-supply investment has been an officially recognized element of rural water strategies, while in the other three areas it has developed as an informal option. Where formalized system household investment has built upon existing traditions, aided by small incentives from government, and with capacity building and some standardization and regulation. Growth of self-supply in the absence of formal support reflects gaps in other forms of supply and a high level of demand and interest by households in improving their water supply.

Keywords: self-supply, rainwater harvesting, government, private sector, NGOs, regulation

Key messages

1. Self-supply is a vital form of water supply everywhere including high-income contexts. It is likely to be a permanent feature of water supply in any countries with universal access to safe water supply services.
2. The self-supply ladder reaches levels that can provide safely managed services including piped water supply using advanced water pumping, storage, and treatment technologies.
3. Across all contexts, performance of self-supply is usually lower than public piped water supplies, suggesting a need for attention and support to self-supply, and a priority towards piped supply connections as and when that gradually becomes possible and affordable.
4. Regulation of self-supply needs to be considered, carefully introduced, and is only a relatively recent practice even in high-income contexts. It can be combined with incentives, such as the grant scheme to improve water quality in private supplies in Scotland.
5. Capacities to support self-supply within both the public and private sectors may be limited and are a critical constraint that needs investment in all contexts. In Thailand, capacities to make rainwater harvesting jars at scale were initially in the public sector before the private sector took over production. In Scotland, there are challenges in relying on private sector suppliers to serve highly dispersed and remote locations, and local authorities must balance provision of support and regulation of private water supplies within a busy workload.

http://dx.doi.org/10.3362/9781780448190.011

6. Strategies to support self-supply need multiple supporting interventions and may include subsidy. Support to self-supply was successful in Zimbabwe, leading to widespread impacts, based on a mixture of local innovation and low-cost technologies, government leadership, piloting and evidence, and subsidy.
7. Promoting alternative technologies likely requires changes and champions at the policy level as well as local innovation and private sector interest. Changes in regulation are hindering growth in the development of manual drilling and rope pumps in Tanzania, for example. Gaps in monitoring and evidence are only likely to be addressed if self-supply is more widely recognized in sector strategies and frameworks.
8. Expectations should be limited from short cycles of project-led innovation on a complex challenge. Progress can be sustained by local organizations and champions when they knit together projects over time, but scaling is unlikely to be achieved without substantial and sustained government and development partners' interest and investment to build on such efforts.

Introduction

The second part of the book provides a selection of case studies contributed by authors engaged in innovating, promoting, testing, researching, and regulating self-supply. There are a wide range of contexts included: high-income settings where all the population has access to improved water supplies; upper middle- and high-income contexts in central Europe and Thailand where self-supply provides an important contribution to high-levels of water supply access; and sub-Saharan Africa country contexts where access to improved water supplies is lower (Zimbabwe, Tanzania, and Zambia).

The case study from Scotland highlights the niche but critical role of small-scale private water supplies to serve areas that are not reached by the publicly managed Scottish Water and its piped networks. From the perspective of the national water regulator, progress and shortcomings in efforts to upgrade private water supplies are reviewed. The central European case study is based on a review of rural water and sanitation services in the seven countries of the Danube region, and sheds light on water supply beyond the realm of utility provision in these countries. Recommendations highlight how self-supply could be a supported model with potential actions taken to regulate and subsidize to improve its performance. In Thailand, rainwater harvesting played a major, if transitional role in developing drinking water supplies based on public and private sector efforts, illustrating how self-supply can include sources other than groundwater.

The three cases of supported self-supply in sub-Saharan Africa highlight the work of local champions and organizations. The National Upgraded Well Programme in Zimbabwe is relatively well-known but remains one of the best examples of government support at scale to grow self-supply. Consecutive efforts led to widespread success in promoting the improvement of upgraded family wells. In Tanzania, technology including manual drilling and rope pumps has been the focus of efforts to provide alternatives for rural and peri-urban communities. While project-supported and private markets have been developed locally, the outlook is uncertain given a lack of government engagement and constraints in the enabling environment and especially regulation. In Zambia, a series of project-led pilots provided an opportunity to improve and test different models for scaling self-supply. These provide insights on the limitations of project-led innovation within short funding cycles, as well as the potential supporting roles of government, NGOs, and the private sector.

CASE STUDY 1

The role of self-supply in Scotland

Matthew Bower

Introduction

Most of the drinking water supplied in Scotland is via the single, publicly owned supplier, Scottish Water. This reaches just over 96 per cent of the Scottish population, concentrated in the lowland areas of central Scotland. In this area many large water supply systems with modern water treatment processes produce consistently high quality water. In the hillier parts of the country to the north and south as well as the many islands in the north and west, a large number of smaller supplies use small-scale modern treatment processes, often membrane treatment due to its scalability.

The quality of the public drinking water supply in Scotland is taken for granted – in 2017, 99.91 per cent of tests on samples from consumer taps met the required standard. Although Scotland is blessed with a wealth of natural water resources, most waters require extensive treatment as they often contain microorganisms and are highly coloured, indicating high concentrations of natural organic matter. This can make the water very expensive to treat on a small scale; hence the creation of a single public water supplier to spread the cost of treating water for smaller, rural communities across the whole population.

Not everyone is connected to the public water supply, however. Some 3.6 per cent of the population, around 196,000 people, rely on self-supply water schemes, known as private water supplies, legally defined as any water supply not served by Scottish Water. There are over 22,000 such supplies across Scotland (Photo CS.1.1 shows an example). Many, but by no means all, are in rural areas beyond the reach of the public water main. They often crop up in some of Scotland's most scenic tourist areas, meaning that the population seasonally relying on private supplies may be significantly larger than the official figures.

The distinction between communities that receive private and public water supplies is certainly not one of size – the largest private supply serves a community of over 1,000 people, while the smallest Scottish Water supply serves only two people. It seems to be a quirk of history that decided the current designation. When the public water supply in Scotland was run by local authorities, it was a matter of local policy that decided which water supplies were adopted, and later transferred to three public water authorities

Photo CS.1.1 A reasonably well-designed and maintained private surface water abstraction in rural Scotland, with a 'stilling pool' upstream and a screen to remove coarse debris
Source: DWQR

during the 1990s and finally to Scottish Water, created by the Scottish Government in 2002.

The quality of public water supplies is regulated by the Drinking Water Quality Regulator for Scotland (DWQR), appointed by Scottish Ministers to act independently to safeguard drinking water. Private supplies, however, are regulated by the 32 local authorities in Scotland. The DWQR does not directly regulate these supplies, but has a role to 'supervise' local authorities.

The nature of private water supplies

Private supplies come in all shapes and sizes, using a range of water source types, categorized by local authorities as part of their regulatory function. Table CS.1.1 shows that groundwater appears to predominate. However, many groundwater sources are influenced by surface water and therefore at risk of contamination from faecal bacteria and other pathogens. In many cases,

Table CS.1.1 Private water supply source types in Scotland

Source Type	No. Supplies
Groundwater Borehole	1,629
Groundwater Spring	15,413
Groundwater Well	1,411
Surface Burn/Stream	3,231
Surface Loch/Lake	462
Surface Rainwater	9
Other	23
Grand Total	22,178

Source: Drinking Water Quality Regulator for Scotland, 2018

'spring sources' are actually shallow collection chambers that fill with water from surface flow and, in some cases, from artificial field drains.

Abstraction and treatment arrangements are often very basic, with some supplies consisting of no more than a pipe buried in a stream above the dwelling. A large number have no treatment at all. Many private water supplies are of poor or inconsistent quality, having minimal or ineffective treatment. The high organic content of many Scottish waters means that ultraviolet disinfection is minimally effective and chlorine-based disinfection risks by-product formation. Other contaminants, mostly natural in origin, are often present.

Table CS.1.2 shows 2017 compliance for those parameters which fail most frequently in regulated private supplies, with the comparable figure for the public water supply. Regulated private water supplies are defined as those suppling more than 50 people or 10 m^3 per day, or supplying a commercial activity, and such supplies are required to meet European Drinking Water Directive standards. Besides microbiology, the other key group of failing parameters is pH and the plumbing metals. These are, of course, connected as many private supplies do not have adequate water conditioning treatment and natural waters in Scotland tend to be low in pH and alkalinity. The extremely soft nature of the water means that corrosion of plumbing metals such as copper, lead, and nickel is often an issue, especially where poor quality or inappropriate materials have been used.

A number of human factors exacerbate risks and inhibit progress in bringing about improvements. These include:

- *Risk awareness*. Many people do not understand or refuse to believe the risks that improperly treated drinking water can present to health.
- *Lack of expertise*. Many owners lack an understanding and interest in water treatment and are consequently ill-prepared to improve and maintain their water supply. There is a very limited number of specialist installers in Scotland, and owners may struggle to find suitable people to work on their supply. This is especially acute in very remote areas.

Table CS.1.2 Compliance for most commonly failing parameters in larger (regulated) private water supplies and comparison with public water supplies in Scotland, 2017

Parameter	Total samples taken	Samples failing regulatory standard	Percentage compliance	Percentage compliance at consumer caps, Scottish Water
Coliform bacteria	2,256	497	77.97	99.76
Colour	2,188	378	82.72	100
Hydrogen ion (pH)	2,226	375	83.15	99.88
E. coli	2,256	260	88.48	99.99
Iron	1,132	122	89.22	99.38
Enterococci	2,178	194	91.09	100
Clostridium perfringens	2,210	151	93.17	99.98
Manganese	987	62	93.72	99.78
Lead	643	30	95.33	99.05
Copper	972	36	96.30	99.93
Nickel	686	18	97.38	99.93

Source: Drinking Water Quality Regulator for Scotland, 2018

- *Lack of resources.* Private supplies tend to be concentrated in remote and rural areas, which have a tendency to be areas of lower income, least able to afford the expense required to properly treat and maintain a safe water supply.
- *Lack of technology.* Many of Scotland's surface waters contain large concentrations of organic material that can be very difficult to remove via conventional means and inhibit the effectiveness of ultraviolet disinfection. There is a need for an affordable, user-friendly, compact and chemical-free treatment process to reliably remove organic carbon.

The regulatory regime

Local authorities in Scotland have regulated private supplies for a number of years and since 2006 have administrated a government grant to improve systems. Regulatory officers are locally based, know the area, and build a relationship with owners and users, gaining trust and leveraging improvements. It is likely that many owners and users would be reluctant to deal directly with a centralized body which they could see as 'state interference' in their water supply.

However, the system has several disadvantages. Regulatory responsibility lies with environmental health departments which have a challenging and wide-ranging remit, delivered with ever-tightening resources. In the face of competing demands private water supplies can become a lower priority, especially in local authorities with relatively small numbers of private water supplies, where the issue is easier to sideline. Moreover, some authorities do not have the expertise to regulate private water supplies effectively and offer advice to users. Finally, there is some evidence that locating support and regulatory enforcement powers in the same place can act as a deterrent to contacting local authorities, as owners and users stay 'under the radar' to avoid the threat of interference or compulsion for action.

In practice, local authorities have been reluctant to use enforcement powers to bring about improvement where other means have failed, preferring to tread softly and maintain relationships, potentially at the expense of bringing about rapid improvements.

DWQR's role as the supervising authority is difficult to define, coming without a clear definition in legislation, audit powers or (until recently) any powers to direct local authorities. Authorities have leant heavily upon DWQR's guidance and expertise, although this has at times been difficult for a small centralized team to provide.

Larger and commercial private water supplies are sampled at least annually by local authorities, with the cost of sampling borne by the supply owner. The number of samples that contain *E. coli* (see Table CS.1.2) is a concern, as this indicates that the disinfection process is ineffective and other pathogens may also be present. As Figure CS.1.1 shows, compliance with regulatory standards has improved little since 2013 despite significant grant payments and concerted efforts by local authority staff. There is evidence that smaller domestic supplies, which may be only intermittently sampled if at all, are of poorer quality still.

Even compliant samples give limited reassurance as they provide only a 'snapshot' of water quality at a specific time and no assurance that the water is wholesome at other times. It seems likely that the analytical results do not tell

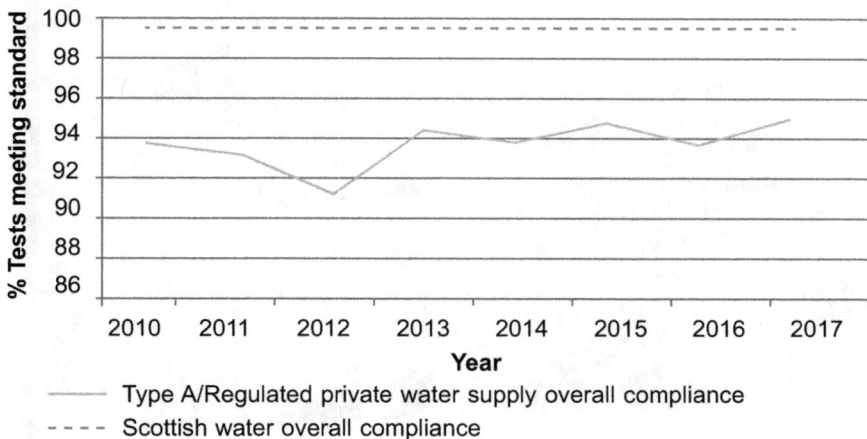

――――― Type A/Regulated private water supply overall compliance

- - - - Scottish water overall compliance

Figure CS.1.1 Overall compliance for samples taken from larger (regulated) private water supplies in Scotland, year on year, with comparison against public water supply
Source: Drinking Water Quality Regulator for Scotland, 2018

the whole story as the quality of water in many Scottish private supplies varies rapidly where they consist of, or are influenced by, surface water. Additionally, the absence of *E. coli* does not guarantee the absence of pathogens such as *Cryptosporidium*, which, based on raw monitoring of public water supplies, is likely to be widely present. For this reason DWQR and local authorities promote risk assessment as the most effective means of safeguarding water supplies on a continuous basis.

What has been tried so far to achieve improvements?

A number of initiatives have been tried in Scotland over the past ten years to support and improve the standard of private water supplies.

A private water supply grant was introduced at the same time as the 2006 Regulations came into force, providing up to £800 per property for improvements to the supply, with more available in cases of hardship. For larger supplies, grants can be pooled with neighbours so that a reasonable sum can be accumulated. The grant is administered by local authorities, which are reimbursed by the Scottish Government. Few restrictions are placed by the government on exactly how the grant is spent, as long as it brings about an improvement in the supply, although some local authorities have introduced their own. Most grant-funded expenditure is on treatment processes (see examples in Photo CS.1.2), although source protection and tank or pipeline replacement would all be legitimate expenses provided the money is spent to improve the supply rather than simply maintain what is there.

| (a) | (b) |

Photo CS.1.2 Two private water supply treatment systems: (a) supplying a large estate and (b) a simple 'point of use' ultraviolet disinfection unit in a kitchen cupboard
Source: DWQR

Scottish Government grants have funded many improvements over the years. In 2017 alone, £429,968 was awarded to improve 347 supplies. They have proven a useful tool for local authorities who might otherwise have struggled to engage with some owners and users. The grant has sometimes been criticized for not being sufficient to cover the cost of an adequate treatment process. In 2006, £800 was theoretically sufficient to fund the most basic treatment such as an ultraviolet lamp but the shortfall was deliberate in the design of the scheme, since it was felt to be important that the owner of the supply made a contribution as this was more likely to ensure sufficient interest in maintenance of the supply.

Although there are undoubtedly many improved supplies that remain of acceptable quality, Figure CS.1.1 provides no evidence that the grant has brought about a sustained national improvement in overall compliance with drinking water standards. It is likely that the frequency and nature of the regulatory sampling programme is insufficient to show sustained improvement at individual supply level. However, it is also likely that substantial sums of grant money have been used to fund improvements without a clear means of committing the owner to ongoing maintenance, and this has resulted in any improvement in water quality being only temporary. There are probably also occasions when the treatment installed is probably not the best solution or has been installed incorrectly.

Many owners do not see a need to take action to improve their private supply. While most people, if asked, would say water was a precious commodity, the reality is that so long as it is reliably emerging from the tap and appears clean there is very little interest in its actual quality. People using private supplies often believe they are getting free, pure water that does not contain the chemicals they associate with the public water supply.

Such perceptions often act as a barrier to making improvements, especially where effort or expense is involved. People often seem unaware of the risks or choose to ignore them on the basis that they have been drinking the water for a long period without ill-effects. Such views are partly understandable but could be considered complacent where non-resident friends or relatives, or paying guests are regularly consuming the supply. And of course, risks and water quality can change rapidly, meaning a previously safe supply becomes contaminated.

It is difficult to directly correlate poor water quality in private supplies with cases of disease. Underreporting of diarrhoeal diseases, the existence of numerous potential pathogen sources in rural areas, and, in some cases, a transient population mean that a direct causal link can be hard to find. Risebro et al. (2012) did not find a significantly increased risk of infectious intestinal disease in older age groups using poorer quality small water supplies; however there did appear to be a stronger link in those aged under ten. Research by the Drinking Water Inspectorate (2014) provides evidence of a link between private supplies and outbreaks of disease, with 12 outbreaks between 2001 and 2009, but in many cases that link is 'probable' rather than certain. Much evidence of risk therefore relies on a number of anecdotal cases of illness.

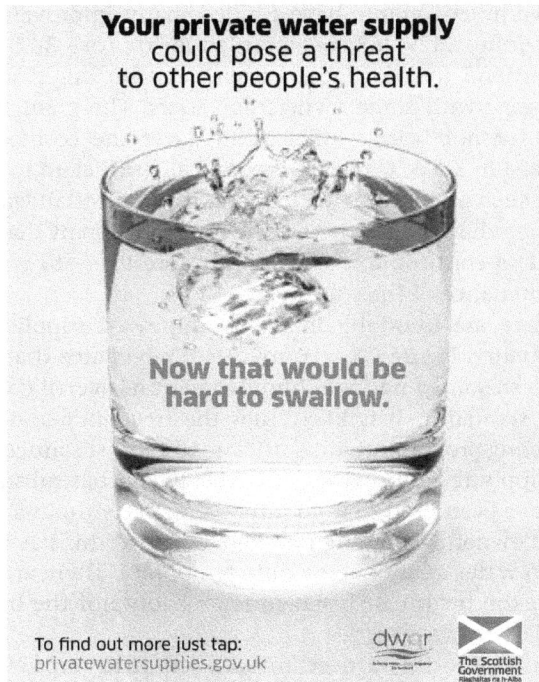

Photo CS.1.3 A leaflet that has been sent to users of domestic private water supplies to raise awareness of risks
Source: DWQR

Work has been undertaken in Scotland to raise awareness of risks, including legislating that tourist accommodation must display a notice informing visitors that they will be consuming water from a private supply. This is designed to initiate a conversation between visitor and landlord, and encourage the latter to ensure their supply is well treated and monitored. Leafleting campaigns (Photo CS.1.3) have been undertaken informing domestic users of the risks and providing support, and local authorities contact thousands of private water suppliers every year offering advice and grant support.

It is hard to determine how effective any individual measure has been in raising awareness, but there is little doubt that publicizing the risks needs to continue.

The role of the private sector

A number of private sector organizations offer treatment solutions for private supplies in Scotland, combined in some cases with maintenance contracts. Some operate successfully and have been established for a number of years. There is not uniform coverage across Scotland, however, and some local authorities report that supply owners in more remote locations have difficulty in persuading companies to visit in order to quote for work. This can leave people with very limited choice in terms of installation options – sometimes just the local plumber. With no accreditation scheme for installers, and a largely uninformed consumer base, there are cases of dubious treatment choices and/or incorrect installation. The advent of internet shopping has increased the number of 'DIY' treatment solutions, sometimes involving quite complex, but inappropriate treatment processes. Local authorities are often the only source of advice to help owners decide on treatment processes, but are often ill-equipped to provide this.

There is anecdotal evidence that supplier/installers, especially smaller ones, find working on private water supplies time consuming and sometimes unattractive. It can be difficult to ensure payment for work done. Reasons include an unwillingness or inability to pay, as these supplies are often in areas of relatively low income or ownership is spread across a number of individuals with no agreement in place for funding improvements. A cultural reluctance to pay for something that 'runs freely off the hillside' exacerbates the situation, reinforcing the case for ongoing education of risk.

What more can be done?

There are currently no plans for a significant programme of extension to the Scottish Water supply, so opportunities for connection will be very limited in remote areas. In the cases where a Scottish Water main already runs directly past a property, connection to the public supply, with the safety and security it brings, is an option that should be encouraged. Barriers include the cost of laying a supply pipe and connection fees as well as ensuring the connection requirements of Scottish Water are understood and complied with. The local authority grant cannot currently legally be used towards the cost of connection, creating a slightly perverse incentive in some cases to remain on a private supply, albeit an improved one. There is clearly scope to make it easier and more attractive for people to connect to the public water supply where this is possible.

Improvements to planning processes could be helpful, by ensuring that a wholesome and sufficient supply of water is a prerequisite for permission for new-build property. Where connection to the public system is feasible, this should be a requirement, in combination with checks post-build to ensure connection has actually place. Forthcoming changes to Scottish planning legislation and guidance make this a possibility.

Fundamental to making further improvements to private water supplies are continued efforts to raise awareness of the risks that private water supplies can present and what can be done to reduce or eliminate these risks. Changes to the grant system are also desirable. Owners could be encouraged to upgrade their supply to a good standard if funding was available to cover the whole cost. This could be in the form of a loan, perhaps set against the value of the property to be paid back once the property is sold. Payment could also be conditional on participation in a suitable maintenance contract – perhaps with some state intervention to ensure it is effective and universally available.

Conclusion

Scotland will always have a large number of private water supplies. These need to be supported and managed alongside the national public water supply system: they are as much part of Scotland's water supply infrastructure as Scottish Water assets. Scotland is committed to compliance with UN Sustainable Development Goal 6, to ensure water and sanitation for all, and this needs to be supported in a way that encourages participation but is fair to everyone in Scotland, including those paying for the public water supply. Making owners and users aware of waterborne risks and helping them to see clean water as a resource worth paying for, while supporting them in taking responsibility for their supply, is essential if everyone in Scotland is to be able to receive consistently safe drinking water.

References

Drinking Water Inspectorate (2014) *A Review of Incidence of Outbreaks of Diseases Associated with Private Water Supplies from 1970 to 2009* [online], Drinking Water Inspectorate, London <http://dwi.defra.gov.uk/research/completed-research/reports/DWI70-2-258.pdf> [accessed 3 February 2020].

Drinking Water Quality Regulator for Scotland (2018) *Drinking Water Quality in Scotland 2017: Private Water Supplies* [online], Drinking Water Quality Regulator for Scotland, Edinburgh <https://dwqr.scot/media/39966/dwqr-pws-annual-report-2017-compiled-report-final-24-september-2018.pdf> [accessed 3 February 2020].

Risebro, H.L., Breton, L., Aird, H., Hooper, A. and Hunter, P.R. (2012) 'Contaminated small drinking water supplies and risk of infectious intestinal disease: a prospective cohort study', *PLOS One* 7(8): e42762 <https://doi.org/10.1371/journal.pone.0042762>.

CASE STUDY 2
Self-supply in the Danube region

Susanna Smets

Introduction

Governments of countries of the Danube region face the double challenge of meeting their citizens' demand for quality and sustainable water services, while catching up with the environmental requirements of the European Union. In general, the bulk of public investments have targeted urban areas, resulting in the improvement of drinking water systems and the development of wastewater collection and treatment infrastructure. This process is largely driven by EU accession and compliance targets and in several countries involves the regionalization of service providers. However, rural areas are lagging behind and significant service access gaps exist in comparison with urban areas. Approximately 28.5 million people remain without access to piped water supply and 22 million remain without flush toilet access in the region (World Bank, 2018), of whom at least 8 out of 10 reside in rural areas.

A seven-country study was conducted in rural areas in the Danube region, to understand whether and how regional water utilities have effectively reached rural areas, and to present lessons and recommendations for expanding and improving the provision of services for rural populations. The countries – Albania, Bosnia and Herzegovina, Croatia, Kosovo, Moldova, Romania, and Ukraine (see Figure CS.2.1) – were selected because they represent a wide range of rural water outcomes, different challenges, and sector reform contexts. Individual self-supply, i.e. households using point sources such as private wells and springs, was found to be an important source of provision, and in the course of the study over 1,200 self-supply households were interviewed. This case study focuses mainly on the study findings related to this type of supply. The full report is available from the Open Knowledge Repository of the World Bank (World Bank, 2018). Other studies, such as the reports by Hendry and Akoumianaki (2016) and Rickert et al. (2016) have also highlighted the important role of self-supply and small private water supplies in Europe.

Figure CS.2.1 Countries included in the review of rural water and sanitation services in the Danube region
Source: World Bank, 2018

The service delivery landscape

Although rural populations in the seven study countries are shrinking, still roughly half of the population, or 30 million people, live in rural areas. Some are served by regional or urban utilities, or by a range of local operators. While access to piped supply ranges from around 90 per cent to nearly 100 per cent in urban areas, the highly dispersed rural population is sharply disadvantaged. In Ukraine, rural piped access is on the decline (34 per cent in 2012). In Romania, access to public piped water services in rural areas slowly increased to 40 per cent in 2016. Moldova, starting from low coverage in the early 2000s, saw progress to 46 per cent in rural piped water supply access by 2015. Croatia and Kosovo have seen impressive improvements with almost 70 per cent of the rural population now served through piped access delivered by public utilities. In Albania and in Bosnia and Herzegovina, rural access to piped water is high (greater than 80 per cent). Access to public service delivery in rural areas is not precisely known in Albania, and is just 36 per cent in Bosnia and Herzegovina. Rural access to flush toilets lags behind urban areas and follows similar country trends, with Ukraine, Moldova, and Romania among the lowest (13–48 per cent) and Albania, Bosnia and Herzegovina, Croatia, and Kosovo significantly higher (85–97 per cent). All these figures include a contribution to rural piped supply through self-supply, as discussed in the next section.

Understanding self-supply

Figure CS.2.2 and Table CS.2.1 illustrate the landscape of rural service provision and the structure of rural piped access delivery in these countries. The contribution of self-supply, either piped or non-piped, is also shown. It is estimated that more than 14 million people are served through self-supply, either piped to the dwelling or to a point outside the home.

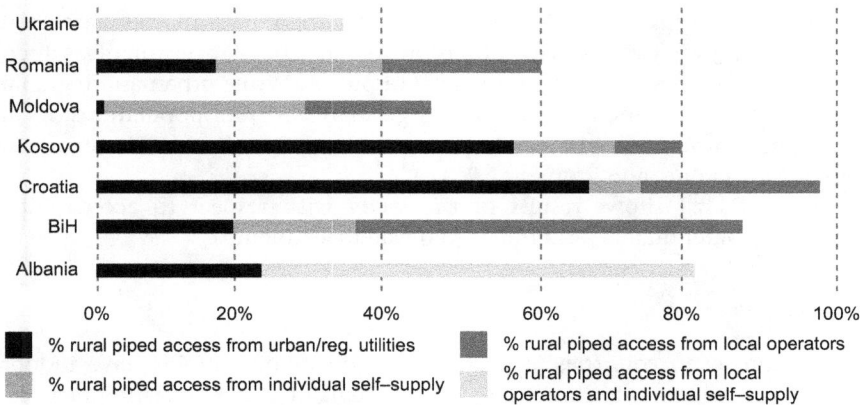

Figure CS.2.2 Rural sector structure and indicative estimates of provision of piped rural services (see Table CS.2.1 for source and notes)

Table CS.2.1 Rural sector structure and indicative estimates of provision of piped rural services

Country	Rural population (millions)	% rural piped access on premises	% rural piped access by utilities	% of rural piped access by local operators	% of rural piped access by self-supply	% of rural non-piped access by self-supply	No. of urban regional utilities	No. of local service providers
Albania	1.2	81	24	57 (split not known)		19	61	unknown
Bosnia and Herzegovina	2.1	88	20	16	52	12	142	unknown
Croatia	1.7	98	67	8	23	2	156	455
Kosovo	1.1	70	55	15	10	20	8	240
Moldova	1.9	46	1	30	15	54	38	1,044
Romania	8.9	60	17	23	20	40	43	1,020
Ukraine	13.5	34	0	34 (split not known)		66	150	1,605

Notes: Individual self-supply is divided into piped self-supply, in which households have invested in piping the source into the home, and non-piped self-supply, in which households need to bring water from sources nearby (these can be either public or private sources and can be within their yards or outside their yards).
Source: Reproduced from World Bank, 2018. Estimates based on national reports from water agencies and regulators, as per World Bank (2018) and survey data

In Bosnia and Herzegovina, Moldova, Ukraine, and Romania, more than 60 per cent of households in rural areas rely on self-supply. Bosnia and Herzegovina have high levels of indoor piped self-supply, while other households rely on wells (mostly private) and springs. There is low coverage by public standpipes. None of the countries studied had an inventory of existing individual self-supply households at national, regional or local level. In rural Croatia, self-supply is estimated at around 25 per cent, in Kosovo about 30 per cent, and in Albania there are no exact figures.

In all countries except Kosovo, decentralization reforms have assigned responsibility for water service provision to rural local governments, which often have poor capacities and financial resources. While urban and regional utilities in Croatia and Kosovo serve large shares of rural populations, local operators continue to play an important role in Bosnia and Herzegovina, Moldova, Ukraine, and Romania.

Figure CS.2.3 shows results of the study with respect to accessibility, reliability, water quality, and household water treatment.[1]

Accessibility

Across the seven countries, a large proportion of households have indoor piped taps, which is an important determinant of better hygiene practices. Most self-supply households in Albania, Bosnia and Herzegovina, Croatia, and Kosovo have invested in a piped conveyance and storage system so that pressured water is delivered into their homes. However, 40–70 per cent of self-supply households in Moldova, Romania, and Ukraine do not have piped water, and only 25–40 per cent have indoor plumbing. Most wells are privately owned, 91 per cent in Moldova, 86 per cent in Romania, and 71 per cent in Ukraine, although some sharing among households takes place. In Moldova, only one in four households has been able to invest in electric pumps, while in Romania and Ukraine around 60 per cent have done so.

Two-thirds of self-supply households in Moldova and around one-third in Romania and Ukraine collect water manually in buckets, increasing the risk of pathogen exposure and the time and energy spent on water collection. Low levels of piped self-supply in Moldova, Romania, and Ukraine are indicative of a weaker ability and willingness to pay for more convenient water supply and related in-house equipment (such as electric pumps, water storage, and indoor plumbing).

Reliability

Water supply reliability is high for self-supply households in the region: around one in four households reporting a service outage over the past year. Self-supply households in Albania and Kosovo experience reliability issues more often: approximately half reported an outage in the past year, typically due to low water tables. However, self-supply is not very prevalent in these two

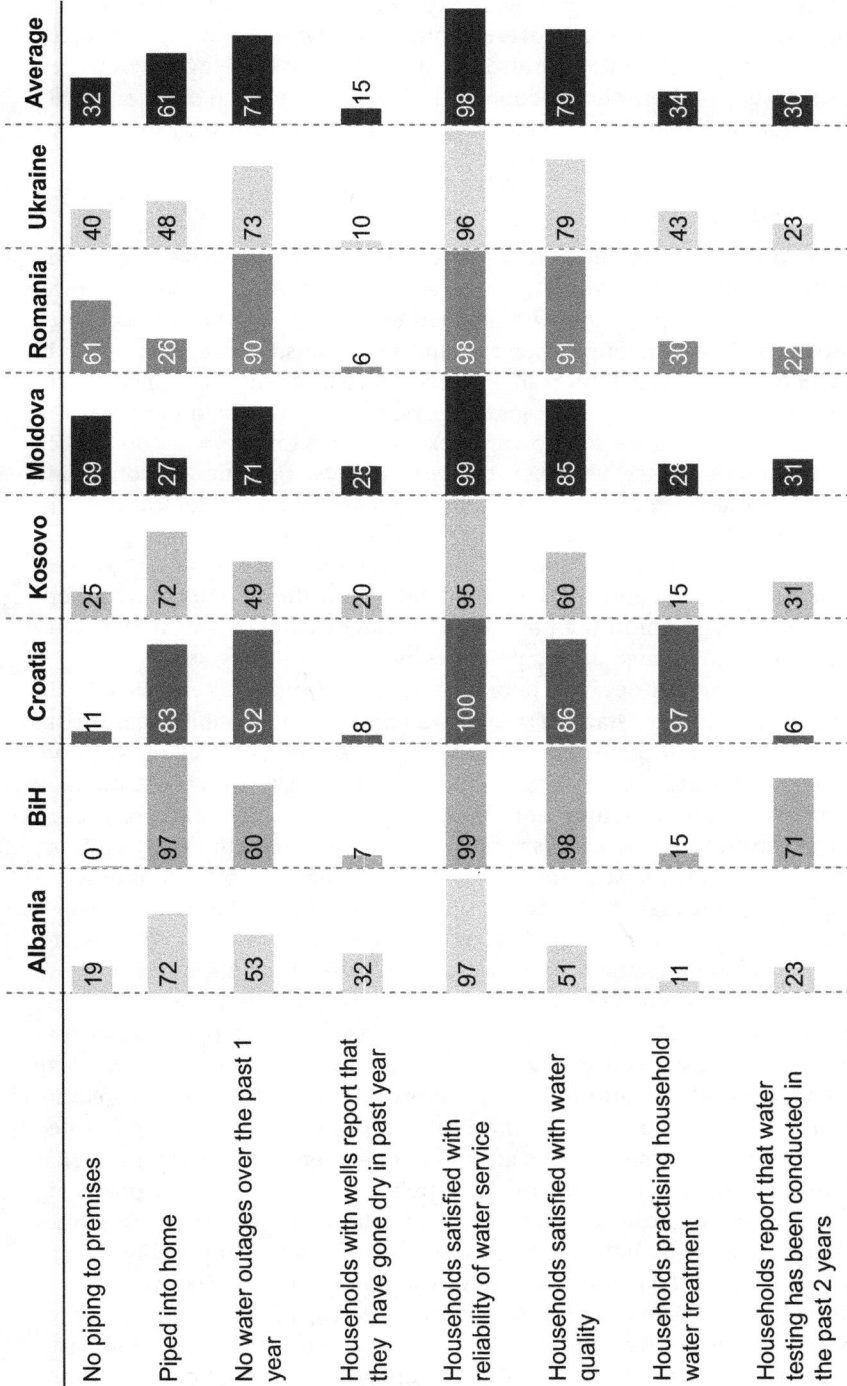

	Albania	BiH	Croatia	Kosovo	Moldova	Romania	Ukraine	Average
No piping to premises	19	0	11	25	69	61	40	32
Piped into home	72	97	83	72	27	26	48	61
No water outages over the past 1 year	53	60	92	49	71	90	73	71
Households with wells report that they have gone dry in past year	32	7	8	20	25	6	10	15
Households satisfied with reliability of water service	97	99	100	95	99	98	96	98
Households satisfied with water quality	51	98	86	60	85	91	79	79
Households practising household water treatment	11	15	97	15	28	30	43	34
Households report that water testing has been conducted in the past 2 years	23	71	6	31	31	22	23	30

Figure CS.2.3 Share of self-supply households and their service level characteristics by management model and by country
Source: World Bank, 2018 based on country-specific household surveys

countries. Although self-supply reliability can be fragile, particularly due to seasonal scarcity or potentially overexploited shallow groundwater resources, satisfaction with reliability conditions is high across all seven countries. This suggests that households cope with occasional service outages, either by using alternative sources or taking measures to repair their own supplies.

Water quality

Satisfaction of self-supply households with water quality (perceived safety and aesthetic acceptability) is generally high (average 79 per cent), although lower in Kosovo and Albania. Households are neither testing water quality frequently, nor, except in Croatia, treating water at home before consumption. Differences in satisfaction with water quality could reflect actual quality deficiencies, respondent bias, varying household expectations, or access to water quality information.

Where households use their own untested sources for drinking, household water treatment (water filters or chlorine tablets) becomes a potentially important protective measure, particularly to reduce microbiological contamination. Only in Croatia is household water treatment commonly practised among rural self-supply households. Low levels elsewhere may relate to access to information, social norms, or the availability and affordability of treatment products. Reasons behind the popularity of water treatment in Croatia could be explored to encourage similar practices in other countries.

Most of these countries have poor data about the public accessibility, availability, quality, and coverage of groundwater. As a result, public health risks for self-suppliers in Moldova, Romania, and Ukraine are not well understood. Adverse groundwater quality conditions that make water less palatable may be due to geogenic contamination of aquifers, such as high levels of iron or hardness. Anthropogenic factors mostly relate to nitrate pollution (fertilizers, manure, untreated wastewater) and microbiological contamination by pathogens, which may result from poor sanitary construction of the wells. Further investigation of groundwater quality may be warranted in some settings to better understand risks for households relying on self-supply.

For countries where self-supply is likely to be an important part of the solution to universal access, a systematic supported self-supply model that addresses water safety concerns and improves water accessibility in the home may be considered. As national and European Union legislation do not require self-supply water quality to be monitored, countries have not promoted surveillance programmes for this group of consumers. The survey finds that local government involvement in self-supply is mostly limited to providing information about drilling companies and pump suppliers to households. Awareness campaigns have reportedly been implemented by public health agencies in some countries. In Moldova, Romania, and Ukraine, where continued high reliance on self-supply is expected, there is some evidence of noncompliance with chemical, nitrate, and microbiological standards. A programme to support self-suppliers to include water quality surveillance (paid for by users), water safety assessment, and measures to encourage correct household water treatment and in-house improvements is called for. This includes strengthening the markets for supply of certified household water treatment devices.

Conclusions and recommendations for supported self-supply

For households with self-supply, the study concluded that:

- The accessibility of self-supply solutions through indoor piping varies by country, while reliability and satisfaction with water quality of self-supply are generally high.
- Self-supply households typically are not connected to centralized systems mainly due to the distance of rural houses from local water supply mains, while some households have opted out of centralized systems due to poor public service.
- In Moldova, Romania, and Ukraine, around one in four households reported the cost of connecting to a centralized system as a constraint. Tariffs are not seen as a barrier.
- Self-suppliers have invested significantly in their systems and a large proportion are satisfied with their water supply. When new rural systems are being built, convincing self-suppliers of the benefits of service connection, specifically superior water quality, requires considerable attention.

If universal access to piped water supply is to be achieved, a supported self-supply model will be a part of the solution, as in many Western countries with dispersed rural populations.

A self-supply model supported by national and local initiatives and policies could mitigate public health risks by improving the quality and quantity of water delivery. The following recommendations are made for introducing such a supported self-supply model:

- Advocate for supported self-supply as a complementary model under a national strategy to reach universal access and mitigate public health risks.
- Register self-suppliers, carry out sanitary and water quality inspections, and analyse results to inform policy and advocacy. Starting with high priority areas, where self-supply is prevalent and public health risks are documented, all self-supply sources should be registered by local or subnational governments.
- Launch communication campaigns and mobile water quality testing services, which could incentivize self-monitoring, as has been done for example in Austria where households were offered testing services close to their home for a modest fee. Local and other subnational authorities would require targeted capacity building from national drinking water quality regulators and sufficient funds to carry out such campaigns.

- Design, implement, evaluate, and scale-up a pilot subsidy scheme for self-supply improvements. Evidence is needed to make a convincing case to decision-makers that supporting self-supply programmes in rural areas contributes to public health outcomes and the SDG achievements. Governments can design and evaluate pilot subsidy schemes in collaboration with local authorities whereby self-suppliers meeting qualifying criteria (and registered) can access a matching grant to improve supply access, safety, and hygiene. Eligible costs could include indoor plumbing, water treatment technologies, and internal water storage to avoid contamination.
- Incentivize connections to centralized piped systems. Self-suppliers should be given incentives to connect to centralized piped systems in their areas to improve water safety and accessibility. This may require a combination of behavioural and economic instruments as self-suppliers have significantly invested in their supply arrangements. Addressing customer perceptions around the benefits of a public service connection is necessary, especially addressing concerns over safe water quality. Where households have reported affordability constraints, targeted financial support may be required to encourage connections.

Note

1. The detailed methodology of the study is explained in the World Bank report. However, household surveys are not statistically representative of all households in rural areas.

References

Hendry, S. and Akoumianaki, I. (2016) *Governance and Management of Small Rural Water Supplies: A Comparative Study* [online], CREW <https://www.crew.ac.uk/sites/www.crew.ac.uk/files/sites/default/files/publication/CRW2015_05%20Final%20report.pdf> [accessed 31 May 2020].

Rickert, B., Samwel, M., Shinee, E., Kožíšek, F. and Schmoll, O. (2016) *Status of Small-Scale Water Supplies in the WHO European Region: Results of a Survey Conducted under the Protocol on Water and Health* [online], WHO Regional Office for Europe, Copenhagen <http://www.euro.who.int/__data/assets/pdf_file/0012/320511/Status-SSW-supplies-results-survey-en.pdf?ua=1> [accessed 31 May 2020].

World Bank (2018) *A Review of Rural Water Supply and Sanitation Services in Seven Countries of the Danube Region* [online], World Bank, Washington, DC <https://openknowledge.worldbank.org/handle/10986/30031> [accessed 3 February 2020].

CASE STUDY 3

The shining example of domestic rainwater harvesting in Thailand

Matthias Saladin

Introduction

People have been collecting and storing rainwater for drinking and domestic purposes for centuries, with documented cases going back to at least the 3rd millennium BC (Smet, 2003). 'In the Northeast of Thailand, a house is not a home if it does not have at least one huge rainwater jar' (Tigno, 2007). In Thailand, climatic conditions are favourable: there is sufficient rainfall across the country, ranging from 800 mm in the north-east to 4,000 mm in the south. Paradoxically, it is in the north-east with the lowest rainfall and longest dry season where domestic rainwater harvesting is most common to supply drinking water. While groundwater is used widely for other domestic uses here, poor quality and high salinity limit its use for drinking.

A short history: from the dragon jar to the Thai jar

In the first half of the 20th century, earthenware vessels holding 50–300 litres were probably introduced to Thailand by Chinese immigrants (Saladin, 2016). They became popular for storing water for drinking and for other purposes, particularly in the north-east. After the Second World War, as import of these jars became difficult, a local industry developed producing jars often decorated with a dragon image. At its peak, there were 200 factories producing 'dragon jars' around the town of Ratchaburi alone (see Photo CS.3.1) and Ratchaburi became known as Jar Town.

In the 1970s, the Accelerated Rural Development Department (ARD) of the Ministry of Interior started working on an alternative to the dragon jar: a larger cement mortar jar that could hold 2,000 litres, later known as the 'Thai Jar' (Hartung et al., 2008). Not only was it larger and more robust than its earthenware predecessors, but it was cheaper and faster to produce.

Thailand's National Jar Programme was launched in 1985 to promote the use of these jars in rural households as a means of supplying clean drinking water. The programme was implemented in all regions of the country, but with emphasis on the north-east where rural water supply coverage was then lowest. Two complementary approaches were employed (Areerachakul, 2013).

Photo CS.3.1 Dragon jars at a pottery in Ratchaburi
Source: Sittha Sukkasi, UpWater project

The first involved training and technical assistance in the construction and maintenance of the Thai Jar for a few people in each village or municipality, complemented with the subsidized supply of key materials. Families also contributed with materials and labour. The second approach involved promoting access to a revolving fund for purchasing jars which were produced by private companies. A retrospective analysis in 2008 found that the revolving fund approach was too cumbersome and slow, only contributing to a minor part of the 300 million jars produced and sold (Hartung et al., 2008).

Through its training programme the government established production capacities at hundreds of locations, and by 1992, the number of Thai Jars in use had increased to about 8 million (UNEP/IETC, 1998). About 6 million of these jars were made under the government programme between 1982 and 1988, with the rest coming from private sector suppliers.

In 1992, the government ended subsidies but production did not collapse. Instead strong competition between producers brought the price of the Thai Jar down. Surviving companies had sufficient capacity to keep producing millions of additional jars and families continued to buy them. Domestic rainwater harvesting became the standard approach for rural water supply: most households had a least one Thai Jar and Thailand became the 'World Champion of domestic rainwater harvesting' (Saladin, 2016). By 2000, 21 million people, about 50 per cent of the rural population, were using rainwater as their main source of drinking water, with the majority living in the north-east. Overall, it is estimated that the Thai Jar Programme managed to put more than 300 million jars into rural households (Luong and Luckmuang, 2002). Nowhere else in the world were such a high percentage of people using rainwater as their primary source of drinking water, and even today Thailand is still among the world's highest rainwater harvesting practitioners (WHO/UNICEF, 2015). This helped Thailand to reach high levels of access to improved sources of drinking water (around 95 per cent in 2005) and to reduce the gap in access levels between urban and rural population and between income groups.

After 2006, the number of people using rainwater harvesting as their primary source of drinking water started decreasing, with rainwater being replaced by piped or bottled water. But the jars have not disappeared and are still used as a secondary source. While data is scarce, because most surveys focus only on the primary source, millions are still being used for other domestic purposes and as a secondary source. Many artisans and small workshops still produce or maintain Thai Jars, although it is a shrinking market. Eventually the jars may only be used in dispersed households where the costs of connection to piped networks are prohibitively high.

Looking back at the growth of the market

The market success of the Thai Jar should not come as a surprise as this well-designed product is durable, affordable, and visually appealing, but it is also possible to identify some socio-cultural, political-administrative, and economic factors that made it possible.

Socio-cultural factors

Two of the most important factors were the high acceptance of domestic rainwater harvesting as a practice and a preference for the taste of rainwater. Surveys have shown that most people in rural Thailand preferred rain as a source of drinking water (Luong and Luckmuang, 2002; Hartung et al., 2008). Additionally, the relative homogeneity of the country where 95 per cent of the population are Thai and 95 per cent are Buddhists, allowed for national campaigns developed under one concept, using one language, to reach the vast majority of the population. Public support for rainwater harvesting by national champions, including the King, and the active involvement of other opinion leaders in its promotion raised the profile of the Jar Programme and further increased acceptance and impact.

Political and regulatory factors

Thailand introduced a set of new policies for rural water provision in the late 1970s which created an enabling environment for rainwater harvesting. Jars and tanks for drinking water, shallow wells for domestic water, and small weirs for agriculture (Areerachakul, 2013) were all recommended for use and management by the user household. Moreover, the National Economic and Social Development Plans of the 1980s foresaw a dual system of water provision, with a limited amount of high quality water (5 litres of water per person per day from sources such as rainwater and protected wells) and a larger amount for other domestic purposes (e.g. from springs and surface water) (Hartung et al., 2008).

There was also a strong and sustained commitment to domestic rainwater harvesting at all levels of government. Over several decades there was little policy change, which allowed a wide range of government agencies to align (Hartung et al., 2008). It was estimated that 26 different government agencies were involved in the promotion and implementation of domestic rainwater harvesting. Interestingly, the main funds for the Jar Programme came through a job creation programme, rather than through a water management or water supply programme. Training of professionals (producers and vendors of the jars) was at the centre of this programme.

Government and international cooperation agencies (e.g. KfW, JICA) invested considerable funds in the Thai Jar Programme. Hartung et al. (2008) estimated overall costs of THB 1,680m between 1986 and 1991, the equivalent of about US$67m at that time, for training and for subsidizing materials. NGOs and the private sector also contributed: for example, one company donated 2,500 tonnes of mortar (Luong and Luckmuang, 2002).

Economics and market factors

Investments in training made in the 1980s, and the know-how that this generated, made it possible to mass produce high-volume mortar jars. After the initial push by the government programme to train thousands of artisans, the private sector (mostly SMEs and micro-entrepreneurs) grew to meet demand. Fierce competition started to kick in, keeping down prices and driving up productivity. Private households took over as the main investors as subsidies were withdrawn.

At around $20 (1990s values), the Thai Jar cost only around 1 per cent of the mean annual income, cheaper than alternatives (such as the dragon jar) and affordable by wide segments of society. With strong economic growth putting money into pockets of rural people, the Thai Jar was one of the best buys on the market – not only for health, but also for productivity, income, and the reputation of a family.

Women play a relatively active role in Thai society, including but not limited to politics, and they have good access to paid labour. Women's labour force participation rate in the 1980s was at 77 per cent, well above other countries in the region (Bauer, 2001). Thailand at that time had a strong, home-based textile industry. However, as in many countries, the task of obtaining, transporting, and managing water for domestic purposes was and is mostly carried out by women and girls. This meant that an investment in a jar could actually

Photo CS.3.2 (a) Thai Jar factory; (b) Thai Jars being delivered to customers
Source: Enterprise Works/Vita

be a money-maker for households: women were able to work and gain income using time that was previously spent fetching water. There was a strong economic incentive for repeated investments in jars – the more water could be stored, the more money could be earned.

The high quality of the jar was important as many people started with only one jar and – based on a positive experience of its durability – later decided to buy additional jars. The relatively low price of gutters, plumbing materials, and corrugated metal sheets for roofing, all contributed to low overall costs for rainwater harvesting.

The ease of transport, combined with the market size, the affordability of the product, and the high demand made it possible to establish mass production, which in turn allowed for a further reduction of the price (see Photo CS.3.2). Even though the government programme was focused on a relatively poor area of Thailand, it was targeted at a large proportion of society, not only the poor. This enabled the programme to grow quickly and reach out to millions of people. Thailand's road infrastructure was also fairly good and most of the land relatively flat making it possible to establish a few production sites and then transport the jars to the users.

Challenges in replicating the Thai experience

Domestic rainwater harvesting has been widely promoted in many countries but it has proved hard to replicate the Thai experience. In nearby Cambodia, Laos, and Vietnam, rural households often use rainwater as a primary source of drinking water but at lower levels than in Thailand.

The 'One Million Cistern Programme' in the north-east of Brazil is another large-scale rainwater harvesting promotion programme. However, despite more than 20 years of significant funding from public and private actors, it has not met its target, and government support eventually was suspended in 2012. Here, the costs of rainwater harvesting are high because low rainfall and long dry periods require large volumes of water to be stored, meaning large roof surface areas are required. Very large tanks – 10–12 m³ –are built on-site, making mass production impossible and requiring the constructors to move to the customer, and material and labour costs are high. Low population densities further limits market development. There is little competition in the market and high prices further limit demand. After more than 10 years of almost fully subsidizing the initiative, the leading government agency made an important adjustment: instead of one tank, two were constructed for each family, one for human consumption and one for livestock or small gardens/irrigation plots. Although this further raised costs, the focus on income generation greatly enhanced the interest of people in participating in the programme and covering part of the costs themselves. The programme became better accepted and progress accelerated. Nevertheless, during a financial crisis (2010–2012) it was decided to stop government funding for this programme.

In Nepal, the government agency responsible for drinking water (Department of Water Supply and Sewerage) has for two decades been promoting rainwater harvesting with partners, both at institutions (schools, health posts, etc.) and for private households. However, in most hilly areas in Nepal it is more cost-effective to install small gravity-driven water supply networks rather than rainwater tanks for each household, and in the lowlands groundwater is readily accessible. Rainwater harvesting is therefore limited to small numbers of households on the top of the hills where supply networks are not feasible. The overall market size is small, with the potential customers scattered across the rural areas and typically hard to reach. Systematic comparison of the contexts in Nepal and Thailand (Bohara and Saladin, 2016) showed that out of 18 factors analysed for both countries, in Thailand 15 were positive and 3 were neutral: in Nepal, 4 were positive, 4 were negative, and 10 were neutral. The four negative factors in Nepal were: rainwater systems not sufficiently affordable, service providers made little profit, providers had limited capacity, and rainwater consumption was out of line with existing traditions and perceptions. In most parts of the rural hill zones, where rainwater harvesting is attractive from a technical point of view, there is no tradition of consuming rainwater, and people prefer to get drinking water from springs.

Many low- or middle-income island states struggle with the similar contextual problems: low population densities, small overall market size, and high transport costs leading to high overall costs and low demand for rainwater harvesting. In many of these islands groundwater resources are too small to cover basic needs even for small populations and rainwater is the most obvious source for many households – but because of these limiting factors, collection and consumption of rainwater continues to be rather the exception than the rule.

Rainwater has been promoted in many countries in sub-Saharan Africa, where access to improved sources of drinking water by the rural population is among the lowest in the world. However, low rural water coverage does not automatically mean high demand for domestic rainwater harvesting.

Consumption of rainwater needs to be culturally accepted, products need to be affordable and available, and rainwater harvesting needs to be more attractive and accessible than alternatives. In sub-Saharan Africa, the country where domestic rainwater harvesting is most common is Uganda, where just 1 per cent of the rural population use rainwater as the primary drinking water source (Ministry of Water and Environment, 2017).

Conclusions

The Thailand experience yields insights on how to align a variety of actors, set enabling policies, establish capacities in the domestic private sector, and unleash market forces to grow and sustain an idea that was initially government-driven. However, Thailand is the exception rather than the rule and many other efforts to promote rainwater harvesting have fallen short of expectations. It has become clear that a large number of necessary factors for scale were in place in Thailand and that in less favourable contexts, the diffusion of the practice will be less effective and costlier. In the wider context of self-supply initiatives, rainwater harvesting promotion in Thailand can be an inspiration, demonstrating that government has an important role to play in establishing sufficient capacities and an enabling environment in self-supply. The leadership provided by Thai government institutions at all levels are an example of effective policy implementation, and the Thai Jar Programme can serve as an example in gradually upgrading water supply service levels to reach almost everyone.

References

Areerachakul, N. (2013) 'Overviews of rainwater harvesting and utilization in Thailand: Bangsaiy Municipality', *International Journal of Environmental, Chemical, Ecological, Geological and Geophysical Engineering* 7(7): 485–92 <http://dx.doi.org/10.5281/zenodo.1087438>.

Bauer, J. (2001) 'Demographic change, development and the economic status of women in East Asia', in A. Mason (ed.), *Population Change and Economic Development in Asia*, Stanford University Press, Stanford.

Bohara, R. and Saladin, M. (2016) 'Difficulties in replicating success stories: the case of domestic rainwater harvesting', paper presented at the *Rural Water Supply Network Forum 7, Abidjan, Cote d'Ivoire* [online] <https://rwsnforum7.files.wordpress.com/2016/11/full_paper_0137_submitter_0046_saladin_matthias.pdf> [accessed 1 June 2020].

Hartung, H., Morgan, M. and Naugle, J. (2008) *Domestic Rainwater Harvesting: Thailand* [online], EnterpriseWorks/VITA, Washington, DC <http://www.rural-water-supply.net/en/resources/details/716> [accessed 1 June 2020].

Luong, T.V. and Luckmuang, P. (2002) 'Household rainwater harvesting – Thailand', paper presented at the *28th WEDC conference, Kolkata, India* [online] <http://wedc.lboro.ac.uk/resources/conference/28/Luong.pdf> [accessed 1 June 2020].

Ministry of Water and Environment (2017) *Water and Environment Sector Performance Report*, Government of Uganda, Kampala.

Saladin, M. (2016) *Rainwater Harvesting in Thailand: Learning from the World Champions*, RWSN, St Gallen, Switzerland <http://www.rural-water-supply.net/en/resources/details/759> [accessed 14 February 2020].

Smet, J. (2003) *Domestic rainwater harvesting* [online], WEDC, Loughborough <https://www.lboro.ac.uk/research/wedc/well/water-supply/ws-factsheets/domestic-rainwater-harvsting/> [accessed 14 February 2020].

Tigno, C. (2007) *Thailand: promoting rainwater harvesting, preserving rainwater jar culture* [online] <http://de.scribd.com/doc/109778391/Thailand-Water-Action-Promoting-Rainwater-Harvesting-Preserving-Rainwater-Jar-Culture> [accessed 17 February 2020].

UNEP/IETC (1998) *Sourcebook of Alternative Technologies for Freshwater Augmentation in Some Countries in Asia* [online], UNEP International Environmental Technology Centre, Osaka <https://www.ircwash.org/resources/source-book-alternative-technologies-freshwater-augmentation-some-countries-asia> [accessed 14 February 2020].

WHO/UNICEF (2015) *Progress on Sanitation and Drinking Water: 2015 Update and MDG Assessment* [pdf], WHO/UNICEF Joint Monitoring Programme for Water Supply and Sanitation, Geneva/New York <https://washdata.org/sites/default/files/documents/reports/2017-06/JMP-2015-Report.pdf> [accessed 1 June 2020].

CASE STUDY 4

The National Upgraded Well Programme, Zimbabwe

Peter Morgan

Introduction

The National Upgraded Well Programme in Zimbabwe led to the improvement of over 150,000 family wells and better water supplies for 1–2 million people through a self-supply approach.

In the parts of Zimbabwe where groundwater is available at shallow depth, wells can be developed using low cost and simple technology (Africa Groundwater Atlas, 2019). Shallow groundwater potential is high or moderate over about half of the country (Chikodzi and Mutowo 2014). By the 1980s, it was estimated that at least 1 million people drew their water from family or community hand-dug wells. In parts of the country, over 30 per cent of the population were using such wells daily. The problem was that many of these wells were either unprotected or poorly protected. Headworks were missing or unhygienic. Wells often became contaminated, either because dirty runoff water could enter the well or because the buckets and ropes used to draw water became contaminated around the wellhead. Many of the wells were open at the top, which also posed a safety hazard for children. Rather than solving these problems, emphasis of official water supply programmes was on installing community boreholes or deeper wells fitted with a hand pump: the Zimbabwe Bush Pump. Despite family wells being widely used, they were not considered seriously by government or other agencies involved in water supply and they were not included in official inventories of water sources.

Rethinking water supply and the role of families

Attitudes to family wells started to change in the mid to late 1980s when researchers at the Ministry of Health's Blair Research Institute (now known as the National Institute for Health Research) highlighted both the extent and popularity of family wells across Zimbabwe. The research also showed that improving the construction of family wells could indeed reduce the risk of well water contamination.

Family wells were found to be preferred by households to communal hand pumps, in part because they were more convenient and promoted self-sufficiency. Many family wells had also been privately improved. Some families had lined wells with bricks, or added well covers, built a surrounding wall to protect the well from contamination, or installed windlasses that kept buckets and ropes off the ground. Trials were built on these practices and indeed, good practices that were promoted within other parts of government. The Environmental Health Department of the Ministry of Health and Child Care had in fact been promoting shallow well use for decades.

The bacterial load in well water was shown to be reduced when hand dug wells were improved. The wellhead improvements (conforming to international standards for improved or protected wells (WHO/UNICEF 2018)) included lining the well with fired bricks, installing a robust concrete well cover and sanitary apron around the well, adding a water run-off channel to lead water away from the well head, a raised collar fitted with a tin lid on top, and a windlass to raise the bucket and to help maintain hygiene of the water lifting equipment (bucket and rope) (see Photo CS.4.1). Table CS.4.1 shows results of testing of well water from unimproved and improved (upgraded) wells. Further evidence of water quality improvement, both for faecal streptococci and *E. coli* indicators were shown through further testing between January and March 1988 during a heavy rainy period (Table CS.4.2).

These tests showed that improvements in water quality could be achieved without the use of a hand pump in shallow wells. The results did not match

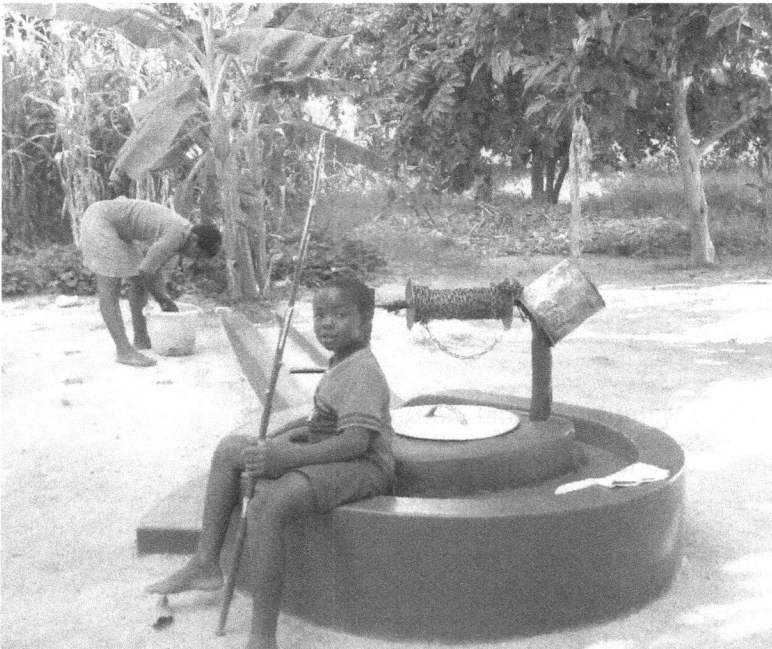

Photo CS.4.1 Well built during Zimbabwe's National Upgraded Well Programme

Table CS.4.1 Levels of contamination (E. coli) for unimproved and improved family wells

Facility	Mean E. coli/100 ml
Traditional well with bucket	266.42 (n = 233)
Upgraded well	65.94 (n = 234)

Note: Averages are potentially skewed by a non-normal distribution and heavily contaminated wells, but more detailed data are no longer available.
Source: Morgan, 1992

Table CS.4.2 Levels of contamination (E. coli and faecal streptococci) for unimproved and improved family wells, January to March 1988

Facility	Mean *E. coli*/100 ml	Mean faecal streptococci/100 ml
Traditional well with bucket	342.48 (n = 85)	579.48 (n = 88)
Upgraded well	84.01 (n = 86)	103.01 (n = 88)

Source: Morgan, 1992

the lower *E. coli* levels found in water delivered by completely sealed hand pumps fitted to wells and boreholes but offered substantial improvement. Importantly, family wells are much simpler and easier to maintain.

Armed with this evidence about possible improvements in bacteriological quality and the better physical safety of improved family wells, a series of pilot projects were initiated by the Blair Research Institute. Between 1988 and 1992, about 5,300 upgraded family wells were built (both new wells and adding headworks to existing wells) with the full backing and support of the Environmental Health Department of the Ministry of Health and Child Care. The first were built in Makoni District, funded by Swedish Sida. At the same time, training teams from the Institute were deployed throughout the country to pass on knowledge about improving family wells to health teams and local builders and to establish demonstration sites.

The National Upgraded Well Programme

Based on the pilots that were under way, the concept of upgrading family wells was studied and debated by Ministry of Health and Child Care officials from all parts of the country during 1988 and 1989. The concept was officially endorsed in 1990 by the Ministry of Health and Child Care and then in 1991 by the Government's National Action Committee (for WASH). It was included at a small scale in their first National Integrated Programme and later, this programme was expanded across Zimbabwe. Throughout the 1990s, development partners such as WaterAid and others subsidized family well upgrading programmes.

Families had to fund the digging and lining of the well shaft themselves, and also pay a builder, but they were supported by a generous subsidy from the government (using donor support) to cover the costs of cement, a tin lid, and a windlass (commercially made). District Environmental Health Officers and their staff supervised upgrading according to the procedures recommended. In order to expand the programme further, Blair Research Institute staff involved in the programme moved to create a new NGO supported by WaterAid. This became the Mvuramanzi Trust (Morgan et al., 1996).

The Institute and the Mvuramanzi Trust upgraded over 38,000 family wells in the early 1990s, and the efforts of other agencies likely brought the total to near 50,000. Additional benefits of the programme were also realized. The wells supported vegetable gardening with water for irrigation, which further supported local economic development (Robinson, 2002). Some commentators at the time reflected on the impact of family wells on community supplies. On one hand, family-based water supplies reduced pressure on community pumps and the likelihood of breakdowns. On the other hand, families with their own well were thought to be less likely to contribute to the upkeep and maintenance of a community pump.

One of the reasons for the success of the National Upgraded Well Programme was that it built upon traditional practices that were already established. It facilitated families to do something for themselves, and provided infrastructure they could build and manage themselves. The well upgrading methods were based on relatively simple, locally tried and tested techniques which facilitated their wider uptake. Private ownership was also an important factor, and the convenience of having a private water supply close to home ·was seen as important. The long-term involvement of the Ministry of Health was also critical. It had the capacity to provide supervisory and training staff at many levels, including in the village. Other ministries would not have been able to do this so effectively.

The private sector played a part in the programme. The windlass was made by commercial businesses in the subsidized programmes, but local entrepreneurs have also made windlasses as they have done for decades, even before the official programmes began. Even in subsidized programmes the tin lid was supplied by informal enterprises. Large numbers of builders were also trained.

The combined and collaborative efforts of the Government of Zimbabwe, NGOs, generous donors, and the private sector helped to achieve a common goal: to improve the quality of and access to potable water for large numbers of people living in the rural areas of the country.

Decline and redesign

From 2000, Zimbabwe entered a troubled political period and has suffered from ongoing economic decline. There was a huge reduction in donor support which affected many developmental programmes including in water supply, and led to a slowdown in the construction of new family wells. At the same time, the performance of family wells in the context of a declining economy and reduced public sector capacities showed the approach still had merit.

With reduced support, community hand pump supplies have been faring worse and perhaps only close to half of hand pumps are functional.

Looking back, support to household water supplies, as well as for community supplies, turns out to have been critical. A review by SKAT, supported by UNICEF and working with Zimbabwe AHEAD, reported on how upgraded family wells had fared in two districts (Makoni and Buhera) in the Manicaland Province of Zimbabwe (Olschewski et al., 2016). The review highlighted the convenience of family wells and the advantages of maintenance by the family. It also noted that the lack of support and follow up was putting earlier achievements at risk as the infrastructure was no longer being maintained properly (see Box CS.4.1). Recommendations were made to invest in the rehabilitation of existing assets, capacity development, and resurrection of the upgraded family well programme.

Box CS.4.1 Construction quality and maintenance

As in all construction, the same ingredients can be used to make structures of varying quality. Family wells require care and maintenance, and good construction helps. Erosion around the well head needs to be checked and built up with new soil. As with any water point that is heavily used, erosion takes place around the well head even with adequate drainage. Poorly made and installed pumps and a lack of routine maintenance can lead to a shorter working life span than pumps which are made, installed, and maintained properly. Morgan and Kanyemba (2012) provide more details on construction methods and Photo CS.4.2 illustrates some of the possible problems.

Photo CS.4.2 Family well showing a lack of attention and maintenance

---

Although the origins of the National Upgraded Well Programme were supported by research, there was a lack of detailed nationwide monitoring to record the successes and weaknesses of the programme. Although many properly constructed wells are still fully functional, some poorly upgraded wells were prone to disintegrate, particularly the important apron, drainage channels, and brick windlass supports.

In the 1980s and 1990s subsidies to families for toilets and wells were common but, over time, the concept of providing quite large subsidies to families has become unpopular with donors and is no longer encouraged by the government. As a result the designs of both the local family Blair VIP toilet and the Upgraded Family Well unit were revisited. Designs were modified to facilitate building in a series of affordable steps and at a lower cost with minimal or no support. The government now promotes the revised method of supporting family Blair VIP construction, known as the uBVIP (upgradable Blair ventilated improved pit toilet). It has continued to use the multi-compartment Blair VIPs in schools. Despite the redesign and some experimentation, a similar step-by-step upgradeable system for family wells has not yet been scaled up.

In Epworth, close to Harare, the suburb where some of the first family wells had been upgraded in the 1980s, local artisans were trained in the new designs and encouraged to train others (Morgan, 2015). The activities were still subsidized as a pilot project, but to a much lesser extent than in the 1990s. Families who wanted to upgrade their well received a bag of cement and two properly treated gum poles with which to support a locally made windlass. It was not seen as compulsory to begin with a windlass and the supporting poles, as these could be added later, and the design of the windlass and its supports was optional. A strong concrete well cover serving as an apron with raised external rim and raised internal rim supporting a lid together with a water run-off channel were seen as essential components. This alternative step-by-step method has not yet gone beyond the experimental stage.

Part of the past and part of the future

While the data available is imperfect, the National Upgraded Well Programme has had major and lasting impacts. The exact number of improved privately owned wells is not known, but may be well lie between 150,000 and 200,000, serving as many as 1–2 million people (a study for UNICEF by Olschewski (2016) found 15–20 people on average sharing each well for at least part of their supply). Where community supplies do not function at their best, self-owned supplies are the only means of survival for many. The concept of self-supply is very much alive in Zimbabwe, even in the cities, where huge numbers of privately owned boreholes have been drilled simply because municipal supplies have failed or do not deliver water of an acceptable quality.

Although the per capita costs of upgrading family wells and community sources might be similar (see Box CS.4.2), there is a more important difference in the financing of costs of investment and maintenance. A community

Box CS.4.2 Costs and financing of family wells

Based upon known costs in Epworth (a peri-urban settlement near Harare), the estimated costs of an upgraded family well in 2015 ranged between $149 and $380 depending especially on lining and whether a windlass was added. Costs include materials and labour, which in rural areas may be slightly cheaper. Tin lids and windlasses and windlass supports can also be locally made. The wells are lined with fired brick. Windlass supports are made with fully treated timber or preferably steel with wooden bearings.

Facility	Total cost (US$)	Per capita cost estimate (US$)
	(including labour)	(assuming 10 persons per well)
No windlass, part well lining	149	15
No windlass, full well lining	299	30
Windlass, part well lining	248	25
Windlass, full well lining	380	38

In comparison, the cost of drilling a 40 m deep borehole and fitting it with a hand pump (Zimbabwe Bush Pump) was about $6,000 in 2015. If the pump serves 250 persons as intended the per capita cost was $24, within the same range of per capita costs as an upgraded family well.

borehole and a hand pump are paid for by the government or a donor, and maintenance largely rests with the government (mainly the District Development Fund). Maintenance costs of a borehole and handpump vary a lot, and performance depends on using and replacing good quality leather seals. In contrast, the near full cost of a family well, including its maintenance, is paid by the family itself.

These economics suggest that family wells will be around for some time. With family wells being restricted to locations with shallow groundwater, while boreholes can be successfully drilled across much wider areas, both approaches are clearly important to serve rural communities (Morgan, 2006).

References

Africa Groundwater Atlas (2019) *Case study: Zimbabwe family well upgrading programme* [online], British Geological Survey <http://earthwise.bgs.ac.uk/index.php/Case_Study_Zimbabwe_Family_Well_Upgrading> [accessed 1 June 2020].

Chikodzi, D, and Mutowo, G. (2014) *Spatial modelling of groundwater potential in Zimbabwe using geographical information systems techniques.* International journal of Water 8(4):422-434 <https://www.researchgate.net/publication/268505753_Spatial_modelling_of_groundwater_potential_in_Zimbabwe_using_geographical_information_systems_techniques> [accessed June 20 2019]

Morgan, P.R. (1992) *Zimbabwe's Upgraded Well Programme: Background Paper,* Blair Research Laboratory, Harare.

Morgan, P. (2006) *Zimbabwe's Upgraded Family Well Programme* [pdf], Aquamor, Harare <https://aquamor.info/uploads/3/4/2/5/34257237/zimbabwes_upgraded_family_well_program.pdf. [accessed 24 February 2020].

Morgan, P. (2015) *Self-Supply as a Means of Bringing Water to the People of Zimbabwe and its Relation to the Hand Pump Program* [online], Aquamor, Harare <https://www.rural-water-supply.net/en/resources/details/751> [accessed 24 February 2020].

Morgan, P. and Kanyemba, A. (2012) *Upgraded Family Wells in Zimbabwe: A Study of Upgraded Family Well Technology and Training* [pdf], Aquamor, Harare, Zimbabwe <www.rural-water-supply.net/_ressources/documents/default/1-703-54-1447081743.pdf> [accessed 1 June 2020].

Morgan, P., Chimbunde, E., Mtakwa, N. and Waterkeyn, A. (1996) 'Now in my backyard: Zimbabwe's upgraded family well programme', *Waterlines* 14(4): 8–11 <https://doi.org/10.3362/0262-8104.1996.014>.

Olschewski, A. (2016) *Review of Self-supply and its Support Services in African Countries: With Findings from Zambia, Zimbabwe and Malawi* [online], UNICEF/SKAT <https://www.unicef.org/esa/media/2151/file/UNICEF-ESA-2016-Review-Supported-Self-supply-Synthesis-Report.pdf> [accessed 24 February 2020].

Olschewski, A., Matimati, R. and Waterkeyn, A. (2016) *Review of Upgraded Well Program in Makoni & Buhera Districts, Manicaland Province, Zimbabwe* [online], UNICEF/SKAT <www.rural-water-supply.net/fr/ressources/details/830> [accessed 24 February 2020].

Robinson, P. (2002) *Upgraded Family Wells in Zimbabwe: Household-Level Water Supplies for Multiple Uses* [online], Field Note 6, Water and Sanitation Program, Nairobi <www.ircwash.org/sites/default/files/WSP-2002-Upgraded.pdf> [accessed 1 June 2020].

WHO/UNICEF (2018) *Core questions on drinking-water and sanitation for household surveys*, World Health Organization and UNICEF (2006) Geneva, Switzerland https://www.washdata.org/monitoring/methods/core-questions [accessed June 2020]

Introducing alternative and affordable technologies for rural water supply in Tanzania

Walter Mgina

Introduction

Njombe District – with its population of 130,000 – is diverse with distinctive highland and lowland climatic zones. The highland areas, with better rainfall, support natural and commercial forestry and agriculture. Rainfall is as low as 500 mm in the lowlands where agriculture and livelihoods are drought-prone. Njombe town (an urban settlement of the district) has grown rapidly, providing a challenge to the extension of piped water supplies in the settlement. Some households have responded by hand digging their own wells, likely using skills and techniques from the lowlands where dug wells are already common. These wells have provided an option to augment the inadequate water supply service in the district, but also showed that groundwater development has a wider role to play in supporting development in highland areas. The privately developed wells are often in use for household water supply as well as income-generating activities like raising cows, pig keeping, poultry, and market gardens, and nurseries for tree seedlings.

Alternative and affordable technologies

In this context, the NGO SHIPO (standing for the Southern Highlands Participatory Organization) started to support the development of traditional gravity-fed water supply systems and introduced hydraulic rams for pumping in the areas around the town. An interest in widening access to water to support more communities and people led SHIPO to search for other, cheaper technologies to develop groundwater, including manual drilling and the rope pump. These can provide an alternative to mechanically drilled boreholes, which, at costs of US$60 to 65 per metre (excluding mobilization, demobilization, and pump costs), are only affordable for externally funded community supplies. Over the years SHIPO has tested, adapted, and demonstrated a wide range of technologies (see Box CS.5.1). With an investment of $100–300 a family can develop a basic dug well with a rope pump and provide water for

---

Box CS.5.1 Alternative and affordable technologies introduced by SHIPO in Njombe Region

Rope pump: a continuous loop of rope with washers at 1 m intervals that fit with a small clearance inside a PVC pipe that is immersed in the well. By turning the wheel, the rope passes around the loop pushing water to the top; several models are available (local cost about $50–130). See Coloru et al. (2012) for more discussion on the performance of rope pumps in this context.

Upgraded dug wells: wells dug using hand tools and ventilation fan developed locally, and improved with basic wellhead protection, a well cover, and hand pump. The wells are lined with bricks to stabilize the walls and the well depth can be increased by underlining if needed (cost around $50–500).

Manual drilling: SHIPO has combined elements of the Bolivian Baptist drilling method with Rota sludge drilling techniques. From 2010, what became known as the SHIPO drilling technique used lighter PVC drill pipes to drill deeper wells in compact clay and semi-hard ground layers up to 48 m deep. Materials are available in local hardware shops and drilling tools are manufactured by local artisans (cost $100–1,000).

Wire cement tanks: These tanks use wire instead of construction steel and local material such as bricks, bamboo, or reed. The cost is 30–40 per cent lower than for ferro-cement tanks and volumes can be 5–50 m³ (cost $40–60).

Well recharge: Tube recharge with rainwater that otherwise would flow away. Use of vetiver grass to slow surface runoff and soil erosion while allowing water to percolate through the soil and into aquifers (cost $5–15).

Siphon filters: A small and very effective water filter; the main component is a high-quality ceramic element that produces 60–80 litres of safe drinking water per day, and it has a lifetime of 7,000 litres. This makes it possible for families depending on both improved and unimproved self-supply wells to access safe drinking water (cost per filter $18–40).

Tippy Tap: A hand washing facility near latrines made of a recycled 5-litre container, a piece of rope, and four sticks. If promoted properly it can improve and motivate hand washing habits for families and schools (cost $1–3).

---

the family (and often also neighbours). Chapter 6 provides more details on a range of technologies related to self-supply.

Solidarity between the Netherlands and Tanzania: building an organization around technology

SHIPO originated from a local community-based organization, Mundindi Development Foundation (Mudefo), set up in the District of Ludewa in 1997. Funding was derived from a foundation in the Netherlands. The objective was to organize communities to solve endemic problems that lead to poverty with water supply top of the list of community priorities, followed by health and primary education. In 2001, activities were relocated to Njombe town and SHIPO was registered and housed at premises provided by the district council. SHIPO continued to develop with support from a growing network of organizations and committed individuals, especially from the Netherlands.

Photo CS.5.1 SHIPO hand-drilling

SHIPO learned about potential solutions to access water at lower cost than conventional drilled boreholes through an article about manual well-drilling and rope pumps in Nicaragua. SHIPO received support from Connect International, who had discussed the same ideas at the Hague World Water Forum in 2000 and worked with the Practica foundation. A first training in Rota sludge well-drilling at SHIPO was organized in 2003 and the first rope pump was introduced to Tanzania. Around the same time (2002–2005), SHIPO received funding from SIMAVI (a Dutch development organization) for community water supply schemes in Njombe. This project allowed SHIPO to use the new drilling method (see Photo CS.5.1) to construct about 22 water points for a community near Njombe town. The community members contributed food, lodging, labour, and some materials, and SHIPO trained community members in manual drilling and rope pump installation and maintenance. The rope pumps were made by a local blacksmith who has continued to produce rope pumps as an additional product from his workshop.

In 2006, Connect International started implementation of the TMF programme (a Dutch Ministry of Foreign Affairs initiative 'Thematische Medefinanciering'), which funded the Tazamo project in three countries (Tanzania, Zambia, and Mozambique). This provided an opportunity to scale up the promotion of such technologies and included the delivery of 450 community water supplies in Tanzania. Practica foundation provided further training with SHIPO in manual drilling and rope pump production, and new manual drilling enterprises were created. Trainees were organized as drilling teams of three persons, receiving assignments through SHIPO. The teams hired the drilling equipment from SHIPO and were paid for a borehole of 24 m depth with a bonus for every additional metre

Photo CS.5.2 Contractors sell low cost options for community projects as well as self-supply, this school supply was installed 15 years ago

up to 30 m. Costs per installation were around $1,500 for each community supply (see Photo CS.5.2). The project also covered the risks of unproductive wells. Communities contributed by providing accommodation, food, storage, and drilling assistants. These were later trained as caretakers for the village water points. Drilling teams were encouraged to register at the local government level as entrepreneurs and potentially gain access to development loans, tax incentives, and other opportunities offered by the government for creation of employment for the youth and the disadvantaged. However, only one graduate of the original drilling and well-digging groups in Njombe was able to make this jump.

The surviving entrepreneur, Laban Kaduma, founded a small registered business enterprise called Umoja wa Uchimbaji Visima Njombe or Uvinjo. Depending on demand he has three to six drilling teams making hand-dug and hand-drilled wells. The technology used has also shifted over time from Rota sludge and Baptist drilling to the SHIPO drilling method. The average depths of wells is 25 m and diameters of the PVC casings are 2, 3, and 4 inch (51 mm, 76 mm, and 102 mm) costing $870 to $1,330 including the rope pump. The deepest tubewell so far is 48 m deep. Some wells have Afridev piston pumps costing around $1,100 but over 95 per cent of the tubewells are combined with a rope pump model. Customers that can afford it have even installed electrical submersible pumps, available from China costing $130–300 depending on pumping head. Since 2015 Uvinjo has also produced its own good quality rope pumps. Mr Laban has reported constructing over 4,000 wells, most of them drilled tube-wells, and Uvinjo is now working on monitoring wells he has constructed as an after sales service to promote his business. Laban says he always travels with parts in case he comes across a malfunctioning pump on his travels. Laban has also provided training consultancy services on behalf of SHIPO and himself in several African countries.

Emergence of self-supply markets

The subsidized wells and pumps – community water supplies – provided by the Tazamo project created a different market. Families, mostly in peri-urban areas of Njombe, Makambako, and other urban settlements, increasingly bought pumps for their own hand-dug wells encouraged by promotional fliers distributed by SHIPO. Around 6,000 families in peri-urban and rural areas were estimated to have bought a pump, without any subsidy, based on estimates made at a manual drillers and pump producer symposium in Morogoro in 2015.

How did this happen? When the Tazamo project stopped (2010), only one out of the four drilling teams continued. Other trainees continued as private independent well-digging artisans but it has been difficult to get feedback on their fortunes. There is occasional news reaching SHIPO about rope pumps in faraway places. Back in 2006, the collapse of the other drilling teams was a learning moment. The drilling teams were paid for their work whatever the result, so they behaved like employees and had little motivation as entrepreneurs. But SHIPO and its partners didn't stop, and later on trainees were selected from artisans who already were well-diggers in the communities and wanted to expand their services to well-drilling.

SHIPO continued its activities, added new technologies at its demonstration site adjacent to the training centre, and increasingly focused on self-supply (Olschewski, 2013; van Donk, 2015). This was rebranded as the SHIPO SMART centre (SMART stands for Simple, Market-based, Affordable and Repairable Technologies). The Tazamo project had included funds (in 2006) for the installation of a training workshop containing space for classrooms, tools, and a fabrication workshop. Over the years, the centre has continued to provide training and follow-up support after projects ended. Different partners have supported the centre, many Dutch (Cordaid, Water Help, DOB, A4A), but also the IWASH project and since 2015 the SKAT foundation. The centre inspired other efforts elsewhere and is part of the SMART Centre Group coordinated by MetaMeta (see Chapter 9).

So called 'Wow' visits demonstrated some 15 low cost water and sanitation technologies. The SHIPO SMART Centre has now trained over 250 people in technical skills (with two consultancy training sessions in other countries) and some 100 people in business skills.

The approach developed under the Tazamo project had already interested other organizations. WINROCK took up the approach in the USAID IWASH project (2011–2015) and funded training and championed the approach. Another USAID-funded project, TAPP (Tanzania Agriculture Productivity Program), through FINTRAC in 2014, contracted SHIPO to train traditional well-digging artisans in four different regions. The approach has reached most regions including Morogoro, Tabora, Arusha, Manyara, Kilimanjaro, Kijgoma, Bukoba, Singida, and Mwanza. There are at least five active drilling/well-digging teams and 11 pump producing companies (including in Njombe, Iringa, Manyara, Morogoro, Singida, and Mwanza) that retain contact with SHIPO. Juma Mape for example is a trainee in manual drilling with previous experience with well ring production and piston pump installation and has travelled as far as Rwanda for assignments. Sara Msofe is the only woman manual driller remaining and has recently registered a private company. These 'second-generation' trainees are likely to be succeeded by a third and fourth generation that have developed without direct support from SHIPO and who are likely making poorer quality wells and rope pumps. But information on diffusion of the approach remains sketchy and there has been no systematic evaluation.

Will regulation of groundwater development spell the end of growth in manual drilling and low-cost pump markets?

Contracts for development of community water schemes were crucial to the development of these businesses, but that is now difficult, and indeed growth of groundwater development using low-cost technologies is threatened by strengthening regulation of groundwater development. This issue has already emerged in the TAPP. The first phase included development of wells for drip irrigation by farmers. Wells were made and teams trained, and in a second phase, it was expected that the trainees would continue as entrepreneurs to deliver the services under SHIPO guidance and then become independent drillers. However, this was stopped following a move by the responsible department to follow up on compliance with regulations for manual drilling in Tanzania. Drilling companies need to be qualified and be registered contractors in the Ministry of Water and Irrigation according to Tanzania's groundwater regulations.

The Water Resource Management Act of 2009 requires drillers to be licensed, retain qualified staff, and pay annual fees. The annual licence for class two (up to 100 m depth) costs $435. The affordable technology artisans that are trained by the SMART centre are awarded certificates of attendance after taking part in the training. But these certificates do not qualify them as drillers by the Ministry of Water regulation standards and the licence is not affordable to those with only private clients.

Summary and next steps for SHIPO

Some 3,000 water points with rope pumps were constructed for small communities based on the example of the Tazamo programme with funding from different NGOs. The spread of the skills to other regions was the result of investment by a series of bilateral projects linked to, supported or inspired by SHIPO, that were interested in the approach of combining low-cost technologies and business development, especially for irrigation. In parallel, over 6,000 rope pumps have been funded by families themselves and installed on hand-dug wells around Njombe and other regions. Over 50 private individuals, farmers, and institutions have commissioned boreholes installed with submersible pumps, so there is also movement up the technology ladder.

Developments in regulation appear to unintentionally threaten further growth of self-supply by limiting prospects for manual drilling. It is recommended that regulations are reviewed, perhaps introducing a third classification of registration for shallow wells up to 45 m deep, and with a registration and drilling permit available at an affordable cost to traditional well-digging and manual drilling artisans.

SHIPO has not yet been able to embark on an advocacy campaign to engage wider stakeholders such as national government and members of the Tanzania Water and Sanitation Network. Opportunities include working with the Water Development Management Institute (WDMI) to introduce training in affordable technologies linked to compliance with regulation for drilling licences, and completing the training curriculum for rope pump production by the Vocational Educational Training Authority (VETA) in Morogoro so as to provide training skills for certified rope pumps production. A national standard for such pumps could also be developed.

References

Coloru, B., Mgaya, S. and Pozzi-Taubert, R. (2012) *A Comparative Study between 'Rope Pumps' and Conventional Piston Pumps on Water Quality and Other Sustainability Parameters* [online], Appropriate Technologies for Rural Water Supply, Fondazione ACRA-CCS and SHIPO <www.rural-water-supply.net/en/resources/details/655> [accessed 1 June 2020].

Olschewski, A. (2013) *Self Supply in Tanzania: SHIPO's Training of Local Drillers and Rope Pump Producers in Makambako, 2012/2013* [online], Skat Foundation report <www.rural-water-supply.net/en/resources/details/534> [accessed 1 June 2020].

Van Donk, M. (2015) *Market Support for Low-Cost, Self-Supply WASH Technologies: Facilitation of Supply and Demand in Tanzania* [webinar], RWSN Webinar Series <https://www.rural-water-supply.net/en/resources/details/651> [accessed 1 June 2020].

The pitfalls and positives of introducing support to self-supply in Zambia

Sally Sutton

Introduction

Three initiatives have been taken to accelerate self-supply in Zambia in the last 20 years. Each has taken a different approach. The first was government-led, the second NGO-led, and the third was private sector-led with NGO support. The most important outcome from these different projects is evidence of the enormous demand to improve household water supply, which is suppressed by a lack of support services and information on how to achieve change.

Zambia has one of the highest population growth rates in the world, a relatively large urban population (41.8 per cent), and a sparse rural one. This context encourages movement into towns but also offers opportunities for growth in rural incomes from selling crops to urban markets with the cash sent back to villages. Rural population densities are low, averaging approximately two households/km² but in more remote districts falling to only one household/km². Rural areas are served by poor road networks and few markets.

Rural coverage in water supply increased by almost 2 million persons from 2000 to 2017, but more than twice as many (4.8 million) remain unserved and a further 0.9 million are only served with a limited supply. Using present coverage trends and National Statistics Office population projections, rates of progress seem insufficient to make a reduction in the number unserved by 2030. Many villages and increasing numbers of households provide their own, often unimproved supplies; over 70 per cent are groundwater sources. It is these trends which have prompted government interest and several moves to explore the concept of self-supply acceleration.

The three separate projects were:

1. DFID-funded research into traditional source improvement (1998–2001).
   A study of existing self-supply in four provinces followed by community-led improvements in six districts supported by advisory services from government health and water sectors.

I. Research with government

II. Piloting in Luapula

III. SME development in Eastern Province

IV. After scaling up/long term

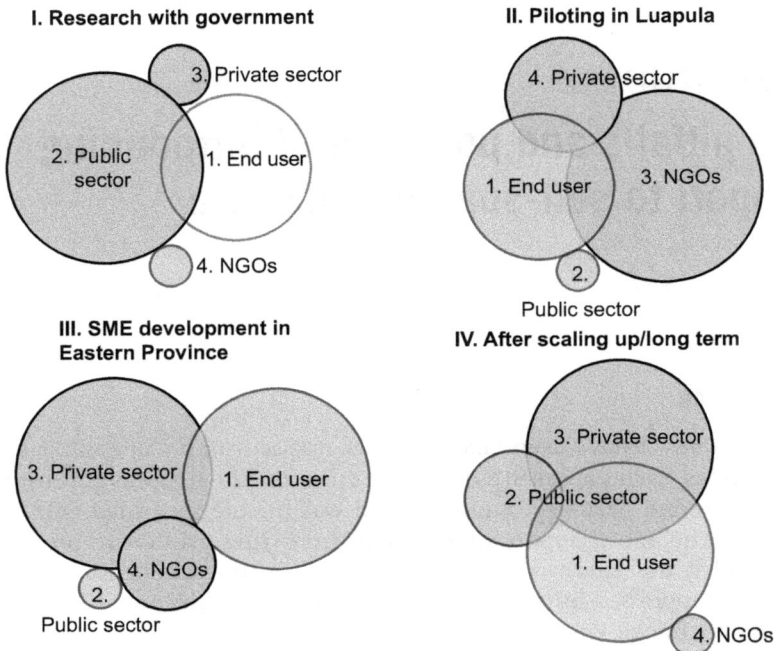

Figure CS.6.1 Stakeholders' roles in Zambian self-supply activities (size of circles reflects size of role)

2. WaterAid developed self-supply support services in a district in Luapula (UNICEF funded 2007–2010) and then a further sub-district (funded by Stone Foundation 2012–2014) with a UNICEF review (2015).
3. Jacana NGO establishment of private sector support services (SMART centre) in two districts of Eastern Province (2017 to date).

Without being part of longer-term programmes, each of these efforts has been faced with a lack of long-term support. Different emphasis has been put on key stakeholders in each project (see Figure CS6.1), allowing a view of the strengths and weaknesses of each approach. But all have the same ultimate aim (Step 4): to end up with an enabling environment for self-supply in which the prime relationship is that between the private sector as service providers and the end-user as the customer. The public sector role, described in Chapter 9, is mainly that of enabler, ensuring private sector capacity and finance where necessary. The NGO is a catalyst whose role diminishes as the relationship between the other three players develops.

Step 1: Research into traditional source improvement, 1998–2001

The Ministry of Energy and Water and the Ministry of Health recognized the need for traditional well improvements in 1997, and so acted as the main player in this DFID-funded initiative. Health risks from unprotected wells and scoopholes and slow progress in increasing rural water supply coverage led to a government request and three years of action research into self-supply and whether its acceleration could be incorporated into government strategies (Sutton, 2002). The national cross-sectoral WASHE (water supply, sanitation, and health education) approach suited this aim well and the committees developed at provincial, district, and sub-district levels, including water, health, education, community development, agriculture, and local government, facilitated inputs from relevant sectors. NWASHE, the national umbrella body for WASHE training and community monitoring, managed the self-supply project with support from the author, an officer from the Department of Water Affairs (K. Nyundu), and a Peace Corps volunteer (E. Kelly).

Both ministries provided personnel for a year-long baseline survey in four provinces. The Department of Water Affairs provided technical expertise in developing low-cost well protection (using two bags of cement), and training for health extension staff who in turn trained local well-digging and masonry artisans in concrete lining and loaned them transportable ring moulds. Zimbabwean masons from Mvuramanzi Trust provided training in brick lining (see Photo CS.6.1). Almost 4,000 water samples were analysed by health or water laboratories supervised by the National Laboratory for Food and Drugs. The participation of government personnel throughout and their

Photo CS.6.1 Family well upgraded in Northern Province Zambia using the training from Mvuramanzi Trust, Zimbabwe

role in design and implementation of the research and promotion were key elements in the approach.

Over 200 sources were improved at owners' cost in the year of pilot implementation, and the growing interest of (especially peri-urban) households meant that many requests were outstanding at the end. A manual entitled *Encouraging Change* (facilitating a PHAST process for low-cost water, sanitation, and hygiene interventions) was produced with the Ministry of Health and later updated and published by TALC Publishing in English, French, and Portuguese (Sutton and Nkoloma, 2011). A second manual on Improvements to Traditional Sources (Sutton, 2004) detailed low-cost improvements to traditional wells. Government inputs and workshops spread understanding of the magnitude of self-supply. Evidence from monitored wells highlighted the potential impact of wellhead improvements by well-owners. At that time traditional sources became an official level of service in the national rural water strategy.

Five years later, little remained from the process that had been set in motion. The Ministry of Health continued to provide small funds in each district for well upgrading, and several districts applied for funds to continue. But responsibility for rural water supply had passed to a new ministry (Local Government and Housing), where few knew of the research and improved traditional wells were dropped from national strategy as being retrogressive. NWASHE was disbanded. DFID, which had requested a proposal for a second phase to scale up, changed its research funding policy without notice from a broad range of KAR (knowledge and research) funds into one consolidated research contract, so the government requested follow-on did not happen.

No exit strategy was therefore in place, and the momentum that had begun to grow in national and local authorities gently faded away as staff moved on and other funded priorities took precedence. Among households and masons however, the basic wellhead protection design became the norm over the following years. There are now several thousand examples. Five of the original improvements made by households were visited 15 years later. Two had been superseded by piped supplies (but the water was still used for washing clothes), and three remained as drinking supplies having provided an uninterrupted supply throughout.

Key lessons learned from this initiative were:

- There was too much emphasis on government and not enough on private sector roles. Personal gain is a powerful factor in sustainability.
- Health personnel most clearly see the practicality of incremental risk reduction and are in the position to promote it.
- The time needed for changes in attitude and support for self-supply to be embedded into the water sector is longer than allowed by short-term (<5 years) projects that are vulnerable to many fundamental changes (policies, funding, staffing) beyond their control.

Step 2: WaterAid Luapula self-supply projects, 2007–2014

WaterAid undertook a two-phase piloting of household-funded source improvements in two areas of one of the poorest districts in Zambia (Olschewski et al., 2016). The first phase in Milenge West was managed by WaterAid and monitored by UNICEF (WaterAid, 2011). In Milenge East, a local NGO (VAREN) provided coordination, selection of artisans for training, and promotion in specific wards. In the first phase artisans had a two-month training period at the provincial trades training institute, and the two best were used to train those in the second phase, with poorer results. Milenge East community motivators (mostly masons) promoted self-supplied sanitation and water using PHAST methods and targeted subsidies to sanitation. The masons were marketing their own services in sanitation first and following up with water supply improvements which triggered a good response, despite high levels of poverty. In an area of such sparse population (less than one household per km^2) the market is limited, materials are expensive, and district and extension worker (agriculture and health) back-up was necessary for marketing, quality control, and training.

Early uptake was slow as the concept in the area was new, but following on from a few early adopters, momentum grew and in 18 months 70 per cent of well owners in the two areas (144, serving 18 per cent of the district population) had made some improvements in well protection, and 40 per cent had reached levels which conformed with JMP 'protected' status. A few were keen to invest in solar panels or low cost pumps but expertise beyond well protection remained to be developed.

The cost of aprons and drainage were a constraint on progress towards JMP standards for some and was partly overcome by the introduction of a loan scheme. This scheme lent an average of $135 per well or around $2.5 per head. Repayment in Milenge East had reached 88 per cent when the project monitoring ceased and the fund was turned into a revolving fund, for which 123 applicants were waiting. Repayment was lower in the West because the first phase project expected some follow-up funding and so had no exit strategy, leaving debtors unsure who to pay back; the trained artisans were ill-prepared to stand unsupported in such a remote area after such a short time in operation.

In 2015, the fund management was struggling and in need of audit, training, and support for costs of meeting up and for topping up losses from bad debts. The best artisans were still in demand but working in isolation, since government had not (or only marginally) been involved. Paradoxically, at this stage there was found to be widespread interest from the present provincial administration offices for water, health, community development and mother and child health, nutrition, chiefs and tribal affairs, who were not previously involved, but saw the need and potential of such household supplies in the context of the scattered housing they were dealing with. There was however no longer any organization to bring them together and develop ways to incorporate support to self-supply into their programmes.

There was also interest sparked at national level by the results of piloting, culminating in the presentation by the Principal Engineer Rural Water and Sanitation, Ministry of Local Government and Housing to an RWSN international webinar (Manangi, 2015).

Some further lessons were learned:

- In piloting new approaches, exit strategies need to be designed into projects from the start, and roles and dependencies monitored regularly to devolve responsibilities over time.
- The low level of government involvement meant that there was no continuity of support as participating NGOs pulled out, leaving little continuous promotion except by artisans constrained by lack of transport.
- Differing strategies, advisory service, and skills need to be in place to cater for the poorest and the richest with a full range of technologies combined with the notion of incremental improvements.
- For those who will not be reached by communal supplies in the foreseeable future and for whom remoteness makes providing their own supply exceptionally expensive, few will be able to reach 'protected' let alone safely managed status without subsidy or long-term loans.

Step 3: Jacana SMART centre, Eastern Province

Jacana is a local NGO and part of the SMART Centre Group. It concentrates on business empowerment and provides training for both water supply entrepreneurs (hand-drilling, well-digging, headworks, and low-cost pumps) and enterprises, which as water-dependent businesses are potential customers. These range from farmers and livestock owners to beekeepers, hairdressers, brick makers, and car washers. The overall aim is to achieve sustainability through financial gain and so the main actors are in the private sector, but NGO advice and help to build markets are necessary for some considerable time.

Jacana used sponsorship funding to subsidize boreholes and pumps to create demonstration supplies (see Photo CS.6.2) for businesses in selected areas whose income is enhanced by water on premises, and who therefore create employment and will be motivated to keep the supply functioning. Most of these supplies also provide water to neighbours. The 24 drillers who have been trained have formed a cooperative (Eastern Manual Drilling) which is registered with the Water Resources Management Authority, saving them the cost of individual registration which would be prohibitive. They have drilled 148 boreholes in their first year as an entity (one-third fully paid for by individual families) and won a trip to Finland as an innovative start-up. Low-cost pumps (rope pumps and now also EMAS pumps) are installed on both existing traditional wells and boreholes.

Photo CS.6.2 Family borehole and rope pump installed by Jacana, in Eastern Province, Zambia
Source: Photo: Rik Haanen, Jacana

Here self-supply is being introduced through private sector initiative but with the ultimate aim of also increasing water supply coverage, especially in remote areas. The transitions between subsidized and unsubsidized supplies and between water supply for business and water supply for drinking water coverage are not easy to achieve. The former will truly test affordability and willingness to pay and may need loan systems or phased incremental improvement of existing wells. The latter requires official recognition of low-cost technologies by government as a level of service for households and small communities if supplies are to form part of sector planning and be eligible for government grants and subsidies. But this may also suppress open market demand unless the guidelines for eligibility are very clear and incorruptible; a Catch-22 situation, but a necessary one if these technologies are to contribute to SDG 6.1.

Jacana has formed partnerships with WaterAid and the EMAS centre. With WaterAid the aim is to collect adequate evidence to present to government to lobby for a lower level of recognized service for scattered and remote households. With EMAS the aim is to broaden the range of technologies available so that investors have a greater choice, and drillers and water businesses have greater skills to sell.

At this stage future outcomes are not predictable. Will government, not involved to date in development of services (accreditation, quality control, monitoring), accept evidence without having been involved in the whole process of introduction? Will markets be able to expand beyond the richest retirees and entrepreneurs? Will lower levels of service be accepted by communities and politicians even where there is no alternative?

Strengths and weaknesses of the different approaches

The main strengths and weaknesses of the different approaches are summarized in Table CS.6.1. As with most research and piloting, for every problem solved several new questions arise and are still to be answered.

The aims and processes of introduction in the three self-supply projects were different. Each tested a different point of entry and different agencies to lead the way. Is any more likely to succeed with a longer time to get established, or is it possible to cherry-pick the strengths of each?

Local authorities are used to being provided with funds, with a belief that eventually enough will be there to cater for everyone. For them to think

Table CS.6.1 Strengths and weaknesses of different stakeholder-led self-supply acceleration initiatives in Zambia

Implementation body	Strengths	Weaknesses
Government	– Easier official recognition of technology and inclusion in coverage statistics – Social marketing through government services – Access to subsidies for vulnerable/poorest – Potential for country-wide scaling up	– Priority given to higher technology and cost options – No motivational incentive to promoters – Budget lines difficult to establish – High vulnerability to political influence and policy changes
NGO	– Flexibility in trying out options – Research, training, and monitoring skills available – Can concentrate all efforts on small areas and few topics	– High dependence on ephemeral motivators – Engagement with communities only while funds last – Impact confined to project areas – Low access to subsidies – Low institutional memory
Private sector (SMEs) with NGO support	– Initial NGO support builds market, technical, and business skills for long term – Sustainable revenue streams provide incentive to grow business – Successful businesses can shed dependence on NGOs	– Dialogue with government limited – Ability to approach donors or banks restricted – Businesses won't reach remote areas without subsidy – Confined time frames for funding usually mean NGOs shed SMEs rather than vice versa

differently requires time for them to analyse how things have gone in the past and what that means in the future, and to examine their own resources and situation. What can they do with what they have and how can they support initiatives rather than fully fund them? When a few households get involved, others copy and change accelerates, but that has often been the time at which funding stops. How can this situation be avoided? What global institute and what donors would be guardians of 10-year processes, albeit at diminishing levels?

The WASHE structures made it possible to get multidisciplinary inputs, which strengthen commitment and expand networks. Elsewhere is it better for health authorities ultimately to play a more major part, rather than to put the onus on those responsible for water supply?

Can other sources of finance, such as remittances and district development funds, pay a greater part? If so how to engage them?

More broadly, are the time frames of global development goals and of donor funding windows incompatible with attempts to introduce new thinking? Are these attempts further hindered by sector-wide planning and budgets which require short time frames and predictable outcomes? This leaves little or no room for iterative attempts to develop new processes and thinking, and for trying out alternatives. It is a recipe for business as usual, despite its inadequacies.

Many lessons have been learned in Zambia, but many questions remain, as does the need and demand for self-supply support. How many times can expectations be raised, demand built up, and projects discontinued before sustainable services have had time to develop?

References

Manangi, A. (2015) 'Self-supply and human rights – rural water challenges in Zambia', presentation to the *8th RWSN Webinar Human Rights and Self-Supply – Potential and Challenges* [online] <https://www.rural-water-supply.net/_ressources/documents/default/1-651-34-1448618726.pdf> [accessed 1 June 2020].

Olschewski, A., Sutton, S. and Ngoma, M. (2016) *Review of Self-financed Water Supply in Milenge District, Zambia* [online], Skat Foundation Report for UNICEF East and Southern Africa Office <https://www.rural-water-supply.net/en/resources/details/754> [accessed 1 June 2020].

Sutton, S. (2002) *Community-Led Improvements of Rural Drinking Water Supplies* [online], Final Report, Knowledge and Research Project (KAR) R7128, SWL Consultants, Shrewsbury <https://www.rural-water-supply.net/en/resources/details/249> [accessed 1 June 2020].

Sutton, S. (2004) *Low Cost Water Source Improvements: Practical Guidelines for Fieldworkers* [website], Health Books International <https://healthbooksinternational.org/product/low-cost-water-source-improvements-2004/> [accessed 25 May 2020].

Sutton, S. and Nkoloma, H. (2011) *Encouraging Change*, 2nd edn, Health Books International/TALC, Rugby, UK.

WaterAid (2011) *Self Supply: A Viable Rural Water Supply Option? Preliminary Lessons from Milenge West Pilot*, WaterAid, Lusaka.

WaterAid (2014) *Zambia Stone Family Foundation Projects: Year Three Report*, WaterAid, Lusaka.

Index

Page numbers in *italics* refer to figures, photos and tables; those in **bold** indicate boxes.

accelerating and supporting 39–42, 215–16, 255–62
  costs 240–3
  developing core support service capacity 217–23
  four-stage framework 224–9
    country experiences 228–9
    government 229–31
      NGO and private sector stakeholders 232–40
    integrating with sanitation 231–2
    objectives 216–17
    summary and conclusion 243–4
adequacy of self-supply 197–9
affordability *see* costs; funding; subsidies
affordable and appropriate response 255–6
affordable technologies *see* early stage technologies; Tanzania: alternative and affordable technologies
agriculture/farming 114–17, 124, 126–7
  food security **118**
  irrigation 151–3, 157–8
  resilience and cross-sector opportunities 261
Albania *see* Danube region/Central and Eastern Europe (case study)
aquifer contamination 168
Asian Development Bank (ADB) 60
Australia 6, 95, **96**, 255
Austria 69, 259, 287

Bangladesh 37, 43, 59, 60, 88, 151
boiling water 177, 180
Bolivia 58, 140, 142–3, 149
boreholes *see* wells
Bosnia and Herzegovina *see* Danube region/Central and Eastern Europe (case study)
bottled/sachet water 87, 90, 175
Brazil: rainwater harvesting 58, 293–4

Canada 64, **96**, 259
Central and Eastern Europe *see* Danube region/Central and Eastern Europe
chlorination 54, 175, 178, 180–1
community supplies
  high-income countries 65–71, *116*
  improved 54
Community Managed Projects (CMPs), Ethiopia 200, **201**
community and self-financed supplies 185–6, 210–11
  differences in thinking as group and as individual 186–8
  intersection between interests 188–90
  user satisfaction and supply sustainability 193–209
  working together 190–2
community-led total sanitation (CLTS) 39, 42, 190
conducive self-supply 29
convenience 112–14, 193–4
cooperatives 68–9, 70–1, *116*
costs 18, 118–19, 200–4, 240–3, 302–3
  low-cost lifting devices and pumps 145–53
  see also funding/finance; subsidies
Côte d'Ivoire 50, 167
Croatia *see* Danube region/Central and Eastern Europe (case study)
cultural aspects of traditional water supply **107**

Danube region/Central and Eastern Europe (case study) 56–7, 62, 64, 281, **281-8**, *282*
  accessibility 284
  recommendations and conclusions 287–8
  reliability 284–6

service delivery landscape and statistics
282–4, *285*
water quality 286–7
Democratic Republic of Congo (DRC)
49–50, 51
Denmark 63, 64, 69, 259
diarrhoeal disease 9–10, 112, 166–9
'disruptive innovation' 262
domestic uses
and agricultural uses 114–18
and multiple uses 32–4
donor(s)
dependence and self-help 260
and international aid agencies 262–3
drilling
conventional rotary and down-the-hole
hammer precision 144
hand drilled wells 139–43

E. *Coli* 69, *70*, 275–6, 298–9
early stage technologies 131–3, 160
accessing groundwater 134–45
higher-level pumps 153–4
introducing and marketing 158–60
low-cost lifting devices 145–53
water use technologies 157–8
education levels 109–10
EMAS Centres **159**, 319
EMAS technologies 148–9, *150*, **150**, 151,
152, 153, 157
enabling environment 40–2, 216–17
energy sector and self-supply **3**
England 64
see also United Kingdom (UK)
enhancing livelihoods 252
entrepreneurial approach 235–7
Ethiopia 15, 20, 43
Community Managed Projects (CMPs)
200, **201**
community and self-financed supplies
191, 192, 199
family well investment **125**
food security **118**
household well *33*
iddr funds 122
investment and education 109, 110
investment and wealth 111, 112
low-cost trickle irrigation *157*
multiple uses 114

ownership 105, *106*
reliability 196–7
rural self-supply 49–50, 51, 54
sharing 106–7
task force 227
unprotected well *136*
urban and periurban self-supply **85**,
88, 93–4
water lifting technologies **152**, 174–5
well water quality 169–70, 174–5
Europe 63–4
group schemes 65–71
regulation 71, 72
WHO survey *63*, 64–6, 72
see also Danube region/Central and
Eastern Europe; Scotland; *specific
countries*

faecal contamination 175–6
diarrhoeal disease 9–10, 112, 166–9
E. *Coli* 69, *70*, 275–6, 298–9
protected and unprotected sources
166–9, *174*
and regulation: Scotland 272–4, 275–6
urban and peri-urban supply 93
farming *see* agriculture/farming
financial issues *see* costs; funding/
finance; subsidies
Finland 36, 68–9, 208, 318
fire-fighting 35–6
fly control studies 10
food contamination 175–6
food microbiology and hygiene 10
food production *see* agriculture/farming
food security **118**
functionality of self-supply 195–6
funding/finance
investment and sources, sub-Saharan
Africa 118–24
loans and grants 71, 72, 73, 276–7
new sources of 256–7
trends and requirements 19–22
types and purposes *222*
see also subsidies

gaps in supply *see* public water supply gaps
gender
-related views on public and private
supplies, Mali **189**

and vulnerability 208–9
  see also women
Ghana 20–2, 37, 54, 120, 140
  community and self-financed supplies
      191–2, 195, 202
  rainwater harvesting and storage *155*
  training 241
  urban and peri-urban self-supply 87,
      89–90
  women 204, 209
Global Analysis and Assessment of
      Sanitation and Drinking-Water
      (GLAAS) reports 37
global perspective 5–7
  urban and peri-urban self-supply
      84–5
government 39–40, 207, 208, 217, *218*,
      229–31
  cost reduction 256–7
  high-income countries 67–73
  Honduras **59**
  India 94, **95**
  Kenya **235**
  middle income countries 62
  NGOs and private sector stakeholders
      232–40
  recommended actions for 263–4
  retirees 124
  sub-Saharan Africa 20, 54–5, 94
  targeting and back-up for remote
      communities and dispersed
      households 257–8
  Zambia 314–16, 320–1
  see also support services; *entries
      beginning* public
groundwater 12, 14, 19, 31–2, 50–1
  accessing 134–45
  improved and unimproved rural
      supplies 6–7, 51
  resources 134
  unprotected 51
group supplies *see* community supplies;
      community and self-financed
      supplies
Guinea 50, 51

hand drilled wells 139–43
hand dug wells 134–9
hand washing 10, 11, 35

handpumps 12
  failure, maintenance, refurbishment
      and replacement 17–18
  history 36
  Mali **189**
  middle-income countries 55–6, 58–60
  and motorized pumps 59, 60, 61,
      106–7, 115, 174–5
  types 153, 174
  user satisfaction 193, 195, 197–8,
      199–200
health
  history 35
  impacts of 'on-premises' supply 9–11,
      112, 113–14
  preventative healthcare 54
  resilience and cross-sector opportu-
      nities 261
  risks 92–4, 166–9, 277–8
  see also faecal contamination;
      household water treatment;
      monitoring; regulation
high-income countries
  rural self-supply 63–73, 74–5
  urban and peri-urban self-supply
      96–7
Honduras 58, **59**
household decisions on water source **191**
household finance, sub-Saharan Africa
      118–27
household water treatment 177–81
household- vs community-level
      benchmarks 8
Human Development Index (HDI) 63
human rights 230–1
hygiene practices/measures 10–11
  wellhead protection 169–73

India 43, 59–60, 264
  urban self-supply 94, **95**, 96
individual supplies
  and community supplies
      see community and
      self-financed supplies
  high-income countries 64–5, 71–3
  Latin America 57–8
  sub-Saharan Africa 48–53
      see also sub-Saharan Africa,
      ownership and investment

International Development Enterprises
(IDE) 157–8
introducing and marketing technologies
158–60
introducing supported self-supply 224–6
investment
ownership and *see under*
sub-Saharan Africa
personal and private 3, 29–32
return on 203, 259
Ireland 63, 67–8, 70, 71, 72, **96**, 208
irrigation 151–3, 157–8

Jacana, Zambia 117, 314, 318–20

Kenya 18, 120, 122, 153, 222
community and self-financed supplies
187, 198, 202, 206, 207
government role in group supply **235**
harambee (self-help tradition) 54,
187, 259
'known-unknowns'
measuring 37–8
researching 264–5
Kosovo *see* Danube region/Central and
Eastern Europe (case study)

ladder of progress/technology ladder 28,
29, 39
landless/tenant farmers 124, 127
Latin America 57–8, 62
latrines 39, 93, 122, 241
EMAS technologies *150*
recommended distance from wells/
boreholes 168
Liberia **16**, *17*, 120
Living Conditions surveys 38
long-term approach 260

Madagascar 91
maintenance and replacement 17–18
costs 202–3
public and private sector 207–8
Malawi 15, 18, 20, 55, 192
food security **118**
ownership and investment *106*, 109,
111, 115, 117, 119, 126–7
rainwater storage *156*
rope pumps 148, 208

SMART Centre **159**
well water contamination 168
Mali 50, 51, 52, 53, 54
ownership and investment 105, 108,
111, 112–13, *116*, 117, 122
public and private supplies **189**, *190*
water uses *116*, 117
management
and ownership 204–8, 250–1
structure 204–6
and support services 207–8
markets/marketing
development 220–1
new technologies 158–60, 309–10
social 42
microfinance services 123
middle-income countries
rural water supply 55–62, 74
urban and peri-urban self-supply 94–6
Millennium Development Goals (MDGs)
5, 8, 166
Moldova *see* Danube region/Central and
Eastern Europe (case study)
monitoring
high-income countries 72–3
and review 223
sub-Saharan Africa 94
motorized pumps 153–4
handpumps and 59, 60, 61, 106–7,
115, 174–5
Mozambique 90
cultural aspects of traditional
supply **107**
rainwater harvesting *31*, *32*
multiple indicator cluster surveys (MICS)
38, 48–50, 52–3, 86–8, 89
faecal contamination 167, 168
water contamination 175–7
multiple uses 32–4

Nepal 10, 294
Netherlands 64
see also Tanzania: alternative
and affordable technologies
(case study)
New Zealand 6, 72
NGOs 20, 39, 58, 207
government and private sector stakeholders 232–40

recommended actions for 264
see also support services; *specific NGOs*
Nicaragua 43, 58, **237**, 260
rope pumps 147–8, 174
Niger
convenience in water lifting **194**
handpump *146*
Nigeria 49–50, 51, 120
urban and peri-urban supply 86–7, 88,
89–90, 91, 92
water contamination 167

'on-premises' supply 9–11, 112,
113–14, 251
overseas development aid (ODA) 20,
119–20
ownership
complex subject of 252
and investment *see under*
sub-Saharan Africa
management and 204–8, 250–1
sense of 104, 204

payment and flexibility of use: urban
sub-Saharan Africa 92
performance: functionality, reliability
and adequacy 195–9
peri-urban self-supply *see* urban and
peri-urban self-supply
PHAST manual and methods 127, 220,
316, 317
piloting and testing support models 226
piped and non-piped rural supplies 6–7
Pitcher pumps 149–51, *152*
policy and strategy development 227
private investment 3, 29–32
private sector
government and NGOs 232–40
see also entries beginning public, private
projected service levels: rural sub-Saharan
Africa 18–19
psychological aspects 127
individual and group thinking 186–7
savings schemes 121–2
sense of ownership 104, 204
public, private and commercial service
delivery *256*
public and private support services
207–8, 216–17

public-private partnerships 32
public sector *see* government
public and self-supply systems: urban
sub-Saharan Africa 91
public water supply gaps 1–5, 249–50
basic challenge 5–7
changing context with SDGs 7–8
informal gap filling 89, 90–1, 92, 93, 97–8
significance of 'on-premises' supply 9–11
PumpAid 109, 208
pumps
food security **118**
higher-level types 153–4
low-cost 146–53
see also handpumps; motorized pumps;
rope pumps

rainwater, artificial recharging with 156–7
rainwater harvesting (RWH) and storage
31, 293–5
Brazil 58, 293–4
Ghana *155*
India 95, 96
Malawi *156*
Mozambique *31, 32*
urban 86, 94–6, 154–6, 293–4
see also Thailand: rainwater harvesting
(case study)
recognizing self-financed supplies 251–2
registration of supplies/contractors 223
regulation 55, 69, 94, 223
high-income countries 70–3
Scotland 274–6
Tanzania 310
Thailand 291–2
reliability of self-supply 196–7, 284–6
remittances 119–20
research institutions, recommended
actions for 264–5
resilience and cross-sector opportunities
261–2
return on investment 203, 259
Roman Empire 34–5
Romania *see* Danube region/Central and
Eastern Europe (case study)
rope and bucket lifting 145–6
rope pumps 58, 117, 147–8, 151–3, 208
rotating savings and credit associations
(ROSCAs) 120–3

rural populations 5–6, 7
  remote communities and dispersed
    households 257–8
  sub-Saharan Africa 14–17
rural self-supply 47–8, 252–3
  evolution of supply related to country
    economy 73–6
  high-income countries 63–73, 74–5
  low-income countries *see under*
    sub-Saharan Africa
  middle-income economies 55–62, 74
  and sanitation 42
  summary and conclusion 76–7
Rural Water Supply Network (RWSN)
  37, 224

sachet/bottled water 87, 90, 175
sanitation *see* community-led total
    sanitation (CLTS); water and
    sanitation (WASH)
savings schemes, traditional 120–3
scaling up support strategies 227
Scotland (case study) 271–2
  improvement grants and risk
    awareness 276–8
  private sector role 278–9
  private supplies 272–4
  recommendations and conclusion
    279–80
  regulation 274–6
sector professionals and household
    perspectives *251*
self-supply
  common characteristics 29–34
  definitions 28–9
  emergence of concept 36–7
  history 34–6
Senegal 120
  hand-augering *141*
  individual vs communal responsi-
    bility **188**
  protected well *137*
  rope and bucket lifting *145*
service delivery
  Danube region 282–4, *285*
  existing self-supply in evolution of
    250–5, *256*
service delivery models 42–3
  middle income countries 61–2
  urban sub-Saharan Africa 92

sharing 106–9
SHIPO *see under* Tanzania: alternative
    and affordable technologies
    (case study)
Sierra Leone 15, 18, *53*, **53**, 54–5,
  126–7, 153
  cultural aspects of traditional supply **107**
  EMAS pumps and technologies
    149, **150**
  water contamination 175–6
  water uses *93*
SMART Centres **159**
  Malawi **159**
  Tanzania 123, **143**, 309–10
  Zambia 318–20
social marketing 42
solar disinfection 180
solar pumps 153–4
South Africa: women's cooperative *116*
South Asia 58–60, **61**, 94
springs 64, 108
  Honduras 58, **59**
  protection 144–5
squatter settlements 85
sub-Saharan Africa 5–6
  combining elements of WASH 13
  improved supply 6–7, 9
  ownership and investment 103–4
    barriers to investment 124–7
    costs and affordability 118–19
    elements of ownership 104–5, *106*
    household financial resources 124
    importance of 'convenience' 112–14
    investment and education 109–10
    investment and wealth 110–12
    microfinance services 123
    potential use 114–15
    productive use 115–18
    remittances 119–20
    savings schemes, traditional 120–3
    sharing 106–9
    studies 104
    summary and conclusion 127
  rainwater harvesting 294–5
  rural community service delivery
    model 42
  rural self-supply 12–13, 14–22, 48–55,
    74–5, *254*
  supported self-supply 29
  trends *11*, *21*

urban self-supply 11–12, 85–94
well water quality 167
see also specific countries
subsidies 203–4, 222–3
  direct 41
  indirect 40
support services 217–23
  delivery 218–23
  elements 40–1
  providers 218, *219*
  public and private 207–8, 216–17
supported self-supply 4, 29
supporting and accelerating *see* acceler-
    ating and supporting
surface water 6, 7, 12, 14, 19
Sustainable Development Goals (SDGs)
    7–8, 181, 251, 253, 260, 266
  sub-Saharan Africa *12*, 13, 22, 112
Sweden 63, 64
SWOT analysis
  government, NGO and private sector
    comparison *320*
  groups/cooperatives vs public supply *71*
  individual self-supply in high-income
    countries *73*

Tanzania 55, 117, 122
Tanzania: alternative and affordable
    technologies (case study) 305
  emergence of self-supply markets
    309–10
  impact of regulation 310
  local community and Netherlands
    collaboration 306–9
  SHIPO 305–6
    drilling *141*, 307–9
    SMART centre 123, **143**, 309–10
  summary and next steps 311
Thailand *56*
Thailand: rainwater harvesting (case
    study) 60, **61**, 289
  challenges of replicating in other
    countries 293–5
  dragon jar to Thai jar 289–91
  economic and market factors 292–3
  political and regulatory factors 291–2
  socio-cultural factors 291
  summary and conclusions 295
time and distance of water collection 9,
    11, 12

toilets *see* latrines
'Tragedy of the Commons' 187
training **159**, 219, 309–10, 315–16
treadle pumps 151–3
trickle irrigation 157–8

Uganda 20, 122, 148, 168–9, 198, 202
  gender and vulnerability in
    WASH **209**
  government support 207, 217, *218*
  rainwater harvesting 295
  task force 227
Ukraine *see* Danube region/Central and
    Eastern Europe (case study)
UNICEF 52–3, 60, **109**, 224
  see also multiple indicator cluster
    surveys (MICS); WHO/
    UNICEF Joint Monitoring
    Programme (JMP)
unimproved supplies
  Latin America 57
  rural 6–7, 51
  South-East Asia 59
  urban sub-Saharan Africa 89–90
United Kingdom (UK)
  England 64
  regulation and funding 71, 72
  urban self-supply **96**
  see also Scotland
United States 64, 66, 69, 149
unserved communities: rural sub-Saharan
    Africa 14–17
unsupported self-supply 28
urban and peri-urban self-supply 83–4
  global picture 84–5
  high-income countries 96–7
  middle-income countries 94–6
  sub-Saharan Africa 11–12, 85–94
  summary and conclusion 97–8
urban populations 5
urban self-supply 32, 253
  individual and group 258–9
user first approach 250–1
user satisfaction and supply sustain-
    ability 193–209

vendors 92
Vietnam 43, 60, 208, 293
village savings and loan schemes
    (VSLAs) 123

water consumption 9, 10–11
water filters, household 178–80
water quality *see* faecal contamination;
    household water treatment;
    monitoring; regulation; well
    water quality
water and sanitation (WASH) 8, 19–20,
    37, 42, 43–4
  combining elements of 13
  gender and vulnerability, Uganda **209**
  integrating 231–2
  middle-income countries 55, **59**, 60
  supporting 38–9
water treatment 177–81
WaterAid 20, **109**, 122, 224
  Zambia 314, 317–18
wealth and investment 110–12
weaning food hygiene 10
well linings 138, *139*
well upgrade *see* Zimbabwe: National
    Upgraded Well Programme
well water quality 165–6, 181–2
  faecal coliform in protected and
    unprotected sources 166–9
  incremental improvement/progressive
    risk reduction 169–73
  low-cost lifting devices 173–5
  point of consumption 175–7
  water treatment impacts, methods and
    recommendations 177–81
  Zimbabwe: National Upgraded Well
    Programme 297–9
wellhead protection 54, 134–7
  and hygiene measures 169–73
wells
  conventional rotary and down-the-hole
    hammer precision drilling 144
  hand drilled 139–43
  hand dug 134–9
  low-cost lifting devices 145–53
    and water quality improvement 173–5
  sub-Saharan Africa 52–3, 55, 105, 106–7
    food security **118**
  urban areas 87, 89, 90–1, 92, 93
WHO
  European region survey *63*, 64–6, 72
  GLAAS reports 37
  Guidelines for Drinking Water Quality 170–3
  water treatment and storage 177, 178,
    179–80

WHO/UNEP 170–3
WHO/UNICEF Joint Monitoring
    Programme (JMP) 9, 12, 13, 19,
    51, *56*, 57, 84, 86, 89, 92, 94
  'improved' well status 134–7
women
  and children's health 113–14
  collective action, Ireland **67**
  cooperatives 68, *116*
  gender and vulnerability 208–9
  gender-related views on public and
    private supplies, Mali **189**
  participation 60, 204
  saving schemes 121, 122, 209
  Thailand 292–3
World Bank: service delivery models
    42, *43*
Zambia 55, **85**, 93–4, 105, *106*,
    108–9, 124
  brick lining for well and drainage
    channel *138*
  concrete well rings *139*
  cultural aspects of traditional water
    supply **107**
  food security **118**
  household decisions on water source
    191, *192*
  household well *136*
  investment and wealth 111
  reliability 197
  return on investment 203
  spring protection *144*
  water uses 114–15, 117
  well water quality 169, 170–3
Zambia (case study) 313–14
  comparison of different approaches
    320–1
  Jacana SMART Centre 318–20
  research into traditional source
    improvement 314–16
  WaterAid Luapula projects 317–18
Zimbabwe 52–3, 55, 117, 138, 169,
    239–40, 243, 260
Zimbabwe: National Upgraded Well
    Programme (case study) 297
  concept and implementation
    299–300
  costs and financing 302–3
  decline and redesign 300–2
  family wells and water quality 297–9

www.ingramcontent.com/pod-product-compliance
Lightning Source LLC
Chambersburg PA
CBHW070902030426
42336CB00014BA/2299